The Contemporary Theory of the Public Sphere

Revised Paperback Edition

NEW VISIONS
OF THE COSMOPOLITAN

Series Editors

PATRICK O'MAHONY
TRACEY SKILLINGTON
University College Cork, Ireland

VOLUME 1
REVISED PAPERBACK EDITION

PETER LANG
Oxford • Bern • Berlin • Bruxelles • Frankfurt am Main • New York • Wien

The Contemporary Theory of the Public Sphere

Revised Paperback Edition

Patrick O'Mahony

PETER LANG

Oxford • Bern • Berlin • Bruxelles • Frankfurt am Main • New York • Wien

Bibliographic information published by Die Deutsche Nationalbibliothek
Die Deutsche Nationalbibliothek lists this publication in the Deutsche
Nationalbibliografie; detailed bibliographic data is available on the Internet at
http://dnb.d-nb.de.

A catalogue record for this book is available from the British Library.

Library of Congress Control Number: A CIP catalogue record for this book
has been applied for at the Library of Congress

Cover image: Kurt Schwitters, *Revolving*, 1919 © DACS 2013.

Cover design by Peter Lang Ltd.

ISSN 1664-3380
ISBN 978-1-78997-248-1 (print) • ISBN 978-1-78997-249-8 (ePDF)
ISBN 978-1-78997-250-4 (ePub) • ISBN 978-1-78997-251-1 (mobi)

This is a revised version of *The Contemporary Theory of the Public Sphere*, 2013,
ISBN 978-3-0343-0146-6 by the same author.

© Peter Lang AG 2019

Published by Peter Lang Ltd, International Academic Publishers,
52 St Giles, Oxford, OX1 3LU, United Kingdom
oxford@peterlang.com, www.peterlang.com

Patrick O'Mahony has asserted his right under the Copyright, Designs and
Patents Act, 1988, to be identified as Author of this Work.

All rights reserved.
All parts of this publication are protected by copyright.
Any utilisation outside the strict limits of the copyright law, without
the permission of the publisher, is forbidden and liable to prosecution.
This applies in particular to reproductions, translations, microfilming,
and storage and processing in electronic retrieval systems.

To Daniel and to the dear memory of Mary and Michael

Contents

List of Figures and Tables	xi
Foreword to the Paperback Edition	xiii
Foreword	xvii
Introduction	1

PART I Normative Theories of Democracy, Communication, and the Public Sphere — 37

CHAPTER 1
The Communicative Constructs of Normative Democratic Models — 39

CHAPTER 2
Rawlsian Liberalism and the Idea of Public Reason — 49

CHAPTER 3
Republicanism and the Cultural Foundations of Public Autonomy — 71

CHAPTER 4
The Radical Tradition: Public Contestation of Subjugation — 91

CHAPTER 5
Political Realism: Competitive Public Communication — 109

CHAPTER 6
Deliberative Democracy and Public Deliberation					129

CHAPTER 7
The Communicative Turn in Democratic Theory					151

PART II Habermas, Democracy, and Public Culture					161

CHAPTER 8
Discourse Ethics, Democratic Discourse,
and the Theory of Society					163

CHAPTER 9
Deontology and Democracy: Limits to the Primacy of the Right					193

CHAPTER 10
Democratic Theories and the Theory of Society					223

PART III   Cognitive Sociology, Collective Learning, and the
Public Sphere					251

CHAPTER 11
Cognitive Sociology, Communication, and Social Theory					253

CHAPTER 12
Discourse, Learning, and Social Integration					281

CHAPTER 13
Cognitive Sociology and the Public Sphere:
Towards a Theoretical Framework					315

PART IV: Democratic Communication, the Cognitive Order, and the Public Sphere ... 353

CHAPTER 14
Public Communication and the Public Sphere ... 355

CHAPTER 15
Generalized Public Communication Media: Mass and New Media ... 373

CHAPTER 16
The Macro-Social Structures of the Public Sphere ... 389

CHAPTER 17
The Dynamics of Public Communication ... 409

CHAPTER 18
Cosmopolitanism and the Transnational Institutionalization of the Public Sphere ... 439

Conclusion: The Public Sphere and Democracy ... 459

Bibliography ... 467

Index ... 487

List of Figures and Tables (in order of appearance)

Figure 1:	Democratic Theory and the Theory of Society	229
Table 1:	A Typology of Political Norms	293
Table 2:	Discourse, Learning, and the Cognitive Order	324
Figure 2:	Cognitive-Communicative Learning	347
Figure 3:	Spheres of Publicity	349
Figure 4:	Forms of Democratic Communication	351
Figure 5:	The Macro-Social Context of Public Communication	391
Figure 6:	Societal Spheres and the Cognitive Order	417
Figure 7:	The Cognitive Framework of the Public Sphere	419
Figure 8:	Communicative Modes of Social Integration	421
Figure 9:	Societal Spheres: Discourse, Culture, and Resonance	430

Foreword to the Paperback Edition

I have not made extensive changes to the original hardback text for the paperback edition. The majority of the changes that have been made are of an editorial nature to improve the flow of the language. I had considered introducing substantial new materials, but in the end reconsidered, because it would have created a type of cognitive dissonance between old and new, requiring substantial changes to the original volume. Nonetheless, there are some revisions to the use of terminology, changes of emphasis in arguments, and a general attempt to align the book with developments in my theoretical position since its original publication, albeit only to a certain level that would not require complex and overburdening elaboration.

More radical changes than those indicated above did not appear to be a high priority. Reviewing the book some five years after its original publication reconfirmed its original rationale. This was to consider the concept of the public sphere, and what it implies for the normative quality of social integration, with modern sociological tools. Neither the once dominant functionalism that continues to be used in building a theoretical context for the public sphere, nor the wide-ranging contemporary implications of the interpretive paradigm, are adequate on their own or in combination for the task. Hence, a book on the public sphere that employs a critical cognitive sociology, retaining a normative-critical edge within a communication theory of society, still seems timely in its original form.

As a work of cognitive sociology, one intellectual matter should be clarified at the outset. The idea of the cognitive is understood here as wide-ranging individual and collective competences for learning and reasoning. At its core, the cognitive consists of the mental and socio-mental mechanisms that are used in such tasks. The cognitive should therefore not be reduced, as it often is due to widespread repetition, to something of another kind, to, non-systematically listed here, the evaluative, the aesthetic, and feelings. So reduced, the 'cognitive' is often thought of today in the human and social sciences as excessively rationalistic and hence needing to be widely supplanted with more creative accounts of mentation. While there is no doubt that such a turn of thought has its point as a corrective to the presumptions about agents that are widely used in both the intellectual and 'everyday' worlds under the concept of 'cognitive', and while use of the concept in this book in some part shares the critique of existing usage, it does not abandon the concept of the cognitive. Rather, it builds upon it and makes it central to sociological thinking, understanding it as the indispensable foundation of signification and, corresponding to C. S. Peirce's observations on logic, to be regarded as inextricably social in its nature.

A further thought is that the book is not complete. Of course, no book ever really is, always contributing to opening up something new rather than being the final word. But this book is also not complete because the tasks within it, the communicative reorientation of sociology, the relationship between normative philosophy and sociology in this light, and the foundations of an adequate critical theory with an intrinsic social science contribution, do not beyond the book receive the attention they merit. And beyond each of these individual tasks, integration across them is still less being given adequate attention. For these reasons, the book's primary contribution may be to open up channels of thinking within and across these tasks. It seems frustrating and bewildering that, as the world we live in appears ever more to need the sustained attention of communicative-cultural thinking spanning a variety of disciplines, this intellectual project appears relatively unready, in spite of decades spent heralding the significance of culture. Viewed from another angle, though, perhaps it is diffusely becoming more ready and the great stirs of thought of the present will in the end converge on a more normatively incisive and more methodologically applicable interdisciplinary theory in this register.

The book, as a type of practice reconstructing theory, is designed to fill a space between theory and practice. So, while there is little in the book on those key issues that make ideas of the public sphere appear so pertinent today, such as populism, war, cosmopolitanism, or the relationship between social media and democracy, it offers a type of multi-level account of the kind of theory of society that could be applied to address any of these phenomena. It is therefore a space of thinking about a different type of sociology, communicative, cognitive, and normative and,

Foreword to the Paperback Edition

ultimately, with methodological intentions whose full expression will have to wait until another day.

A final point is that the author's work on critical cognitive sociology has, of course, gone on since 2013. It is now, building on foundations offered in the current book, taking the form of a comprehensive sociological statement on communicative reason. Such a project, building both from Peirce's semiotics, critical theory, and cognitive sociology, just to mention the major influences, aims for an integrated statement on how reason, the public sphere, and the communication theory of society are conceptually intermeshed. For this purpose, a semiotic restatement of both Peirce's and discourse ethics' guiding ideas in sociological light will be fundamental, opening towards a different way of cognizing both intellectual-political objects and aims. The interdisciplinary foundation of this work are ineluctable, and, if the years have taught me anything, it is just how much gets lost by the self-insulation of disciplines. But, of course, premature and superficial attempts to correct this state of affairs will not suffice, even if correction is essential. A concept like the public sphere demands interdisciplinary thinking, even listing possible disciplines that must contribute would go on a long time, and, hence, as much as philosophers and sociologists, I will welcome the thoughts on this project of others beyond these disciplines, including those outside specific disciplinary identities.

Kilbrittain, Summer 2018

Foreword

This book has been some time in the making. It is composed of elements that have received attention at different periods over the last fifteen years, each generating their own intermediate output of various kinds while also moving in a general direction. Whether these now come together in a satisfactory way is for the reader to judge. But, for the author, it feels like a long road where a destination is at last reached. The destination is one of those that might have been expected as the journey began, but it was far from altogether clear at the beginning. It only became clearer with the passing time.

The motivation to write this book owes as much to a sense of impotence as anything else. This above all derives from the feeling that if only a number of theoretical and methodological currents in different disciplines could combine to advance common understanding of democratic culture, how much better scholarship in the field would be, and perhaps the world would be a little better too. Of course, it's understandable that disciplines and fields of scholarship go about their business in their own ways, building up knowledge traditions that have standing for intellectuals and the world generally. But contemporary challenges appear to make both necessary and desirable some relaxation of borders, between disciplines, between individuals and groups, and within individuals. So, this book is partly dedicated to the realization of a kind of freedom that is based upon a responsibility to learn from others.

Though the book is not specifically addressed at methodology in any recognized sense of the term, it has a methodological intention at its core. This intention is to develop the kind of theory that can guide research, and learn from it, without sacrificing theoretical foundations. The goal is to understand what is at stake in public discourse so as to open a path towards better researching this discourse. And the intention is not just to do so to enable social actors generally to better see their contributions, but also to enable better academic interventions into public argumentation.

Leaving aside the relatively poor integration of normative horizons and research approaches general in the social sciences, a focus that is intrinsic to the public sphere, there are some promising research methodologies that could tell much about how discourses shape understandings, creating opportunities or closing them down. And some frustration arises from how little this has really been able to be done, given shortage of resources, across the vast universe of possible issues and spheres of application. Perhaps the difficulty in finding these resources has something to do with the limitations of the ambition. What, after all, is the true value of the kind of research that hides its own perspectives and denies itself the right to be anything other than a mirror of culture?

The concern for democratic inquiry, as Dewey saw a long time ago, could unite philosophical and social scientific inquiry with the discourses of all the other agents who shape the world for better or worse. The very good idea Dewey had was that democratic inquiry could make these discourses better and thus make the world better. So, in fact, by working from the perspective of the good of publics, whatever that may turn out to be, it is possible to have both normative and methodological intentions that support one another. And it might be the case that, in raising our sights in this way, academics that are concerned with normative questions might form a more acute sense of the relevance of what they do. And, then, they might be less inclined to leave what counts as publicly relevant research, the kinds of research that publics might interest themselves in, to the many kinds of research 'realists', even if they too make a valid contribution. And the first and most important task, beyond apathy, despair, and cynicism, is to draw attention to the discursive power of these publics, both the power they have and the power they should have, mindful of the fact that this power, like all power, must have limits.

In the gestation of this book, a number of people have been inspiring in many different ways. I would like to single out my colleague, Piet Strydom, who has been a in every way a major inspiration over many years and who has been a permanent, indispensable presence in my intellectual milieu. Intellectually, he has blazed a trail by developing a form of cognitive sociology from which this book has greatly benefited. This local milieu is small and I am greatly indebted to it for its remarkably high intellectual quality.

Another colleague, Tracey Skillington, has used her penetrating critical talents and general theoretical insight to good effect on my work over the years. My political philosophy colleague, Cara Nine, patiently and knowledgeably helped my education in this area. I am also greatly indebted to a number of postgraduate students who have contributed so much to making this milieu, though small, also vibrant. These include Roddy Condon, Mark Cullinane, Ronan Kaczynski, Richard Milner, Kieran O'Connor, Marie O'Shea, Siobhan O'Sullivan, April Park, Leonard Reidy, and Annie Schueler. Beyond this milieu, and yet part of it, I would like to single out Klaus Eder for being such a galvanizing presence during his many visits to Cork and, generally, for doing so much to develop the sociological dimension of critical theory. Jim Bohman's single visit was later, but during that visit and a return visit I made to St Louis he has made a considerable contribution to the ideas in the book.

On both a personal and professional level, I would like to offer special thanks to the copy-editors of this book, Sarah Bologna, Nicholas McMurry, Ronan O'Brien, and Siobhan O'Sullivan, who contributed not just to the improvement of the style and the clarity of the language but also, through their acute comments, to the ideas themselves. Further gratitude is due to Ronan for being there right to the end when needed. Finally, I would like to thank my editor at Peter Lang, Christabel Scaife, for her helpful contributions and great patience.

On a personal level, I would like to thank Kate Kalin and Klair van Haght for sorting out my organizational deficiencies and improving my decision-making capacities so as to make it possible to do this book at all. I thank Kate also for delving into the motivational foundations of this Irish academic and helping to change them. My dear dogs, Emerald, Leo, and Ruby, were great company throughout, though they might not say the same in return about these last months. At another motivational level, I owe an indescribable amount to Daniel and Mary, who were my companions at the book's origins. This book is dedicated to Daniel, who is a continuing presence, to my mother, Mary, who has since passed away, and to the dear memory of my father, Michael.

Introduction

The concept of the public sphere asserts the centrality of communication by an enlightened public to democratic politics (Fraser, 1992; Fraser, 2007; Habermas, 1989). In contemporary sociology and social theory, this concept is regarded as important, but it is nonetheless poorly elaborated. It has acquired a kind of pragmatic coherence, achieved through the sum of the multiple ways in which it is deployed. This applies not just to its sociological usage, but also to its usage in philosophy, politics, geography, and the humanities. One important factor explaining the absence of profound theoretical elaboration is that the concept of the public sphere draws from many disciplines in circumstances where interdisciplinary theory building is not highly developed. In this light, at the core of this book is the attempt to harness the combined potentials of two disciplines that are intrinsic to the study of the political public sphere, philosophy and sociology, to advance the goal of better theoretical elaboration. If the main concentration is on the sociological theory of the public sphere, it is recognized that the normative core of the concept is critically depend on philosophical ideas.

In one respect, the fate of the concept of public sphere parallels that of many core concepts in sociology. Concepts such as class, state, institution, and system that once claimed privilege in *explaining* social organization have become substantially redefined. Redefinition is expressed through the rise of a different conceptual repertoire, embracing such concepts as interaction, fluidity, dynamics, contingency, and relationality, which give priority to process over structure, innovation over stabilization. This development is part of the micro-sociological recapturing of the sociological imagination, which has significantly changed assumptions about the relative importance of macro-structures and micro-processes (Delanty and O'Mahony, 2002; Emirbayer, 1997; Rehg and Bohman, 2001).

The concept of the public sphere appears suited to this shift. It resonates with conceptual *complexes* such as epistemological multi-perspectivism, non-linear thinking, creative ferment, and dislocated, disempowered subjectivity. Yet, such concepts emphasize only one important dimension of the concept of publicity, which regards it as contingent, open, pluralistic, and contestatory.[1] The other important dimension, referencing classical and neo-classical traditions in sociology and their shared concerns with political philosophy, emphasizes society as a normatively structured reality. Translated into a communication theory by Habermas, such a normative perspective holds that modern society has to potential to reliably, transparently, and legitimately institute just and transparent organizational principles by the dual means of public discourse and democratic deliberation (Habermas, 1996).[2]

These two orientations draw from contrasting, yet interconnected, conceptions of society for which discourse is commonly central. The first emphasizes the erosion of any project of societal integration based on overarching 'universalistic' normative commitments; the other holds to a continuing enlightenment belief in the capacity of society *as a whole* to know and organize itself in the normative medium of morality, ethics, and law. Yet, generally, these approaches appear as incompatible alternatives. Sociologically, there is a further difficulty spanning both conceptions that has hindered the adoption of the concept of the public sphere. The discipline's primary critical mode is that of *critique* of macro-structures and the agents assumed to control them, whereas the normative reach of the public sphere concept, in the prominent line of the later Habermas

---

[1] The principle of publicity upheld from Kant onwards the idea that 'all actions affecting the rights of other human beings are wrong if their maxim is not compatible with their being made public' (Kant, 1917).

[2] The term 'public discourse' is preferred in this book to the more generally used term of 'public opinion'. This preference, amongst other reasons, follows Splichal's point about the term 'public', which, when used in combination with opinion, appearing merely as an adjective to something that is subjective, 'opinion' (Splichal, 1999). 'Public opinion' thus suggests a public translation of something originally private; 'public discourse', by contrast, suggests an entity that is intrinsically public in nature. These two terms characteristically emerge from different eras; the first from pre-war political science, closely associated with the birth of opinion polling, and the second with the general rise of the term discourse, associated with the constructivist epistemology that consolidated itself in the second half of the twentieth century.

at least, encompasses not just critical but also 'affirmative' and disclosing normative moments. The affirmative normative moment attends to those institutional capacities of modernity that should be defended, and the disclosing moment to another kind of capacity, that of envisioning possible normative progress. For modern critical theory, these three normative moments are central to grasping the role of public discourse.

The divided orientations of sociology, as they respectively shape scholarship of the public sphere, emanate from what are assumed, historically, to be opposing intellectual projects. The first, more actor-centred approach, corresponds to certain lines in contemporary sociological theory, partly inspired by post-structuralism, together with particular strands of radical political theory and stresses the purely critical and transformative normative moment. In one important approach, political authority appears as an empty space to be temporarily filled by the institutionalization and de-institutionalization of discourses shaped in the crucible of power struggles (Lefort, 1988: Nash, 2007; Von Trotha, 2006). By contrast, the other, more normative and structured, drawing off strands of deliberative, liberal, and republican theory stresses an enduring, if evolving, democratic project at the core of the normative culture of modernity. This partial affirmation of the normative culture of modernity is in critical theoretical writing joined by critical and disclosing normative moments. In some other theoretical traditions, for example, some versions of liberal political theory, these normative moments are either absent or are less emphasized.

Such different currents of academic opinion on the relationship between political practice and potentials for normative integration are engaged in a kind of strife that permeates writing on the public sphere and, more generally, on democracy. There is manifest contention between the emphasis on non-institutional politics and the creativity of political discourse on one hand and, on the other, on institutional politics and recognizable and reproducible procedures of political justification, though, as will be argued in later chapters, it is theoretically and empirically unproductive to draw the line too sharply in either direction.

One implication is that the public sphere is a challenging and underdeveloped concept in sociology, due to the interdisciplinary contexts in which it finds itself and the general intra-disciplinary reorientation. Sociology draws on both currents of thought sketched above and sometimes manages to creatively combine them. Its thought operates within an inescapable interdisciplinary context that ever more reaches into the core of the discipline. Any primacy it might claim for elaborating and applying the concept of public sphere, arising from the at least partial provenance of the concept within the discipline, has therefore to be qualified by the powerful impact of the interdisciplinary context, as well as the intrinsic difficulty it has found in theoretically explicating the concept *within* the discipline.

This book is primarily concerned with the role of the public sphere in relation to normative foundations of the democratic project of modernity. It is assumed that certain necessary values such as equality, legitimacy, publicity, fairness, legality, dignity, esteem, and freedom are intrinsic to this project. Moreover, it is assumed that the quality of democratic discourse within public spheres is intrinsic to the meaningful realization of these values. For this task, it takes its cue more from the sociological orientation concerned with the processes of building a just and responsible macro-social normative order, but now strongly guided by the constructivist, political impulses of the first orientation and wider interdisciplinary horizons. It is concerned with how the public, through many forms of participation in the public sphere, is intrinsic to the possibility of a normatively well ordered, just, and responsible society, even if it still remains far from that. In its concern for normative order, the book returns with changed register to the macro-normative focus of classical and neo-classical sociology that itself was in debate with the liberal philosophy of its time (Honneth, 2011; Seidman, 1983).

Normatively well ordered is not understood as a one-sided product of an existing public reason vested in a political elite in the sense of John Rawls (Rawls, 1993). It is, rather, conceived as the fragile but real achievement of good justification in the complex and pluralistic actuality of modern society. From the perspective of the contemporary theory of the public sphere advanced in this book, society can only be normatively ordered, unlike Rawls's conception, by means of extended public discourse that, rather than taking its lead from an elite public reason, instead specifies the latter's agenda. Only a public reason shaped by a fully democratic process of learning and justification involving all reasonable political agents can satisfy standards of being fully inclusive, fair, and effective, and hence make for a normatively well-ordered society (Habermas, 1995; Habermas, 2001).

The conscious shaping of a just and responsible social order is an achievement of a discursively formed *general* public will. Such a view of democracy not only differs from the restricted Rawlsian conception of public reason, but also from the view that politics involves continuous contestation, whether conceived in liberal or agonistic terms.[3] While contestation is absolutely central to the conception of politics offered in this book, it is regarded as only one part of a wider political process. Rather, in the tradition of certain strands of deliberative theory, the achievement of standards of justice and responsibility is taken to depend on the capacity to generate publicly justified principles and procedures that can be instituted with relative stability in the complex, contingent, and unpredictable conditions of modern society.

A fully developed sociological approach to communicative politics can demonstrate how the legitimate and effective operation of the public sphere can create a normative bridge between democratic politics and its societal environments or, indeed, demonstrate why such a bridge fails (O'Mahony, 2009). Normative principles and procedures are temporally and spatially subject to ongoing revision given the contingencies of the modern social order. Deontological commitment to such principles and procedures cannot be simply dogmatically asserted across time and place, as they are constantly subject to challenges arising from altered contexts and interpretive practices; hence, they must be redefined on an ongoing basis (Honneth, 2011). This sociological understanding of deontological commitment follows the *discourse ethical project* of the linguistification of Kant's ethics of duty. Foundational moral commitments, worked out through the discourse of affected agents, underpin democratically organized modern societies – for example, standards of relative equality, dignity, fairness, and freedom. Such commitments are consequentially qualified; their interpretation and relational significance may change through processes of public justification animated by capacities for collective learning that lie within and beyond formal political contexts.

---

3 Speaking generally, agonistic political theory is committed to the view that utopian and universalistic ideas of societal integration are misplaced and diminish the significance of spaces and kinds of contestation driven by human passion.

Full public justification is the key mechanism for constructing normative culture. This culture is both a guiding input to and outcome of the multi-level organization of democratic communication. Sociology, working closely with other disciplines, can show how such communicative organization, using Nancy Fraser's criteria, can be not only legitimate, but effective (Fraser, 2007). Just as fundamental a task, and one that expresses the very essence of a theory of critical publicity, is to demonstrate the formidable impediments to full public justification that lie in pathologies afflicting normative cultures. In Forst's terms, these can lead to bad justification that sustains relations of domination (Forst, 2007a, 2007b). Conceptualized in this way, the sociology of discursive democracy has an important contribution to make to democratic theory. It can broaden its range by showing how democratic justification and the formation of normative culture in learning processes take place in social spheres beyond formal democratic institutions. For this task, the restriction of justification to these institutions and the associated restriction of the counterfactual imagination should be transcended – and the enduring contribution of Boltanski and Thévenot, who drew attention to the wide range of justificatory standards and relations that permeate modernity, fully recognized. It becomes clear, too, that the sociological account of democratic justification by publics must no longer be left on the margins of democratic theory.

The remainder of this introduction identifies the critical issues and debating lines that form the context of the book's intended contribution. In so doing, it first offers a short overview of the public sphere concept as developed in the debate opened up by Habermas's early *Structural Transformation* (Habermas, 1989) and, drawing on this overview, concludes by outlining the steps followed in subsequent chapters towards realizing this contribution.

The Public Sphere: History of a Concept from Structural Transformation to the Present

Few deny the pioneering significance of the contribution of Jürgen Habermas to articulating the modern conception of the public sphere. This arises as much from Habermas's own efforts to advance the concept as from the criticisms and contributions by others in response. Reconstructing these important debates even briefly and selectively presents difficulties, not least in following timelines operating across two linguistic communities, German and English, that were, in the immediate aftermath of the publication of *The Structural Transformation of the Public Sphere* in 1962, and for several decades to follow, largely insulated from one another.[4]

For the first extended era, following the original publication of *Structural Transformation* in the early 1960s right up to the early 1990s, two fundamental crystallizing nodes of critical reception emerged, that offered by Negt and Kluge within the extensive German debate in the 1960s and 1970s, and by Nancy Fraser within the English language debate that followed the book's English translation in 1989 (Negt and Kluge, 1993; Fraser, 1992; Habermas, 1989). These distinctive contributions of the first era of reception highlight fundamental theoretical issues that still remain alive, notably to do with equality of status, the division between private and public, the range of public spheres, the degree of separation of state and civil society, the nature of cultural production and reception, and different readings of critical publicity. The second era is defined by Habermas' revised account of the public sphere in *Between Facts and Norms* in the 1990s. A number of key themes characterize this second era, notably the growing relevance of the transnational context for the public sphere and the enhanced importance attached to the relationship between democracy and political communication.

Habermas's *Structural Transformation* saw the category of public sphere as lying between state and civil society. The idea of a public that could not alone demand accountability from political authority, but could regard itself as the arbiters of the legitimacy of that authority, was intrinsically associated with the emergence of civil society as an autonomous sphere of private citizens who assert the public relevance of their opinions (Calhoun, 1992).

---

4   Several of Habermas's books will be regularly referred to throughout the text. Therefore, the following shorthand conventions will be used. For *The Structural Transformation of the Public Sphere: An Inquiry into a Category of Bourgeois Society*, the term *Structural Transformation* will be used. Similarly, for *Between Facts and Norms: Contributions to a Discourse Theory of Law and Democracy*, the term *Between Facts and Norms* will be used; and for *The Theory of Communicative Action Volumes 1 and 2*, the term *Communicative Action* will be used.

At first, private citizens acted publicly and politically through the medium of loosely structured exchanges of ideas in particular locales – coffee or tea houses are often instanced – that were, at least in principle, unbound from social status. Gradually, these unofficial and sometimes even secretive gatherings led to the formation of political associations that became bolder and more open in their activities. The goal of such associations of would-be citizens was to assert and maintain the autonomy of civil society as a forum for 'rational-critical' discourse that would be free from political domination and thereby could establish values of freedom, equality, and publicity as the basis of a democratically transformed politics.

This discourse owed its origin and transformation from non-public to public opinion to the formative experience of participating in literary debate, an experience that over time and in certain conditions of political opportunity gradually became extended to address the political status of civil society itself. The centrality of such rational-critical discourse to the gradually refashioned relationship between the political and social spheres draws attention to the enduring legacy of Habermas's development of the concept of public sphere, together with the concept of the public in a longer intellectual lineage that amongst others embraces Tönnies, Park, Dewey and Mills (Dewey, 1927; Mills, 1968; Park, 1972; Tönnies, 1992). In this tradition, modern society does not simply depend upon the procedure of voting as an aggregation mechanism for establishing legitimate political authority and reaching political decision. It depends more fundamentally on the communicative process of the formation of reasonable public will by means of rational-critical discourse. The latter is more fundamental as it embraces the indispensable ethos of democracy, an ethos that must be constantly communicatively replenished and without which it could not endure.

The innovation of the concept of the public sphere was to emphasize how democracy depended on agents capable of common and respectful reasoning. In so doing, it drew attention to the centrality of the public to the legitimacy and efficacy of democracy. Moreover, it did this in a sociologically potent manner, not simply axiologically asserting the sovereignty of the people or the constitutional guarantees of citizenship, but also demonstrating how communication media, networks, and practices converge in differing social conditions and institutional configurations to generate public will. Above all, it emphasized how a rational-critical public was vital to democracy, one capable of respectful, transparent, explicit, and epistemically cogent public reasoning.

Perhaps the most contentious claim raised in *Structural Transformation* was that enacting the classical bourgeois ideal of publicness involved a bracketing of status differentials. In Habermas's early account, this egalitarian bourgeois public sphere had a short lifespan and subsequently degenerated into the 're-feudalized' assertion of private, corporate hegemony over the technologically advancing communication media during the nineteenth and twentieth centuries. The idea of the bracketing of status differentials that Habermas attributed to the original bourgeois idea was an essentially Kantian view of the moral status of practical reason. Practical reason in this account required ineliminable commitment to truth, impartiality, and publicity, if the necessary conditions for a free and rational society were to be met. Habermas transposed the 'regulative idea' of practical reason into the moral-normative foundations of democracy, manifested in the disinterested ethos that must attend democratic participation. To a multitude of critics, the idea that 'bourgeois men' – what some critics claimed was Habermas's default category – could act for the good of all, was an unsustainable idea, something of an overly abstract and implausible fiction.

In his 1992 essay, 'Further Reflections on the Public Sphere', Habermas explains that he had been trying to draw out the connection between the ideals of bourgeois humanism – articulated in the key principles of subjectivity and self-actualization, rational political will formation, and political and personal self-determination – and the institutional framework of the constitutional state (Habermas, 1992). In *Structural Transformation*, Habermas claimed that these bourgeois ideals reached beyond historically achieved constitutional orders and continued to offer utopian horizons though, in the end, they were substantially negated in the practices of modern society, in large part a product of the structural transformation that led to the degeneration of the public sphere (Habermas, 1989). However, in his 1992 chapter, Habermas revised his account of the bourgeois public sphere in *Structural Transformation*, considering that it ran the risk of over-idealizing a set of norms and value orientations that actually proved historically ambivalent, even cynical, about democratic commitments. He instead proposes the invariant standard of the intersubjective commitments arising in ordinary communication, commitments that do not depend on hypostatizing the normative achievements of any historical era.

In moving to ground normative standards in the various commitments to validity used in ordinary communication, Habermas encountered further criticism directed at what was assumed to be an even greater degree of abstract idealization. To the critics, turning to the formal pragmatic validity commitments of ordinary language result in normative standards that float above social and political life and that are impossible to realize in practice, or alternately generate utopian potentials that so disregard the actual conditions of political practice as to be pernicious.

The criticisms of Habermas's model of the bourgeois public sphere as over-idealized, disembodied, and impartial raise important issues for the understanding of the public sphere. Yet, can the critics have it both ways? In spite of his own distancing from them, some degree of defence of the normative claims inherent in Habermas's 1962 account of bourgeois ideals may be useful, even if these normative claims are concretely tied to a particular social project. This point should properly be defended in the full context of the debate that followed the English translation of *Structural Transformation* but, in the interests of brevity and clarity, some concise theoretical remarks will here suffice.

In the first place, if the role of democracy is to generate binding social rules based on morally defensible procedures, these rules must be given primacy in social organization. Social rules emerge both from the substantive framework of rights, liberties, entitlements, and obligations and from instituted procedures and public discourses. Such rule-forming standards and processes have to be consciously carried by agents capable of acting for the good of all, or at least what they perceive to be the good of all in a given time and place. The fact that the good of all applies only to a given ethical community of citizens qualifies but does not remove universalistic intentions. Though bourgeois ideology, as Marx originally argued, was universalistic in intention but often highly particular in application, its universalistic intentions were not necessarily exhausted by its practices. At least some of the intentions lying behind these ideals, to use Forst's phrase, could still be reciprocally and generally justified. And even in those many cases where the establishment of rules favours a particular social group, they nonetheless have to be defended from a general standpoint, thereby illustrating the power of the counterfactual argument in favour of universality that recurs again and again in modern politics.[5] Beyond Habermas, the very idea of the public as rational-critical and universalistic, and opposed to the crowd or the mass, consistently appeared in early twentieth-century theorizing as the democratic project of universalization gathered pace, becoming gradually more socially immanent. That many of these writers could also bemoan what Dewey called the 'eclipse of the public' did not invalidate its counterfactual and partly realized status as the carrier of a universalistic principle (Dewey, 1927; Mills, 1968; Park, 1972; Tönnies, 1992).

In the second place, if democracy is to be regarded as an achievement that can be built upon, however imperfect its concrete manifestations and however much potentially attainable ideals may be regarded as reaching beyond its current status, then the historical genesis of this achievement together with its evolving normative validity must be recognized. This implies that the bourgeois democratic revolution contained important utopian moments that, beyond their ongoing future potential, *actually were* moral-normatively institutionalized. This is an important strength of Habermas's early account of the public sphere even if, as discussed above, the argument over-strongly endorsed the actual bourgeois public sphere, a position he would later try to correct by using the quasi-transcendental ideal of communicative rationality. These observations of course assume that bourgeois democracy actually was an achievement, a view that can be defended from the vantage point of history only in a highly qualified manner.

The above remarks presage an important theme of the book, the dialectic between quasi-transcendent counterfactual standards and social

---

5 The counterfactual idea of acting for the good of all is complicated in modern societies, not least by the anchorage of political parties in ideologies and particular social milieus. But 'real' counterfactuals carry that sense of the general good by taking a negative form; nobody can afford to ignore that certain classes of action must be defended as being for the general good, even in those cases where the actions are not so motivated.

immanence. Counterfactual ideals can only be institutionally realized when they are supported by social experiences of varying kinds. These experiences could be a sense of the moral infringement of a particular group that give rise to claims to recognition and associated social conflict along the lines proposed in Honneth's recognition theory or Bourdieu's theory of classification struggle; they could also be more general experiences of democracy that are based on making counterfactuals institutionally real in structures of private and public autonomy, though without exhausting their further potential (Bourdieu, 1984; Honneth, 2011). The younger Habermas of *Structural Transformation* advanced a more historical sociological account of the latter process, which is sometimes unjustifiably lost sight of, not only in his own later work but, as Honneth more generally points out, in political philosophy after Hegel (Honneth, 2011).

Structural Transformation defined the debate in the public sphere in Germany in the 1960s and 1970s. Its publication in English began a further round of debate in the English-speaking world. In what follows, major issues in these debates are briefly recapitulated, first of all addressing the contribution of Negt and Kluge's *The Public Sphere and Experience*. It goes on to consider the influential reception of the concept of public sphere into the English-speaking debate by Nancy Fraser, then returning to Habermas's later reworking of the concept, before addressing the distinction between normative and empirical public legitimacy raised by Bernhard Peters that crystallizes important issues taken up in this book. The concluding section of the chapter considers the theoretical implications of these issues in terms of the unfolding argument of the book.

Negt and Kluge's Critical Cultural Sociology of the Public Sphere

Negt and Kluge's text, *The Public Sphere and Experience*, originally published in German in the early 1970s, shares an intellectual atmosphere with Habermas's *Structural Transformation* (Negt and Kluge, 1993). Both books advance a neo-Marxist critique of the negative impact on public life of the capitalist form of the social organization of economic production and distribution. Both develop a critical perspective on capitalism, less with respect to social consequences of inequality and exploitation and more to its colonization of the collective imagination that is a prerequisite for such consequences. The industrialization of consciousness that springs from the capitalist massification of cultural production and the generally alienated nature of social relations formed in a capitalist production system does not result in an active public keen to participate in political communication. Instead, the colonization of will by a sensationalist media combines with the lack of participatory opportunity to create a predisposition towards a reified, instrumental rationality that can be technocratically managed.

The difference between Habermas and Negt and Kluge is nonetheless significant, particularly with respect to the normative foundations of the public sphere. This difference rests on the respective evaluations of the bourgeois public sphere, notwithstanding Habermas's changing position on this question, outlined above. Negt and Kluge, continuing Adorno's critique of enlightenment reason, take the view that the bourgeois public sphere does not simply degenerate as Habermas claimed, but that it is flawed from the outset because of its abstract and general quality that destroys all particularity, especially the capacity to make sense of and act on everyday life experience. The normative architecture of Negt and Kluge's critique of the bourgeois public sphere parallels Adorno's critique of the false synthesis ('totality') of bourgeois ideology and parallels it, too, in the strategy of asserting the potential of creative cultural production dredged from the flows of experience to act against such an ideology.

By means of a productivist paradigm, Negt and Kluge establish symmetry between the capitalist production system and the bourgeois public sphere secured in constitutional law. Just as the capitalist economic system separates the person from ownership of the use value of their labour, ineluctably leading to the atrophy of the positive experience of labour within an overall life context, so the bourgeois public sphere also separates the authentic producers of use value and social experience from the tools that enable collective will to be produced. The analogy rests on the idea that the bourgeois public sphere has a predominantly illusory notion of publicness, a publicness that is permanently enthralled to the mechanisms of private control that characterize bourgeois society.

In the private sphere of production, the control mechanism is to be found in the organization of labour, a control mechanism that is extended by private culture-producing organizations to the control of consciousness. In this way, the possibility of authentic publicness may be asserted, in that all can equally contribute to public debate and will formation, yet there are no means that enable this to happen. What the bourgeois public sphere is adept at, therefore, is the 'illusion of participation by all members of society', an illusion that inhibits dissent and whose very illusory quality, leading to public assent on disadvantageous premises, is one of the foundations of 'social discipline' (Negt and Kluge, 1993, p. 56). This is sustained by the formal emptiness of bourgeois constitutional ideals that hide wide disparities of social power and opportunity.

Negt and Kluge do allow that the public sphere is not entirely an illusory experience that exclusively facilitates bourgeois and post-bourgeois domination of social life. The existing public sphere is a form for expressing use values, even if the bourgeoisie determine them. The form allows for the 'idealistic revolutionizing' of the public context by those subordinate to the bourgeois organization of democratic participation and public communication. Such non-bourgeois elements continuously produce use values and have worked at creating forms of human relationship, modes of social intercourse and intellectual constructs. In a somewhat ambivalent formulation that relies mostly on a footnote, the authors claim that the form of the bourgeois public sphere contains 'emancipatory auxiliary phenomena' that should not lead to seductive incorporation, but also should not be 'radically' rejected. This formulation creates space for the 'positive' moment in the authors' work where they develop the idea of counter-public spheres – the proletarian public sphere is the most prominent example – in which dominant forms of publicity can be subverted and experientially authentic communication practices can redirect the potentials of communicative media. They understand this process of subversion to be carried by a bricolage of disparate semantic elements generated by innovative production techniques. These subvert the intention of control built into the form of established media and anticipate later formulations about the emancipatory potential of the new internet-based media.

Negt and Kluge's difference from Habermas lies, too, in how they identify significant normative potentials immanently in the bourgeois public sphere. Habermas's judgement in this regard is, in certain respects, not specific to a particular historical moment, but is inscribed in the very potential of the constitutional democratic frame itself. Clearly present in Habermas's early account is the idea – and this is confirmed in his later work – that constitutional democracies must contain at least some of these normative potentials and, offer in their model of communicative power, however imperfectly, a springboard for more (Habermas, 1996). Though Habermas has always acknowledged the social critique of inequality and alienated living conditions, he does not regard the reality of these conditions as pointing to the complete negation of established constitutional democratic principles. In fact, he argues that the constitutional democratic state, admittedly via the paradoxical and dependency-inducing model of the social welfare state, results in reduced levels of inequality. As a consequence, an egalitarian orientation has become incorporated into political ideologies and governance programmes, even if they are presently subject to challenge. Negt and Kluge hold, by contrast, that the structure and extent of social domination and alienation arising from capitalist organization makes impossible anything other than a form of democracy that is also a mode of domination and which they provocatively entitle the dictatorship of the bourgeoisie.

Negt and Kluge and Habermas therefore provide radically different estimations of the historic contribution of democratic constitutional models to social justice and authentic life experiences. Their estimations mirror an important divide in the general literature on the public sphere. What is a tendency in the early Habermas, the communicative rationality that is immanently built into democratic forms by virtue of the institutionalization of communicative power, is a motif in the later Habermas. While he predominantly defends this position by means of the counterfactual device of the ideal speech situation, he also believes that democratic communication must operate legitimately and effectively in actual empirically observable societies. The communicatively reproduced constructions of normativity that find their way into the democratic regulation of social life thus, in his view, must exhibit a historical pattern whose mechanisms are socially immanent. But Habermas neglects to systematically address internal mechanisms for building normative culture, and at considerable cost, for it is they that give rise to the capacity for collective learning – as opposed to Habermas's emphasis on individual learning (Strydom, 1987) – through the medium of political discourse that feeds into and renovates democratic institutions.

Nonetheless, Habermas's framework implies a two-track model of related innovation and institutionalization of democratic ideals as an ongoing, historically evolving process, though this idea is not concretely developed and sits uneasily with his strong counterfactual assumptions. In this understanding, the defensible normative content of democratic arrangements is not merely transcendentally projected into a possible future state of society. It is also immanent in existing democratic arrangements, even if potentially surpassed by critical judgement and normative projection. This double conception of democratic normativity, immanent and projective, frames Habermas's conception of the public sphere.

Negt and Kluge do not operate with a strong thesis of normative learning in this sense. Rather, they conceive of learning as transposing into public view capacities collected in the body, in the unconsciousness, and in collective cognitive structures. They develop a critical account of meaning that is emancipatory in the sense of equipping agents with the capacity to generate authentic self-expression. But their analysis does not extend to how learning achieved in this register could lead to transformed normative structures. Negt and Kluge tie symbolic emancipation to material justice. Many writers on democracy and the public sphere, such as Nancy Fraser and Chantal Mouffe, pursue a similar tack in assuming that the temporal and conceptual affinity between symbolic liberation and material justice drives democratic innovation, usually without historically and empirically demonstrating the mechanisms of how democratization has developed, or might develop, in this register.

Beyond this, Habermas's difference from Negt and Kluge's brings to bear another important divide in contemporary social theory, two opposing interpretations of the nature of contemporary communication societies. On one side, Habermas still operates with the idea that collective identities and new political cultures can be communicatively constructed with positive normative implications for the complementary development of state and society. His more recent remarks on feminism, for example, illustrate how values that arise in the private sphere of society ultimately acquire innovative political significance (Habermas, 2001). It is this estimation of the normative significance of a historically unfolding democratic constitutional project that most decisively distinguishes Habermas from his critics, both in the earlier and later work. The status of the constitutional state and its relation to the public sphere and the identity projects of civil society therefore emerge as a major theme in the scholarship of the public sphere.

On the other side is to be found an architecture stressing the ongoing circulation of semantic contents and the play of difference. When developed as a social semantics in the hands of Derrida and Luhmann, this approach appears to minimize the role of agents as creators of meaning. While Negt and Kluge have, by contrast, an emphatic sense of emancipatory agency, this agency appears to lack any long run institutional implications, largely because they have a negative estimation of the hitherto existing achievements of democracy.

In this sense, and given affinities with a post-structuralist concept of power as disciplining domination, the authors are not completely separated from the de-agentialized conception of much of the post-structural account of meaning. Agents may generate meaning in the liminal conditions of the late bourgeois world, but this meaning merely gestures to some future possible state of society that is impossible to conceive of in any concrete sense. Further to this point, the proletarian lifeworld and public sphere celebrated by Negt and Kluge has progressively weakened in the thirty five years or so since the original German text and no longer serves as a rallying point for a transformative idea of justice, as it once did for many.[6]

The work of Negt and Kluge still reads as modern and relevant in its ideas of fragmented consciousness, normative dislocation, and the identification of counter-public idioscapes, even if the 'proletarian' identity project on which it is based is no longer tenable on its own as a catalyst and

---

6   This conception of justice centrally contributed to the establishment of higher levels of social equality over the course of the twentieth century, a trend that is currently being reversed.

criterion of social transformation. And to the proletarian public sphere of Negt and Kluge has been added a multitude of other public spheres, such as the feminist and black public spheres (Hansen, 1993).

The Multi-Stranded Critique of Nancy Fraser

Many of the themes developed by Negt and Kluge, such as their critique of the bourgeois model, the multiplicity of public spheres, and the constitution and significance of counter-publics, arise again in the reception of Habermas in the English-speaking world. In many respects, the often cited essay by Nancy Fraser, 'Rethinking the Public Sphere: A Contribution to the Critique of Actually Existing Democracy', is prototypical of this appreciative, but still strongly critical, reception (Fraser, 1992).

Fraser raises four points against what she calls Habermas's 'bourgeois masculinist' account of the public sphere, each of which she believes to be supported by revisionist historiography. The first is one that has been addressed briefly above: the claim that status differentials cannot be bracketed in the political public sphere and that political equality cannot be achieved without social equality. Claims to act in the good of all are always compromised by political power relations that mirror actual social inequality. It is hard to argue against Fraser's empirical accuracy. The example she gives of the communicative diminution of women's contributions in a professional – and, it might be added, in an everyday – context is abundantly confirmed over and over again by any sensitized observer. This is, therefore, a point of great importance for the empirical-theoretical and normative analysis of real public spheres.

Objections can, however, be raised when this position is overextended to suggest that the bourgeois ideal had no conception of subordinating particular interests to the common good. Universalistic ideas were important, particularly when articulated with respect to the dignity and autonomy of individual persons, equality before the law and the sovereignty of the public – even if their full import for the political participation of different categories of people and cosmopolitan citizenship were still far from realization. It is not that Fraser cannot see this; it is simply that the argument from the vantage point of social exclusion needs to be balanced by consideration of what has been achieved and how much it owes to the idea of universalization first institutionally articulated in bourgeois constitution-building. An important further issue here is the assessment of the contribution of liberal and republican constitutional philosophies, owing their genesis to bourgeois ideals, to the public equality of contemporary societies. These issues are dealt with more systematically in Part I.

The second point raised by Fraser is her objection to the idea that the proliferation of competing publics within multiple public spheres is always to be regarded as democratically inferior to a single, comprehensive public sphere. This point allows her to introduce the term *subaltern counterpublics*, a term that closely echoes the ideas of Negt and Kluge two decades earlier. Once again, empirically, this should be regarded as an important idea. Indeed, Fraser's claim that what is needed is a critical political sociology that addresses multiple but unequal publics, and that this means to theorize the contestatory interaction of publics and to identify the mechanisms that render some of them subordinate to others, is a clear statement of a constructivist sociological task that has yet to be properly fulfilled. Moreover, the idea of publics intrinsically differentiated by identity, and the importance of intercultural translation in common forums are also highly pertinent points that provide insight into the present conjuncture.

Essentially the same issue, however, arises as in the case of the first criticism: how could the outcomes of such interaction be described in terms of the moral-normative integration of society? Do competing and differentiated publics ever come to an understanding and sometimes even to a fully reasoned consensus? If so, what is the nature of such a consensus and how important is it for the influence of democracy on social integration and change? Or, indeed, can forms of consensus and dissensus be more generally described and linked to a single framework for the establishment of political will within a given political community (Miller, 1986; Miller, 2002; O'Mahony, 2010; Splichal, 1999)? And what would be the consequences of the absence of such a general process of political will formation? It is not enough simply to draw attention to what lies beyond the idea of a single overarching public sphere without considering the wider institutional implications for the possibility of a well-ordered and just common life. The kind of difference- and conflict-theoretical tools used by Fraser are not in a position to do this, though they *are* well equipped for exploring excluded discourses and innovative challenges.

Fraser's third point opposes the assumption that discourse in the public sphere should always be discourse about the common good and that the appearance of 'private issues' and 'private interests' is always undesirable. In the course of her exposition of this position, she makes two important observations. The first is to clarify that acting in the common good does not necessarily have to entail discourse about the common good. The latter she describes as a civic-republican position and she ascribes such a position to Habermas. By contrast, she claims that deliberation for the common good does not necessarily entail a commitment to a single all-encompassing 'we' as in the republican position; it has to be held open as a principle that parties to any kind of deliberation may hold different interests and that these interests may not be reducible to any version of the common good in the strong sense. This position, though Fraser does not say so directly, appears to attach more force to the liberal emphasis on bargaining than she thinks is allowed for in the degree of primacy that Habermas attaches to moral consensus. It bears a close relation to what Max Miller describes as 'rational dissensus', where opposing parties come to an understanding about the nature of their differences, but do not agree except in the sense of agreeing to disagree (Miller, 1992; O'Mahony, 2010). However, unlike Fraser, Miller ties such rational dissensus to the possibility of collective learning – or the capacity to resist learning – through the medium of public discourse, thereby explicitly tying a conflict-theoretical position to one of social integration.

Fraser also raises the shifting boundaries as to what should constitute matter for public discussion. These boundaries have been revised significantly in the case of gender issues – wife-battering is Fraser's example – particularly where matters that were once regarded as private are now regarded as public and subject to legal regulation, illustrating how problematic ideas of what is and is not publicly relevant can be sustained by dominant worldviews. Fraser correctly claims that the early Habermas failed to identify the particularity entailed by the 'bourgeois-masculinist' domination of the *public* agenda and hence did not recognize the repression of women, historically relegated by forced exclusion to the *private* sphere. The later Habermas, himself a product of his times, has given a greater degree of attention to gender issues and, generally, work on the public sphere is vitally important for examining the mechanisms of conscience-formation through moral learning and the manner in which it becomes socially relevant (O'Mahony, 2010).

The final point raised by Fraser is to oppose the idea that the democratic public sphere requires a sharp separation of civil society and the state. Here, Fraser draws a distinction between strong and weak publics. Strong publics, such as parliamentary bodies, have decision-making power, whereas weak publics can merely indirectly influence decision-making through the formation of public will. She claims that the bourgeois conception of the public sphere that she attributes to Habermas institutionalized this distinction and thereby created a categorical divide that excluded the general public from having a real say in decision-making. James Bohman makes a similar point in his critique of the public sphere model that the later Habermas elaborated in *Between Facts and Norms* (Bohman, 1994).

Fraser uses this distinction to call for an exploration of the relative appropriateness in given situations of direct and representative democracy and to suggest the possibility of 'hybrid' forms. This observation highlights the extent to which democratic theory is grappling with the contemporary crisis of representative democracy in both empirical – evident malfunctioning – and normative terms – conceptions of its appropriateness in the context of alternatives (Young, 2010). Fraser further ties in the territorial level at which democracy and the public sphere can operate in a way that is mindful of the mass media induced de-territorialization of the public sphere that Negt and Kluge had already observed. Today, the impact of new media on territorial opinion and will formation, the role of the public at different territorial levels of democracy, has become an urgent issue for public sphere theory and research (Bohman, 2004; O'Mahony, 2009; Splichal, 2010).

In a later article, which is still concerned with the critical reception of *Structural Transformation*, Fraser continues the exploration of issues of territorialization when she sets out to criticize and displace the Westphalian model of the public sphere (Fraser, 2007). She sees this public sphere model as occurring within the boundaries of clearly defined nation-states, and as a typical, and yet mistaken, assumption of earlier theories of the public sphere, embracing Habermas and his various critics including Fraser herself. Fraser questions what happens if the public sphere breaks out of the Westphalian frame. In particular, what becomes of the critical function of the public sphere for checking domination and democratizing governance? This formulation is, in fact, strikingly similar to that of Habermas in *Postnational Constellations*, where the nation-state is represented as a contingent accompaniment rather than essential telos of modernity, and one whose era of domination is coming to an end, with significant implications for the relationship between public will formation and governance structures (Habermas, 2001).

Both writers essentially call for a strengthening of cosmopolitan consciousness that Habermas views as the completion of an evolutionary learning process which originally moved from the local and dynastic to the democratic consciousness of the self-legislating national public. Fraser expresses the view that public sphere theory must envision new transnational public powers that can be made accountable to new democratic transnational circuits of public opinion. Habermas additionally poses the question of the kind of intercultural learning that would ground a cosmopolitan identity able to address issues that reach beyond national self-interest. He sees this as requiring the construction of overlapping lifeworlds that meaningfully penetrate one another so as to be able to generate a common will on pressing trans-societal issues (Bohman, 2004; Trenz and Eder, 2004).

The issues raised by Fraser's early article crystallize the debate on Habermas's conception of the political public sphere at a particular point in time. However Fraser's arguments are judged against those of Habermas, her article clearly summates critical issues in the theory of the public sphere. While this offers a normative challenge, it also raises important theoretical-methodological issues for historical and empirical research on the public sphere. She raises questions of inclusion and exclusion, territorial scale, multiple arenas and publics, logics of identity formation, boundaries of public and private, and forms of democracy. In so doing, she continues a tradition of criticism first initiated by Negt and Kluge in the German debate. At the centre of this debate is a radical rethinking of the public sphere that, some twenty years later, may be identified as making an important contribution.

Development of a Theory: The Later Habermas and the Public Sphere

The later work of Habermas on the public sphere is distinguished not only from his own earlier account but also, and decisively, from the direction of criticism represented in a trajectory from Negt and Kluge to Fraser and many others. There are two pivotal differences. The first is that Habermas has developed a comprehensive theory of the constitutional state as a complex shaped in its normative foundations by the two-sided rationalization of modern society. This theory advances a version of the old Marxist account of reification in the thesis of the potential colonization of everyday life by the systemic 'steering media' of power and money that carry the danger of weakening its communicative foundations. He also identifies a countervailing force in an even more fundamental process of communicative rationalization affecting modern society as a whole. In its democratic-political version, this communicative rationalization shapes the internal working of the constitutional state. The fully developed account of the constitutional state means that Habermas now transposes assumptions about the incipient universalism of the bourgeois public into a qualified confidence about the degree of real universalism attained in the modern legal-political order

While Habermas is more inclined to defend these developments in the abstract, counterfactual discourse ethical terms of the ideal communication community, they also represent a historical learning process that emphasizes the significance of enlightenment universalism. Habermas separates himself from his own earlier self by the comprehensiveness of the treatment of the communicative constitutional state. He separates himself from some of his critics, too, by the insistence that learning episodes in the public sphere do not always point forward to possible realization in a distant future but, in certain crucial instances, have already taken form in the practical rationality of the democratic constitutional order.

The second theoretical development with significant implications for the theory of the public sphere is the way that, from the 1980s onwards, Habermas develops a two-track theory of society, emphasizing system integration through the steering media of money and power, on the one side, and social integration through the communicative generation of meaning in everyday life, on the other. From a normative-political standpoint, the steering media of money and power must be sufficiently autonomous to organize the play of interest-driven positions in formal spheres and yet secondary to the resource of social solidarity emerging from civil society.

In the decentred conditions of modern society the norms that underpin social integration cannot directly programme the operations of purposive-rational systems. Instead, they must be continuously discursively elaborated in terms of functional implications and normative appropriateness by means of episodes of political will formation in the public sphere. The relationship between forms of social solidarity and functional organization is established via the outcomes of such episodes. In this sphere, too, Habermas takes care to interrelate the macro concerns of societal integration with the dynamic processes of discursive elaboration. Law becomes an essential mediating force between the generation of resources of social solidarity and the embedding of these resources in the operations of social systems. Public discourse therefore has to be filtered through legal discourse and legal norms play the dominant role in the steering of differentiated social systems and action spheres.

Habermas's account of the public sphere in the 1990s has to be understood in relation to the above formulation of the requirements of social integration. Social integration is achieved by virtue of a differentiated and yet inter-dependent normative-political complex, composed of deliberative, administrative, and judicial bodies, which channels resources of social solidarity. Social solidarity enjoys primacy over the functional organization of society, though the latter must be granted appropriate autonomy. The public sphere is the forum for the distillation of social solidarity; innovative discourses let loose on the societal periphery undergo a complex transformation process in that public sphere – in order to become institutionally significant they must be carried anonymously, divorced from their initial sponsors. It makes no sense to conflate the creative dynamism of the societal periphery with the stringent consistency and rigour required of the legal and decision-making core.

The concept of communicative power advanced in *Between Facts and Norms*, describes the process whereby the public comes to influence legal-administrative programmes and policies (Habermas, 1996). In the so-called sluice model, public discourse washes into the legal-administrative context of decision-making, forcing continuous justification of norms rather than merely effective application within it. Issues are initially worked up in the *context of discovery* of the public sphere and become refined for purposes of application in the *context of justification* taking place in the legal-administrative political core. Borrowing a schema of Bernhard Peters, Habermas describes the interaction between the public and the administrative core as the constitutional circuit of power (Peters, 1993).

The advantage of the later Habermas's highly complex and sophisticated model is that he places the concept of the public sphere both within the overall theory of society and then within the constitutionally regulated governance order. He therefore embeds public discourse in the general context of normative integration. The communicative model of society that underpins this conception conceives of public discourse as circulating around the various arenas for the operation of publicity in such a way that pragmatically, morally, and ethically conditioned political will can be seen to shape legally achieved societal steering.

Habermas, therefore, does not see it as sufficient to assert the diagnostic critique of the societal periphery as the principal rationale for public discourse without a concerted attempt to relate it to a wider normative framework conceived on the basis of the theory of society. This implies that he views the constitutional framework for the realization of communicative power as an achievement, albeit an incomplete and contradictory one. Through his account of the public sphere, Habermas holds to the conception of the communicative power of the public in which the legal-political steering of society can be conceived, in part actually, and in part potentially, as normatively well ordered. But how can communicative power be secured in complex social and political conditions? The answer lies not simply in advancing normative arguments for comprehensive communicative power, but in understanding the empirically manifested mechanisms that enable or block it.

Bernhard Peters: Normative and Empirical Dimensions of Publicity

As Habermas himself has frequently pointed out, there are no longer any metaphysical guarantees in a post-metaphysical world that can shape the direction of societal development. It follows that there is no progressive teleology built into the normative foundations of the public use of reason that stand above and direct countervailing processes of irresponsible power and runaway complexity. Only the fragile resources of public argumentation and accumulated normative learning can be arrayed against the apparently unceasing capacity of contemporary societies to generate unjust and irresponsible conditions and syndromes. In this context, of great importance for the theory of the public sphere over the narrower remit of theories of deliberative democracy, are the actual communicative mechanisms for the generation of political will, spanning what Fraser describes as strong and weak publics, which, in the end, must be democratically defining (Fraser, 1992).

Bernhard Peters, in an essay on deliberative publicity written for Habermas's seventieth birthday festschrift, draws attention to some of the tensions between the normative and empirical accounts of public discourse in assessing two different concepts of legitimacy (Peters, 2001). From a normative standpoint, a political order or decision is legitimate when specific reasonable and transparent justifications and obligations are present. From an empirical standpoint, legitimacy extends beyond the general compliance with a political order to its status as a kind of active assent or loyalty. In the latter sense, it is composed of phenomena such as custom or affective identity with a given tradition – national identity is a good example – which can only be weakly normatively justified. The empirical concept of legitimacy is, in certain respects, more comprehensive than the normative one, as it can include the normative concept as an element within the overall process of legitimating a political order.

Following on from the distinction made by Peters, it does not take much reflection to see that contradictions may arise between these two accounts of legitimacy. A political regime may be empirically legitimated for non- or even anti-democratic reasons. This could arise, for example, where a regime is accorded legitimacy by a majority precisely because it suppresses a minority regarded as ethnically or socially different. Hence, there is no a priori guarantee that deliberatively produced normative legitimacy will prevail over democratically indefensible forms of legitimacy that may still enjoy the support of some of the public. This is one factor that leads to the necessity of differentiated judgements on the normative status of different contemporary public spheres and on the intrinsic tensions within them between normative and non-normative – or weakly normative – sources of legitimacy.

Peters goes on to explore the actual contribution of public discourse to societal reproduction and innovation, a contribution that is at some remove from the rather circumscribed assumptions of deliberative approaches. While he accepts the deliberative position that society cannot operate without at least some consensual foundations, he is more interested in the fact that public discourse frequently tends to produce a greater diversity of positions rather than arriving at a consensus, contra to the tendency of the deliberative model – such as Habermas's account of will formation processes in *Between Facts and Norms* – to assume a narrowing of differences. Peters instead emphasizes that conflictual outcomes and disagreement can actually lead to the emergence of new ideas and norms that are the product of a higher level of rationality. Crucially though, such normative or ideal emergence may be based on the retention of differences, taking the form of agreement to disagree, rather than overcoming them through moral consensus.

This is a point made by quite a number of authors. It bears on Fraser's point about the significance of discourses that are not necessarily oriented to the general common good. And Hauser draws attention to the rhetorical foundations of public argumentation that results in a sense of communal solidarity, though not necessarily consensus (Hauser, 1998). Max Miller speaks of the infrequency of consensus and the greater incidence of what he terms rational dissensus, where contending parties actually understand and recognize their differences (Miller, 1992). In addition to this, there is a lively debate in the tradition of discourse ethics about whether moral discourse constitutively depends on an impartial standpoint or whether it can also be articulated as interest-bound speech (Mansbridge et al., 2010). An important distinction bearing on this issue is that between what Rawls calls 'constitutional essentials' and the everyday activity of moral argumentation, which often emerges from what is initially an interest-bound perspective before being transposed into a reciprocally binding moral commitment. Hence, consistently with the former, the moral framework of democracy as a constitutional structure of rights and obligations is morally universal, but the raising of a new moral perspective in argumentation will not initially, and in some cases perhaps never, enjoy universal status.[7]

Innovative moral and ethical argumentation may generate a new level of practical rationality that nonetheless leaves constitutional essentials unchanged. Such a new level of rationality may emerge in the way in which public discourse reproduces and transforms a public culture, a particular repertoire of claims to knowledge, norms, and values. Such knowledge, norms, and values may be collectively shared or held only by certain social groups. The prior existence of a certain level of collective rationality in public culture is a precondition of argumentative public discourse, but this level of rationality can be changed as a result of that discourse. The level of rationality of public culture in this sense can decide between appropriate and problematic forms of legitimacy and determine the capacity for innovative societal learning that in successful cases might eventually lead to a yet higher level of rationality. Such new levels of rationality, which may be based on compromise in conditions of disagreement, generate an orientation complex for public culture, a cultural model, beyond what is

---

7 These issues of consensus, rational dissensus, and the status of moral judgement consistently recur throughout the book.

institutionalized. Indeed, contemporary society exhibits a systematic differentiation between its effective public culture, taking the form of competing but yet also compromising ideologies, and its formal and informal constitutional framework. This differentiation, which could in some cases be regarded as a contradiction, has been enhanced by globalization but, given the relatively long-run crisis symptoms of contemporary democracy, by no means determined solely by it (Bobbio, 1984; Streeck, 2009).

These remarks, following on from Peters, expand theoretical consideration beyond the narrower confines of the deliberative model. This perspective invites the basic question that while it might ideally be hoped that public discourse will generate adequate epistemic, evaluative, moral and legal capacities to address contemporary problems, can it in fact do so in existing conditions? As Peters observes, a point reiterated by Honneth, this kind of question can at best only be partially addressed by the agora model of face-to-face communication, even where this is counterfactually extended in the manner of a Rawls or a Habermas (Honneth, 2011). This is the essence of Peters' treatment of empirical legitimacy with regard to the rationality standards of public discourse. It implies that the study of the public sphere must be approached with the will to combine normative and empirical-theoretical perspectives and, furthermore, that the contexts of public discourse and deliberation must be creatively related to one another. Recent work suggests some moves in both these directions, though it remains at a relatively early stage (Ferree et al., 2002a, 2002b; Parkinson and Mansbridge, eds, 2012).

The Public Sphere: Central Themes and Approach of the Book

The overview, outlined in the preceding sections, of a small, symptomatic selection of literature on the public sphere, within the Habermasian frame of reference, crystallizes into a pivotal orienting premise: the mutual indifference between normative-philosophical and empirical-theoretical approaches must be overcome. Normative-philosophical approaches rely on implicit theories of society and empirical-theoretical sociology engages normative frameworks. Their respective influence on one another can no longer remain merely latent. Intellectual exploration needs to reach across these disciplinary frameworks rather than simply operate within them.

From his early work onwards, Habermas developed the concept of the public sphere with a normative reference that, notwithstanding its wide empirical range, continued to determine his overall project. His later discursive-deliberative approach remains the most comprehensive account of the normative use of public reason within the framework of the theory of society, a perspective that Axel Honneth is now also developing (Habermas, 1996). In pursuit of this approach, Habermas ranges across political philosophy, incorporating key dimensions of liberal and republican theories into his overall discursive-deliberative framework. For him, political philosophies do not only clarify dimensions of the normative use of reason, but they also feed in to the constitution of political cultures (Habermas, 2006). Ferree et al. also seek to establish a framework for relating normative models of the public sphere to one another and also in this case seek to directly employ them in the analysis of abortion politics (Ferree et al., 2002a, 2002b). The work of Boltanski and Thévenot on modes of justification may also be regarded as making practical various characteristic kinds of philosophical justification with, by now, an extensive sociological programme to support it (Boltanski and Thévenot, 2006).

In the light of the issues raised in this introduction so far, both Habermas and Ferree et al. offer valuable starting points for grasping the relationship between central strands of normative political theory and the empirical-theoretical analysis of public culture. For the purpose of advancing this work, the point raised by Peters should be brought centre-stage; normative theory is not above societal argumentation, but is rather part of it (Peters, 2001). It is not simply a question of how the public should normatively reason, but of how it actually does, or of how it could in better circumstances. Given challenges of complexity, scale, and inclusiveness, the collective learning is a diffuse process that depends on discursive exchanges between multiple social positions. These exchanges may in episodes of successful learning combine to produce new levels of institutionalized collective rationality. The sociological study of societal discourse and its structural outcomes is essential for the task of judging whether rationality standards are appropriate on both a normative and a functional plane. Even with the aid of the empirically supported insights of the social sciences, what 'appropriate' actually entails is always open to critique and revision. For social actors always remain participants, capable of arguing for certain principles, but within the contingency generated by an epistemically complex and socially differentiated present and an uncertain future. It is these actors who actually employ the normative insights of political philosophies and it is they who remain the principal vehicles of their construction and reconstruction. Developing normative standards and empirical-theoretical knowledge is not a didactic task of educating the public, but a vital common enterprise shared with it.

In the light of this, the book is centrally concerned with how communicative politics both carries and reconstructs the normative culture of democracy. It pursues this goal by means of a *cognitive sociology* that emphasizes the socio-cognitive and communicative modalities involved in the construction and critique of normative culture. It therefore pays primary attention to the theoretical-methodological task of exploring these modalities, which form the core of democratic communication. This is a circumscribed task, intensely challenging in its own right, which addresses other heavily emphasized dimensions of public sphere research that are in this book not given equivalently sustained attention. This includes such important considerations as what constitutes authoritarian, manipulative, and 'good' publicity; the relation between the public sphere and political institutions generally; variations in publics and public spheres; normative and material preconditions for the possibility of a public sphere; eras of the public sphere; media agenda-setting and agenda-building processes; communicative inclusion and exclusion; and the democratic redesign of public spheres and of political institutions generally.

These kinds of considerations are woven into the text that follows but they are nowhere treated systematically. Rather, the focus is on addressing the theoretical lacuna in sociological and interdisciplinary public sphere scholarship by centrally attending to the interplay of public discourses, publics, and cultural structures within the broader contexts offered by the theory of society and normative democratic theory. With this emphasis, the book addresses theoretical-methodological problems related to how empirical and normative considerations arising in sociology and other related disciplines are interlinked within a broadly critical approach. The critical approach employed combines 'conservative' horizons with transformative horizons; past achievements must be preserved, and built upon, as well as injustice criticized and new potentials identified.

The first part of the book, covering Chapters 1 to 7, explores the communicatively relevant normative constructs of key political philosophies with a view to later placing them within a societal-theoretical framework. It reviews these communicative constructs in order to establish a stronger relationship between normative models of the public sphere and empirical-theoretical scholarship on public discourse and normative culture. It provides an account of the communicative constructs of political philosophy within five classical democratic paradigms that include the social liberalism of John Rawls, republicanism, radical democracy, realist liberalism and, finally, deliberative democracy. These five approaches offer distinctive normative-philosophical perspectives, respectively, a restricted account of public reason, the ethical contextualization of public communication, pragmatic accounts of repressed subject positions, competitive election-oriented communication, and intersubjective public reasoning. These five communicative constructs, placed in the broader context of the normative concerns of contemporary political theory, indicate the emergence of a communicative turn in at least some dimensions of that discipline. This communicative turn, anticipated by Apel in his *Towards a Transformation of Philosophy*, epistemologically moves the discipline so as to become more compatible with the social sciences that have also moved in a similar direction (Apel, 1980). And, perhaps, the most notable effect of this, one that is a central concern of this book, is that normative culture should be regarded not as coming out of the minds of political philosophers or sociologists but, instead, should be regarded as the product of *public* discourse of which philosophical discourse is one important component. Normative culture, therefore, comes from 'below' and not from 'above', as Axel Honneth stresses (Honneth, 2011).

Part II, building from the outline of normative philosophical perspectives offered in Part I, turns to assess the degree to which Habermas's discursive-deliberative approach, incorporating an account of the discourse ethical perspective he shared with Apel, can provide foundations for a better integrated political philosophical and societal theoretical approach to public communication that guides both normative and empirical analysis. In this part, accordingly, the basic contours of Habermas's and Apel's communication theory of society are developed. Building on Kant's transcendental philosophy of practical reason and the theory of signs of the American pragmatist, Charles Sanders Peirce, Habermas and Apel develop a theory of society as a communication community reproduced and elaborated by the speech and actions of sign-using agents, who are capable of offering reasons for their actions and who, on this basis, are also capable of learning. Human identities are constituted by experiences gained in such a communication community.

The capacity for reasoning and learning is dependent both on the historical foundations of existing forms of public culture and the capacity to problematize it through future-oriented discourse that reaches beyond the existing, real communication community to the unlimited communication community of argumentation that is always already presupposed, and thus virtually present, in the real communication community. In the last chapter of Part II, the various streams of Habermas's work are pulled together into a societal theoretical framework that is then applied to the normative philosophical approaches outlined in Part I. This leads to an encompassing, admittedly idealized, perspective on the political order of modernity, its structure, and its dual modalities of reproduction and transformation. The various democratic-theoretical perspectives clarify indispensable dimensions of the normative, counter-normative, and rationalist prerequisites of modernity, which are combined in various ways in the normative cultures of actual society in such a way as to generate the foundational normative question of how they might be made minimally compatible in given historical eras.

The normative framework that thus emerges attempts to satisfy the challenging task, currently most advanced in the work of Axel Honneth, of identifying the conditions of the well-integrated and at least minimally 'good' society. For this task, the book takes a strong lead from philosophical perspectives but also, in the interests of empirical-theoretical analysis, tries to go beyond the kind of abstract foundations that they offer.

The philosophical perspective as currently developed is unfruitful for the analysis alike of the communicative mechanisms and cultural-structural constellations that make possible the self-thematization, self-critique, and self-correction of modern societies. The problem with the philosophical perspective on its own is not abstraction per se, but rather the kind of abstraction that cannot be connected to the critical relationship between communication and democratization, the central concern of the theory of the public sphere viewed in relation to its capacity both to understand and to influence social change.

The manner in which abstraction and application can be made work together is developed in Part III, by outlining an approach that emerges out of a re-elaboration of discourse ethics for empirical-theoretical purposes, already underway in Part II. This approach, building from discourse ethics, and yet critical of it, is associated with three sociologists in particular, Klaus Eder, Max Miller, and Piet Strydom, but profits from consideration of a wide variety of authors not directly concerned with discourse ethics as such. Following the direction offered by the internal critique of discourse ethics, the approach moves from Habermas's predominantly normative-universalist presuppositions to a cognitive and learning theoretical perspective. This approach offers the distinct advantage of relating public communication to democratic culture in such a way that the latter does not immediately become reduced to an ideal-theoretical and transcendental formula for generating justified norms. Rather the socio-cognitive context of various kinds of democratic norm, that is to say, how they are culturally constructed, is made manifest.

The universes of meaning built into the multiple dimensions of the socio-cognitive order variously provide quasi-transcendental 'frames' that reflexively structure communication both in normative and other domains of modern societies. The term 'cognitive' as used here runs the risk of crashing against the barriers of its dominant pre-interpretation to mean formal-logical competences and, thereby, to exclude moral, ethical, and aesthetic competences based on other presuppositions. Such a restrictive view of the cognitive entails an equally restricted reading of the cognitive revolution that confines cognitive processes to the domain of mental mechanisms for establishing factual truth and neglects the wider import of that revolution.

Introduction

From such a wider vantage point, it may be asserted against this narrow reading that what works in diverse social practices is the product of reflexive and generative competences, collective as well as individual, that form within diverse universes of meaning, moral, ethical, and aesthetic as well as truth oriented. These reflexive competences operate are of a second-order nature and they make first order social practices possible. The cognitive order, in the social brain of society as well as the individual brain, is a suite of post-conventional generative competences that make conventional rule-governed action possible – or problematize this action to such a degree that it is no longer possible.

The cognitive order, on the one hand, identifies categorically distinct social capacities and competences, but this does entail that these categorical frames that reflexively structure communication, breaking with systems theory for reasons clarified later, remain operatively closed to one another. The respective frames or principles combine in the building of cultural models that are composed from these frames and from different 'takes' on them springing from the plurality of social positions that modern society throws up. The compositional mechanism of these cultural models is discourse. The discursive mobilization of the various dimensions of the cognitive order, composed of those reflexive principles – frames – that orient modern life, guides the process of building agreement, including reasoned disagreement, which can claim general and reciprocal standing. Through such a cognitive approach, basic presuppositions of modern social thinking such as non-linearity, contingency, complexity, difference, and future-openness are made intrinsic to reflection on the cultural foundations of social order.

Chapter 13, the concluding chapter of Part III, brings together this cognitive-learning-communication approach to the generation and implications of normative culture. The approach, drawing from a variety of social theories, combines transcendent and immanent horizons; it also combines mediation processes on two levels, vertical – micro, meso, macro – and horizontal – the various cultural spheres of modernity; it specifies discursively generated innovation, variation, learning, and selection processes; and it accounts for accompanying cognitive structure formation with its implications for norm building. This approach is carried into Part IV and there integrated with the framework combining normative philosophy and the theory of society, already developed in Part II.

Part IV begins with a restatement of the theory of critical publicity, drawing on the preceding chapters. It then moves on to consider how the role of new and old media might be reinterpreted in the light of this theory. On the basis of these additions, the sociological framework offered in Part III is expanded by means of a detailed account of the interplay between cognitive and cultural structures and communication dynamics as they contribute to the formation of the normative order. The concluding chapter of Part IV clarifies how this framework can be applied by addressing a major contemporary issue, the role of the public sphere in the context of the emerging cosmopolitan order of transnational democracy. The book finishes with a short conclusion drawing together the critical themes.

PART I

Normative Theories of Democracy, Communication, and the Public Sphere

CHAPTER 1

The Communicative Constructs of Normative Democratic Models

Normative theories of democracy are pivotal to both the academic understanding and practical operation of the public sphere. Reconstructing the normative claims of democratic theories is the first step towards making explicit what often remains implicit, namely, the profound effect of these normative claims on reproduction and change in democratic, public culture. Explicating these claims is the first step towards clarifying both how they shape the design and functioning of democratic institutions, including public spheres, and an important part of what of what is considered relevant in public discourse. Normative theories of democracy are actualized in political systems and their public spheres in the various ways described by Ferree et al., providing characteristic orientations to the what, who, where and how of public discourse and hence shaping the conditions, mechanisms and outcomes of politics (Ferree et al., 2002a, 2002b). The second step, taken up at various points in the remainder of the book, is to show how as part of the modern cognitive order these normative theories are themselves responsive to and altered by public discourse.

How do such abstract normative entities as political philosophies become effective in the actual practices of everyday politics? Pettit draws a distinction between currents of normative ideas such as political philosophies as opposed to ideologies that guide actual politics (Pettit, 1999, p. 2). Political philosophies operate as enduring background phenomena that structure what appears to be politically possible. They play a big part in deciding what is regarded as normatively legitimate and feasible in a particular political culture. Political issues are deemed relevant or not by the normative grip of a particular political philosophy, or by a combination of several of them. An example of this logic of inclusion and exclusion may be found in the respective normative statuses of private property and the common good in the discourse and implementation of justice in various political systems. These differences can be led back to relatively long-run orientations carried in institutionally embedded political philosophies. The latter do not occur in the singular in specific public cultures; they are combined with different degrees of emphasis on specific tenets. For example, all modern public cultures combine republicanism and liberalism in some degree, often selecting 'packages' that varyingly emphasize particular tenets *within* each political philosophy, as well as showing a general, overall preference for one or the other. Such an interest in the practical influence of political philosophies is rarely systematically considered in political philosophy itself.[1] This is primarily concerned with arguing what normatively should be the case, rather than what is actually present as established practice or cultural horizon as a downstream effect of philosophical – and legal and political – theorizing (Berg and Geyer, 2002).[2]

1   The social scientific – mostly political science – concept of social model offers a promising path towards considering the relationship between theoretical and applied political philosophies. The concept of a social model is used to describe the organizational principles of a society with respect to the balance between private and public spheres. Two aspects of the balance in particular are stressed: (a) that between economic efficiency and social justice and (b) the relationship between democratic institutions and systems of interest intermediation. Perhaps the most famous example of the use of the concept is Esping-Andersen's account of three worlds of welfare capitalism, liberal (English-speaking world), democratic corporatist (Germany, Austria, France and Italy) and social-democratic (Scandinavian countries) (Esping-Andersen, 1990). The latter two are heavily influenced by a republican conception of politics. In particular, high levels of organized neo-corporatist participation characterize the Scandinavian model, which is consistent with a republican political style.
2   A recent development in political philosophy may indicate something of a shift in priorities relevant to this task. Perceptions of *injustice* are increasingly being given priority over systematic or transcendental theories of justice. This theme is re-visited briefly following Amartya Sen below (Bufacchi, 2012; Sen, 2009; Shklar, 1991, 1992). The idea of a situated political philosophy that was sceptical of any attempt to fix or absolutize values was already anticipated by Deweyan pragmatism with its critique of what he understood as the empty formalism of Kant's Categorical Imperative. Dewey criticized the Categorical Imperative insofar as it tries to reach moral conclusions without presuming anything to be good – even if it could have a role as an inclusive

There is increasing social theoretical interest in applying political philosophies because of their orienting role in structuring actual democratic cultures and providing standards to adjudge them. Habermas, for example, attempts to clarify three normative models of democracy, liberal, republican and deliberative (Habermas, 1994). In the liberal model, the mere aggregation of the plurality of pre-political interests through the political process loses all reference to the normative core of the public use of reason. Whereas the republican model gives genetic primacy to politics as communicative will formation, its current communitarian manifestations over-substantialize the pre-existing ethos of community in a manner that could only colonize public discourse. With respect to his preferred deliberative position, he claims that democratic will formation draws its legitimating force not from a 'settled ethical conviction' as in the republican position, but 'from the communicative presuppositions that allow the better argument to come into play in various forms of deliberation and from the procedures that secure fair bargaining processes' (ibid., p. 24).

In a return to this theme in a 2006 essay, Habermas claims that each of these positions give a different weighting to the three elements of the institutional design of modern democracies, namely, the private autonomy of citizens to pursue their own life plans, democratic citizenship as the inclusion of free and equal citizens in the political community and the independence of the public sphere that operates as an intermediary system between state and society (Habermas, 2006). The liberal tradition reveals a preference for the liberties of private citizens, the republican tradition stresses the political participation of active citizens, and the deliberative tradition emphasizes the formation of considered public opinion. Moving beyond his earlier position on normative models of democracy, he goes

---

principle of moral inquiry. Dewey also had reservations about the transcendentalism of Kantian moral theory, developing a three-dimensional moral theory encompassing teleological, deontological, and virtue-oriented approaches whose insights were not authoritative in themselves so much as offering hypotheses for experimental inquiry (Anderson, 2010; Dewey, 1985; Koopman, 2009). A further historical source for recent developments is the ideology-critical, praxis-oriented philosophy stemming from Marx.

on to claim that these strands of political thought carried by the theoretical traditions impact in different ways on national political cultures and generate characteristic relations between theory and practice in each case. The varying emphasis that citizens of different nation-states place on the normative elements of democracy, rights and liberties, inclusion and equality, and public deliberation and problem solving 'determines how they see themselves as members of their political community' (ibid., p. 412).

Ferree et al. further illustrate the empirical utilization of political philosophies, in this case to analyse the normative-philosophical traditions emphasized in different public spheres (Ferree et al., 2002a, 2002b). Their approach is to put normative models to work by exploring to what degree national public spheres conform to the ideal type representation of four models. These four models are representative liberal, participatory liberal, discursive and constructionist. An account of these models is provided under a number of criteria including civility, detachment, popular inclusion, empowerment, deliberativeness, and outcomes. They break down into criteria of who participates, in what sort of process, how ideas should be presented, and outcomes of relations between discourse and decision-making. In general, the authors claim that only the representative liberal tradition regards publicity as flowing from top to bottom. In this model, citizens delegate and as part of the delegation contract they have a right to know what their representatives do on their behalf, but they observe rather than participate. Each of the other three traditions tends to view publicity as flowing from bottom to top in one form or another. This framework is then used to empirically diagnose the nature of political communication on abortion issues in Germany and the United States. It is claimed that Germany conforms closely to a model of the public sphere consistent with the elitist representative liberal tradition, whereas that of the United States has more of a participatory liberal quality.

Boltanski and Thévenot (Boltanski and Thévenot, 2000; Boltanski and Thévenot, 2006) provide another example of the sociological utilization of political philosophy for the analysis of public culture. These authors, describing what they do as a competence model, attempt to reconstruct the categorical framework that underlies the ordinary sense of justice used by social actors. The approach starts from the different grammars of justice used by these social actors and then explores the differences and points of convergence between them. These different grammars, if they were merely reconstructed from observation of the competent performances of social actors, could not reach a sufficient level of generality to ground their validity. The authors therefore took recourse to linking the empirically observable reality of actors' performances with formal models of justice that they derived from political philosophies.

The approach is unusual in the breadth of the understanding of the regimes of justification that emerge from the conjunction of ordinary competence and formal models. These give rise to six primary regimes of justification, or as the authors call them orders of worth, market, industrial, civic, domestic, inspiration and fame to which, over time, has been added further more tentative regimes of information and green (ecological). These orders of worth are cultural structures that guide communication between social agents, generating conflicts of rationality across their boundaries – for example, civic versus domestic, industrial (bureaucratic) versus poetic (inspired) – and also generating convergences taking the form of compromises between them. Such conflicts and convergences shape the characteristic rationalities of public cultures and public discourses, providing a powerful means of analysing public spheres.

The various orders of worth identified by the authors are not entirely consistent with more standard accounts of political philosophy. They are drawn from diverse sources. For example, both Hobbes and Augustine are used in describing the order of worth of fame. The authors succeed in raising the question of the plurality of sites of justice and discourses of justification, throwing forth a challenge to the restriction of ideas of justice and public justification to the formal political sphere, a challenge that is also posed in a different way by Axel Honneth (Honneth, 2004). That challenge is in part taken up below in the account of the radical tradition. It returns in subsequent chapters in the attempt to link political philosophy and the theory of society to provide a framework for the analysis of public discourse.

Finally, an in-depth study of liberalism as an enduring meta-narrative is offered by Margaret Somers (Somers, 1993, 1995a, 1995b). Somers outlines how what she calls 'Anglo-American Citizenship Theory' – proceeding from Locke – has shaped politics in English-speaking countries over the course of modernity. Developing a historical and cultural sociological version of political sociology, she emphasizes the long-run socio-political significance of systems of normative ideas rather than the play of materially grounded interests. In this account, what matters are historically embedded views about the normative role of politics that evince a 'narrative structure' connecting past, present and future in depicting what is politically desirable and efficacious. She claims, for example, that the characteristic way in which the relationship between public and private are considered in Anglo-American citizenship theory, the public realm seen as necessary but coercive and in tendency threatening individual freedom and the private viewed as the source of political good, operates as a 'meta-narrative' that imaginatively constrains what is politically possible. This viewpoint is similar to the idea of social imaginaries, a concept developed by Taylor to describe the moral foundations of democracy in the principle of consent, once again proceeding from Locke (Taylor, 2004).

Somers's historical sociology of concept formation, and its further development as citizenship theory, or the work of Taylor and others on social imaginaries, will not be expanded on further here. Rather, the line of inquiry opened up by Habermas and Ferree et al. is followed by providing, in the remaining chapter of Part I, an overview of the communicative constructs of selected political philosophies. With respect to this selection, whereas Habermas's work has a path-breaking quality in not just comparing three political philosophies – liberal, republican and deliberative – but linking them to visions of society, and Ferree et al. provide a comparative typology of the intrinsic constructs of the public sphere in four political philosophies, some dissatisfaction remain. Neither Habermas nor Ferree et al. make any reference to Rawls in their surveys, Habermas does not include the radical tradition, or rather subsumes it into republican and deliberative positions, and Ferree et al. problematically integrate republican and deliberative philosophies into one position (Ferree et al., 2002a, 2002b; Habermas, 1994).[3] The reviews below cover the four main political

---

3   This is not to deny that Ferree et al. have significant support for combining republican and deliberative philosophies, as contemporary political philosophers such as Bohman, Forst and Sunstein in certain respects also do. The distinction between

philosophies most commonly used in the philosophical literature, liberal, republican, radical, and deliberative. A fifth, 'political realism', will be added. In the main, political realism is a variety of liberal theory that is distinct from Rawls to the point that, in some recent manifestation, its focus is on a critique of the claimed idealism of his theory. These five traditions represent a selection that is partly driven by their apparent centrality to debates in political philosophy and theory, but also by their suitability for the goal contained here, that is, to show how selected philosophies clarify in a social theoretically productive manner the relationship between normative culture, communication and agency in complex, pluralistic societies.

Normative-philosophical theorizing has an important contribution to make to social theory and has always been intrinsic to the theory of the public sphere. The latter has suffered though as a consequence of lying in the borderlands between normative and empirical-theoretical disciplinary orientations and will continue to suffer until there is greater integration between them. As a modest contribution to this task, it is proposed in this chapter to identify distinct communicative constructs associated with each of the five political philosophies as they emerge from their respective normative contexts and, later in the work, to show how they can provide an interrelated framework for combined normative and empirical-theoretical analysis. The idea of clarifying the communicative constructs of distinct political philosophies is in part derived from what is assumed to be a communicative reorientation of political philosophy, a reorientation that proceeds in different ways and at different speeds in different traditions. It is a task for political philosophers themselves to explore such a reorientation in depth, if that is what it is. Nonetheless, there are certain manifest and significant indications that point in this direction, including the intersubjectivist cast that Rawls has given contemporary liberalism, the rise of a distinct deliberative tradition, the renewed importance of Dewey and pragmatism in a variety of thinkers from Rorty to Honneth and Bohman, and the manner in which Habermas has tried to communicatively

---

some versions of republican and deliberative traditions is hard to draw, but it is not so hard a distinction between communitarian republican traditions and deliberative democratic theories. This issue is taken up further in Chapter 3.

ground political and social theories in an integrated manner (Bohman, 2010; Dewey, 1927; Habermas, 1996; Honneth, 1998; Rorty, 1982). The task here remains a modest one. It is to establish some communicative baselines in the normative constructs of political philosophies so that the boundaries between them and the social theory of the public sphere are not so strongly drawn. On this basis, as suggested in the introduction, bridges may be built between empirical-theoretical and normative accounts of the communicative foundations of the key democratic ideal of popular sovereignty, thereby assessing the actuality and potentiality of this ideal.

In what follows, therefore, the communicative constructs of five traditions in political philosophy will be outlined.[4] These are, respectively, the idea of *public reason* in Rawlsian liberalism; the ethical foundation of *public autonomy* in the republican tradition; the idea of *public contestation* in the radical democratic tradition; the *competitive communication* model of the realist tradition; and, finally, the *public deliberation* model of the deliberative tradition. The distinctions are far from watertight and do not entail that there is no overlap between them. For example, Rawls and liberalism have much to say about public autonomy; there is a distinct blurring of boundaries between liberalism and republicanism in recent decades; modern forms of republicanism are heavily influenced by the deliberative turn; republicanism and for that matter deliberative theories lay claim in some instances to being radical democratic; and all the other political traditions, with the exception of the realist, often advance a claim to being deliberative in their approach. Identifying and specifying these communicative constructs is a matter of emphasis rather than absolutes, but the task is guided by the fact that political philosophies still exhibit ontological and epistemological differences that shape their interpretations of the proper

---

4   As indicated above, the choice of which political philosophies to include took much consideration. In addition, the choice of philosophers – and social theorists – to populate these philosophical 'containers' was equally difficult. The review is far from comprehensive, a herculean task, but instead guided by the intention of showing broad family resemblances amongst certain kinds of political philosophy and meaningful differences between these and other such kinds. It is also the case that the framework that appears in Part II, Chapter 10, conditions much of the selection decisions made in the chapters of Part I.

normative foundations of democratic politics and the good of society. These interpretations are increasingly influenced by how they accommodate communicative constructions within their existing frameworks.

In conclusion, there are several kinds of rationale that can be offered for this exercise. Following Habermas, political philosophies in practice in certain respects are not as they often appear in theory, that is, they complement rather than compete with one another. Elements of these traditions combine within the constitutional framework of modern democracies, whether that framework is understood formally or informally. This way of thinking turns attention away from internal disputes within and between political philosophies, however important these may be, and towards using the concepts and world interpretations of these philosophies to build a picture of the multiple kinds of normative structuring of society. As the book evolves, it will be seen that this provides a mode of describing normative commitments of different kinds. Further, this description then makes possible evaluation of how these normative commitments are formed into patterns through the effects of multiple kinds of public discourse. This pattern forming operation on normative commitments achieved through discourses takes place on a different plane to normative institutionalization, that is to say, moral, ethical, legal, and pragmatic norm application that guides social action. It takes place on a socio-cognitive plane where the 'mind of society' is engaged in sense-making practices, variously involving acts of diagnosis, prognosis, agreement, disagreement, repression, representation, and critique. The growing tendency within political philosophy to address public communication is one index of the slow decline of the previously entrenched third party, objectivist paradigm, in which philosophers proposed normative principles on behalf of society. Moving with this change in the orientation of political philosophy, and building on it, allows the constructive and reconstructive moments associated with a cognitive-communicative-learning theory to become apparent. This by no means denies the efficacy of the normative level of analysis. Rather, it examines the process whereby normative commitments on this level are discursively formed, revised, and adapted. Such an approach is the vehicle whereby a constructivist understanding of the public enters political philosophy and whereby the deep understanding of patterns of normative commitment, present in political philosophies, may in turn come to inform sociology.

CHAPTER 2

Rawlsian Liberalism and the Idea of Public Reason

Not alone is John Rawls frequently credited as the preeminent political philosopher of the second half of the twentieth century, but his work is also credited with giving the discipline a new relevance. Even though, somewhat ironically, his 'ideal theory' is now criticized in some quarters for excessive detachment, one of Rawls's key innovations was to link political philosophy to the state of society, to make it serve as a guide as to how to design political institutions on the basis of determinate principles of justice. In certain respects, Rawls was both a figure of his time and a harbinger of intellectual currents to come. In the first instance, he reflected a general confidence, present also in structural-functional sociology, that enduring values could be identified that would substantially stand beyond social change. In the second, his methodology of political constructivism in certain respects anticipated the general constructivism that was beginning to grip many disciplines from the end of the 1960s onwards. It could in the end be said, once again with some irony, that this wider constructivism is currently partly turning against Rawls.

Given Rawls's centrality to political philosophy, and his Kantian emphasis on the normative significance of the public use of reason, he is an unavoidable figure in thinking about the public sphere, though not always recognized as such. Rawls is fundamental to understanding how the constitutional values present in a society, and represented in the political conception of justice, acquire public legitimacy. In his theory, the idea of public reason is basic to securing legitimacy and this idea has an important part to play in conceptualizing the public sphere and in grounding a communicative theory of democracy. This chapter outlines some core ideas of Rawls and is designed to grasp his significant contribution in these dimensions.

Rainer Forst, whose work encompasses an authoritative reading of Rawls, identifies three core principles of liberalism: personal liberty, where liberal principles are safeguarded by negative freedoms; social pluralism in which liberal principles emerge as an agreement of reciprocal tolerance due to the incompatibility of citizen's conceptions of the good; and political constitutionalism in which liberal principles can be understood as norms that can be generally justified by those subject to them (Forst, 2002). These principles may overlap in particular theories. Social equality and popular sovereignty are not basic principles, but have to be constructed from the above.

These core and supplementary principles are reflected in the predominating liberal idea of freedom as non-interference in private life plans. Social equality and popular sovereignty must be constructed in such a way that they do not endanger individual freedom. There is a major difference of emphasis between different kinds of liberalism with respect to these supplementary principles. To take the extreme contrast, that between right-wing libertarianism and social liberalism, the former asserts that the state should be as minimal as possible and that, since they own themselves, individuals should gain what their own efforts entitle them. By contrast, what is sometimes termed modern social liberalism, often associated with Rawls, puts its emphasis on a significant measure of publicly achieved equality.[1]

---

1   Social or egalitarian liberalism, which is of greatest interest from the standpoint of a communicative theory of democracy, also includes such figures as Dworkin, Ackerman, and Larmore. Forst distinguishes between Dworkin's individualist liberalism in which equality is understood as the negative equality of rights-bearers from Ackerman's non-rights-based and hence more contextual account based on 'a dialogical model of justifying political and social distributions of power' (Forst, 2002, p. 33). For Ackerman, the most important of the three grounds for the formation of liberal principles is that of neutrality – the second in the main text above – and this reflects the pluralism of society. Larmore's is the most procedural of the three, offering a Kantian universalistic account of rational dialogue in the sense of the third 'constitutional' formulation of liberal principles. Of the three, this offers the greatest interest from the standpoint of a communicative theory of democracy. Finer distinctions are not made here between the social liberalism that accommodated itself to egalitarian currents in the twentieth century and Rawls's theory of justice.

Rawls's two principles of justice conform to the distinction between core and supplementary principles of liberal political theory (Rawls, 1971, 1993). The first principle is given priority. It stipulates necessary political liberties for a just, democratic society and is consistent with the negative right to freedom as non-interference. The second principle, which has proven more controversial, along with specifying the principle of fair opportunity reveals an egalitarian intention in stipulating that social and economic inequalities are so to be arranged as to work to the benefit of the least advantaged. This should be achieved by a structure of equal opportunities that extends to affirmative action to combat existing discrimination. The second principle, the difference principle, endorses policies that mitigate inequality and hence entails a commitment to social solidarity.

In his later work of the 1990s and early 2000s, Rawls does not abandon the egalitarian commitments of the difference principle, but they play a lesser role (Rawls, 1993, 2001). The fate of the difference principle is bound up with his recasting of the status of the overarching standpoint of justice as fairness, first developed in *The Theory of Justice*. In *The Theory of Justice*, justice as fairness is advanced as a superior moral theory to its main rival of utilitarianism, continuing the dominant debate in moral philosophy. Through the device of the original position, participating citizens, who are expressly denied knowledge of how any principles they agree would affect their own interests, would select justice as fairness as the basis of the political conception of justice that should shape the basic structure of their society. The basic structure consists of fundamental social institutions such as the judiciary, the economic structure, and the political constitution. The problem the later Rawls identifies with this earlier work is that it failed to distinguish between moral and political theory and presents justice as

---

While Rawls was generally regarded as a social democrat he distanced himself both from the capitalist providential welfare state and the rule of the market. While in his view justice has priority over economic goods, the welfare state doesn't correct the structural inequalities of societies. In this respect, Rawls offers a kind of mediation between classical liberalism and social liberalism. Audard not alone clarifies this point, but also provides an excellent general overview of liberalism (Audard, 2009).

fairness as a legitimate *comprehensive* moral conception of justice rather than as a more overarching yet restricted *political* conception of justice.

In his later work by contrast, then, justice as fairness emerges from a reshaped device of the original position, and understood as a political conception of justice derived from but also distinct from the many existing reasonable comprehensive doctrines. In this way, he separates the moral perspective of reasonable comprehensive doctrines from the moral perspective of a political conception of justice. Such reasonable comprehensive doctrines are systems of moral beliefs about the subject of political institutions, but also about wider subjects such as how to live one's life and what virtues to uphold (Rawls, 1971; Rawls, 1993). In his later work, Rawls claims that a legitimate political conception of justice, justice as fairness, should emerge from the overlapping consensus of reasonable comprehensive doctrines. Comprehensive doctrines exhibit moral and other commitments that proponents of these doctrines cannot reasonably expect others to share, though if such comprehensive doctrines are in fact reasonable then elements of them may support a neutral, overlapping conception of justice. Rawls calls the latter a political conception of justice and it is based upon liberal principles and values. A reasonable interpretation, derived from Rawls's multiple formulations of the problem and his prioritization of the components in *Political Liberalism*, is that a political conception of justice consistent with justice as fairness has a foundational moral component derived from constitutionally founded individual rights that should be consistent with the equal rights of others (first principle of justice), a strong component associated with fair equality of opportunity (second principle of justice, part one) and a weaker component composed of the commitment to least possible inequality (second principle of justice, part two).

This shift in Rawls's position from regarding justice as fairness as a dominant comprehensive doctrine to regarding it as the political conception of justice involves some degree of 'desubstantivation' and proceduralization of his conception of justice. This does not so much affect the status of the first principle specifying equal liberties. It affects more the second principle of justice, and here especially that dimension (part two) dealing with acceptable levels of inequality. The limited congruence of the right and the good present in the third part of *A Theory of Justice* is thus weakened in *Political Liberalism* (Rawls, 1971; Rawls, 1993). The fact of reasonable pluralism, that is to say, a plurality of reasonable comprehensive doctrines whose different emphases have to be morally recognized as of equal standing, creates the possibility of a political conception of justice forged by means of the standard of publicity of public reason. The difference principle as a substantive commitment to the good, which was easier to sustain when justice as fairness was regarded as a comprehensive doctrine in *The Theory of Justice*, is 'architecturally' retained in *Political Liberalism*, but it is rarely mentioned in the text. To be in conformity with the standard of a shared political conception of justice, citizens need only be provided with certain material minima derived from an adequately fair basic structure of society. Such provision would enable them to effectively follow public reason, and the operation of public reason should both protect basic liberties and prevent social and economic inequalities from being excessive (Rawls, 1993, p. lvii).[2]

The relationship between the two principles draws Rawls into the complex terrain of the relationship between the private autonomy deriving from the first and the institutional collective action required for the second. In his later work, the idea of public reason as an expression of the latter kind of public autonomy is introduced so as to deal with the question of how the values of least possible inequality and maximum responsibility before a public can be sustained. Public reason therefore emerges as a procedural response to the fact of reasonable pluralism. The vision of a society socially integrated by basic liberties, equal opportunity and a demanding substantive principle of equality – the difference principle – is now partly supplanted by a modified vision; that of a society that has the wherewithal to establish and maintain a political conception of justice that is subject to variation in application arising from the interplay of reasonable comprehensive doctrines within the framework of public reason.[3] Citizens need only be

---

2 Rawls's influence in these respects is manifested in recent work in critical political philosophy, for example, Forst's treatment of the interplay of a basic structure of justification and a justified basic structure (Forst, 2007a, 2007b).

3 It is not always easy to be clear about what follows what in Rawls's schema. The establishment of justice as fairness as the political conception of justice in the original position antedates any later overlap between reasonable comprehensive doctrines

in possession of those primary goods that enable them to act in conformity with a political conception of justice. In this account, confirming the procedural turn, the difference principle is excluded as a constitutional essential and along with fair opportunity is 'to be decided by the political values of public reason' (Rawls, 1993, pp. 228–229).

The political conception of justice therefore has two principles composed of (a) principles of justice for the basic structure drawn from the values of equal political and civil liberty, equality of opportunity, social equality, and economic reciprocity and the common good and (b) guidelines of inquiry which are principles of public reasoning and modes of evidence in the light of which citizens are to decide which principles properly apply and to identify laws and policies that best satisfy them. In the latter, citizens should evince both reasonableness and the moral duty of civility, 'which as virtues of citizens help to make possible reasoned public discussion of political questions' (Rawls, 1993, p. 224).

Rawls development of the idea of public reason marks a communicative turn in his theoretical development. The combination of justice principles and the idea of public reason can take many forms; many possible liberal conceptions of justice differ from one another in their combination of these two basic elements. Public reason provides a conduit from the sense of justice of citizens who hold comprehensive doctrines to the principles of a political conception of justice. The political conception of justice therefore strongly qualifies the a priori principles deduced from the pre-social foundations of reason in the natural law tradition, instead giving them a constructed quality deriving from the sense of justice held by citizens as part of a public political culture and achieved by a process of *public reasoning*.[4] The emphases on the historical construction of liberal political

---

that would modify it in any way. Rawls explicitly advances the idea that political socialization consistent with justice as fairness would have the implication of reducing or eliminating the perceived need for such modification.

4   Rawls's understanding of public reasoning, developed further below, is relatively confined as it is tied to the institutionally realized normative framework of justice, the political conception of justice, and is generally referred to by means of the noun form 'public reason', as distinct from the verbal form of 'public reasoning'.

culture and on citizenship indicate also a move towards accommodating republican motifs into his theory.[5]

Rawls confines the core domain of public reason to judges, politicians and political candidates, and higher public officials.[6] He erects a boundary between the relative stability of public reason, on the one side, and the plurality of comprehensive voices associated with public discourse in the public sphere, on the other.[7] Public reason in Rawls's sense is the mechanism for producing the fundamental moral-political core of democratic justice and therefore its use must be procedurally well regulated. Public reason, he points out, does not determine or settle particular matters of law or policy, but rather the terms in which they are to be politically decided (Rawls, 1993, p. li). Such public reason is clearly distinguished by Rawls from the non-public reason of civil society that takes place in churches, universities, associations and professional groups. Rawls's account of public reason is a 'weak' account. Normative claims to preferred principles of justice, and an appropriate kind of reason to sustain them, rest on the historical formation

---

5   Rorty defends Rawls from his communitarian critics on the grounds that Rawls offers a version of the situated self in the original position. Rorty claims that Rawls abandons the Kantian idea of the transcendental self in favour of a more historicist and empirical account of the self in his later work and hence that communitarian criticisms of Rawls, directed at the former account, are accordingly misplaced (Rorty, 1991). For comments on this viewpoint and an account of contrary views, see Baynes (Baynes, 1992).

6   Gutmann and Thompson, for example, offer an instructive contrast of a 'strong' version of public reasoning, taking the form of actual deliberation by citizens (Gutmann and Thompson, 1996).

7   Rawls partly accomplishes this in *Political Liberalism* by regularly distinguishing between the normative claims of justice as fairness and public reason from sociological considerations arising from the use of public discourse in civil society where comprehensive doctrines reign. As argued later, he does not establish a clear and ongoing conduit between these spheres. Rawls's position has some similarity to how Turner criticizes the use of the relatively new concept of 'normativity' in philosophy that, in his view, similarly distinguishes itself from the existing normative order by demarcating a higher sphere or 'ground' for normativity that cannot be empirically accessed (Turner, 2010, p. 5).

of liberal values animated by a sense of justice arising within a national political culture, and not on the shorter-run dynamics of public discourse.

The 'cultural a priori' contained in the idea of a long-run sense of justice and the relative downplaying of public discourse may be associated with his general reluctance to trust too much to discourses arising from the fractious and polarized American civil society of the last thirty years (Isaac, Filner, and Bivins, 1999). For Rawls, the transfer of values from civil society to principles of justice is a slow one. The transfer of values from his standpoint is much more likely to work the other way around, through the socialization of members of civil society into the values of justice as fairness. This 'weak' account of public autonomy that arises from his understanding of public reason is illustrated below by means of two themes: firstly, Rawls's relationship to deliberative democracy and, secondly, his account of the original position and its relation to the historical grounding of political culture. These two themes bring out how Rawls forges a particular understanding of the relationship between political communication and the normative grounding of democratic culture.

Public Reason and Public Deliberation

A recurring issue, Rawls's status as a deliberative theorist, clarifies important dimensions of the relationship between communication and democracy. In his essay, 'The Idea of Public Reason Revisited', Rawls specifies the essential elements of deliberative democracy as public reason, a framework of constitutional democratic institutions that specifies rules for deliberative legislative bodies, and 'the knowledge and desire on the part of citizens generally to follow public reason' (Rawls, 1993, p. 448). He also asserts that his own theory of a well-ordered constitutional democracy should be understood as a deliberative democracy, though full deliberation would be confined to constitutional essentials (Rawls, 1997, p. 772). In part, there has been a sceptical reaction to this claim.

Gaus, for example, claims that 'in many ways' political liberalism and deliberative democracy are distinct doctrines where the former 'stresses justification of basic political principles that can be the focus of an overlapping consensus among irreconcilable comprehensive doctrines' and the latter stresses 'an open-ended discourse that validates political claims' (Gaus, 2003, pp. 197–198). Gaus considers Rawls's paradigm case of good deliberative democracy, the US Supreme Court, and questions whether such a 'highly elitist procedure' may be best for discovering what the people '*would* agree' (ibid., p. 198; italics in original). For Gaus, the idea that a discourse confined to nine lawyers could offer a satisfactory basic for validating norms only makes sense counterfactually, and here not very plausibly. Gaus adds that notwithstanding the difficulties of achieving it, the deliberative democratic ideal of discourse between all those to whom a norm could apply provides a firmer link between public reason and '*democratic deliberation*' (ibid., p. 198; original italics). This claim is broadly consistent with Habermas's criticism of Rawls on this point, which is that democratic deliberation should depend on discursively achieved 'acceptability' by a public, rather than mere acceptance by them of what emerges from the procedure/s of public reason (Habermas, 1995).

Benhabib accepts that there is an overlap between Rawls's idea of public reason and deliberative democracy in that both envisage democratic procedures being open to a public to scrutinize, examine, and upon which to reflect (Benhabib, 1996). But she identifies three significant 'philosophical divergences'. The first divergence is that, whereas the agenda of deliberative democracy is in principle open, 'Rawls restricts the use of public reason to deliberation about a specific subject matter', 'constitutional essentials' and 'questions of basic justice' (ibid., p. 75). The second is that public reason, as indicated above, is not a process of reasoning so much as a 'regulative principle imposing limits upon how individuals, institutions, and agencies *ought to reason about public matters*' (ibid., p. 75, italics in original). And, thirdly, in drawing a distinction between non-public and public reason, Rawls restricts the spaces in which public reason is exercised, distinguishing between the background culture of civil society and public, political culture. On this third divergence, Benhabib comes to the telling conclusion that for Rawls, the public sphere 'is not located *in civil society but in the state and its organizations, including first and foremost the legal sphere and its institutions*' (ibid., p. 75; italics in original). Benhabib further claims that while these three points are adequate to distinguish Rawls's idea of public reason from deliberative democracy, there are problems in the strict separation that Rawls establishes between public reason and civil society. Civil society is also structured according to public norms that make it difficult to restrict the operation of public reason to particular themes and constituencies. In her view, it makes more sense to regard public reason as continuously and dynamically shaped by its interaction with civil society, though certain established norms and modes of reasoning may endure for long periods.

Saward also argues against the idea that Rawls is a deliberative democrat (Saward, 2002). He does this by defining core ideas of deliberative democracy, notwithstanding extensive differences between its various theorists. The core ideas are that deliberative democracy entails adequate deliberation by representative citizens before voting; deliberation of another kind, in non-state public forums, should also be publicly facilitated; that deliberation, particularly of the first sort, should be clearly linked to actual outcomes; and, finally, that formal deliberation should satisfy standards of equal respect and inclusiveness. Saward's argument against Rawls's status as a deliberative democrat is similar to Benhabib's in that he regards Rawls as restricting the agenda and the space of public reason too much to match the criteria he sets for deliberative democracy. He adds the idea that Rawls, both in his account of the actual practice of public reason and in the counterfactual norm-building process of the original position, envisages public reason as a monological, internally directed kind of deliberation that is associated with no manifest communicative process. He associates this with the basic tenets of Rawls's account of reflective equilibrium.[8]

Gutmann and Thomson have similar doubts and for similar reasons (Gutmann and Thompson, 1996). They claim that the earlier Rawls defended an essentially monological account of deliberation. While his theory leaves room for deliberation, it emphasizes 'a solitary process of reflection, a kind of private deliberation' (ibid., p. 37).[9] They rightly claim that Rawls's specification of the principle of reciprocity that is a guiding

---

8 Reflective equilibrium is discussed in more depth in the chapter on republicanism, Chapter 3, with respect to Pettit's use of the methodology.
9 These comments also bear on the methodology of reflective equilibrium.

principle of public discussion in his later writings is a significant move towards deliberative democracy. As Nussbaum also emphasizes, against Gutmann and Thomson as well as Habermas, Rawls's idea of public reason includes all moral arguments, including such arguments from comprehensive doctrines as can be shown to be consistent with reciprocity.[10] This does not crucially affect Gutmann and Thompson's conclusion, though, that Rawls's argument remains 'constitutionalist' in the priority it gives to principles of justice over the process of deliberation.

A further interesting treatment of Rawls's account of deliberation and public reason, where the critique of Rawls is more indirect, comes from Erin Kelly (Kelly, 2011). Kelly follows Sen's critique of 'transcendental institutionalism', of which Rawls is an exemplary later figure who is prefigured by Locke, Hobbes, Kant, and Rousseau, in its mistaken search for a comprehensive system of justice – a social structure of political, social and economic institutions within which people are entitled to certain rights, liberties, and opportunities (Sen, 2009). According to Sen, reasonable people won't agree on such principles and such principles anyway don't help in making comparative judgements between real possibilities. For Sen, the advancement or retreat of justice is to be achieved by tracking actual social realizations of justice rather than offering unrealized or impossible to realize ideals.

Kelly draws attention to Sen's emphasis on the 'discursive features' of society. Wide discursive participation closes the gap between justice and democracy, as citizens are enabled to hold governments to account by

---

10   Nussbaum (Nussbaum, 2011) argues against the critique of Rawls, broadly developed by these authors, that he excessively diminishes the role of the public. In Rawls's theory, according to her, citizens can appeal to their comprehensive positions at any time and he does not introduce any sort of moral idea concerning how they should speak to one another. Nussbaum does not develop her critique of the critique further, but I assume it to mean that apparently more inclusive theories such as those described in this section, which do not establish clear boundaries between public reason and the non-public reason of comprehensive doctrines, constrain this non-public reason too much and diminish its possible creative import for public reason. Reasonable arguments from comprehensive positions can actually find their way into public reason proper by satisfying the test of reciprocity.

bringing public opinion to bear on their agendas and actions. Discursively open societies make for the minimization of injustice through the maximum social realization of possible justice. For Sen, public reason is to be understood as the situated capacity for public reasoning. Higher procedural capacity for such reasoning underpins the greater likelihood of also achieving just substantive outcomes. Kelly follows Sen, and also Joshua Cohen, in 'not equating the norms of public reason and democratic government and will instead refer to the discursive features of public realms and their association with the values of membership, participation, dialogue and public interaction'. (ibid., p. 4). Going beyond Sen and the residual individualism of the capabilities approach, she advances the idea of a *collective capability* for making possible 'just social realizations' through discursive interaction (ibid.).[11]

The above positions, critical of the strength of Rawls's deliberative orientation, draw attention to the fact that his position is both hard to internally grasp and to externally compare if he is treated as a deliberative democrat, at least in the generally understood sense of that term. The fact that his theory partially accommodates deliberative moments does not make him a deliberative theorist. Addressing why Rawls is not, at least in a strong sense, a deliberative democrat clarifies how deliberative democracy is dependent on a broad communicative theory of politics, not just on the institution-bound reasoning of political actors. Instead of moving in a deliberative direction that would result in the communicative fluidization of political culture *as well as* its selective stabilization, Rawls redraws his theory to ground it in a historically formed, stable, territorial, normative culture. Rawls is nonetheless right to believe that territorial regimes of justice have enduring qualities and that these regimes have powerful implications for concretely understanding how limits and possibilities of justice become manifest in given times and places.[12]

---

11   See footnote 2 above on social models.
12   The relationship between territory and the public sphere is addressed in more depth in Chapter 18.

Public Reason, Culture, and the Original Position

Rawls develops the idea of the original position as a counterfactual model of how co-operating individuals could rationally decide a fair distribution of primary goods for society from behind the veil of ignorance, where they are unaware as to what the outcomes of their decisions would be for themselves in their actual social position. The original position is designed around what Sen describes as transcendental institutionalism envisaged as that which should guide the construction of the idea of perfect justice and of perfectly just institutions (Sen, 2009, pp. 4–10). It requires commitment to the higher goal of impartially advancing the principles of a just society, rather than acting in pursuit of one's own personal interests. While in designing the device of the original position Rawls wishes to emphasize the standpoint of a non-partisan framework for justice, it is difficult to see how the original position as he frames it – Habermas describes the orientations of the actors in it as 'egological' – could produce principles of justice for a contemporary world in which identity issues are given equal standing to distributive issues (Habermas, 1995). The priority given to distributive questions more accords with the society of the 1970s, compared to present-day society in which volatile identity issues are more prominent. Desirable outcomes tend to be far from clear and require the active participation of the relevant actors. The problem for the original position is that these participating actors could not exhibit public reason due to his circumscription of who might be expected to command it.[13] Recourse to the device

---

13 Both Schapiro (Schapiro, 1986) and Sandel (Sandel, 1996) identify Rawls with Keynesian macroeconomics and the social democratic welfare state era that reached its zenith in the middle third of the twentieth century. Schapiro speaks of Rawls's Keynesian moment, understanding Keynesianism as managed capitalism with a human face for which Rawls's theory appeared particularly well adapted. Similarly Sandel, implicitly critical of what he regards as the social conservatism of 'procedural liberals' like Rawls who believe in the neutrality of the state, follows Brinkley in interpreting Keynesianism as an abandonment of the more radical versions of the New Deal and committed to the latter's contribution to the survival of capitalism without radical alteration to its organization (Brinkley, 1995).

of the original position would be optimistic if is assumed that it would be possible for participating actors to adequately epistemically grasp and morally agree on what should constitute a political conception of justice for a stable, as well as just, basic structure in contemporary conditions.[14]

The problem, therefore, with the design of the original position is that actors acting in a disembodied, disinterested and future-oriented manner cannot do justice to how situated actors in complex and contradictory contexts of experience might wish to represent themselves. The original position is concerned with distributive interests that could be impartially assigned. Such a procedure could not reach how actors account for their experiences in first person terms and thereby engage in reciprocal moral learning processes adequate to the challenges posed by their differences. At issue here is not alone the relationship between the demands of reasoning on different issues, that is, issues of distribution versus issues of identity, but the methodological difference between reasoning on behalf of others – a third-person perspective – and immanent reasoning by the parties themselves – first- and second-person perspectives.

Rawls's position in substantial part depends on the third party perspective of ideal theory – the principles of justice to which all might agree are defined by the academic commentator or the detached law-giver beyond societal participation, notwithstanding the strictly counterfactual use of the device of the original position. While Rawls claims his approach is based on intersubjectivity, the latter is weakly defined because public reason and its key practitioners are so clearly distinguished from the public discourses of citizens that the latter are frequently described as 'following' public reason rather than actively shaping it (see, for example, Rawls, 1993, p. xlix). The intersubjectivism is thereby both socially and, following Gutmann and Thomson and Benhabib, constitutionally circumscribed. In this respect, Rawls inclines towards the legacy of liberal thought, including Kant and Hobbes, and the idea that the moral legitimacy of the social order stands

---

14   Strydom describes Rawls's constructivist criticism as a transcendent form of critique: 'On the basis of a consensual form of justification, it involves the construction of normative principles beyond society which allow a criticism of social institutions' (Strydom, 2011, p. 168).

beyond social institutions. The device of the original position as Rawls's transcendent ideal standard, nominally fully inclusive, actually insulates the formation of justice principles from society, insofar as one can speak of forming anything in a wholly counterfactual manner.

Nonetheless, at least in outline, elements that could orient an empirical-theoretical as well as ideal position on the normative use of reason are present in Rawls in various ways, manifested in how he understands embedded 'comprehensive' social positions, the need for interplay between these positions, a methodological standard in public reason for good political discourse, and, most importantly, a sense of the principles of justice that might sustain a democratic form of social integration. These are potentially insightful for a sociological understanding of normative culture, a potential which disciplinary boundaries on the whole has so far occluded. And, as outlined in later chapters, a form of transcendentalism, immanent-transcendence, is implicitly or explicitly intrinsic to sociological – and philosophical – argumentation in much of the critical theoretical tradition. In this respect, Rawls's trancendentalism, fused with an account of the basic structure of society, could he highly profitable for political sociology, if taken up in a modified form that would embed Rawls's framework in a multi-level sociology that would give a central place to communicative *action*. The problem is, as many critics have pointed out, that his strongly transcendent – and third party, objectivist – emphasis on what ought to be the case precludes real focus on immanent *mechanisms* of intersubjective communication and learning. Rawls's idea equates a national 'sense of justice' with the 'outcome' of the experiment of the original position in a given society. But without sustained attention to ongoing intersubjective processes of communication and learning, for which transcendently evolved capacities would be immanently available, normative order or change cannot be adequately explained.[15] As a consequence, the device of the original position as the source of Rawls's transcendent ideal standards, nominally fully inclusive, actually insulates the formation of justice

---

15   For a broadly consistent account of some limitations of Rawls's approach, see Bohman (Bohman, 2000, pp. 80–83).

principles from society, insofar as one can speak of forming anything in a wholly counterfactual manner.

Rawls is aware that there has to be a concrete socio-historical process in which justice-supporting reason is formed. It would be possible to reinterpret the original position in deliberative terms as an ongoing forum to reflect on what justice should be, that would not just be a transcendent counterfactual mechanism, but also a socially immanent one in which wider justice principles are brought to bear on concrete challenges. But this is not how Rawls views the role of the original position. The original position derives from more settled political values. Individuals bring certain rational intuitions, a sense of justice, to their deliberation in the original position that derives from the pre-existing public political culture of societies of which they are members. It is from within this shared normative framework, adequately insulated from recourse to their self-interest, that they are able to perform the intersubjective labour of filling out a political conception of justice. As Apel observes, in his revised understanding of the original position, Rawls goes beyond the Hobbesian model of the purposive-rational pursuit of egoistic interests to the intuitive capacities of the participants, their sense of justice. But this sense of justice can only be regarded as universalistic in a limited sense, since its socio-genesis and context of application lie within a given national political culture (Apel, 1993; Rawls, 1985). This amounts to a hermeneutic emphasis on a nation-centred 'universalism' that Rawls confirms in his later *Law of Peoples* (Rawls, 1999).

Rawls: Public Reason and Public Autonomy

In his later work, Rawls claims that his theory finds a balance between public and private autonomy, though he heavily qualifies the former. The public is by and large excluded from ongoing processes of justification, except through delegates who in any case float free of them through their capacity, beyond the public, to use public reason. The public has had its counterfactual say in deciding principles of justice in the original position, a device that corresponds to no actual political process. The cultural anchoring of its idealized participants in a common sense of justice guarantees its outcomes. It is hard to discern in this a rationale for the original position that is not already present in national citizens' intuitive sense of justice. This intuitive sense of justice would ineluctably generate the justice as fairness that Rawls endorses. What is neglected in Rawls is attention to the *political process* that could generate real innovations in both the space and remit of citizens' deliberations. At various points in his theory construction, Rawls minimizes the creative involvement of the public.[16] Civility is reserved for public reason, where proper and full respect for all interlocutors can be practiced, and it is distinguished from the more raucous nature of discussion in the public sphere. The space of politics in public political institutions is likewise separated from the idea of the community which, contra Dewey, is separated from the state (Dewey, 1927). The notion of reasonableness is merely extended to comprehensive doctrines as a moral-political necessity, but little attention is given to how such reasonableness is generated and reconstructed through participation in the political process. Like the original sense of justice, reasonableness in comprehensive doctrines is simply assumed to exist in order to ground a political conception of justice as fairness.

Yet, even if Rawls could be regarded as 'anti-political' in the sense of diminishing the creative political involvement of civil society in shaping the moral foundations of politics (Dryzek, 2000, p. 16), he is not anti the public realm per se in the sense that Margaret Somers taxes liberal theory in general – she calls it Anglo-American citizenship theory (Somers, 1995a; Somers, 1995b; Somers, 2008). In most respects, Rawls finds good arguments against the communitarian critiques of social atomism or the alleged self-contradictory assertion of ethical neutrality. He does this, on the one hand, by incorporating some elements of the critique, for example, the

---

16   In *Political Liberalism*, Rawls distinguishes between the requirements of modes of reasoning, which must involve certain common elements such as judgement, principles of inference, rules of evidence and much else from, as he puts it, 'perhaps rhetoric or means of persuasion'. He then goes on to say that 'we are concerned with reason, not simply with discourse' (Rawls, 1993, p. 220).

manner in which a sense of justice is culturally grounded, or by advancing the idea of a political not metaphysical conception of the person. He does it, on the other hand, by elaborating his arguments more convincingly where he has strong grounds against communitarianism, for example, impartiality understood as full intersubjective reciprocity between reasonable comprehensive doctrines (Forst, 2002).

Wellmer claims that the real difference between liberals and communitarians is what participatory democracy and a democratic form of ethical life can mean in contemporary societies (Wellmer, 2000). The tragedy of modern life, already seen by Hegel, is that it can no longer aspire to the reconciliation of the whole, since it is irredeemably fragmented into the plurality of gods and demons of Weber's famous diagnosis. For Wellmer, the aspiration of civic republicanism to any form of substantive communal reconciliation of the whole has to be let go. Rawls is therefore right to advance the view that any idea of the common good can only be a relative one faced with the plurality of individual and associational goals, projects, and conceptions of a good life. In the face of such plurality, the only ultimate standard of the common good is that embodied in democratic, normative cultures. But commitment to these normative orders does not come ready made; it has to be nurtured as the virtues of a fully inclusive, liberal, and democratic tradition.

In his commitment to a national form of life as the incubator of such virtues, Rawls in the end, though principally a liberal, does embrace civic republican motifs. Given his prioritization of liberty, belief in ethical neutrality, commitment to the moral foundations of justice, and confidence in institutionalized public reason, he clearly belongs predominantly to the liberal camp. On the other hand, in a manner that stretches his liberalism in certain republican directions, he emphasizes the importance of national citizenship, attaches importance to a collective ethos that gives rise to a sense of justice, and is committed to a relatively strong version of social equality. He is in some ways a classical embodiment of a point raised in Chapter 1 above; political philosophies draw off one another and are not as typologically separated as they sometimes appear when designations like liberal or communitarian are utilized. The logics that force often unacknowledged overlaps frequently do not lie in the philosophies themselves, but arise from the fact that they have a real existence in the social and political world that does not always respect the self-understood grounds of their differences.

Rawls and the Public Sphere

What are the implications of Rawls for the theory of the public sphere? As indicated above, Rawls does not provide inspiration for creatively exploring the relationship between public reason and the discursive formation of public will. In his architecture, public discourse does not recurrently lead to the transformation of the grounding norms and agendas of politics. Charney acknowledges this in defending Rawls account of the public sphere (Charney, 1998). What is crucial he argues, following Judith Shklar, is not where the distinction between public and private is drawn, but that it should be drawn in order to distinguish between the legal-political sphere governed by public political values and the non-public sphere of private life where conventional values prevail. In a classical liberal sense, clearly restricting the sphere of government allows freedom to prevail in private life. Charney therefore suggests that Rawls is right to assume that the capacity for public reason does not apply to citizens, except when they vote in elections in which constitutional essentials and matters of basic justice are at stake. Those who by contrast promote the idea of a politically active civil society force a kind of over-politicized self-understanding on individuals and associations and impede their capacity to cater for the distinct and particular identities proper to private life and guaranteed by the structure of negative rights. Charney, on the other hand, criticizes Rawls for setting the bar too high in his expectations of the democratic reasonableness of comprehensive doctrines, an expectation that in his view obscures the clarity of the distinction that Rawls establishes between public and private.

Charney's defence of Rawls returns to problematic classical liberal assumptions about the necessity of a depoliticized civil society. Repeated historical experiences from classical democratic revolutionary movements, to decolonization movements, to the democratic movements of Eastern

Europe, and to those of the 'Arab Spring' in the Middle East attest to the critical political role of civil society. Civil society has not just a revolutionary role where democracy is not yet established, and occasionally a transformative role even where it has been, but it *always* has an important political role without which the concept of public sphere has no meaning. Hence, contrary to Charney, it matters where the line between public and private is drawn and the *political* associations that comprise civil society must be regarded as public, muddying distinctions between public and private. This view, different from some of the literature, entails a restricted reading of civil society. It breaks from the idea that it consists of everything in society not in the actual public complex of governmental institutions. In fact, beyond this public complex may be found not just civil society, understood as the sphere of political and voluntary association, but also a distinct sphere of private life and another distinct sphere of systemically structured formal organizations. The overall architecture sustaining these distinctions is later on systematically outlined in Part IV of the book. Rawls's own idea that the public conception of justice arises from the interplay of reasonable comprehensive doctrines implicitly accepts the existence of a politically relevant civil society in which such doctrines take form, but, as argued, he does not analyse its dynamics and implications.

While recognizing that Rawls does have a political conception of civil society, this conception is nonetheless too implicit and even contradictory. The contradiction arises in that the public political conception of justice articulated through public reason must emerge from the interplay of reasonable comprehensive doctrines in a historical process about which there is no reason to suppose that it has stopped. The limitations of this merely implicit recognition of civil society affects Rawls's understanding of public discourse in the public sphere and its separation from the higher order concept of public reason. Though Rawls regularly alludes to the public sphere in *Political Liberalism*, public discourse in it is assumed not to impinge on public reason and hence on the public political clarification of constitutional essentials and basic justice. Insofar as a clear purpose can be discerned for it in Rawls, the public sphere operates through the framework already established by public reason. The avenues whereby learning proceeds from the outside in, from civil society to political institutions, is strictly limited in this conception, ultimately leaving it as a kind of mystery how historically significant innovations in justice, such as civil rights or gender equality, emerge and become effective. The only possible answer is to envisage public discourse as identifying problems that require the use of public reason as a solution, a weaker version of institutional learning than Habermas's two-track model of discursive will formation and deliberative justification. In the end, the focus on constitutional essentials at the core of Rawls's theory insulates the assumed pre-political framework of negative rights from the incursions of public autonomy arising from mass publics.

While in this sense Rawls neglects the creative contribution of public discourse, he does provide a vivid intellectual construction of institutionalized political values and public reason in the political core. If his model of civil society is too implicit to capture political inputs, and his model of process too static to capture dynamics, his model of the possible conditions for fair political process is important. Because Rawls never empirically specifies how such political conditions do in fact regulate political processes, his overall architecture is best understood as a counterfactual model of such conditions. Here, the notion of *political values* might be understood as an encompassing category. These determine how Rawls understands the substantive framework that express both principles of justice that have acquired constitutional standing and the procedural values that link democracy and justice, which are in part carried by means of public reason. In this general sense, Rawls sharpens our sense of what reasonable foundations of political processes might look like, but not the processes themselves.

CHAPTER 3

Republicanism and the Cultural Foundations of Public Autonomy

Like liberalism, there are many versions of republicanism, ranging from critical communitarianism such as Sandel, non-state-centred, neo-Aristotelian communitarianism such as McIntyre, and various versions that are close to liberalism such as Pettit's neo-Roman and Sunstein's deliberative version (Arendt, 1958; McIntyre, 1981; Pettit, 1999; Sandel, 1996; Schnadelbach, 1987; Sunstein, 1988). The concern that unites these versions, though with considerable variation, is the centrality to politics of its ethical context. Democratic culture derives from the ethos of a way of life that is in turn sustained through appropriate politics. Such a politics makes possible the democratic formation of public will and thus directs social and political institutions to serve the common good. In its classical formulation, republicanism expresses the voice of society or sub-societal communities, articulated in the form of collective political will, and directed towards political authority. As both Habermas and Pettit observe, it is a contestatory vision of politics, permanently directed towards the state as the source of modern political authority (Habermas, 1994; Pettit, 1999). Nonetheless, republican theory is on the whole not anti-state and, though not in all versions, generally recognizes the state's potential as an agent of the collective good, and its role as either itself the embodiment of ethical community or the facilitator of such community at other social levels.

The significance of a historically established communal ethos permeates civic republican philosophy. Such an ethos is composed of the values that emerge from the experience of sharing a common world. In communal life practices, these territorial, political, and expressive values are combined into a distinctive normative culture that directs social organization. The emphasis on ethos is directed variously against the liberal ideas of the 'asocial' moral individual, the ethical neutrality of law, the separation of ethics and politics, and the separation of ethics and morality in justification (Forst, 2002). Critique is therefore respectively directed at the notion that the individual can have moral capacities that are divorced from her experience of socialization, at the idea that the law and the state can be neutral in its ethos, that ethical preferences lie beyond politics in private life, and that moral questions can be separated from ethical questions in general justification. The general thrust of the critique is that political activity is embedded in a general culture, which is not pre-political; on the contrary, it can only be brought about, reproduced, and changed through political activity. Liberalism as political theory mistakenly ignores this central insight, though liberalism as practice – viewed as an ideology – does advance a distinctive and successful, though mostly unacknowledged, general cultural model. Hence liberalism is accused of advancing damaging disjunctive visions of a depoliticized private realm separated from the public realm, of individuals divided into moral political agents and self-interested social selves, and of justification that depends on distinguishing the moral supremacy of the right from communal articulations of the good.

Sandel offers the most sustained and referenced version of this critique (Sandel, 1984, 1996, 1998). He does not deny the wide diffusion and efficacy of liberal ideas, but critically evaluates the consequences for contemporary America. In accepting the efficacy of liberalism as a political philosophy, he does not find liberalism wanting with respect to its realistic description of a world it has itself created but, instead, normatively criticizes it for destroying the republican spirit of early American democracy. The standard provided by this republican spirit, like the early Habermas's account of the public sphere, is the superior, practically relevant, normative philosophy of an earlier time (Habermas, 1989). This philosophy allowed for an egalitarian and humane spirit to permeate social and political institutions in which rights and responsibilities were integrated into sustaining communal values. Crucial factors were the extent to which practical, communal philosophies shaped the direction of politics and were themselves reinvigorated by political discourses. By contrast, the advent of the 'rights revolution', which Sandel traces to the actions of the courts in the early twentieth century, freed individual rights from their communal constraints

(Sandel, 1996). This rights revolution prioritized an ethos of individualism over that of the collective good – priority of right over good – and led to the 'ethical' ills of 'monadic' individualism, destruction of the communal ethos of solidarity, and a minimal 'procedural' republic oriented by a de-ethicized idea of morality carried by autonomous individuals.

Much of the contemporary revival of Republican thinking in line with Sandel is based upon critique of the separation of politics and society. The general formula is the need for a new 'ethicization'. The nature of any such ethicization leads to very different prognoses, ranging from the overall modernity critique and corresponding validation of culturally integrated small-scale life contexts of McIntyre to Sandel's appeal for a republican revitalization of modern society. Republicanism is animated both by the conservative critique of the enlightenment and by the recovery of an alternative modernity. In both versions, the form taken by modern society is a cause of dissatisfaction. In the conservative counter-enlightenment tradition, modern life as a whole represents a problem that *somehow* needs to be transcended (Koselleck, 1998). In the modernity critical tradition, which different from Koselleck generally regretfully accepts that the direction of modern societies cannot foreseeably be reversed, inspiration drawn from the past cannot be rediscovered in the complex, differentiated, and pluralistic societies of the present. Both versions, therefore, exhibit a critique that is unable to clearly demonstrate a way forward.

Sandel, along with Pettit, McIntyre, and Taylor, disagree with the deontological standpoint they associate with liberalism (McIntyre, 1981; Pettit, 1999; Taylor, 1989). This critique of deontological arguments is grounded on an interpretation of the relationship between the self and the social world. The general republican argument is that deontological arguments rest on an asocial assumption when they assert that foundational moral principles guiding political justice are located in the moral capacities of individuals. Individuals in the liberal tradition appear as socially detached monads that are a priori entitled to a set of rights guaranteeing their moral and political autonomy. The collective good is then to be achieved by co-operation between these rights-bearing individuals. Moreover, such rights-bearing individuals, and the rational actions that can be expected of them in depoliticized private realms, allow a moral conception of justice to be presented as underpinning an ethically neutral law. Such a conception of justice is formal and minimal and effectively ignores the 'thick' contexts generated by cultural forms of life, the collective action they generate, and the consequences of this action for politics.

The republican position stands in stark contrast in assuming the *social* production of a collective ethos that then leads to the formation of individuals compatible with it. It therefore emphasizes how spatially and circumstantially differing contexts of social practices both generate and reflect variation in ethical systems. The plurality of ethical systems is a premise of republican theorizing. The emphasis on the importance of the virtues of ethical community in no sense leads either to factual agreement across different societies or, for that matter, normative agreement between their academic interpreters. Republican philosophies seek grounding in different kinds of ethical community – small-scale local communities, nation-state communities, ethnic communities, and transnational communities – and in different, valued dimensions of these communities, for example, common cultural belonging or egalitarian qualities. What unites these evaluations is the importance attached to the thick, multi-stranded quality of collective ethical commitments at different times and places.

Pettit's Reorientation of Republicanism

In his assessment of Sandel's *Democracy's Discontent*, Pettit claims that Sandel offers a cogent account of the influence of a previous era of republicanism in American political life (Pettit, 1998; Sandel, 1998). But, according to Pettit, Sandel leaves unclear how the valued republican ethos – for example, constraining the profit motive to protect labour – could be revitalized. Following Pettit's logic, Sandel needs an 'independent' normative standard to evaluate modern institutions and, in his own work, Pettit proposes the standard of 'non-domination'. The idea of non-domination echoes not alone an important historical current within republican thinking, but also the normative standard of the early Frankfurt school that continued into

Habermas's early account of the public sphere, captured there in the idea of the legitimacy generated by a rational-critical public (Habermas, 1989; Horkheimer, 1982). The standard of non-domination is unusual in modern Republican thinking by virtue of its negative status, the emphasis on what should not be the case. In this sense, it is like the liberal principle of non-interference but, in another sense, it is more encompassing in its egalitarian interactive and communal implications. In his critique of Sandel who, by contrast, remains attached to a positive standard of the common good, Pettit claims that he is unable to demonstrate how such positive – and also egalitarian – 'republican' values, historically displaced in American political life, could be re-established. Pettit's solution is to propose the principle of non-domination as a standard, but not to attempt to socio-historically concretize it in substantive, institutional values (Pettit, 1999).

The standard of non-domination amounts to equalizing the power of citizens, so that they could jointly and individually influence political authority. On the input side, citizens would shape the agenda of the state to pursue policies that in turn lead to the continued realization of non-domination as an egalitarian good on the output side.[1] In an afterword to the 1999 paperback edition of his book, Pettit stresses the priority of process over policies that he says became 'blurred' in the original book (Pettit, 1999, p. 288). Process refers to how things should be decided in political life. In this formulation, Pettit is very close to a 'procedural' position of the kind that Sandel finds problematic. Due to the danger of the state dominating its citizens it should confine itself to addressing only their 'common, recognizable interests of the rule of law, the dispersion of power, the representation of different classes and so on'. According to Pettit, the policy commitment should only commit the state to promote domestic peace and external defence and perhaps 'other goods' like the system of land distribution that James Harrington called 'the agrarian' (ibid., p. 288; Harrington, 1992).

---

[1] Both Goodin and Michelman draw attention to the importance of considering both input and output sides of political procedures (Goodin, 2003; Michelman, 1997).

Pettit's republicanism, based on the negative standard of non-domination, generates a dilemma. His account of political process takes account of wider issues than the liberal position – dispersion of power, balanced representation of class interests – but it is not clear how the state, with a narrow remit on the output side, could actually create the kind of society that would guarantee a politics based on non-domination on the input side. Pettit's critique of Sandel asks whether substantive goals for collective action in contexts of complexity and pluralism can still be understood as actually securely embedded in orienting value systems, or at least whether there exists a foreseeable potential in this regard. Pettit answers this question only indirectly by advocating a process model of politics that would obviate domination. However, without showing a demonstrable relationship between such a process model and the actual production of a non-dominated society this answer submerges a central question in republican political theory; where the ethos that carries non-domination is located and who would carry it? Pettit's thinking could be adapted to support a promising virtuous republican circle: ensuring progressively greater levels of non-domination on the input side of politics leads to the construction of the most egalitarian ethic possible to guide the collective pursuit of a good and non-dominated society on the output side, and that such a society would in turn improve non-domination on the input side, and so on. This virtuous circle lies at the heart of Michelman's critique of Habermas. According to Michelman, Habermas only attends to the conditions of consensus on the output side of politics, the setting of norms to which all could agree, but such consensus on the output side is bound to operate as consensus on basic important political values on the input side, even if this input side consensus is always likely to be revised or transformed through deliberative political processes (Michelman, 1997). The question that arises is how is this input consensus forged in the first place?[2]

---

2   This observation of Michelman bears on the nature of the cognitive order and sociocultural models developed in detail in Part III. There, a position is taken that accept Michelman's point on the importance of the input side, but the understanding offered of the input side is not restricted to consensual values.

Pettit's own work does not go down this route of clarifying the input and output conditions that must attend a political process that would generate a non-dominated society. Instead, he offers a version of political proceduralism in his account of legitimation through contestability. Contestability, the idea that multiple publics should be in a position to scrutinize the laws once they are produced, is in his view superior to the notion of popular will, because it does away with any idea of a unitary communal ethos that would over-substantialize politics and carry the risk of majority tyranny. Hence, the notion of the public as the subjects of law is altered to the public as the potential critics of law. Pettit's theory of republicanism seeks thereby to retain some of its participatory vitality, but it breaks the link between a guiding substantive ethos and political activity. This account of republicanism consciously weakens the core idea of public autonomy as constitutive of politics and understands the role of the public as reactive to a political agenda constructed elsewhere. He variously describes his account of politics as deliberative and dialogical, but he provides nothing analogous to Habermas's integration of deliberative politics with discursive will formation in the public sphere, or Gutmann and Thompson's account of the multiple forms of public participation, or Bohman's dialogical account of public deliberation, to name but a few contrasting examples (Bohman, 2000; Gutmann and Thompson, 1996; Habermas, 1996).

Pettit's Critique of Deontological Arguments

Generally, republican theories challenge the way liberals employ the deontological standard of foundational human rights. Liberals regards these rights as substantively pre-existing the democratic process and legitimating a particular form of individual autonomy as the freedom enjoyed by rights-bearing individuals. Republicanism begins the other way round and asks what kind of social institutions guided by which value standards could best promote 'society-enhancing' kinds of autonomous individual? The desired republican outcome would not only be the generation of individual autonomy, but also that autonomous individuals would be imbued with a sense of responsibility for the collective welfare. The republican standard is hence consequential or teleological and not deontological, confirming the primacy of values formed in a wide conception of the political process rather than originating in anything approximating to the state of nature. In Pettit's view, all the main figures of the republican tradition 'treat the question of which institutions do best by freedom as an open, empirical issue, not as a question capable of a priori resolution' (Pettit, 1999, p. 100). He argues that it is not the comprehensive, a priori derivation of constitutional norms that is to be sought, but the institutional configurations that best realize a specific normative standard, in his own case the standard of non-domination. Even deviations from constitutional norms could be tolerated 'if the cause of maximizing non-domination does require such departures from the perfect constitution' (ibid., p. 102). He claims that in a consequential approach of this kind, a wide range of institutional variation is possible depending on what is needed to realize the particular social goal, whereas a deontological approach would circumscribe such variation because of its restrictive commitment to formal constitutional standards that apply at all times and places. In this formulation, Pettit suggests that a republican consequentialist approach is superior to a liberal deontological one, because it better serves the potential for institutional and social learning.[3]

Pettit goes on to ask the question of could we be sure departures from the perfect constitution would not 'prove repugnant to our moral sense' (ibid., p. 102)? To answer this question, Pettit invokes the test of the Rawlsian standard of reflective equilibrium and suggests that a teleological republicanism would pass it. Reflective equilibrium requires of an ideal to prove, after reflection and 'perhaps after revision', that it 'equilibrates with our judgements about proper political response'. He adds that a teleological republicanism 'would fail to satisfy reflective equilibrium if it required intuitively objectionable arrangements' (ibid., p. 102). Teleological

---

[3] See Chapter 9, and Parts III and IV generally, for critical remarks on some aspects of the deontological tradition that bear on Pettit's observation. In the end, though, the conclusion is to find a balance between the two approaches.

republicanism with a consequentialist commitment to freedom as non-domination would pass the test, because 'it is in equilibrium, in this reflective way, with considered intuitions about how things should be politically organized' (ibid.). Pettit's account raises the questions of by what standards and by what process would reflective equilibration take place?

With respect to standards, he suggests that morality is grounded in an intuitive sense of what is right, but that such a sense cannot be specified in advance according to deontologically grounded principles; it rather comes into play in the flux of the political process. With respect to process, reiterating the point above, it is not clear from Pettit's account how reflective equilibrium would take effect other than by political activity in a generally understood sense. In Rawls's account, a distinction is drawn between broad and narrow reflective equilibrium (Rawls, 1993, p. 384). What Rawls describes as narrow reflective equilibrium, by which we take note only of our own judgements, appears to equate with Pettit's account. Of course, 'our' could be understood in the sense of one or a number of people sharing a common position. By contrast, what Rawls describes as wide – or full – reflective equilibrium comes into play when citizens, having duly considered all available conceptions of justice, come to affirm a common public conception of political justice. He goes on to say that 'this equilibrium is fully intersubjective; that is, each citizen has taken into account the reasoning and agreement of every other citizen' (ibid.). By contrast, to follow Pettit, some kind of unspecified, political agency must be at work in deciding the political agenda – the primary agent throughout his work is the state. Rawls holds that citizens must decide the public conception of political justice by means of an intersubjective process of reflective equilibrium. This intersubjective process would include reflective consideration of rival political conceptions of justice in arriving at a common, minimal, political conception of justice. Nothing in this decision would preclude further consideration of 'comprehensive' philosophies of justice – for example, freedom as non-domination – in order to assess how they would influence the common political conception of justice.[4] Understood through their respective interpretations of the political usage

---

4   In actuality, such comprehensive philosophies in any case find their way into political programmes as ideologies, since much of what is politically instituted in actual

of reflective equilibrium, Rawls's position on the role of public autonomy is actually stronger than Pettit's.

Pettit's consequentialist account assumes the necessity for a comprehensive political position, freedom as non-domination, to guide political action. Such a comprehensive position depends on the widespread diffusion of this ethic so that political authority can shape society in conformity with it. Pettit is vague about what could be described in Sen's sense as the 'social realization' of such an ethic on the input side (Sen, 2009).[5] Moreover, following Michelman above, without a widely diffused ethic guiding *both* input and output sides of political action, no normative consistency on anything like republican terms could be imagined. Further, for a general as distinct from local standard of non-domination to apply by means of the principle of contestability that Pettit advances, which consists of the right of publics to contest political outcomes, a form of societal argumentation would be required that would lead to common alignment of normative possibilities with socially distributed preferences. Such alignment by no means excludes continuing differences and also does not require the presumption of prior value consensus, as over-substantialized communitarian theories tend to assume (Habermas, 1994). In this light, republicanism no longer has to depend upon a single institution-directing ethos anchored in a communal life form. It can postulate a plurality of ethical systems that play out their differences and yet achieve some kind of more or less satisfactory resolution of them in the cognitive structures, cultural models, and normative orders of modern societies.[6]

---

democratic politics will exceed what has been 'consensually' agreed in advance as a minimal, common conception of justice.

5 There is a clear affinity between Pettit's idea of the ongoing re-design of institutions to fit consequential goals and Sen's notion of social realization with its strong conception of agency. The latter does stress agency quite actively, while it remains a latent and under-developed category in Pettit. In addition, a common interest in institutional design to remedy manifest injustice or domination may be discerned.

6 A cognitive sociological approach along these lines is developed in Part III of this book.

Pettit's principle of freedom as non-domination represents, in Rawls's term, a reasonable comprehensive doctrine that would give new force to an egalitarian reading of the republican tradition. From a substantive viewpoint, in distinguishing between non-domination and non-interference, it presents itself as more radical than the liberal position by expanding the scope of politics and emphasizing the centrality of power. However, what would be required to make this substantive commitment politically effective is not clear, since he neither demonstrates how a societal ethos such as non-domination might operate in practice as Sandel does, though only in a historical sense, nor does he argue for the extension of the mechanisms of political participation into civil society. In fact, in dismissing what he describes as Arendt's populism, he explicitly inverts the relationship that the radical democratic tradition drew on in situating the state as servant and the people as master. Pettit suggests that, by contrast, the state should be regarded as trustee and the people as trustors. They would, above all, trust the state to pursue the general interest within a framework of law in a non-arbitrary manner.

Republicanism and the Public Sphere

The republican tradition generally finds it difficult to maintain key principles and remain relevant to the contemporary world. Modern republicanism appears to weaken its core commitment to public autonomy, arguing, as does Pettit, for output legitimacy in the principle of contestability or defending the integrity of a disappearing and unrecoverable historical ethos in the communitarian tradition. Yet, the guiding intuition of the theory is to expand the scope of politics beyond the narrow formal core emphasized in liberal theory and show how it actually depends, and should further depend, on the wider normative culture of civil society. Against the proceduralism of modern liberal and deliberative theories, most formulations of republicanism argue for inclusion of some kinds of substantive principles of the good life. As a tradition that seeks as wide a scope for politics as possible and that generally argues that public autonomy is foundational for democracy, it is critical of the effect of modern political institutions on the vitality of ethical traditions, including egalitarian ones. Notwithstanding problems of fit with modern conditions of life, republican philosophy continues to advance the case for a normatively wide-ranging politics that would address dimensions of democratic and social justice that lie beyond the minima of the rights that confer autonomy on individuals and the merely aggregative effects of social co-operation by these autonomous individuals. In short, recurrently throughout a long tradition, it proposes the reconciliation of the collective good, communicatively achieved by the autonomy of publics and their institutions, with the individual values that it regards as one-sidedly emphasized by liberalism (Seidman, 1983; Walzer, 1990).

Republicanism encounters real problems in explaining modern cultural forms in either descriptive or normative registers in a manner that would be theoretically productive. As Pettit argues, its consequentialism commits it, in terms of the relationship between the political system and other social spheres, to argue from the outside in as well as the inside out (Pettit, 1999). Variations in its own account of factual and normative worlds already attest to different evaluations of various kinds and facets of ethical community. Such evaluations have to squarely face not just the problems of the origins and jurisdictional authority of isolated, virtuous communities, such as ethnic groups or culturally homogenous nation-states – which are problematically assumed to represent ethically unified cultures – but also to address the conditions of modernity in which differentiated cultural orientations prevail within and across political communities. Even within a given political community, the term 'community' itself not only should refer to the plurality, as opposed to the singularity, of ethical communities, but also to legal, moral, and political communities, all of them characterized by different processes and rules, and all of them interacting in complicated ways (Forst, 2002).

Ultimately, the lack of fit between republicanism and the conditions of modern life is to be traced back to the understanding of communalism that underpins many versions of the theory. This kind of communalism understands citizens as conventionally embedded in the contexts of life in which they are socialized. This preexisting cultural infrastructure is assumed to provide them both with meaning and a sense of collective purpose. But the idea of culture as an overarching superstructure that primordially precedes and shapes the formation of individuals has a naturalistic and holistic quality to it that does not do justice to modern conditions characterized by the plurality of communal contexts and collective identities. Republicans could argue, as much communitarianism does, that from the standpoint of the good of society it would be better if there was such a holistic and integrating communal ethical system available, and insofar as it doesn't exist in modern societies those societies have problems. But republican philosophy has not taken up the challenge of specifying what would comprise a contemporary communal ethical system. To adequately do this, it would have to provide not simply normative diagnosis and prognosis but undertake to demonstrate the mechanisms whereby the – pessimistic – diagnosis and – optimistic – prognosis could take effect. Taking on the task of demonstrating the mechanisms of culture formation would immediately mean jettisoning the anachronistic idea of an encompassing and singular territory-based group culture formed at a defining point in history. Ethical communalism, no longer understood as springing from such a culture and determining political values, would instead have to be located as one type of politically relevant community amongst others, and one moreover subject to mutation in the process of social change. This is indeed what Sandel does, but he does so only looking backwards and with a predominant emphasis on socio-economic life.

Generally, the relationship of the republican political tradition to the category of public sphere is a peculiar one. The centrality to the tradition of the idea of public autonomy, of the public as the authors of the laws that bind them, suggests that republicanism should be at the forefront of demonstrating how both the spaces and the participatory modalities of politics might be expanded. The theory and practice of public participation and communication should, therefore, be core concerns. Yet these concerns are at best only hesitantly and indirectly present in much republican writing. As already observed, and perhaps serving as part of the explanation, the focus of at least the influential communitarian strand of republicanism on an established communal ethic tends to deny the significance of political process. This is the more problematic given that the idea of a historically embedded substantive ethos capable of being remobilized in the contemporary conditions of territorial communities lacks plausibility. Even what some might regard as a beneficent ethos within the nation-state such as solidarity cannot be assumed to endure in existing forms, as the social and spatial locale of solidarity is subject to ongoing reconstruction.[7]

These observations lead to two further points that press in different directions. The substantive commitments of republicanism to the production and reproduction of a justifiable ethos on the input and output side of political processes is important to any account of the public sphere that, using the concepts of Peirce, does not trump the real communication community with the counterfactual ideal of pure deliberative procedures that are one-sidedly understood from the transcendent standpoint of the unlimited communication community. Such substantive commitments, with echoes of Hegel, involve the historicization of reason, a historicization that in any foreseeable political conditions must be shared between procedural and extra-procedural dimensions of political life. This observation raises questions about the epistemic status of deliberation that will be taken up in addressing deliberative theories below. Similar to the value of Rawls's identification of the principles that an order of political justice should follow, the republican commitment to the importance of ethical systems in politics has real value. In sociological terms, these ethical systems are expressed through what Lamont and Thévenot describe as the pragmatic culturally anchored repertoires that make possible various kinds of communicative practices (Lamont and Thévenot, 2000). More generally, following Bourdieu, such pragmatic repertoires are given persistent structural shape by the social fields in which they are inset and contribute to the 'structuring structure' that these fields represent (Bourdieu, 1985). In certain respects, these latter sociological traditions involve republican thinking applied to understanding the cultural foundations of social practices,

---

[7] James Bohman notes that it is largely an empirical question whether nation-states can maintain specific policies such as the social rights of the welfare state (Bohman, 2007, p. 22). On the future of justice and territorial rights in conditions of globalization, see Cara Nine's *Territory and Global Justice* (Nine, 2012).

and in part draw off the Durkheimian tradition, emphasizing collective representations, which itself has republican roots.[8]

Like liberalism, republicanism is a broad political family. One variation on republicanism that diminishes its communal ethos in favour of emphasizing the relationship between communicative freedom and normative statuses and powers is that of Bohman (Bohman, 2004; Bohman, 2007). Ethos is retained in a normative form in the idea of a legitimate public law that is rooted in a political community. Only in the context of such a community can the genesis and continuing validity of human rights be understood. But this community is constituted and replenished through the exercise of communicative freedom. This version of republicanism, which is immediately congenial to a communicative idea of politics, uses the standard of non-domination as does Pettit, but it does so with a stronger institutional commitment to bringing about the societal conditions that would actually realize it. This would be achieved if individuals were equipped with those necessary normative statuses and powers, what he terms the 'democratic minimum', which would enable them to democratize complex interdependencies and secure a good common life (Bohman, 2007). This vision of democracy in action is true to the pragmatist vision of the capacity for individual and collective action that could resist the power of domination by other actors, by structural forces, or by both in combination. This would operate by virtue of a communicative epistemology that could comprehend the play of interdependencies and normatively distinguish legitimate power from arbitrary domination. This vision of democracy, which advocates deepening the reflexivity of institutions through communicatively carried learning processes, is one in which democracy is never formally stable, but instead subject to ongoing democratization.

Such strong assumptions about the normative powers constructed out of communicative freedom, on the one hand, makes the republican tradition more compatible with a dynamic, institutionally resonant conception of public discourse. On the other hand, Bohman offers an explicit critique of the self-legislation model that is at the core of classical republicanism, and

---

8   This dimension of the substantive ethos of republicanism will be developed later in the book with a view to making it sociologically fruitful.

which is also associated with grounding claims to group self-determination in liberalism too. He argues that the range and multi-directionality of interdependencies are such today that territorially bound publics cannot minimally morally order them to create conditions of non-domination. What *is* possible is a spectrum of legal communities at different spatial levels that would be democratically bound by mobilized publics who insist on the communicative redemption of their political and human rights by constructing reticular public spheres.

These ideas raise a profound challenge to the orientation of the republican tradition to the model of self-legislation, which has the normative connotation of self-rule, and the ethical connotation of a spatially located, usually territorial, collective identity. In a general, descriptive sense, Bohman's ideas on the likely innovative effects of communicative freedom make sense given the challenges created by the multiple and competing flux of interdependencies that characterize functionally and culturally differentiated modern societies. These ideals also have a kind of dynamic, normative virtue in the sense of encouraging democratic innovation as opposed to imagining that existing, deeply troubled democratic institutions can solve the 'old' problems of citizen detachment and distrust they confront within national political communities and the 'new' problems of ordering post-national interdependencies.

Nevertheless, Bohman's radical vision unnecessarily neglects intrinsic and defensible aspects of established democratic cultures that are guided by the ideal of self-legislation. It remains true, notwithstanding the pace of globalization, that interdependencies between citizens are 'thicker' in established territories. Attempts to normatively regulate these interdependencies then give rise to what Christiano describes as a 'common world' in which strong, reciprocal expectations of justice and responsibility prevail (Christiano, 2008; Mead, 1934; Nine, 2013). As interdependencies and corresponding normative regulation increase on the transnational level, at least some of the features of a democratic normative culture can be expected to emerge. Later in the book, it will be argued precisely why such a culture remains necessary in spite of the dangers of citizens excluding non-citizens.[9]

---

9   Bernhard Peters, writing in 2001, observes that most of the legitimacy of European institutions derives from what he describes as empirical legitimacy to distinguish

Such dangers have to be overcome, because a normatively weak, functionally integrated polity will, in the end, be more likely to practice the kind of ethnocentric exclusion that is today quite far developed even in the countries of the European Union that was built from the ashes of such calamities, not to mention at the level of the Union itself (Skillington, 2013b).[10]

With respect to the general fork in the republican road, insofar as Bohman endeavours to move beyond territorially concentrated normative cultures he moves towards the procedural assumptions of deliberative democracy. This reveals the deep fissure within theories that all describe themselves as republican, between the substance-oriented republican legacy taken up in communitarianism and the desubstantialization and proceduralism emphasized in modern deliberative theory – and decried by Sandel amongst others.[11] Deliberative republicanism corrects the 'peculiarity' of

---

it from formal legitimacy. Empirical legitimacy in this sense is consistent with the degree to which nation-states are integrated through symbolic attachment to the nation (Billig, 1995; Peters, 2001). It might be observed from the vantage point of a decade later that this kind of legitimacy on the European level has proven to be largely illusory, though this observation is not meant to deny its historical role within the nation-state and more generally (Delanty and O'Mahony, 2002).

10 Not everybody is so concerned with negative consequences of insider/outsider distinctions. Such distinctions are based upon claimed common, ascriptive characteristics of members of national or other territorial entities, and the argument is made that these should serve as boundary markers for normative inclusion. At least some theories of nationalism claim that national cultural loyalties, which inevitably depend on insider/outsider distinctions, actually create the conditions for democratic institutions (Greenfeld, 1993).

11 Difficulties with distributing authors to particular traditions are illustrated by the case of Sunstein (Sunstein, 1988). He identifies four essential features of republicanism, comprising of deliberation, equality – especially democratic equality – universalistic orientation to the common good, and participatory rights of citizenship. A reasonable interpretation of Sunstein's account is that, of these four, the most characteristic and important is that of deliberation as it provides the means to realize the other three. Along with blurring the boundaries between republicanism and deliberative theories, Sunstein also claims that his version of republicanism is not in tension with liberalism, but that it is, in fact, a liberal republicanism. In the end, this kind of boundary blurring does not create the kind of difficulties for the typology developed here as might first appear. Distinctions between positions will later be interpreted from within a societal theoretical framework that is precisely intended to show how

republicanism with respect to the public sphere alluded to above, public autonomy without a theory of mechanisms for its realization, but it does so in a way that is to the cost of understanding how the substantive theory of some versions of republicanism contributes to understanding the public sphere. This kind of republicanism draws attention to what *normative cultures* do, though it less than clear about the mechanisms associated with their formation and operation. Sociologically translated, these normative cultures consist of the outcomes of collective learning processes that result in the varied interplay of democratic regulative ideas, cultural models, and institutional rule systems. Republican substantialism, thus sociologically translated, clarifies how public autonomy can be supported by legitimate normative cultures that incorporate principles of justice into forms of social co-operation. Contra the communitarian idea that such normative cultures can only be generated by ascriptive, communal identities such as ethnicities or nations, they should instead be regarded as also having a moral dimension that opens them to general and reciprocal justification (Forst, 2002; O'Mahony and Delanty, 2001). They should therefore be permanently revisable in fair conditions of pluralism and publicity.[12] It can be seen already in this choice of language how such a sociologically translated and ethically

---

they contribute to particular societal spheres and how these spheres interpenetrate in social practice.

12 Honneth's interpretation of Dewey whom he regards as having elucidated the relationship between the normative foundations of democratic theory in deliberation and the normative foundations of social co-operation in the division of labour provides some guidance as to the relationship between democratic procedures and normative cultures (Deranty, 2009; Honneth, 1998). Honneth's interpretation rightly attaches great importance to the epistemic dimension of it being clear to the public in general how individuals fit into the system of co-operation and that its terms are fair. This is achieved by fostering a reflexive relationship to the system of co-operation. In this way, Honneth, following Dewey, opens up the issue of the respective relationships between social and democratic theory and social and political philosophy. Both Dewey and Honneth favour the widening of democracy beyond the formal political system. In contemporary conditions of complexity, such widening depends very much on democracy's epistemic capacity to understand other social spheres and hence generate feasible as well as just normative interventions (O'Mahony, 2009, 2011b).

pluralized republican substantialism requires the support of a Rawlsian idea of morally grounded principles of justice. The two together then go a significant part of the way towards clarifying the normative culture that must be understood as the complement of deliberative reasoning. This connection is addressed in more detail in Chapters 10 and 13.

The challenge facing contemporary republican theory from a communication-theoretical standpoint is assessing the form and the strength of normative culture in the light of the communicative mechanisms that constitute it. Approaches like that of Sandel emphasize the necessity and necessary stability of such a normative culture; approaches like that of Bohman understand this normative culture as a weaker form and emphasize its subordination to those communicative mechanisms, especially deliberation, that operate with communicative freedom to reflexively change normative rules. The proposal here is that both are needed; normative cultures are more stable than Bohman supposes, but communicative mechanisms more immediate and dynamic in their transformative implications than Sandel imagines. If a relatively stable normative culture is requisite for democracy, then republicanism must face the question of territorial limits and transgressions, if it doesn't want to argue for a world government. For such purposes, territorially bound normative culture should not be equated with ethnos, or with an ethnically conditioned theory of the demos. This dimension of republican theory in a contemporary world characterized by ongoing processes of deterritorialization and reterritorialization can only be satisfactorily addressed from within a theory of cosmopolitan solidarity in which normative culture is seen as a moral as well as ethical achievement (Brunkhorst, 2005).[13]

---

[13] The critical issue of cosmopolitanism is developed in Chapter 18.

CHAPTER 4

The Radical Tradition: Public Contestation of Subjugation

In important respects the radical tradition starts from and attempts to go beyond republicanism. Its most important affinity with republicanism is the common emphasis on public autonomy, with the public as subject of the laws that bind them, with the important caveat that, for the radical tradition, in actual political conditions the public struggles to assert either public or private autonomy. It is concerned with the status of civil society and its political influence and, correspondingly, with the importance of political identity as an expression of standpoints within this civil society. By contrast with republicanism, it places greater emphasis on subjugation, and responses to the experience of subjugation, and shows less interest in the institutional dimensions of politics. At least it has less affirmative interest in institutional politics, though it is thoroughly engaged with political institutions at the level of critique. Insofar as radical democratic positions are concerned with the experience of and response to subjugation, in Haraway's sense the preference for the rights and truth claims of subjugated knowledge, these theories are latently or manifestly concerned with the communicative construction of *public contestation* (Haraway, 1991).

What is distinctive to the radical tradition can be hard to specify since the republican tradition already lays claim to the inheritance of radical democracy with its emphasis on participation and popular will, even if this in practice is mostly understood in a limited, institutional sense, though with exceptions such as Bohman (Bohman, 2004; Bohman, 2010). What is intended here by the term 'radical democracy' is an emphasis on both the enduring and politically creative nature of conflict. The agonistic tradition associated with writers such as Mouffe, Honig, and Laclau emphasizes conflict's constant political presence. As Honig puts it, political settlements always leave a remainder that generates new grounds for contestation (Honig, 1993). Within its emphasis on contestation, agonism rather hesitantly introduces an institutional dimension, as when Mouffe suggests there is an affinity between radical democracy in her sense and the building of liberal institutions. Nonetheless, echoing a theme of Marx, she claims these institutions should be more consistent with their grounding principles (Honig, 1993; Laclau, 1996; Mouffe, 1990). Fraser, who also understands herself as standing in a critical, constructive relationship to the liberal tradition through her commitment to thick deontological liberalism, distinguishes between normal and abnormal justice. She speculates that the latter, in which both the substance of justice and the very grammar through which it is expressed are not well defined, is historically the most common (Fraser, 2008).[1]

One of the most distinctive features of the tradition is the disinterest in theorizing the normative foundations of a democratically just and well-ordered society.[2] A general starting presumption is the pressing need for radical social change. This is originally derived from the critique of a society assumed to be unfairly organized on capitalist lines, but this is now extended to other social arrangements deemed exploitative and subjugating. Democratic politics must respond to this need and not imagine that it has already met it or that it can somehow exist in a 'neutral' space beyond it. The notion of resistance to subjugation as a theme begets the question of the source of that subjugation. In the radical democratic tradition three kinds of critique are prominent. The first is the critique of social injustice; the second is the critique of impersonal domination, whether in the form of authoritarian, bureaucratic, or capitalist domination; and the third is the critique of the subjugation of legitimate socio-cultural identity. These three kinds of critique have historically succeeded one another in modern radical democratic theories. This does not mean that the social critique

---

1   The account of the macro-cognitive order provided below is relevant to this point of Fraser's. It suggests, additionally, that constant interplay between normal and abnormal justice is to be expected.
2   In this respect it has distinct affinities with Sen's theory briefly alluded to above (Sen, 2009).

disappears to be replaced by newer emphases of critique. Rather, it means that the entire landscape of socio-political critique is comprised of multiple foundations that can be separated or combined in different ways.

The Dialectic of Rationalization and Subjectivation

If there is one fault line in modern culture that more than anything defines radical democratic theory, it is what Touraine, echoing a dominant motif of Max Weber that is also to be found in Marx and Durkheim, calls the dialectic of rationalization and subjectivation (Touraine, 1995; Touraine, 1997). Touraine understood the advent of a rational subject that arose with modernity as the carrier of democracy. Such a rational subject advocated and institutionalized universal laws, principles, and rights that protect the liberty and guarantee the equality of individuals and also provide them with the capacity for enhanced individuation. Touraine's modern subject remains capable of rationality in the sense of the capacity for action so as to construct, sustain, and change a democratic society. But Touraine sees progressive *rationalization* in a manner consistent with Adorno, Foucault, and Weber amongst others as escaping the powers of rational democratic subjects by means of the institutionalization of regimes of conduct, understood variously as instrumental, disciplinary, or purposive. Building on Touraine, the contemporary rational subject, not yet consolidated as a subject in such a way as to be adequate to the times, has to face the significant challenge of freeing itself from dangerous forms of rationalization in the unstable conditions produced by social, ethnic, gendered, and racial pluralism amidst growing functional complexity.

Individual subjects, and the subject writ large as a collective, historically constructed the public, participatory resources of modernity to solve the problem of living together across difference in an increasingly pluralistic society. Touraine perceives the reconciliation of liberal and republican positions, respectively focusing on rights and active citizenship, private and public autonomy, as essential to grounding a common democratic culture. If, in this respect, Touraine is close to Habermas, he also stands in some contrast to him and also, in different ways, to Rawls and Luhmann in not understanding legitimacy as justification through procedure. While defining the *problem* in broadly similar terms to at least Habermas and Rawls – irreconcilable comprehensive doctrines producing identities in need of reconciliation that leave no neutral transcending perspective – he instead emphasizes the importance of sustaining and appropriately changing the substantive democratic culture of civil society. Such a democratic culture depends on the *social production* of both the kinds of subjects, and the associated kinds of intersubjectivity, that would enable the democratic project to meet the challenges of the times. It could only do so by ongoing processes of democratization of which social democracy in the twentieth century serves as one prominent example (Touraine, 1997).

Touraine's interdisciplinary emphasis on subject formation illustrates the extent to which the radical democratic standpoint draws off multiple disciplinary sources, including social theory, psychoanalysis, feminist theory, and literary theory, as well as the 'classical' sources of political philosophy and political theory. A social theorist with a viewpoint similar to Touraine is Cornelius Castoriadis, who also extensively draws off multiple disciplines (Castoriadis, 1998). Like Touraine, Castoriadis is suspicious of the authoritarian potential that he associates with overarching concepts of political community and ideas of cultural homogeneity. He develops instead the idea of the self-institution of society. Society understands itself as a collective subject that is dynamically constructed by conflicting collective social positions that contend with one another in democratic processes. The result of this contention is the construction of an institutional imaginary, which substantively orients democratic politics and is close to Touraine's own concept of historicity. The institutional imaginary is formed in the movement from contention to institutional resolution. It is never stable, because it is ultimately a product of the framework of political contention, in other words, the balance of forces and ideas that sustain it. As a social imaginary, it is partly immanently instituted and partly a horizon that reaches beyond existing institutional projects as a set of aspirations carried by society. Important for Castoriadis is that the mechanisms of producing an institutional imaginary are not planned and foreseen; in its contentious self-examination and interdependent networks of action, society 'exceeds' itself, since its collective self-interpretation runs ahead of what any one subject, individual or collective, can know. Later on, these innovative currents are explicated, sifted, and institutionally structured. The influence of Castoriadis can be seen in the French political philosopher, Claude Lefort, with his distinction between 'the political', as the symbolic framework of political action, and 'politics', as the everyday space of political activity (Lefort, 1988).

From the point of view of a general appreciation of radical democracy, Touraine and Castoriadis introduce key motifs that are addressed at finding the appropriate relationship between rationalization, subject-formation, and conflict, on one side, and possible creative outcomes of these processes on the other (Joas, 1993). Touraine's notion of the rational subject, both with its historical and future importance to democracy, offers one standpoint. Castoriadis's emphasis on collective autonomy, which he offers, as does Touraine, with the proviso of not impinging on individual liberties, provides a broadly compatible diagnosis. Across all accounts of radical democracy, the perceived need for a new kind of subject, alternately understood as the full realization of the capacities of existing subjects, attest to the perception that addressing structurally embedded injustices, organizational irrationality, and the pathologies of everyday life require a new kind of agency.

The focus on the subject has a different emphasis in other radical democratic theories. In agonistic theories, such as those of Laclau, Mouffe, and Honig, it is not the rational subject that is seen as the desideratum, but passionate, embodied, and situated subjects who bring with them the concrete circumstances of life, who can speak without mediation from social experience, and who can bring this sense of their irreducible otherness into the political domain. The idea of the subject as rational is regarded as an effect of rationalization, a rationalization that Mouffe views as carried right into the heart of modern political theory in the deliberative proceduralism of Habermas and Rawls. Mouffe criticizes both of them for what she claims is the attempt to insulate politics from the pluralism of values, claiming that both 'try to fix for all time the meaning and hierarchy of the central liberal-democratic values, instead of allowing what might be assumed to be 'healthy' continuing contestation concerning the interplay of private and public autonomy and the boundaries between them (Mouffe, 2000, pp. 92–93). While agonistic theories like Mouffe embrace the creative role of conflict, this conflict is not designed to annihilate the other, but to express the deep wellsprings of difference. Politics has a discursive and even deliberative moment, and liberal institutions and values are important, but she is opposed to what she perceives as the consensualism of the deliberative positions of Rawls and Habermas. Politics should not lead to consensual closure, but should always be open to difference.[3] Recognition of the value of conflict does not point in the direction of the reconciliation of the subject with political authority, but the freeing of the subject to politically express the counter-rationalism of authentic experience. The subject is thereby in Connolly's work ir-rational in the sense of bringing into play that which is beyond the politically instituted (Connolly, 2002).

Lefort's notion of 'the political', which he understands as the symbolic framework of political activity, ties in closely with this position (Lefort, 1988). When the political is regarded as closed for business, no longer open to the contingency of the world, is denied its capacity to create newness, danger lurks for democracy. Society has to be alive to its own inner differences, and the political is the repository of meaning that draws these differences together and, like Castoriadis's institutional imaginary, gives form to politics. In Lefort, civil society is the locus of the political, and new symbolic frames arising in civil society compete for the absent seat of power. Political power is always in principle open; it is a vacuum waiting to be filled with whatever socio-historical meaning emerges in the political. The rules of the political game, shaping both what counts as politically meaningful and the open competition to provisionally fill the empty seat of power, are provided by the constitutional founding act of equality of rights (Forst, 2002). On this minimal basis, the political fills in the ethical orientation of political activity, providing it with content. The content of the political is of an ethical nature; it results from the radical freedom of political agency that is expressed by means of a collective, but pluralist,

---

3   This formulation is close to how the 'constructionist' position is described in Ferree et al. (Ferree et al., 2002a; Ferree et al., 2002b).

ethos. Hence, in the radical democratic approaches of Castoriadis, Lefort, Laclau, Mouffe, Connolly, and Honig, there is an overarching commitment to pluralism, a pluralism that should comprehensively reflect the range of experiences arising from the social structures of society.

Nancy Fraser uses a formulation that is in some respect similar to the imaginary institution of the political, joining together Castoriadis and Lefort, when she speaks of a society's 'hegemonic grammar of contestation and deliberation' (Fraser and Honneth, 2003, p. 207). Like Castoriadis's idea of an imaginary institution and Lefort's idea of the political, the idea of a hegemonic grammar indicates the existence of a cultural order that specifies what counts as politically relevant, both with respect to present actuality and future potentiality. Fraser understands hegemonic grammar as decentred discourse formations that are expressions of moral disagreement and social protest. These do not belong to any one set of social subjects. They are 'transpersonal normative discourses that are widely diffused through democratic societies' (ibid.). They are folk paradigms of justice that create a common political grammar with which to consider political questions.[4][5]

The reference to social subjects by Fraser captures another ontological assumption that is widespread in radical democratic theories. Cultural forces shape subjects, but this does not deny these subjects a capacity for agency. Ontologically, it is neither an individualist position like that of much of liberal political theory, nor is it a socially derived identity as with much republican theory. Rather, it is a mediated position in which the

---

4   In describing these folk paradigms of justice as 'decentred' normative discourses, Fraser distinguishes her more procedural, deontological position from what she considers to be Honneth's subject centred one (Fraser and Honneth, 2003). It would be an interesting exercise to explore to what extent this gives Fraser's position a different foundation to other radical positions, but this cannot be pursued here.

5   Both Fraser's concept of hegemonic grammar and Castoriadis's account of the institutional imaginary have similarities with the concept of cultural model outlined later. Touraine's account of cultural model is taken up at that point, but further profit is taken from Castoriadis and Fraser, as well as the general radical stress on contention. All of this is placed in the context of the radical dissensus that is a key 'compositional' mechanism for building cultural models out of the the cognitive order. For an account of rational dissensus, see Miller (Miller, 1986, 1992, 2002).

micro-reality of the subjective world is assumed to constantly engage with an objective cultural world, and in which the two worlds are mediated by social forms of communication. Illustrating these social forms, Gottweis refers to subject positions, understood as social constellations or milieus that constitute subjects. These subject positions are constantly subject to alteration (Gottweis, 1998). The subject is therefore not the clearly bounded entity that animates politics as in the liberal tradition, but an entity that is formed by multiple kinds of experiences that produce varied, potentially unstable, and sometimes internally contradictory outcomes.

Radical Democracy and Institutional Politics

Lefort is typical of many radical democratic theorists that are happier to speak of the symbolic forms of politics, the subject writ large, than to explore the institutional formations that could translate symbolic forms into normative orders. The specification of immanent institutional forms has a troubling quality for these theories in that it detracts from the sense of politics as unlimited possibility and also suggests the danger of domination, even authoritarianism, through the immunization of political power located in institutions from the capacity of society for symbolic learning.[6] Suspicion of the politics of norm formation complements the contrary idea of the creative subject operating in pluralistic social spaces. The idea of freedom in the latter register as the unlimited possibilities of resisting domination through contestation – some echoes of Pettit here – is threatened by any kind of normative closure that appears to enshrine the hegemony of the right over the good. Political closure is the great fear of radical positions like those of Lefort and Mouffe. For Mouffe, it lurks in the rationalist

---

6   The emphasis on the symbolic in many radical democratic intellectual thought indicates its close relation to various lineages of the philosophy of consciousness including psychoanalytic and phenomenological.

consensualism of Rawls and Habermas and it lurks in liberal political ideas generally that always tend to confine power to an entrenched elite.

Nonetheless, in a 1996 essay, Mouffe suggests that the under-theorized institutional dimension of radical pluralist theory was there all along in the form of liberal institutions (Mouffe, 1996). She explores the possibility of a virtuous relationship between liberal democratic ideals of equality and liberty, republican ideas of the common good, and radical pluralist ideas of the need for constant struggle against subordination. The principles of liberalism in her view contain the political language of 'many struggles against subordination' that have been won and of others yet to be fought. But she criticizes liberalism in practice for anti-political tendencies in its reduction of politics to instrumentally mobilized private interests and calls for the corrective recognition of civic virtue, public spirit, and political community. Nonetheless, republicanism too generates its own dangers in the oppressive idea of a single, substantive common good. She also stresses in a pluralist register, drawing off Carl Schmitt, the importance of collective identities – that she claims liberalism does not recognize – and the struggles in which they are always fated to engage in constituting the political. In this way, Mouffe generally argues against the dichotomous manner in which liberal and republican theories separate politics into private and public, arguing instead for recognition of the common symbolic form of the political that enables them to relate to one another.

In some contrast to Mouffe, Fraser takes the institutional question further in advocating participatory parity as the single moral principle that underlies the cultural complexity of modern society (Fraser and Honneth, 2003). The principle of participatory parity suggests that politics should be so organized that participation is genuinely open, comprehensive, and fair. It should be open in the sense of meeting far-reaching requirements of publicity, comprehensive in its range of participants and themes, and fair in its treatment of these participants and themes. Participatory parity is derived from the deontological norm of universal equality, an equality that can only be secured by adequate participation. But in what spheres could participatory parity be applied? According to Forst, in Fraser's account, it could be applied to either or both of, in a minimal sense, justification processes in which all members of a society could decide on which institutions under which they are to live and, in a maximal sense, full justification of a basic structure, that is, 'a basic structure that grants those rights, life chances and goods that citizens of a just society could not reciprocally deny each other' (Forst, 2007a, p. 297).[7]

The ideal of participatory parity aims to specify conditions of full political inclusion. It would apply not simply to the powers of existing democratic institutions, but also to those institutions that would be needed to remedy domination in society. It represents a deontological, procedural standard for realizing full democratic justice. Mixing theories, it could be understood to procedurally translate the political in the sense of Lefort and Mouffe into deliberative institutions. Forst suggests that in the maximal sense of justification, participatory parity, because of its wide implications for justice throughout society, could be regarded as having a teleological standing as a weak, substantive specification of the good (ibid.; Fraser and Honneth, 2003). Participatory parity translates the overarching context of possible political meaning, organized into paradigms of justice, into a procedural framework that could generate just material norms.

But the idea of the political retains something more than what could be procedurally translated in this way; it contains the diffuse and eclectic ideas of the good that society is able to generate about itself in its contestation and deliberation and that guide its political actions. This is what the residual, pluralistic sense of the good may still be taken to mean. In this way of thinking, the good is what society wants before it seeks to politically institute it, the locus of the new, the expression of a complexity that precedes and exceeds the attempt to democratically order it. Democracy, and its normative culture, always get so far and must always seek to get further, but the normative order never can completely encapsulate or entirely restrain society's capacity for innovation. Were this to happen, as Lefort stresses, democracy would become ossified and dangerous, regulating social

---

7 Full justification of a basic structure in this reading goes much further than Pettit's account of collective action that is achieved through the state. If non-domination is in any sense to be thinkable for social arrangements as a whole, then more radical normative standards for its realization than Pettit offers must be sought. The same could be said of his account of contestability as a procedural standard.

life too closely, coercing it in the name of a sham utopia that is merely a cloak for authoritarianism (Lefort, 1988).[8] From the vantage point of theories of the political, like Lefort, participatory parity would, at least to some degree, potentially operate as a normative restraint on society's capacity for innovation whose most important creative wellsprings lie beyond formal institutions. The problem for these theories is to explain where expressions of the political 'go'. Theorists of 'the political' rightly want to preserve the gap between the creativity of popular democracy and institutional democracy, while also wanting a productive relationship between them. It is at this point that a cognitive-communicative-learning theory of public culture of the kind outlined later in this book comes into play. Such a theory fills in the central dimensions of how discursive mechanisms and the cognitive order translate between popular and institutional democracy.

Even though Axel Honneth is regarded as holding a position at variance with that of Nancy Fraser as a result of their 2003 debate, his work can be seen to close the gap between predominantly deontological procedural theories, like those of Fraser, and predominantly teleological constructions, like the idea of the political in Lefort. Honneth's Hegel-inspired idea of three modern standards of recognition, love as a standard of intimacy, equality as a legal-political standard, and achievement as a standard of accomplishment, are aimed at articulating the modern framework of the good life from within, that is to say, locating in the institutional forms that guide the immanent practices of modern life forms. Honneth contrasts his own reading of modernity as a recognition order to those who would, like Fraser, too readily read off deep-lying pathologies from manifest forms of social protest and those who would, also like Fraser but Rawls and Habermas too, seek to provide a merely procedural response by means of the minimal putting in place of comprehensive relations of justification in Forst's sense (Honneth, 1996, 1998, 2004, 2007, 2011).

Honneth shares much with accounts of the political imaginary, such as those of Castoriadis, in that he establishes reflective standards that are both inputs to – in the sense of creatively mobilizing experiences of

---

8 See also Touraine (Touraine, 1997) for a similar position.

non-recognition – and outcomes of recognition struggles. Through the three-fold structure that adds standards of intimacy and achievement to the 'traditional' philosophically emphasized – over-emphasized according to Honneth – standard of legal equality, politics is understood to span all social spheres, and is not confined to a formal political sphere. Honneth takes Hegel's lead to show how normative standards that guide both the diagnosis of pathological deformation in forms of life, or the prognosis of better levels of self-realization and moral integration, are located within society, not before it or beyond it. Building from Hegel, he shows how these standards become socially formulated and applied in the medium of social struggle, revealing a conflict-theoretical orientation that is at the core of the radical democratic tradition (Honneth, 2011).

The above-sketched theoretical positions, ranging from Mouffe to Fraser and Honneth, explicitly or implicitly advance the case for extended forms of political participation, perhaps in the form of the discursive designs put forward by John Dryzek or the associative designs proposed by Claus Offe (Dryzek, 1987, 1994, 2000; Offe, 1992). In this vision, politics should be widened to incorporate diverse constituencies and the structure of interests should become institutionally more dispersed and decentred. The associational structure of civil society and a vital public sphere are viewed as intrinsic to democratic practices. This position is frequently asserted against what is claimed to be a minimal liberal position, focused on basic rights and formal procedures. As already outlined, for example, Benhabib, amongst others, opposes Rawls's strong distinction between public and non-public reason on the grounds that too strong an ideal of public reason fossilizes into principles without processes and fails to show how civil society can influence politics. Politics is constituted by interaction between embodied and situated agents, rather than characterized by the veil of ignorance associated with being in the original position.

In common with many radical democratic positions, Benhabib asks that visions of the good life and the play of collective identities be given a role in shaping politics (Benhabib, 1996). In line with this viewpoint and in keeping with feminist writing in general, Benhabib criticizes the making of too strong a distinction between public and private, given that these boundaries are subject to constant change (Landes, 1988, 1995). The too strict separation of public and private ascribes a hegemonic role to the formal core of politics, a position that is likely to maintain unjustifiable power differences, make movements against subjugation difficult, and overly restrict the domain of politics. Stronger forms of participation beyond formal political representation, including changes to the form of representational politics itself, would lead to the realization of meaningful democratic justice (Young, 2000). Radically questioning the distinction between public and private reaches beyond the present structure of politics to ask whether the predominantly state-centric model should be sustained. In a tradition stemming from Negt and Kluge, Young raises the issue of multiple publics and multiple public spheres (Negt and Kluge, 1993; Young, 2000). Black American women, for example, could use a certain kind of restricted market for goods as a basis for a public sphere. She also draws attention to the different rhetorical modes characteristic of different groups and the need to accommodate these in appropriately designed political forums (see also Hauser, 1999).

At the core of these suggestions lies the pivotal issue of power. As political chains of influence within the existing political system become extended and weaker on the path from core to periphery, it becomes less likely that the full range of positions on the periphery will be adequately taken into account. Some issues may simply not feature. In other cases, political groups do not adequately represent the diversity of positions within their ranks and privilege one or more of them in their arguments. Young's point, therefore, resonates with the call for greater levels of direct democracy by Barber amongst others (Barber, 1984). The greater the degree to which individuals or groups can represent themselves and not become submerged in diffuse coalitions, including political parties, in which the voices of the disempowered and the unjustly treated are not properly heard, the less likely will be gross maldistribution of power in politics and society. Such an understanding of power follows Lukes in identifying the centrality of its agenda-setting dimension, the cognitive and perceptual power to define what is relevant for politics (Lukes, 1974; Skillington, 1997). The power to set agendas should be combined with a greater range of forums to consider such agendas and the outcomes of such forums would in turn lead to greater power over decisions by affected parties.

This standpoint on direct democracy takes on a self-consciously utopian caste given the impact of systems of economy, science, and law that, in Habermas's term, 'colonize' the everyday lifeworld (Habermas, 1987). Radical democrats call for an equivalently strong political system to regulate them in the public interest, but rarely advocate a stronger state, at least not without the corresponding strengthening of participatory institutions. Willke follows Luhmann in viewing social systems as spanning society and directing behaviour, yet he addresses how such systems interpenetrate one another and how within and between their various operations affected citizens could influence them. He therefore traces both the need for, and emergence of, symptomatic, horizontal action systems that exist either within or between systems, incorporating a human dimension into the autopoietic logic of system interchange proposed by Luhmann (Willke, 1992). Willke's intention is not to promote extended participatory democracy. Yet, the manner in which he combines a decentred theory of politics with citizen involvement in solving 'interpenetration' problems between – he assumes systemic autonomy to be essential – social systems does begin to address the often asked question of whether the participatory, radical visions of politics can resist the charge of unrealistic utopianism and find some support in the empirically observed conditions of modern society?[9]

As outlined already in the introduction, such a decentred vision of politics is, at least in some respects, consistent with the work of Negt and Kluge and their subsequent interpreters who call for a plurality of public spheres. Associated with this call is the idea of the public not as a mass of citizens who mutely legitimate political authority, but as composed of publics in the plural who actively ease the transition between contexts of experiences, such as that between formally organized social systems and lived contexts of life. In a way at least consistent with Willke's differentiation-theoretical *description* but with a different *normative* orientation,

---

9   Though in *Between Facts and Norms*, Habermas criticizes this account of Willke because of its denial of the normative force of an overarching public sphere, he essentially shares a decentred description of the political system, though with very different assumptions about the need for normative binding through discursively produced collective will and deliberatively produced law (Habermas, 1996).

radical democrats aspire that such publics, in the words of Joas, might democratize differentiation and render it compatible with the normative foundations of citizen 'self-rule' beyond coercive or patronizing institutions (Joas, 1996). Such a design is not necessarily inconsistent with the idea of an encompassing public sphere, understood as a public sphere of public spheres. Part of the intention lying behind the advocacy of such a 'variable geometry' is to allow space for, in Fraser's phrase, subaltern counter-publics to crystallize, develop oppositional discourses, and ultimately become politically influential in the mass public sphere (Fraser, 1992). The return to the mass public sphere of such oppositional discourses is not essential; counter public spheres can simply make for the expression of autonomous identity and self-organization in civil society (Hirst, 1993).

Radical Democracy and the Public Sphere

The public sphere is intrinsic to radical democracy, whereas the issue of how it features has to be teased out for many versions of republican and liberal political philosophy. The different manifestations of radical democratic political philosophy unite in acknowledging the importance of publicly empowered subjects that both give witness to existing, usually unsatisfactory, social relations and also attempt to change them. The focus on the politicization of subjects, and the importance of suitable spaces for its political expression, draws attention to power relations that are in need of exposure. The corresponding normative critique is directed against the widespread repression of the legitimate rights and influence of dominated subject categories within the existing political order. The tendency to focus on the democratic limitations of the political order, rather than domination in other social spheres such as the economy and the state's bureaucratic apparatus, has grown since the decline of Marxism and the partly related decline of social philosophy. Both unjust domination and the antidote of normative innovation are now presumed to predominantly take place within the domain of politics, extended to include the formation of participatory associational structures in civil society, rather than through the kind of socio-institutional reconstruction that the critique of capitalism once promised. Both the general diagnosis of institutional-political deficiencies and the specific focus on new mechanisms of political mediation, point towards a prominent role for the category of the public sphere or public spheres as a vital structural element of building a socially equal and democratically just society.

The reference to public spheres in the plural draws attention to the significance of publicity within this tradition. Democratically adequate standards of publicity include the right to a voice and to be heard, wide-ranging inclusion of themes, and socially diverse modalities of communication. Furthermore, special arrangements should be made to hear the messages of those who cannot speak for themselves. The critique, especially prevalent in feminism, of the dominant 'reasoned rationality' of the public sphere through legitimating this rationality as a 'civilized' normative standard is aimed at exposing the hidden operation of power.[10] Central to this critique is not the orderly structure of argumentative deliberation, but that the overall ensemble of voices, themes, and modalities of speech and listening, can lead to a collective reconstruction of the canons of what is politically relevant (Warren, 2007).

Moreover, politics is assumed to take place in a wide range of institutional and extra-institutional domains, the latter attesting to the extent to which the impacts of institutional politics should be reoriented or opposed in alternative or counter public spheres. Counter public spheres emerge from the associational structures of civil society and from personal experiences arising in counter-normative milieus that render agents either available for political mobilization or at least open to counter-normative political resonance. Public spheres understood in this way, as in the theory of the new social movements to which they are closely related, have a double reference; on the one side, they act as a conduit between subaltern publics and dominant political institutions and, on the other, they provide forums

---

10   Thomas McCarthy, aiming to unmask the operations of power in the midst of claims to reason, offers a critique of Rawls's ideal theory claiming it shows a systematic blindness to the problem of race (McCarthy, 2001).

for identity formation and facilitate a different kind of civil societal politics (Touraine, 1981; Touraine, 1995). This double political reference is not simply left liberal; it can also take libertarian-right, populist, and other political forms (Canovan, 1999; Kitschelt and McGann, 1997).

CHAPTER 5

Political Realism: Competitive Public Communication

A survey of democratic theory addressing the various ways in which it explores the forms and impacts of public communication cannot be complete without considering a variety of traditions of political thought that, in one way or another, raise doubts about ambitious democratic theories on the grounds of their lack of, or limited, practical feasibility. What distinguishes the democratic theories outlined so far is their high valuation of public will, even if the process of realizing such will is understood in very different ways. As Peters puts it, the 'political and legal regulation of social affairs' is not thought of in these other traditions as social engineering on behalf of political elites, aided by technical know how that is supposed to serve as a neutral arbiter of alternative 'decisions' (Peters, 2008, p. 17). In various ways, these theories claim that democratic institutions can be designed to protect the primacy of public sovereignty while doing justice to realist criteria of efficiency and effectiveness in the governance process. Representative democracy and formal-rational bureaucracy are thus envisaged as supplements to democracy's basic idea of popular sovereignty that would guarantee its relevance in an ever more complex world.

By contrast with this picture, realist theories claim that the democratic constitutional state has proven incapable of meeting its manifest goal of institutionally expressing popular will. Peters outlines another challenge to the idea of politics as the realization of popular sovereignty posed by anarchist, Saint-Simonian, and Marxist traditions. These postulate the ultimate disappearance of law and politics, which are given the status of transitory historical phenomena that are intrinsically repressive. He considers this tradition 'unrealistic', even if it remains a major wellspring of radical political ideas that question the political neutrality of the state and also, in some cases, its very form. By contrast, he considers the 'realistic' tradition associated with Weber, Michels, Lippmann, and Schumpeter more fruitful. This tradition examines the disjunction between normative theories and political practices on both theoretical and empirical grounds and finds a systematic gap between them that calls into question the normative principle of popular sovereignty – other than through periodic elections, at least. In these traditions, a conception of democracy is to be found in which politics is strictly seen as a mechanism for the aggregation of interests, a position that is today most associated with the theory of rational choice. Peters draws attention to the increasing scepticism in a variety of theories of the value of collective action co-ordinated through the state, especially in the form of a comprehensive welfare state regarded as the source of further democratization. Some modern diagnoses echo older theories and point to the need for a more pessimistic view of the scope of democracy as a form of collective action, and especially for a weakening of overblown claims to popular sovereignty. He wants to balance the disillusioning claims of realist theories of these kinds with both the intrinsic value and empirical hold of normative accounts of democracy.

Peters poses a productive question that is taken up in various versions of realist theory: how can the reality of contemporary politics be aligned with assumed normative foundations of democracy? Some realists would, however, disagree that it is a productive question, being dismissive of the historical over-inflation of political expectations generated by certain lines of democratic theory, spanning Locke, Kant, Rawls, and Habermas. Nonetheless, it is a question that is implicit in realist theories that deny that the public can be the final arbiter in contemporary politics. Instead, political realism proposes a model of politics whose normative reach is confined to minimal and formal procedural rules that protect the integrity of politics as a competitive, electoral struggle. In this competitive struggle, political communication takes the form of *rational, competitive communication* between rival political programmes that vie for an electoral mandate and associated governing power (Schumpeter, 1942). This kind of communication can be associated with the liberal idea of the 'free marketplace of ideas' and with the general economic theory of democracy (Down, 1957).

Realism and the Critique of Ideal Theory

Galston claims to identify a new realist movement in political philosophy that embraces a variety of different approaches, but appears to be most unified in its attempt to distance itself from what he describes as Rawls's 'high' liberalism (Galston, 2010). This realist standpoint that Galston sees as incorporating thinkers of such diversity as Williams, Hawthorne, Honig, Philp, Elkin, and Mouffe recapitulates some long-standing critiques of Rawls's 'ideal' theory (Elkin, 2006; Honig, 1993; Mouffe, 2000; Philp, 2007, 2010; Williams, 2005).[1] An overarching critique is to suggest that Rawls constructs politics as a branch of moral theory that generates a priori principles of justice with which political action should comply.[2] This moral framework is grounded in the primacy of right over good, a position that realists do not accept. But, unlike some communitarians, they do not hold to the idea of an encompassing good and accept Rawls's pluralism. This pluralism, however, should apply to justice as well, which should not be assumed to take the form of consensually accepted principles that trump all else. Consensualism of this kind obviates the very essence of what is political, a capacity to forge an order that is part moral, part ethical, and part pragmatic out of distinctly political processes.

There are no moral foundations anchored in the rationality of individuals or a time-transcending sense of justice beyond what is achieved in the political process. In the account of Williams, political philosophy is not just applied moral philosophy or legal philosophy. It must instead use distinctive political concepts such as power and legitimation. Accordingly, the authors advance the view that an overarching, morally grounded and

---

1   Honig and Mouffe have already been included in the radical democratic tradition outlined above. They form part of the critique of Rawls's ideal theory, but for reasons taken up further below they have entirely different reasons to the kind of liberal realism that will emerge as the dominant concern of this chapter.
2   As outlined above, the later Rawls does distinguish moral and political theory, but the realist objection is better understood as directed at the transcendental moralism that they impute to him, once more resonating with Sen.

'extra-political' concept of justice distorts the key political imperative of the maintenance of order, since justice achieved at the expense of order will not mean very much. In Elkin's view, there is no substitute for politics, 'if by politics we mean the various ways in which we arrive at collective, authoritative decisions in a world in which people legitimately hold different views about the purposes of government and the manner in which it should be carried on' (Elkin, 2006, p. 257).

Galston asserts that political realists eschew the deontological, liberal standpoint of achieving co-ordination through consent in the absence of gross asymmetries of power. They deny the possibility of consent in this strong sense, asserting that co-ordination will require coercion or the threat of coercion. In this respect, at least some realists show an inclination to turn away from the tradition of consent of the governed in the Lockean tradition towards recognition of the necessarily compulsory nature of authority in the Hobbesian tradition that flows forward into classical statements of political realism such as Weber and Schumpeter. In this tradition, political realism is focused on the mechanisms of legitimate domination. Unlike the Hobbesian version of legitimate domination, in which the dominated, recognizing the threat of chaotic anarchy, permanently consent to the absolute power of the sovereign, modern legitimate domination is consistent with ongoing contestation over power. Politics is understood as a struggle to secure the right to exercise such legitimate domination. The procedural rules that regulate political contestation are taken to ensure that modern politics is ethically legitimated. Against the view imputed to Rawls, the outcome of such competition will not be the assertion of a singular political morality derived from a pre-political ethics, nor need it necessarily result in the permanent domination of one group over others, so much as generate a modus vivendi taking the form of an unending series of compromises. Realism in this sense is a bleaker view of the possibilities of politics than that of Rawls. The coercive force of order-securing law is mitigated through a legitimate politics of power rather than, as with Rawls, moral-institutional designs and the moral-political socialization of citizens that come before the coercive use of power. But, in its proponents' view, realism has descriptive adequacy whereas ideal theory in the tradition of Rawls does not. Political realism prides itself in not reasoning from abstract and unrealizable principles to the detriment of building a minimal normative order on the basis of what is politically feasible and consistent with actual political practices in which contestation over power is the distinctive characteristic.³

Political Realism and Liberalism

Some of the thinkers referred to above, Honig and Mouffe for example, are generally engaged in a critique of Rawls, but they do so from a radical democratic standpoint that contrasts with the realism described here. They are part of a critique of what Sen calls the 'transcendental idealism' of Rawls (Sen, 2009). Political realism in this sense, already explored in the description of the radical democratic tradition, serves as a critique of the alleged denial of the role of power and of passion in politics, a denial that is assumed to be related to the a priori of a transcendentally grounded and unrealistic idea of popular consent as consensus. This movement of ideas has real value as a corrective to the excessive idealization of procedure, though it goes too far in its restriction of the moral dimension of politics. It engages with a moral standpoint only as critique and generally does not address the status of moral norms already institutionalized in both formal and informal constitutions. The denial of any 'affirmative' moral evaluations, which must stand as the necessary obverse of any moral critique, results in what Apel terms as a 'performative contradiction', a condition that assails much of the critical tradition in this respect (Apel and Papastephanou, 1998).

---

3   In political sociology, the Weberian theory of power and the associated theory of legitimacy have always been influential, but recently they has been coupled with new elements such as a stronger commitment to the effects of contingency and the importance of war and violence (von Trotha, 2006). It is tempting to suggest that a new paradigm that is opposed to the liberal deontological project is emerging in a variety of disciplines and that the term political realism offers a kind of banner for it.

While the relationship between realism and critique is of great importance, and indeed forms an important theme of the remainder of the book, of greater interest in this chapter is the alternative and opposed version of political realism. This version understands itself as liberalism without illusions and is closely associated with democratic elitism. It represents an alternative liberal tradition, less concerned with specifying and realizing moral principles of justice and more with the conditions of realizing political order within a minimal, legitimate state. In general, this tradition, most influential in political science and in the actual societal reception of political ideas in the twentieth century, views politics as a process of coercively achieved order, with interest conflicts ultimately held in check by compromises – 'modus vivendi' – as its principal content, and electorally achieved legitimacy as the basic formula.

Liberalism of this kind defends the clear separation of public and private realms. In much of the realist liberal formulations of the twentieth century, it emphasized a relatively minimal state and maximal, private autonomy.[4] Pluralist theories of interest group competition acted as a supplement to the basic theory, connecting private and public realms with a new account of organized interest intermediation. In more realist accounts of liberalism of this kind, the focus is on pre-political interests, whereas in normative accounts such as those of Rawls it is on pre-political moral intuitions guiding a sense of justice. Both versions of liberalism draw off the first wave of early modern liberal theory within the natural law tradition that gave form to the distinctive problem of social order in modernity. The problem of order arises in the new kind of normative co-ordination challenge that emerges from the social facts of freedom, equality, and plurality underpinning modern civil society, a civil society that most obviously gains its identity in economic terms as a putatively free space of market exchange. It is delineated as a question of how egocentrically calculating

---

4   This kind of 'realist' liberalism with its emphasis on reducing the size of the state and maximizing individual autonomy was at variance with the strain of social liberalism that dominated much of the twentieth century – though this social liberalism was only indirectly politically influential – but in the last quarter of a century it gained unexpected political influence in the period of neo-liberal political hegemony (Audard, 2009).

private individuals can generate outcomes that are to the good of all. The would-be free citizens of the emerging seventeenth-century civil society also asserted political claims that began with Hobbes and Locke and were shared over the following centuries by others such as Kant and Paine. The essence of such social contract theories in the words of Habermas was that 'society as a whole could be understood as the intentional complex of a free association of originally autonomous and equal members' (Habermas, 1996, p. 44).

Social contract theory emerged from early modern social conditions of land-holding and commercial property owners that exhibited high levels of social, cultural, and political compatibility, though also ethnic, gendered, and racial exclusions. It is not so hard to imagine the founding of the modern idea of democratic consent in such a community, even if from this distance it is also easy to underestimate its radical import compared to the entirely different authoritative and transcendental justification of feudalism and church authority that both preceded it and, for a long time, in no small measure accompanied it. The existence of such a community generates a kind of realist political epistemology, in which the close integration of economic status, culture, and forms of political co-operation amongst the dominant political elite underpins the construction and observation of political institutions that are seen to have reliable social effects over time. The status derived from natural law theory of the consciously willing 'intentional' individual gains additional force by virtue of the kind of resources of property, education, and cultural compatibility that certain kinds of individuals could acquire in seventeenth-century society. The preservation of such individual powers, free as far as possible from the alien danger of a diffuse and threatening collective, has consistently guided a libertarian stream in liberal political theory.[5]

---

5   These brief remarks on the relationship between social position and cultural orientation surrounding early modern political thinking diffusely draw off the theory of the habitus, which explores the relationship between personality and social structures, and is given much prominence in interpreting this historical era especially as applied to early Protestantism (Merton, 1936, 1938; Weber and Kalberg, 2001). The modern theory of the habitus is most closely associated with the work of Pierre Bourdieu. For a version of the relationship between social structure, identity and political

Individual causal determinism in the above sense, which proved highly significant for shaping the connotations of the concept of freedom, could not strictly rely on an asocial conception of individuals, for it had to locate such individuals in social arrangements, above all law, that generated intersubjectively valid norms. These norms, whose dependence on intersubjective processes could be taken for granted and hidden from view in a settled and excluding political community, emerge as the focal point of a permanent tension in the modern, liberal tradition with respect to mediating the relationship between freedom and order, the individual and the collective. Rawls provides one way of dealing with it through the fictive device of the original position and the continuing confidence, without actually demonstrating the actual mechanisms, that individuals who can support an appropriate moral sense of rights and obligations can be forged from contemporary social and political conditions. Another way of addressing the same problem, associated with the liberal strand of political realism, is to acknowledge that freedom and order are only indirectly connected and that both must be left run an autonomous course. In this second way of thinking, there is no close relation between societal morality and politics, only a continuous struggle between interests that can claim no moral legitimacy beyond their own perspectives, guided by certain formal procedural rules to orchestrate the struggle.[6] Hobbes already anticipated this, albeit in his case in the absolute domination by a sovereign, and it became a premise of

---

orientation see his essay 'Social Space and Symbolic Space' in his collection on practical reason (see also Bourdieu, 1985; Bourdieu, 1998). Related to this, Nine makes the interesting argument, not least from a sociological perspective, that Lockean theory ultimately depends on collective rather than individual rights to territory. She argues that the problem of the justification of territorial rights is ultimately transferred from a question of the rights of property holders to the jurisdictional rights of sovereign collectives. This in turn raises the question of what underpins these collective rights and introduces issues of the meaning of self-determination (Nine, 2008; Nine, 2012). The meaning of self-determination can also be extended in a cultural direction in a way that integrates the theory of the national habitus (Delanty and O'Mahony, 2002; Elias, 1992).

6 In one respect the later Rawls can be seen as engaged in an ongoing argument with respect to these assumptions, articulated in his acceptance of public autonomy and

twentieth-century 'disenchanted' political sociology and political science. In this view, norms that make possible a common life are legitimated only by procedures for managing political power and by their effectiveness and efficiency in organizing political processes.

A rough and ready distinction may be made between two versions of political realism. In one version, politics as contestation is closely associated with radical democratic theories and increasingly also some versions of republicanism. In another, at issue in this chapter, politics is understood as the interplay of interests and order in a way that is still to some degree in line with the premises of early modern liberalism. This interplay is examined without significant concession to the idea that public communication could be regarded as a shaping force. Instead, the account operates by means of strong epistemic assumptions concerning the intentional rationality guiding the assertion of interests and the competitive, strategic rationality that guides the selection of outcomes. This is all pursued in the face of a scarcely dubitable fact of contemporary social and political analysis, that successive historical stages of increasing social complexity – for example, the extension from the late nineteenth century of formal-bureaucratic rationality, the advance of functional and stratificatory differentiation, the emergence of a multi-stranded system of intermediation – have rendered the relationship between intentionally held interests and the outcomes of political processes both unclear and unpredictable. In actual fact, a further variation on the second strand of liberal political realism breaks with the assumptions of rational action theory and views the relationship between political inputs and processes and outputs as largely arbitrary, though they are procedurally critical. This strand of political realism, which can loosely be termed democratic elitism, has exercised a dominant hold on the political imagination for much of the last seventy or so years. With this authority, it has cast doubt on the normative status of popular sovereignty and denied the rationality of public communication, instead largely imbuing it with negative connotations.

---

yet the imposition of strong limitations on it through the manner in which he separates comprehensive doctrines from public reason and morally privileges justice as fairness.

Political Realism as Democratic Elitism

Ian Schapiro (Schapiro, 2005), operating within a broadly liberal, realist idiom, that also includes some republican elements, proposes to make democracy more effective by improving the prospects for genuinely competitive elections as a means of controlling unwarranted domination and radically improving the responsiveness of governments to electorates. In making way for such a position, he argues against libertarian and rational choice theories that advance aggregative theories of democracy and seek to reduce the scope of collective action because of its assumed tendency to excessively restrain individual freedom. Rational choice theorists argue that the general will as the aggregative outcome of the preferences of each voter cannot be demonstrated to result from electoral processes. Schapiro argues that even if this is conceded, majoritarian governments formed on the basis of competitive elections have other important advantages. They encourage competition in ideas and institutionalize the permanent possibility of upsetting the status quo, hence improving the prospects for democratic stability by allowing election losers anticipate a different future outcome. He also argues against the idea that preferences can be changed through deliberation, claiming that this lacks realism for dealing with complex, large-scale decisions, especially because of inattention to the importance of conflicts of interests whose substantive form cannot readily be changed in deliberation. He also claims that deliberative theory neglects the significance of power relations for politics.

In general, Schapiro argues that aggregative and deliberative conceptions of democracy are problematical to the extent that they respectively relate to the common good. While aggregative conceptions of democracy may show that the common good does not follow from voting procedures, not as much follows from that as they assume, partly because of other good features of majority rule and partly because assuming that there could be a direct, unmediated relationship between individual preferences and political outcomes is over-ambitious. And in affirming the desirability of a common good outcome arising from the deliberative process, deliberative theories underestimate the extent to which underlying interest conflicts and power relations can be communicatively transformed. Reviewing the work of Gutmann and Thomson at this point, he argues that experimental, deliberative procedures cannot sustain the weight of the expectations placed on them.

Schapiro proposes that Schumpeter's approach in the famous text, *Capitalism, Socialism and Democracy*, overcomes the lack of realism of these theories while also having normative advantages over them (Schumpeter, 1942). He claims that Schumpeter's argument rests on two claims (1) that structured competition for power is preferable both to Hobbesian anarchy and to the power monopoly that Hobbes saw as the logical response to it; and (2) that of the choices that Hobbes saw as the logical response to anarchy, monopoly and competition over power are the only meaningful possibilities.

While Schapiro's account is a reasonable statement of Schumpeter's general intentions, the latter makes no direct reference to Hobbes in *Capitalism, Socialism, and Democracy* (Schumpeter, 1942). Like Schapiro, Schumpeter begins by attacking the idea of the common good as the union of individual wills, which he regards as the pillar of the classical doctrine of politics. He goes on to offer an economic theory of democracy where electoral competition is conceived of on the model of the theory of economic competition. Organized competition is regarded as always better than either anarchy or monopoly (ibid., pp. 100–101). Here, the model of 'consumer sovereignty' through electoral competition trumps not just ideas of democracy as the direct expression of popular will, but also representative ideas of democracy that view it as an accurate conduit of the will of the people. The very idea of the will of the people can only be procedurally interpreted as the mechanisms for the replacement of the government of one political party with another. Schapiro equates Schumpeter's preference for such an economic theory of democracy with the intentions of the divisible theory of power of republicanism, which he advances by using Hamilton's phrase that 'ambition will be made to counteract ambition'. For him, the value of such a republican conception of electoral competition is that it could offer a means to avoid domination by legitimating the kind of collective action to remedy injustice that would not be countenanced in more libertarian liberal philosophies.

Schapiro certainly combines different motifs in his theory. Schumpeter is normally categorized as a liberal in the tradition of democratic pluralism, but he may be interpreting him in the context of the New Deal era with its greater acceptance of collective action and thus reorienting the theory in a more republican direction. In any case, he instances two kinds of objection that could be used to diminish the force of Schumpeter's argument. Electoral competition tends to be oligopolistic rather than fully competitive and it is biased to the wealthy as a result of the system of campaign financing, but concludes that these do no obviate its overall advantages. Conceived of as a market, electoral transactions are actually more purely competitive than economic markets because each voter is endowed with the same initial resource, a single vote. Schapiro admits that Schumpeterian competitive democracy can ultimately be understood as a thin version of the common good, understood as what those with an interest in avoiding domination share, but not the expression of a unitary will. In his conclusion, Schapiro gives some rather sparse attention to the communicative dimensions of the competitive electoral model. He claims that structured competition for power is desirable 'also because it is geared to institutionalizing argument rather than agreement' (ibid., p. 149). He argues that agreement is an over-rated concept and that the liberal notion of the free market place of ideas is superior to and threatened by the growth in consensus – which he says, following Mill, is a breeding ground for 'slavish conformity'.

Schumpeter himself actually fills in more fully the cultural and communicative presuppositions of his notion of competitive democratic competition (Schumpeter, 1942). His version of democracy is actually to be understood in the tradition of democratic elitism in which 'the masses' choose between different elites. At its core, early elite theory in the twentieth century drew from a generalized cultural critique of mass society that advanced a pessimistic understanding of the political capacities of citizens. Schumpeter outlines his view of the apathetic and indifferent citizen, illustrating his account by comparing the high reasoning capacities of educated professionals in their vocations compared to their woeful and immature understanding of politics. This understanding of the limitations of the citizen, reflecting findings of the empirical political sociology of his time (Bohman and Regh, 2002, p. x), is at the heart of his break with the classical account of popular sovereignty. Moreover, such apathetic and incompetent citizens are at the mercy of the new techniques of political communication that generate volition without will. In this respect, Schumpeter repeats a twentieth-century motif of the degeneration of the subject's capacity for reason, overwhelmed by the flood of sensory and emotive stimulation generated by the new means of communication. Competitive democratic elitism emerges from this understanding as an almost despairing attempt to preserve a liberal democratic society by means of the procedure of selecting and deselecting the rule of alternative coalitions of elites and supportive experts. Its concept of *public* communication is therefore pessimistic and mainly confined to electoral processes. Even in these processes, communication by the public should only play a limited role for the low political competence of the public could only result in poorly evaluated choices.

Political Realism and Systems Theory

The idea of the superior practicality and hence normative desirability of a 'disillusioned' realism remains a constant motif in twentieth-century political theory. Its most prominent contemporary form is the critique of the viability of extended deliberation, especially new kinds of participatory public deliberation whose possible contribution Schapiro pessimistically assesses. Such an assessment can be viewed as part of the long debate on the extent to which politics can be founded on a strong version of the classical ideal of consent, which implies a view of social and political institutions as supporting a citizenry that would not simply be formally equal but also equally politically competent. Such competence, still regarded as possible by political theorists in the Kantian tradition, like Habermas and Rawls, even if usually defended only counterfactually, is abandoned by a realist theory that, whatever the merits of its arguments, has had most influence on the self-understanding of twentieth-century politics. Given the inescapable fact of a functionally complex, socially differentiated, and culturally pluralistic world, political realism argues against the possibility of a universalistic ethics of participation in the Kantian tradition. In the face of the challenges of the modern world, an ethics of principle cannot be generalized to the political community as a whole and can only retreat to a series of maxims to guide private non-political conduct (Zolo, 1992). Zolo argues further that the universal and impartial character of categorical ethics clashes with the 'particular and partial nature of the criteria of exclusion and hierarchical subordination on which the 'protective' function of any political order, whether ancient or modern, is founded' (ibid., p. 60). Here, Zolo repeats the fundamental preference of this kind of political realism, giving evidence of its Hobbesian roots, for recognition of the primacy of political order. This preference is allied with impatience towards moral universalism that is seen to distract from the real mechanisms that guarantee such order, and which indicates that even initially defensible utopian ideologies may in the end prove misleading and dangerous.

In *Between Facts and Norms*, Habermas documents the shift in focus from intentional to non-intentional forms of sociation that underpins this modern form of realism, ultimately anchored in the idea of the objectivity of a social order that cannot any longer be consciously steered (Habermas, 1996, p. 45). In this account, political economy from Smith to Ricardo became the disciplinary catalyst that revealed society as anonymously integrated by exchange mechanisms that take effect behind the backs of its participants. This insight pluralizes the idea of social integration; it proceeds not only from the voluntary and conscious association of individuals in civil society, but also by means of anonymous systems that function independently of the intentions of its members (Habermas, 1987). This shift explains the loss of the central role of the category of law in theoretical analysis, as the reproduction of social life appeared far too complex to be comprehended in the 'meagre normative motifs of natural law' (ibid., p. 45). Habermas goes on to explore how Marx tried to preserve the vantage point of conscious sociation via a teleological account of the historical process that projected conscious control over the conditions of material life on to the future association of producers. The objectivism of the Marxist account of society actually goes so far as to reduce norms, values, communication, and law into mere illusion. As Marxism loses the last vestiges of optimism bequeathed by a philosophy of history that might one day come right, the totality of society becomes negatively constructed as a compulsory order integrated only by power.

Habermas goes on to outline how with Luhmann the functional view of systems loses the critical character it had in Marxism and becomes affirmative. Luhmann conceives of society as taking the form of multiple, autonomous systems. He can even outdo the 'realism' of the Marxist model by subsuming the observer into the vantage point of the system. There is no longer any privileged standpoint from which systems can be observed from the outside; all acts of observation are dependent on the encompassing system from which the observation is made. It is in this respect that Luhmann's break with what he pejoratively describes as 'old European' modes of thinking can be understood. These modes of thinking were based on the autonomy of the subject and a morally integrated society (Luhmann, 1998). Subjects in fact disappear from view in Luhmann and it is only the evolution of the semantics of systems that is anonymously triggered by social communication that counts (Luhmann, 1980). Luhmann retains neither of the two approaches, respectively opened up in the early modern period via Locke and Hobbes. In a polycentric society of multiple autonomous social systems, the political system is neither to be understood as a moral community based on consent, nor an organized body with unlimited powers of command delegated to a sovereign.

As depicted by Lange and Schimank, Luhmann defines the special function of the political system for society as the ability to make collectively binding decisions based on the code of power as a generalized medium of communication (Lange and Schimank, 2004). As they put it, for Luhmann 'gaining power, increasing one's power, or at least preventing its decrease, is what politics is about' (Lange and Schimank, 2004; Luhmann, 2004, p. 64). In formulations that have an affinity with those of Schumpeter, Luhmann describes the reality of modern politics as not based on the will of the people, but on a representative system that detaches the public from decision-making, rendering whether their communication is relevant or not depend on resonance with the system code of power (Luhmann, 2000). Such a systemic logic will exclude non-relevant forms of communication in the form of moralized expectations about the role of politics. Moreover, like Schumpeter, the struggle for power itself takes the form of competitive elections between political parties and continues in the institutionalized form of government and opposition.

Lange and Schimank, along with Luhmann himself and other systems theorists, identify a new development in modern society that make the systemic logic of power more difficult to realize (ibid.; Bora, 1999). Sections of the public are no longer content with the outcome of the 'normal' circuit of power, where government and opposition are formed through electoral processes. Political parties can no longer present programmes that satisfy the heterogeneous demands of multiple publics and actually pursue their varied concrete interests – aggregated into collective actors – through the political cycle. In order to accommodate this, various modes of contact have been established between publics and political administration. This is both a problem for neo-Schumpeterian accounts of political realism, and as Luhmann observes, it is also an expression of a rising demand for wider public participation in political issues. Luhmann sees the interventionist welfare state as the paradigm example of this political trend. He regards this development negatively as an overloading of the political system that is now forced to take on board the inclusion problems of the other social systems.[7] This happens by means of the simultaneous inflation of the three mechanisms of political intervention in society that take the respective forms of money, law, and political power. According to Luhmann, the welfare state generated chronic inflation and state debts as money was used to solve social problems; social life has been extensively juridified and yet the acceptance of law has declined; and the increasing influence of bureaucracy has stifled market forces and other forms of societal self-regulation. Luhmann's solution, which has at least some compatibility with neo-liberalism, is to reduce the size of the political system based upon a strict refusal of welfare state policies (Luhmann, 1990).

In one respect, as Lange and Schimank point out and as others also claim, Luhmann's account of the role of politics could be understood as

---

7   Alfons Bora provides a systems theoretical account of the overloading of the function system of law with demands for participation and for the inclusion of 'non-legal' discourses, demands that the legal system rejects in order to preserve its own communicative coding and ultimately autonomy (ibid.).

a minimal kind of liberal, societal self-regulation (Gerhards, 1997). This carries forward a theme that is reasonably consistent across the realist account of politics offered here, and that goes beyond the radical kind of critique of ideal theory. It is generally strongly associated with a political liberalism that emphasizes competition and struggle given the challenge of cultural and social incommensurability, though without imagining that the minimal necessary constitutional foundations will obviate the need for politics, a position that is attributed to Rawls's high liberalism. And not just any politics, but a politics that would be efficacious through its understanding of political objectives and their settings, the measurement of costs, the evaluation of consequences, and the estimation of risk (Zolo, 1992, p. 81). With Luhmann, the spectrum of realism is extended beyond the art of politics itself to a circumscription of appropriate, realistic relations between politics and other social systems.

Luhmann also offers a typically irreverent account of how public communication can be understood within a broadly realist account of competitive party politics, which is organized by the binary code of government and opposition. While the dominant, authoritative coding of political communication is that between acquiring and defending power and opposing it, the public, influential through public opinion, also enters in as a parasitic, external third value. It is parasitic because it is secondary to the struggle over power that characterizes the dominant code of the political system. Public opinion reminds power holders that their power is only secure until the next general election in the course of which the public ceases to be an external third value and enters intrinsically into the binary logic of politics by choosing who will next hold power and who will not (Luhmann, 1990).[8]

These remarks on Luhmann only confirm the distance that has been traversed in realist political theories away from the idea of a normative politics of popular sovereignty. In a favourite word of Luhmann, this distance is an expression of 'disappointment' at the fate of politics, a disappointment that from the standpoint of the theory can be turned to good account if

---

8 Strydom (Strydom, 1999) provides a critique of Luhmann's account.

it leads to a commitment to a workable politics and to a relevant political theory. In the realist account, normative constructs become emptied of will – and reduce to learning and following expectations derived from the performance of systems – and retreat to a minimalistic proceduralism taking the form of basic constitutional guarantees coupled with procedures for exercising and transferring power to different groups (Bobbio, 1984; Sartori, 1987). Politics, as the only means of reaching binding collective decisions that take effect through law, is both compellingly necessary and must be pursued to the full and yet at the same time must withdraw from overarching claims to rectify the ills of society. It must allow for the competition of interests within the limitations set by the complexity of the world.

Political Realism and the Public Sphere

Political realism is inconsistent with the normative status of communicative politics generally followed in this book. It does have a distinct version of political communication, but this version opposes the idea that the public sphere discursively crystallizes public will. Political realism goes back to the idea of the rival presentation of political programmes by elites within a circumscribed understanding of what is politically possible. The implementation of the victorious programme decided by the principle of majority rule is supplemented by the 'relief mechanism' that is offered by the system of political intermediation. This entails the building of a secondary sphere of communication *within* the political system, but one that is not a properly *public* sphere in that it is largely secret and hidden from view. The presumption of the public's lack of competence ensures that it should be so. Except in relation to political campaigning, communication involving the public plays a secondary role, even for Luhmann the parasitic one, of reminding governments that they remain accountable at the next election.

This view of Luhmann encapsulates the general vision of a political realism that has lost its illusions. The public is denied normative significance other than as a mechanism for selecting political elites and it is not clear on what grounds they might do so. The key is that from the vantage point of democratic elitism, it doesn't matter as long as the elites themselves offer rational programmes. Political realism, contra Schapiro's idea that it can be made compatible with republicanism that in its many different forms always depends in some meaningful way on the rationality of the public, in fact depends on the rationality of elites. If the reasons for choosing elites are arbitrary to the extent that electoral campaigning and voting as the modality of selecting them are arbitrary, then these elites stride on the stage as the only possible defenders of democratic principles. Pluralism as interest intermediation then serves as a relief mechanism, by allowing for ongoing inputs from the private sphere and civil society, which prevents politics from becoming merely unbridled ideology expressed through majority rule and instead capable of 'disinterested' and 'neutral' decision.[9] Given the general view of the public throughout this process, the idea and ideals of a communicative politics have low standing. Only Luhmann offers an extended account of political communication, but this vision constitutively excludes normativity. The public has a job to do, but after that must lose any illusions of having ongoing influence. The problem, as Luhmann and others see it, is that though political realism has the complexity, obscurity, and chronic apathy of modern society to lend credence to its vision, the public has never quite gone away and remains a normative threat, ever in need of being further disappointed by a systems rationality that has become detached from everyday life.

9   Representative elitism bears the hallmarks of post-war confidence in the value foundations of elites whom, it was assumed, are socialized into an appropriate kind of habitus that carries the values that Merton attributed to science, impersonality, disinterestedness, organized scepticism, and openness (Merton, 1973). It is something of an apparent paradox that part of the animus of contemporary realism represented by Galston, Philp, and others is opposed to this kind of idealization, but it remains to be shown from within this standpoint how defensible democratic values otherwise enter the political process and become stabilized therein. Within the sociology of science in a way that has wider political connotations, Michael Lynch provides a valuable account of changed presuppositions that critically interrogate and find wanting Merton's idealized values as applied to the actual practices of science (Lynch, 1997).

CHAPTER 6

Deliberative Democracy and Public Deliberation

Of the various traditions covered in this review, the deliberative tradition is in many ways hardest to specify. This is in some part because it is the newest tradition whose main lines have only been outlined over the last quarter or so of the twentieth century reaching up to the present, notwithstanding famous forebears such as Dewey (Dewey, 1927). As a new tradition, it both borrows from more established traditions and at the same time sets itself up as their rival. As a rival, it corrects their deficient understanding of the importance of deliberation. Some proponents tentatively claim that the theory of deliberative democracy might offer a comprehensive theory of democracy in its own right. Assessing the claim of whether it is itself a comprehensive and alternative theory of democracy, or whether it calls for a modification of existing theories to make space for a greater emphasis on deliberative processes, is a major issue in deliberative theory. This fault line between a more radical, participatory version of deliberative theory and deliberation as a component to be better integrated into existing theories is not exactly what it seems. For the call for deliberation to be a comprehensive theory of its own in one line of interpretation necessarily brings it closer to what existing theories do – showing the normative import of voting systems, for example – and hence towards theoretical ecumenism. The terrain is further confused by the very success of the deliberative turn. While it would certainly not be true to say that everyone is a deliberative democrat now, well known representatives of major political philosophies such as Rawls as a liberal, Sunstein and Pettit as republicans, and Dryzek as a radical theorist, describe themselves and their traditions in these terms. While, in some cases, as already seen with respect to Rawls, this self-ascription is contestable insofar as *actual* reasoning by the public is not treated as an intrinsic democratic mechanism, the degree to which there is debate about whether the term should be ascribed to particular cases indicates its power.[1]

Two loosely interrelated lineages of deliberative democracy can be delineated, one within political philosophy itself and the other in broader epistemological shifts that have characterized the social and political sciences over the course of the twentieth century.[2] With respect to the first, Rainer Forst defines deliberative democracy as a 'political practice of argumentation and reasoning among free and equal citizens, a perspective in which individual and collective perspectives and positions are subject to change through deliberation and in which only those norms, rules, or decisions which result from some form of reason-based agreement among the citizens are accepted as legitimate' (Forst, 2002, p. 346). He sums up deliberative democracy in the simple phrase of 'the rule of reasons'. The two key elements are that a certain kind of political communication in an appropriate forum may result in a change of preferences among the deliberating citizens and that the actual substance of the communication that results in this change should be reason-based. To counter the immediate objection that 'reason-based' implies a reductive rationalism confined to

---

1   Of course, the identification of 'actual reasoning by the public' tout court as a hallmark of deliberative theory is itself contestable, but it is certainly consistent with the idea of 'public' deliberation that is the title of this chapter.

2   These distinctions partly correspond to that made between deliberative democracy type 1 and type 2 by Bachtiger et al. in an overview article (Bachtiger et al., 2010). The authors distinguish type 1 deliberation as the classic, consensus-oriented, counterfactual standard of Habermas's discourse ethics from type 2. Type 2 is the more 'realistic' strain of deliberative theory that focuses on deliberation in real situations. The authors find important insights in both type 1 and type 2. Type 1 shows the importance of counterfactual standards and type 2 is actually suited to the analysis of the wider spectrum of reasoning that could in some sense be understood as deliberative. In the same edition of the *Journal of Political Philosophy*, a second article by Mansbridge et al. argues that deliberative theory has evolved away from the first phase assumption of the necessity of reasoned agreement and towards a second phase embracing the idea of the necessity of accepting disagreement, including the non-reducibility of opposing interests to consensus (Mansbridge et al., 2010). In a very broad sense, both articles are consistent with the arguments advanced later in Parts III and IV of this book.

established 'reasoners' and forms of reasoning, reason can be taken to mean no more than that all are open to be persuaded by the arguments of others. This is a basic definition that reaches across different interpretations of deliberation, leaving aside for the present the pivotal issues of under what circumstances and by what modalities this is most likely to happen.

With respect to the second, the very idea of deliberative democracy attests to the rise of a communicative epistemology in the human and social sciences. Reaching beyond the antagonistic alternatives of 'holistic' macro-level or individual determination of social phenomena, a communicative epistemology that is indebted to the pragmatist inheritance emphasizes the process-related space of mediation between them. In fact, the dynamic emphasis on the process of communication creates three foci, individuals, transsubjective culture and communication itself. The central innovation of deliberative democracy may be regarded as focusing on the 'meso-level' of communicative process. It seeks to embed this standpoint into theories that are more static and 'structural' in their overall composition such as liberalism and republicanism, and especially into their respective alternative, but potentially complementary, emphases on individuals and trans-subjective culture.

The above philosophies regard the political process as on the whole shaped by structural factors that decisively limit their form and scope. This can be said of the idea of the individual foundations of the preferences that become aggregated within the liberal tradition and of the predominant emphasis on a collective ethos in the republican tradition. Again, speaking broadly, the former assumes the centrality of pre-political preferences (Dryzek, 2000; Shapiro, 2005; Sunstein, 1988), and in some of its forms the latter substantializes ethical values (Habermas, 1994). In the respective contributions of Rawls and Sunstein to these traditions, process-oriented thinking becomes more prominent. On the whole, though, within liberal and republican traditions, this is still done hesitantly without sustained attention to the actual intersubjective *mechanisms* that transform preferences through the giving and taking of reasons. This hesitancy to embrace process suggests that structural thinking is inbuilt into core assumptions of these theories, whereas deliberative theory, especially where the emphasis lies on *public* deliberation, embraces process as central.

That they take a deliberative form has long characterized basic assumptions about judicial and parliamentary law making. Law is assumed to be legitimate because it is justified and applied according to transparent deliberative procedures. The idea of deliberative democracy asserts that what was previously assumed to only apply to core aspects of the institutional democratic process has been broadened out to incorporate citizens, hence the term *public* deliberation. So instead of merely voting and letting others deliberate on their behalf, the recent turn understands citizens, or publics generally that do not enjoy the status of citizens, as intrinsic to the deliberative process. Public deliberation, in line with the rise of constructivist epistemologies across the social sciences, assumes that agents make reality rather than merely observe its law-like formation. It is not surprising in this respect that democratic theory should be revitalized by the participatory emphasis of public deliberation, a revitalization that resonates with its most fundamental founding idea, that of popular sovereignty.

The founding idea of popular sovereignty, even when positively reevaluated, can give rise to many different positions on what the public should actually do within the democratic process. The radical tradition on the whole places a strong emphasis on participation and on the necessary institutional innovation to realize it. Institutional redesign is accepted to a greater or lesser extent in most deliberative theories, but differences arise on how radical this redesign should be (Bohman, 1998; Dryzek, 1994, 2000; Fung, 2002). These differences in turn spring from different estimations of the normative and practical contribution of representative democracy, ranging from relatively poor in the judgement of 'participatory deliberativists' to requiring significant but feasible deliberative modification (Bacqué and Sintomer, eds, 2011). These estimations of existing democracy lead back to wider estimations of the relationship between democracy and society, generating the fundamental question, given contemporary patterns of injustice and social change, of whether it requires radical or gradual alteration. Sometimes this fundamental question has to be inferred, as mostly in democratic theory interpretations and evaluations of the state of society are indirect.

Deliberative Democracy and Communicative Politics

The idea of deliberative democracy ultimately rests on a communicative understanding of politics. Its proponents often contrast its active and process-based philosophy with the aggregative conception of democracy that rests on voting, pluralism, and majority rule. Normative claims for it rest on the superiority of mechanisms that lead to deliberative will formation over those based on the outcomes of preference aggregation. The normative pre-decision in favour of deliberation underlies the corresponding description of the political process that tends to view democratic politics as predominantly deliberative in form (Habermas, 2006).[3] Normative commitments of sufficient range, revisability, and intensity cannot be derived from the politics of the vote. An understanding of the primacy of communication for politics is also required in understand the capacity for responsible action that is entailed in voting. Essential epistemic and normative dimensions of politics can only be realized communicatively. Only through effective and normatively appropriate forms of communication can citizens acquire the knowledge they require about political principles and issues and be empowered to assert their distinctive standpoints. Deliberative theories thus attach great significance to the normative implications of its claimed epistemic superiority *as a communication theory* over other democratic theories (ibid.).[4]

The idea of communicative politics that in one way underpins the theory of deliberative democracy in another way generates a considerable challenge to it. In the first instance, while deliberative theory clearly responds to the paradigm of communication and derives its rationale from it, its main line of development in democratic theory on the whole exhibits

---

[3] The wider context of these deliberative claims is shaped by communicative politics in the public sphere, though in much of the actual literature on deliberative democracy this mainly forms a background context that is largely not explicated.
[4] For a good discussion on this point see Bohman's survey of deliberative democratic theory (Bohman, 1998).

ambivalence about radical institutional redesign to increase public participation. The question that frames this ambivalence is, what does it mean to say that citizens deliberate? Within communicatively oriented democratic theory, attention has gradually shifted from the dominant goal of realizing extended participatory democracy that was the centre of attention three or so decades ago (Barber, 1984; Pateman, 1976). Enhancing the legitimacy, fairness, and effectiveness of existing democratic institutions by making deliberative procedures stronger is now also regularly advanced as a goal. Formal democratic institutions should operate as far as possible through the deliberative 'rule of reasons'. While deliberative democrats rarely speak against the value of extended participation, the shift amongst many deliberative theorists towards greater recognition of the deliberative quality of existing institutions still amounts to a change in emphasis. To complicate matters, it is not at all the case that the argument for including formal democratic institutions more strongly in deliberative theorizing is taken to exclude consideration of experimental and participatory deliberative designs.

Deliberative theory, viewed as a whole, therefore appears unsure as to whether its normative claims should result in fundamental change to the existing level of democratic participation. It proposes that existing institutions would better realize values of publicity, impartiality, comprehensiveness, epistemic rightness, accountability, and reciprocity associated with public autonomy by incorporating stronger deliberative procedures. Nonetheless, the actual implications for the design of democracy as a system of interacting institutions are not clear (Parkinson and Mansbridge, eds, 2012). In this respect, the evolving literature on deliberation and participation reveals a tension between the values of participation and deliberation; extending participation will gain representativeness in one sense but due to the complexity of co-ordinating large-scale participation could, in another sense, threaten deliberative values (Cohen and Fung, 2004). These values stand as 'real counterfactuals' in deliberative theory. It is not argued that deliberation according to these values is – or perhaps ever can be – fully institutionally realized, but they are interpreted as forming guiding horizons that critically inform *existing* political designs and processes. They constitute the irreducible procedural ethos of democracy. The balance to be struck between deliberation, participation, and other democratic mechanisms depends upon what constitutes a justifiable institutional realization of democratically relevant counterfactuals standards; what relative importance should be accorded to fundamental political values such as publicity, freedom, participation, legality, procedure, respect, and dignity.

Those advocating stronger participation as a component of deliberation most acutely feel the possible tensions between the values of deliberation and participation (Dryzek, 2000; Sintomer, 2011). The case for stronger participation is articulated in a broad coalition spanning political science and sociology and it also encompasses some radical kinds of democratic theory. In this loosely defined coalition, existing institutions are criticized for not including adequate levels of direct public participation. It is generally proposed that new institutional designs are needed to address deep-seated problems of democracy, including citizen apathy, power differentials in agenda setting and decision making, corruption, democratization outside formal democratic spheres, and the weakening of popular sovereignty through bureaucratization (Dryzek, 1994). A key aspect of this second deliberative perspective from a socio-historical vantage point relates to the nature of the societal challenges that democratic institutions are assumed to have to address. The arguments therefore work less from the vantage point of institutionally bounded democratic processes, than from the perspective of the 'needs' of society arising in the spaces beyond existing formal democracy. The challenges of the times characterized by pronounced ethical differences, individualization, and the internationalization of interdependencies, not alone generate turbulence in the societal environment of democracy but also offer opportunities for its radical extension. Prior to the rise of deliberative theory, a major fault-line in democratic theory lay between those who advocated stronger participation, at least in part inspired by the civilizational crisis of the 1960s (Touraine, 1971), and those who sometimes shared its diagnosis but feared the consequences for democracy (Bobbio, 1984; Sartori, 1987).

Disciplinary preferences are apparent between these versions of deliberative democracy. In the first case, the deliberative versions that may be closely aligned with existing liberal and republican accounts of political philosophy by and large stay within the framework of existing normative orders, essentially radicalizing the public autonomy component of democratic process over against the classical liberal emphasis on private autonomy. Deliberative democracy is here – often implicitly – interpreted as potentially consistent with aggregative mechanisms that are properly applied, such as majority rule and, perhaps, by implication the party system and the relative power of government over against parliament (Barry, 1995; Dewey, 1927; Nino, 1998). The challenging edge of this first perspective broadly consists of radicalizing the premises of political argumentation by increasing the self-consciousness of political agents of their dependence on deliberation with and before a public. Such self-consciousness would also have reflexive consequences for political institutions that should give new prominence to deliberative norms of inclusion, reciprocity, generality, publicity, and accountability. Such a renewed deliberative conception of political institutions and processes could therefore beget evolutionary changes to institutional designs that perhaps in the end, over a long period, might amount to radical innovation.[5]

By contrast, the second option, which closely associates the deliberative turn with extended political participation, is carried more by disciplines, such as political science and sociology, that couple a normative perspective with an empirical diagnosis (Dryzek, 1994, 2000; Jacobs, Cook, and Carpini, 2009; Sintomer, 2011). As already outlined in Chapter 2, the fit between these two perspectives, normative and empirical-theoretical, is not straightforward. Instead of extended reflection on this tension – Dryzek is an exception – the latter disciplines tend to gravitate to fine-grained

---

[5] There is nonetheless a question of judgement as to what radical institutional redesign might be taken to mean. The distinction in question is that between institutional innovations achieved through adding further deliberative elements to existing formal democratic systems, as opposed to the transformation entailed through proposing new institutional configuration. These might, for example, include reducing the importance of representative institutions in favour of direct democratic institutions. From a comparative perspective, there are already a large variety of democratic mechanisms deployed in democratic systems across the globe as, for example, the different institutional designs of democratic corporatist as opposed to liberal pluralist political systems. These differences, along with the many small-scale experiments in deliberative designs, offer foundations for empirically assessing potentials for democratic innovation.

exploration of cases of democratic experimentation, which is part of a general enthusiasm for democratization through extending participation. This version focuses on unresolved societal problems that are taken to pose significant challenges to democratic arrangements and require democratic innovation for their adequate treatment. It includes critical currents that associate existing problems of democracy with general problems of modernity, economic inequality, environmental degradation, patriarchy, the particular instituted form of individual autonomy, and many more. Above all, it carries a belief that the problems of democracy cannot be rectified predominantly on the basis of current democratic institutions though, in most cases, it assumes that existing institutions will continue to have an important role.

According to Bohman's 1998 review, deliberative democracy has matured as a theory of democracy that extends from innovations such as deliberative polling right through to proposals for a deliberatively shaped type of majority rule (Bohman, 1998). While the range of deliberative theory has progressively expanded and deepened, it is perhaps optimistic to suggest, as he does, that it is approaching a full theory of democracy. While the normative imagination of deliberative democracy, in the range of deliberative arenas and procedures it countenances, has significantly widened – even more than when Bohman was writing – its relative incapacity to integrate empirical-theoretical with normative perspectives, not to mention the general cultural context consisting of societal discourse and learning, leaves it some way short of a full theory of democracy. From a practical standpoint, the moral core at the heart of deliberative theory, contained in the idea that democratic institutions should be fully inclusive with respect both to themes and publics, is far from realization. It is only through counterfactual devices and rather selective identification of empirical-theoretical problems that such a claim can in any way be asserted, even as a feasible potential (Habermas, 2006). To illustrate this point, consider the deliberative deficiencies in the manner in which substantive governmental programmes are decided and implemented through majority rule systems.[6] These programmes have the greatest influence in shaping the focus

---

6 Some systems that are understood in majority rule terms have the same powers though, in practice, consisting of the rule of the largest minority. First past the post

and scope of politics. Yet they are decided in a manner that is epistemically vague with affected citizens and sometimes even the initiators of these programmes, such as socio-political movements and political parties, unclear as to long-run implications as they embark on wide-ranging 'reform'. They are also frequently either excluding or divisive from a normative perspective. This is both a concrete problem of democracy and also a problem for deliberative theory that in some measure still insulates itself from the task of a satisfactory empirical-theoretical relationship to such issues.

The second current within deliberative theory is right in its belief that these problems cannot be solved on the basis of the empirical-theoretical assumptions of the first tradition of deliberative theory. They reflect the inescapable problems arising where democratic institutions meet other social spheres and make apparent the characteristic and unsatisfactory theoretical and practical tension between formal democracy and a possible alternative to it that would be achieved through 'deepening' or 'widening' democracy. This is of course not to deny that this gap can only ever be theoretically grasped and creatively bridged by means of the counterfactual imagination which, though arising from immanent practices, reaches beyond them and returns to challenge them. Deliberative theory is preeminently the counterfactual imagination of contemporary democratic theory, even if its counterfactual imagination remains circumscribed from the vantage point of the relationship between democratic theory and the theory of society that is developed in subsequent chapters.

Speaking across its various versions, deliberative theory seeks both to extend the scope of deliberation and to embed it in other institutionalized

---

systems like that of Britain are of this kind. In that system not much more than 40 per cent of the total vote will guarantee single-party government in which parliamentary debate forms part of wider discourse more than deliberation leading in any meaningful sense to co-decision through the exchange of reasons. It is also, of course, an empirical truism of many contemporary political systems that an electoral mandate does not simply generate representative agency by parliamentarians, but produces cabinet government often insulated from parliamentary deliberation by clear majorities.

democratic procedures.[7] It therefore advocates institutional innovations that extend inclusion and improve the quality of reasoning. This might lead to cumulatively far-reaching democratic innovations such as deliberative polling, public hearings, citizens' juries, mediation processes, long-term planning commissions, in-depth consultation, participatory local democracy, and wider public access to influential agenda setting media. Surveys of the actual variety of communicative political processes, such as that of Burns, emphasize the wide range of innovative democratic or proto-democratic mechanisms that are actually employed. In some cases, they also advocate a corresponding new role for representative institutions to monitor and regulate this diversity. This work adds empirical support to the viewpoint of contextually embedded deliberation as a cumulative innovation, as does the work of Callon et al., delli Carpini and many others (Barthe, Callon, and Lascoumes, 2001; Burns, 1999; delli Carpini, Cook, and Jacobs, 2004). Deliberative innovations are not generally understood as direct democratic *replacements* for existing representative institutions. They instead progressively make possible more meaningful deliberation by the public as opposed to deliberation on behalf of a public. Meaningful public deliberation is impelled by the new kinds of normative claims-making arising with issues such as environmentalism or the future of family relations. These exceed the limits of existing knowledge and capacity for agreement and impel deliberative democracy in all its forms to consider how the reasoning of affected agents might be better accommodated. Differences within the

---

7   Though neither the terminology nor its application to the terrain is particularly easy, a further distinction may be made between the deontological proceduralism of much deliberative theory and the teleological influences that still characterize much radical democratic thinking. In egalitarian terms, this often presents itself as a distinction between a predominant or exclusive emphasis on democratic justice as opposed to a combination of social and democratic justice. This distinction is partly one about the proper functional remit of democratic politics, more narrowly or more broadly. It is associated with another distinction about what constitutes the proper foundations of democratic values, that is, whether they should be regarded as political procedural values alone or a combination of substantive values and procedural values. The status and changing significance of Rawls's difference principle encapsulates many of the issues in this debate.

theory tradition relate to how radical deliberative innovation needs to be, if it is to lead to greater levels of public, democratic influence.

Deliberative Democracy, the Communicative Turn, and Popular Sovereignty

Both social theory and philosophy experienced a communicative turn in the 1970s. This communicative turn entered political philosophy maybe a decade or so later, where it took the form of an emphasis on procedures for the public use of reason that is inseparable from the rise of deliberative democracy (Emirbayer, 1997; Emirbayer and Mische, 1998; Rawls, 1993; Habermas, 1996; Wenzel, 2005). Rather than procedure being understood in a strictly formal and realist sense as the selection of governance regimes based upon political preference formation amongst electorates, procedure could now be understood instead as reasoned deliberation that would be fully inclusive, reciprocal, and public. The renewed interest in the idea that democracy is ultimately grounded in popular sovereignty raised interest in the investigation of deliberative procedures that could meet such a demanding principle. How could deliberative designs meaningfully connect politics to publics in a context where political programmes could be electorally legitimated, though they remained epistemically vague, normatively divisive, and functionally incoherent? And how could such deliberative procedures form part of a feasible democratic process that would also be normatively defensible with respect to the inclusive, reciprocal, and public premises implied in the idea of public sovereignty?

The first answer to this question is an apparent paradox; deliberative procedures form part of a feasible democratic process by not forming part of it. Instead they operate counterfactually as cognitive expectations about deliberation that political actors could be held to at any time. These conditions could be internalized as intrinsic to democratic action, even though institutional conditions for fully realizing these expectations are rarely met. Nonetheless, the normative expectations of democracy may sometimes be fully procedurally met, for example when the regulative idea of equal, democratic entitlements to voice and to be heard is denied to some or all of a political community, and those excluded are fully aware of this denial and successfully argue against it. Justice is most likely to be procedurally realized when subjects capable of rectifying action perceive it as not being realized. Pure procedural justice, in Rawls's sense, where the procedure is fully determinative of the justice of its outcomes, is realized when the counterfactual assumptions that underpin deliberative practices are fully realized within procedures (Tschentscher, 1997). Such procedural justice depends on participating agents who have a clear sense of what fully inclusive procedure would consist. Procedures are only as good as the epistemic and normative competences of those who participative in them.

The second answer to the question opens up more contentious issues in the theory of deliberative democracy to do with the claims of deliberative procedures in relation to other democratic choice-making mechanisms. The institutional forms of contemporary democracy are unequivocally mixed mode; they are part discursive will formation, part populist, part deliberative, and part decision-oriented. Deliberative theory generally operates in abstraction from these conditions of mixed mode democratic forms. Deliberative democracy, accordingly, can only provide partial answers to the question of the extent to which public sovereignty might be realized in contemporary conditions. Such partial answers correspond to the distinction between those conditions when the exacting procedural conditions of deliberation could conceivably be fully met and the much more common cases where they are not. Deliberative theory currently is increasingly concerned with its wider context and with the multiple kinds of argumentation that compose it. It is becoming apparent that the hegemony of the normative-philosophical account of deliberation in a rationalist idiom, emphasizing the comprehensive and co-present giving and taking of reasons, is not adequate by itself. This is where the wider communicative and constructivist turn in the social sciences can help place deliberation in its societal context, rather than leaving it to be restricted to a largely self-sufficient account of procedures.

One example that might serve to illustrate the above point is the debate over epistemic reliability (Bohman, 1998; Estlund, 1997). Here, the issue of whether epistemic outcomes should be judged as right from a procedure-immanent or procedure-independent standard is less fundamental if the reality of existing democratic structures and processes is taken into account, where epistemic standards because of external constraints are to a great extent procedure-independent. The more compelling questions from a contextually expanded perspective are to what degree do deliberative procedures actually add to *general* epistemic reliability, and to what extent could deliberative democratic innovations make epistemic standards more procedure-immanent?

A further example of the necessity to attach more importance to the societal context is the status of morality in deliberative procedures. Recent writing on deliberation is moving away from a principal focus on the moral-procedural standard of rightness as consensus. Arguments that qualify the latter arise both in the sense of acceptance of the legitimacy of deliberative forms that allow for the sincere articulation of individual interests for Mansbridge et al., hence for compromise as an outcome of deliberation, or for the mixed argumentation modalities that Bachtiger et al. call type 2 deliberation (Bachtiger et al., 2010; Mansbridge et al., 2010; Parkinson and Mansbridge, Ed., 2012). These new foci are indicative of an attempt to place deliberative procedures in a broader societal context. The universalistic moral rules of publicity and inclusion, underpinning the deliberative ideal, cannot be exclusively redeemed within any foreseeable deliberative procedures. Therefore, moral outcomes must be assumed to derive from a wider range of deliberative and other participatory procedures in combination. Deliberation must not be assumed to be the sole democratic location of moral learning processes. These learning processes not alone go beyond deliberation to other institutional forms of participation, but they also go beyond it to the discourses, cultural structures, and formal and informal constitution-forming processes that form its context. The latter are foundational for public autonomy, and they are also critical preconditions of deliberation. The application of norms, in complex ways interacting with their justification, also generates moral learning and is, therefore, also critical to the moral basis of public autonomy (Alexy, 1993; Günther, 1993; Habermas, 1993).

While the above remarks appear to point, along with Dryzek, towards the need for a more radical and innovative deliberative theory, two qualifying notes should be entered. The first is that deliberative theory should address rather than avoid how existing institutions might be conserved and adapted as well as in some instances transformed. This applies in particular to aggregative institutions, like voting systems, which continue to be essential to democratic legitimacy and effectiveness. But the status and importance of voting systems might change if they are inset into a more discursively as well as deliberatively shaped context. If, for example, a radically different and more inclusive kind of political argumentation carried by a transformed system of political communication could be envisaged, then voting systems might appear in a different light to how they often function today, where they often serve as conduits for ideological hegemony with the weak proviso that this hegemony can be changed by the collective actions of publics in further episodes of voting.

The second qualification relates to the limitations of participatory theories of deliberation. Accounts of participatory democracy mostly contain a strong deliberative component, but this literature on the whole tends to be rather specific and case based, animated by the assumed normative superiority of participation. It does not yet amount to a comprehensive theory of a more participatory democracy that would indicate how existing and new institutions could in combination lead to a feasible and normatively defensible model of wider democratization. The contemporary debate on deliberative democracy actually appears very promising if conceptualized less from the ideal counterfactual standpoint, though that will always remain important, and more from the socio-historical circumstances in which counterfactual standards fuse with immanent reasoning and potential institutional innovation.[8]

The challenge to deliberative democracy therefore requires all of the existing resources of deliberative theory and more. The 'more' arises in developing as a 'regulative idea' a model of democratization that would extend the range and institutionally deepen the deliberative goal of the 'rule of reasons'. Attempting to develop the theory of deliberative democracy by only exploring the deliberative deepening of existing institutions

---

[8] This issue is explored in some depth in the cognitive-communicative framework developed in Parts III and IV of the book.

cannot properly address the contemporary challenges facing democracy. What are expressed in part as disciplinary differences, the defence of a legitimate model of democracy, on the one side, that can be adapted to meet new challenges, as opposed to the critique of the presumed insufficiency of this model, on the other, inhibit a common effort to address contemporary problems of further democratization that is at the heart of the idea of public deliberation. The study of deliberation as a kind of democratization whose potentialities can only be fully explored from the standpoint of a communication theory of society is currently underdeveloped. Only by moving in such a direction can an adequate vantage point on democratization be gained, that is to say, it can be gained only by viewing democratic institutions, processes, and outcomes in the context of their multiple societal environments.

Deliberative Theory and the Theory of Society

The idea of addressing both evolutionary and transformative versions of deliberative theory in conjunction with the theory of society certainly has an unusual feel in the contemporary intellectual landscape, given that the theory of society as opposed to social theory generally has fallen into decay. While it may be argued that the theory of society needs to be revived for many reasons, even in its present condition it can still provide a description of society that is compatible with a normative democratic theory. A normative democratic theory consists of the assertion of preferred normative commitments that are either already, or should be, socially realized. Its claims to validity depends on being able to argue that, where those preferred normative commitments are realized, they improve the state of society or, where it is argued they should be realized, they would improve it. For almost all democratic theories both claims, which are present to a greater or lesser extent in different theories, depend on an *implicit* rather than an explicit description of a state of society in which the actual or desirable normative commitments are held to operate, or to be capable of being realized. The only obvious exception to the merely implicit or 'background' account of society in democratic theory is that of Habermas where, as addressed in later chapters, the theory of society that corresponds to his democratic theory is at least partially explicated.⁹

While these observations apply to all the traditions of democratic theory reviewed in Part I, they apply particularly to the deliberative tradition. This is because that tradition is tied to the actuality of a communication theory of society to which its account of normative commitments corresponds. The other traditions, with the possible exception of some versions of political realism such as those built upon systems theory, in one way or another can more easily seek to evade, if never successfully, the description of society that must correspond to their normative commitments. Such evasion can be achieved through the liberal device of ideal theory, the republican reconstruction of a past than cannot be recovered or a standard of non-domination with no societal explication, and the radical account of a symbolic container of political power that is always only potentially, but never actually, filled.¹⁰ Deliberative theory, by contrast, is bound to a communicative description of society that it can only evade by retreating into the normative fastness of a self-sufficient democratic theory.¹¹ Such a retreat diminishes the creative political role of social spheres other than the formal political core. As will be developed in subsequent chapters, these other politically relevant social spheres comprise of formally organized systems, the everyday lifeworld and civil society. They not alone

9   Rawls has a strong implicit theory of society that to my knowledge is still unfortunately waiting for its interpreter. Axel Honneth's account of social freedom is without question a major new development in the combined scholarship of political philosophy and the theory of society (Honneth, 2011).
10 In the latter case, the claim that it is 'never actually filled' indicates unwillingness to address how this power container might actually be filled. In other words, the theory has little to say about the institutional outcomes of the contention of political forces.
11 The extent to which deliberative democracy may be regarded as a largely self-sufficient democratic theory, as opposed to one requiring a supportive and interacting social theory, goes back to the distinction made earlier between deliberative democracy and public deliberation, and also to the issue of whether Rawls is or is not a deliberative democrat.

have pivotal roles as the 'environment' or 'periphery' of the formal political system, but they stand as political, and thus democratic, complexes in their own right.

The value of introducing the theory of society may be illustrated by consideration of a recurring debate in deliberative theory that also has wider resonance in comparative political philosophy. This has to do with the status of the consensual foundations of morality and its relation to the ethical neutrality of the state, an issue that has from many sides been used to criticize Rawls and Habermas. For example, republican theory has criticized Rawls and modern liberal theory generally for its claim to the ethical neutrality of the state (Sandel, 1984). In both Rawls and Habermas, this ethical neutrality is the expression of the moral core of legal-political institutions that is distinct from any 'comprehensive' ethical doctrine, even if it interacts with them in complex ways. For republican communitarians in particular, this is an untenable position. They regard ethical neutrality as impossible. Liberal assertions of its necessity merely mask the normative preference for an individualistic way of life. For the radical position, such theories abstract too much from the social positions of concrete persons and their emotional drives. The dynamics of social positioning leads to positional conflicts that constitute the political, a process animated by evolving ethical perceptions of social arrangements.

Within deliberative theory, Mansbridge et al. provide an illustrative account of some recent tendencies (Mansbridge et al., 2010). They argue against its first phase focus on impartial moral consensus and for its extension to consider appropriately argued interests in negotiation and bargaining processes. Deliberation should be understood as an exercise in generating binding decisions in an inclusive, reciprocal, and open manner that could range from disinterested consensus, for example on certain constitutional matters, to appropriately argued interests in other settings. These different procedures would be commonly characterized by such regulative ideals as inclusion of all those affected, comprehensibility, truthfulness, civility, and the absence of coercive power. Furthermore, deliberative theory should not be seen as the antithesis of aggregative mechanisms of decision-making that in the end do depend on coercive power. Rather, the interplay of deliberative and non-deliberative decision-making mechanisms should be examined together. This approach indicates a broadening both of the range of deliberative mechanisms brought under consideration and of their potential application to a range of social situations. In this way, the theory of public deliberation tentatively begins to address the relationship between democracy and other social spheres (Bohman, 2000).

Notwithstanding these advances, consideration of the implications of various deliberative mechanisms, and the extent they might contribute to a better moral level of social integration, remains generally absent in deliberative theory. Until these implications are systematically addressed, it remains unclear what problems consensual, bargaining, and other deliberative mechanisms are supposed to address and whether they actually are efficacious in dealing with these problems. In other words, deliberative theory needs to work with a corresponding theory of society to adequately demonstrate its societal implications. By coupling deliberative theory with the theory of society, it can be demonstrated what role consensus forming, bargaining, and other deliberative mechanisms can play in making normatively well-ordered co-operative schemes possible. It can also be demonstrated what problems and normative diagnoses remain unmet and in need of normative prognoses, including innovation in democratic institutions.

The perspective of the theory of society brings in its wake the issue of the relationship between justification and application. The latter distinction associated with authors such as Gunther, Alexy, and Habermas separates the ideal justification of a norm, where all affected parties have full opportunity to deliberate on it, from its application, where issues of appropriateness arising from its employment in a concrete situation must be impartially taken into account (Alexy, 1993; Günther, 1993; Habermas, 1993). Justifying deliberation on the basis of its societal contribution would therefore go beyond the deontological commitment to fair procedures to also include the actual implications of real justification processes. This would mean taking account of interrelated democratic processes of the discursive formation of public will, deliberation, and application. It is only in this way that the contribution of the deliberative model of democracy to real political processes, spanning inputs, processes, and outputs, can be properly assessed with respect to two crucial axes; the diachronic axis – its contribution to socio-historical development – and the synchronic axis

– its contribution to problem solving and co-ordination within a given democracy-society structure.

Mansbridge et al., in an early footnote, draw attention to the regulative ideals that should guide deliberative democracy, specifically instancing the existence of a plurality of regulative ideals and possible tensions between them, for example, the potential tension between liberty and equality (Mansbridge et al., 2010). The status of regulative ideals is addressed by these authors only from the standpoint of the theory of democracy. While they are right to consider the question of the interplay of plural democratic regulative ideals and their potentially tension-laden relationship, this is only part of the overall picture. Insofar as deliberative processes are inset into extended societal communication systems that have democratic import, then the regulative ideals that guide these spheres, for example, economic efficiency and cultural authenticity, have to be considered along with deliberative and wider democratic ideals. Without losing its concern for political institutions, deliberative theory as part of a communicative theory of politics should also concern itself with wider social spheres that both constitute the societal environment of the formal political system and, in their own right, constitute political contexts of action. This is the import of Honneth's combination of social theory and political philosophy (Honneth, 2007; Honneth, 2011).

Public Deliberation and the Public Sphere

The relationship between deliberative theory and the theory of the public sphere is based upon the communicatively mediated relationship between democracy and other social spheres. From a political standpoint, the most important of these social spheres is civil society. Civil society, treated at more length in Part IV of this book, is the sphere of political associations of all kinds. Deliberative theory generally assumes a dynamic and reciprocal relationship between civil society and democratic institutions, taking leave of Rawls's more static and closed assumptions. Generally, the public sphere is not understood as playing a pivotal role in that relationship. A strong assumption of 'classical' or type 1 deliberative theory, which permeates much normative-philosophical reflection, is that the public sphere can be made consistent with the requirements of a deliberative democracy. Properly organized deliberation can substantially supplant the 'wild' reasoning of the public sphere. In this formulation, the gap is closed between the real and the counterfactual and the public imputed an idealized role, capacity, and status.

There are three characteristic responses to this formulation that loosely correspond to traditions of deliberative thinking, though they can be variously combined in different theories. The first is to privilege this ideal formulation and to tie it closely to fully deliberatively justified law as the source of normative authority. This helps to make the theory plausible, because law offers the best potential for full deliberative justification. Deliberative democracy, in this first tradition, consistently requires a high capacity for collective reasoning and counterfactually incorporates the public. This approach is at least implicit in Joshua Cohen's by now celebrated account of the grounding principles of deliberative democracy (Cohen, 1989).[12] The second, to be developed more in the next part of this book, is close to the first with respect to the ideal counterfactual status of deliberation

---

12   Cohen's principles of formal deliberative democracy are summarized below (Cohen, 1989):

   1. A deliberative democracy is an ongoing independent association whose members expect it to continue into the indefinite future.
   2. The citizens in the democracy structure their institutions such that deliberation is the deciding factor in their creation, and the institutions thus created allow deliberation to continue. Free deliberation amongst equals is the basis of legitimacy for these citizens.
   3. A deliberative democracy is a pluralistic association. The members are committed to the respect of a pluralism of values and aims within the polity.
   4. The citizens consider deliberative procedure as the source of legitimacy, and prefer institutions in which the association between deliberation and outcomes is evident and easily traceable to the deliberative process.
   5. Each member recognizes and respects other members' deliberative capacity.

and the role of law, but understands the public sphere as the mechanism for discursive mediation between periphery and core (Habermas, 1996; Habermas, 2006). In this formulation, legitimacy is formally conferred on deliberative institutions by means of the discursive formation of public will.

Finally, the third response has a fundamentally different understanding of the relationship between deliberation and the public sphere. In this case, the public sphere is understood as the overarching context of deliberation. The approach, therefore, combines public discourses and public deliberation; in fact, deliberation appears here as a variation on public discourse and is conducted through multiple modalities of argumentation, that are variously understood as more emotive and subject specific than is the case with the first approach to deliberation (Eder, 2006; Mansbridge et al., 2010; Parkinson and Mansbridge, 2012; Warren, 2007; Young, 2000). It is not that in the first two approaches such issues are not considered; the difference has to do with the relative importance to be attached to them. This constitutes a major difference in that, in the third response, the normative power of law is no longer regarded as unassailably primary. Nor is the counterfactual assumption retained that affected political agents are always co-present in deliberation; for deliberation is a process that is in reality spread across multiple arenas of communication. Such an approach changes how the relationship between deliberative democracy, civil society, and the public sphere should be understood. In line with the different emphasis of this third tradition, the cognitive-communicative approach of the kind outlined in detail in subsequent parts of the book finds its place. The import of this is not to dilute the significance of the normatively regulated exchange of reasons in strong deliberative contexts; it is to show how strong deliberation of this kind is not the whole of public reasoning, or even the whole of public deliberation. And, in any case, it too is contextually embedded in the wider context of public discourse in the public sphere.

CHAPTER 7

The Communicative Turn in Democratic Theory

The normative models of democracy reviewed in Part I are selections from a very wide field. They nonetheless indicate a communicative turn in democratic theory. This turn is real but not dominant, since it promises to disturb other well-entrenched foundational assumptions. These include assumptions about the self-contained autonomous individual whose powers of reflective reasoning sustain the values necessary for democratic politics; about the homogeneity of individual or collective actors that become fused in concepts like self-determination, the explanatory power of institutional structure built around states, and the civic culture of societies; about the self-evident standards underpinning critique; and about the confident distinction drawn between what is political and what is not. The communication paradigm comes with a range of challenging assumptions: *intersubjectivist* assumptions about the nature of political interaction; *constructivist* assumptions about the multiplicity of valid public perspectives that must be both identified and recognized to avoid domination; *mediated* assumptions about the interplay of different levels of analysis; and *non-linear, processual* assumptions about the dynamic and contingent nature of political development. The reorientation of much of democratic theory along these lines is nonetheless ongoing and, in some respects, revitalizes latent traditions of the normative status of popular sovereignty, partly reassessed as the democratic importance of inclusion in political communication.[1] This reorientation arises at least as a question to be addressed in all the reviewed traditions,

---

1   For a valuable discussion on citizenship and communicative inclusion from a systems theoretical perspective see Bora and Hausendorf's contribution to their edited collection on citizenship talk (Bora and Hausendorf, 2006).

even where, as in some versions of the realist tradition, its credentials as a truly productive question are challenged.

The communicative turn may be giving rise to greater congruence between at least some of the five traditions, especially variants of the dominant traditions; liberalism in its Rawlsian variant building on Lockean and Kantian ideas; republicanism, emphasizing public autonomy as a route to non-domination; and radical ideas emphasizing a participatory widening of the political space. One major reason for this is the advent of a distinct theory of deliberative democracy, which has raised to theoretical view the question of *public* deliberation. The socio-epistemic roots of the deliberative turn may be traced to a variety of societal preconditions, including new media technologies, the epistemic import of the communicative paradigm in the human and social sciences, new concepts of the self, but perhaps most fundamentally of all the rise of new movements. These movements raise suppressed issues of recognition, highlighting the dissatisfying implications of groups being spoken for rather than speaking for themselves, and thus specifying their own conditions for the realization of justice and non-domination. Though these changed societal foundations have affected all democratic traditions, the rise of a deliberative tradition has crystallized the issue of reflexive democratic communication in the sense of the importance of individuals and groups representing themselves. The idea of deliberation, spreading through liberal and republican traditions also, has diffused a sensibility for the cognitive and normative premises of public communication and revitalized the idea of popular sovereignty as it does so.

The implication for current concerns of the increasing significance of intersubjective communication in various traditions of political philosophy does not lie in the expectation of the radical diminution of normative differences between them. It lies in the possibility that the reflexive import of the communicative turn might at least lead to greater agreement on the conceptual range and shared concerns of political philosophy, following an argument of Bourdieu on reflexivity where he claims that recognizing the legitimate voices of others should inspire greater self-scrutiny of one's own (Bourdieu and Wacquant, 1992; Pettit, 1999, p. 2). Such a language would create new possibilities for agreement on the spectrum of meaning, even if the spectrum of normative validity remained disputed. Despite the fact that political philosophies assert normative autonomy through being embedded in political cultures and epistemic communities that sustain their differences, greater epistemic co-operation in defining problems and potentials of democracy, derived from paradigmatic sharing of at least some dimensions of a common communicative reorientation, may lead to productive revisiting of normative differences. This will not lead to normative consensus, but it may lead to an enlargement of the spectrum of normative rationality, and the possible emergence of greater levels of rational dissensus in which at least the differences can be understood and a common course of action made possible amidst them.[2]

One necessary concomitant to such potential ecumenical developments would be that the perceptual horizons of political philosophies are turned outwards and 'positivized' by deeper engagement with the social sciences. As was already clear to Dewey, the optics of political philosophy must empirically expand if it is to play a leading role in mitigating and reversing the crisis of democracy (Dewey, 1927). The present generates challenges similar to the period of its early modern re-establishment in that democracy's primacy for the organizational shaping of social institutions has to be reasserted. Such primacy is not to be achieved by the 'technocratic' means of governance afforded by the steering medium of power overseen by public or private bureaucracies, or by the steering medium of money overseen by market provision. To the extent that these technologies of bureaucratic or incentivized monetary steering have conspicuously and successively failed, democratic institutions can no longer retreat to a procedural minimum and either delegate the organization of society to bureaucracies or allow it to happen by self-organizing markets. Democratic institutions must incorporate greater epistemic capacity to relate to other societal environments, with that capacity resulting not in the rule of experts, even if they play an important role, but in the rule of reasons. A communicative theory

---

2   The idea of rational dissensus is a key idea of this book and is further developed in subsequent chapters. It represents a commitment to generate agreement across differences on the part of alternative and otherwise conflicting political perspectives. It is reflexively applied here to the capacity for agreement and learning in political theory itself.

of politics founded on the normative premise of deliberative democracy must reconcile reason and expertise and must extend this reconciliation into public contexts beyond formal political institutions, building new kinds of reflexive institutions as it does so. The resources of a transformed sociology of public communication can make such a task more visible, while also contributing to its fulfilment.

Comparative Political Philosophies and the Public Sphere

From an internal standpoint, the landscape of political philosophy appears as a complicated, variegated, and contested terrain. From an external standpoint, asking how varieties of political philosophy enter into the self-understanding of political institutions and subjects and with what practical consequences is no less challenging (Audard, 2009). Yet the latter by and large receives less attention, even though, viewed from comparative and evolutionary perspectives, societies select and combine political philosophies in constituting their political cultures.[3] The very invocation of the term 'political culture' in this way suggests that democratic societies achieve some kind of cultural and normative stabilization, in various parts achieved through political inclusion, contained disagreement, agreement, and ideologically mobilized social power. But, as in previous epochs of democratic transformation, this normative order appears today highly mutable. The terms of the relationship between political order and political change appear to be reversed to such an extent that order appears to be the provisional outcome of modalities of change, rather than the latter merely indicating incremental disturbances that can be institutionally assimilated.

---

3   Sandel illustrates this process, whether one agrees or not with his normative perspective, in criticizing the liberal values he claims are dominant in American political culture.

Subsequent chapters will explore what the combined resources of political and social theory have to say about this situation, proposing that a communication theory of society specifically addressing the relationship between politics and other social spheres is the key to generating insight and guidance into how the dynamism and fragmentation of the contemporary world need not lead to normative agnosticism or worse. Above all the other political traditions, this is a challenge that deliberative theory poses for itself. However, deliberative theory still needs the resources, capacities, and insights of the other traditions if its contribution is to be fully made. In its fullness and variety, democratic theory develops a political language needed to understand the depth structure of the normative logics underpinning democracies. These can be discerned through the normative concerns of particular theories and partially in overlaps, borrowing, and arguments between them. Subsequent chapters, then, will explore how normative-philosophical theories in combination provide a normative core for the communication theory of society, without prejudice to the continuing philosophical and practical-political debate and disagreement over which normative preferences should be made immanent in social arrangements.

The task that opens out from this approach is shared between a social theory of communicative politics and a democratic theory of public deliberation. For this task, the communicative focus of each of the traditions reviewed above has a place. With respect to Rawls, his idea of public reason addressed at applying basic principles of justice can appear to take on elite connotations, especially with regard to the restricted range of its social carriers. But the idea of public reason, when made socially inclusive, clarifies what counts as good standards for democratic argumentation as it reaches into spaces where agreement, rational disagreement, and compromise can be forged. It adds more demanding criteria for such argumentation compared to the more neutral, sociologically derived term of public discourse. The later Rawls in particular contributes to understanding how a substantive normative culture – a political conception of justice forged from reasonable comprehensive doctrines – is formed.

What Rawls does for the moral and legal components of culture, some versions of republicanism do with respect to the 'substantialization' of ethical culture. This substantialization, taking the form of boundary forming ethnic, national, and religious identities, has been ever present in modernity, of great import for its development and yet laden with danger. The republican themes of the importance of group ethos and solidarity resonate through modern thought. In this connection, some parts of political philosophy in a way that unite such adversaries as Sandel and Rawls, extending also to the critical social philosopher, Axel Honneth, ask a question that is of great importance: What is the relationship between ethical identities and moral-legal normative commitments? And this republican theme also inspires the further question of how can such commitments be understood to be formed and transformed given the social theoretical reorientation towards a constructivist epistemology?

The radical position, in some respects close to republicanism, draws attention both to the subjugation wrought by the interplay of social and political power and resistance to it. At the very core of its contribution is the concern for struggle between different habituses – including the sociogenesis of new kinds of habitus associated with the emergence of distinctive subjects. These subjects are the products of identity forming communication that shapes otherwise diffuse experiences into patterns. The construction of political subjects involves creative communicative processes, in part directed against the kind of ideological hegemony that impedes subject formation, and in part serving as the realization of modalities of being not previous foreseen. Subjects are finally formed, as further elaborated in Part III, when the changing outcomes of communication become socially and cognitively stabilized into aligned social and mental structures. These subjects then become a resource for wider political assertion and bring a distinctive kind of communication to bear on the wider political system. The advent of such subjects is disturbing. They have the potential to deeply influence, using Touraine's concept, the direction of historicity understood as the manner in which a society's priorities will be reflected in its cultural models. New political subjects can significantly change both the input and output sides of politics. Subject formation, its possibility, its achievement, its negation, and the opposed projects of different kinds of subject, is at the core of the idea of an impassioned, embodied, concrete, radical politics.

In Chapter 5, political realism disperses into a number of variations on classical liberalism, in the end united by the claim that normative standpoints are either irrelevant or counterproductive. Political realism argues that the continued assertion of such standpoints in public communication is a problem rather than a solution, given that the social facts of complexity and fragmentation render the intertwined ideas of publicly sustained morality and epistemic rightness illusory. This interpretation of the normative generates similar problems for democratic theory that the power of nationalism in distributing rights of citizenship does in another way. Disillusioned realist theories describe something real even if they overstate it. Contemporary political outcomes, consistent with their diagnosis, are more shaped by the competition of political ideologies to achieve legitimate domination than it is by any kind of deliberative procedures. This is not to say that competitive politics works without reference to principles of justice, the ethos of substantive forms of life, or distinctive kind of ethico-political subjects. But, insofar as the discursive formation of will and norm setting procedures are institutionally weak, competing political parties acquire considerable freedom to shape public opinion so as to support their ideological programmes. Though this tradition is dismissive of the role of public discourse in favour of a strategic model of power struggle, much of this struggle is in fact conducted in the medium of such discourse. The ideals of political realism tallies closely with what Ferree et al. describe as representative elitism, though such elitism is dependent on the play of other forces that constrain it in multiple ways (Ferree, Gamson, Gerhards, and Rucht, 2002).

The core concern with communicative politics makes the deliberative tradition central to this book. In part, the book proceeds to consider the claims of this tradition, firstly, with an emphasis on discourse ethics and in the broader context offered by other democratic traditions in Part II and, then, in Parts III and IV, as qualified by the still broader context of a cognitive sociological theory of discourse. Viewed this way, it explores the intuitions that lie behind the renewed theoretical interest in *public* deliberation as an approach that might satisfy the potentials associated with the intersubjectivist, constructivist, processual, and mediated epistemology, which is emerging in political philosophy and that has much promise for collaboration with the social sciences.

Such an epistemology can be extended to engage the reconstructivist and multi-level methodology of critical theory. From a reconstructive standpoint, critique in its conserving, disclosing, and opposing moments is guided by a rational intuition about what is wrong or about to be made wrong by specific actions or unplanned consequences. It is also guided by a sense of how social institutions can be so arranged as to better serve various standards of justice such as care, equality, and autonomy, and other standards such as environmental responsibility. The theory of public deliberation – interpreted through the social and democratic theory of discourse ethics in the next part of the book – emphasizes the 'meso' level where intersubjective political discourse is located. Deliberative theory assumes that deliberative discourse at this level can both make critical judgements and establish agreed upon norms.

The theory of deliberative democracy privileges this meso-level of deliberative procedures and, for various complex reasons to be developed in Part II, this leads it to neglect the macro dimension of normative culture and the micro dimension of subject formation. Accordingly, from the vantage point of the argument developed here, deliberative theory should be repositioned within a version of the theory of society that can fully do justice to these different levels. Part of that repositioning exercise is to take profit from the insights of the other democratic traditions. Through the various dimensions of the democracy-society relationship these positions emphasize, they generate important considerations to be taken up by the theory of society, such as the nature of non-procedural moral foundations, the role of collective identities, the relationship between morality, ethics and law, the possibility of non-domination, the import of subject formation and social positioning, and the inescapable facts of pluralism and complexity. These standpoints force attention to the 'hard facts' that attends the democracy-society relationship. It is not just pluralistic and complex in practice; this reality demands complexity and pluralism on the theoretical plane too.

This approach does not attempt to show how deliberative theory can, internal to democratic theory, embrace and modify the contributions of other traditions. It rather aims to show how democratic theory as a whole can contribute to establishing normative standards for the theory of society. In this way, the strange separation of normative theories of democracy, which are necessarily also theories of the democracy-society relationship, from a normatively oriented theory of society can be confronted, and at least preliminary lines of fruitful interchange established. In turn, this work requires the kind of social theory that could advance the normative intentions thus revealed. Such a social theory must show how society is normatively constructed and reconstructed by attending to communicative mechanisms, learning processes, and cultural structures that go towards realizing – or blocking – appropriate kinds of subjectivity, intersubjectivity, and structure formation within the democracy-society field.

Such a social theory profits from the normative standards that political philosophies elucidate. But it breaks with the dominance of the normative perspective that informs them. A multi-level cognitive-communicative social theory views society as an equivalently multi-faceted reality in which normative logics – whether 'good' or 'bad' – are set within complex discursively elaborated contexts. These contexts are composed of the multiple communication arenas of the public sphere and the ensemble of cognitive models and structures that enter into public discourse. These contexts specify criteria for the relevance, legitimacy, justice, and efficacy of norms. Norms are hence not bound to institutional procedures, reflecting one tendency of political philosophy but, reflecting another, neither are they entirely unbound from such processes and formulated in the free space of the political. This cognitive recontextualization of norm-building processes proposes that normative innovation is first anticipated and shaped in this cognitive circuit of discourse, learning, and cultural structure formation. But this process should not neglect the intrinsic importance of norm-setting procedures. The cognitive approach developed here therefore agrees with the deliberative insight that norm-setting procedures are of great importance for the finalization of norms, even if also proposing that they stand in a real – and not just counterfactual – relationship to the public sphere and normative culture generally.

The public sphere cannot be viewed as a mere filter of discourses so as facilitate normative finalization. It is a permanent and pervasive context of norm building. It determines the cultural relevance of such norm building by recognizing the nature of social differences that can only sometimes, and usually as part of a long learning process, be fully reconciled. Reconciliation is, however, usually only partial. Reconciliation of this partial nature – giving rise to what Miller calls rational dissensus – should not be confused with the compromise-based sway of alternative political programmes in the realist tradition. While that, too, is a mechanism of culturally specifying the normative agenda, the idea of partial reconciliation contains the key idea that differences can be recognized and yet sufficiently overcome to allow norm setting procedures to operate. Consensus as full reconciliation and rational dissensus, and compromise as partial reconciliation, of social differences are therefore alternative, but potentially complementary, ways of specifying cultural models that would allow norm setting to proceed.

The central claim being raised here about the limitations of deliberative democratic theory with regard to the public sphere is that it neutralizes the cultural variation – both pragmatic and semantic – that follows from the nature of public discourse and cultural structure formation. It neutralizes it by diminishing the situated, social forms that actually shape such discourse, which can only be grasped from the balanced constructivist and reconstructivist perspective of a social pragmatics rather than the dominant reconstructivist perspective of a formal pragmatics. If formal pragmatics belongs to the deliberative theory that springs from discourse ethics, the same intuition takes other, in this respect, similar forms with the general deliberative bias towards procedurally secured democratic justice. This amounts to a bias to the counterfactual that trumps the immanent context of a differentiated and pluralist society. Such a society specifies many valid standards for evaluating different forms of action that must be somehow harmonized enough to allow institutional selection to take place. In the parts of the books to follow, recognition of the normative insightfulness of political philosophy must therefore be balanced by its constructivist and substantive limitations viewed from the standpoint of a communication theory of society.

PART II

Habermas, Democracy, and Public Culture

CHAPTER 8

Discourse Ethics, Democratic Discourse, and the Theory of Society

Part II of the book builds on the review of philosophies in Part I. It places Habermas's theory of democracy in the context of the five approaches to democratic theory outlined there. Habermas is unusual amongst those who practice political philosophy in combining his democratic theory with the theory of society, beyond the tendency to treat 'society' as a mere backdrop. In *Between Facts and Norms*, he combines the communicative theory of society with the theory of deliberative democracy, employing the normative insights of liberal, republican, and, latently, radical political philosophies within a social theory that follows on from *The Theory of Communicative Action*. The task that opens up for Part II is to critically interrogate dimensions of the relationship between normative philosophical theory and the theory of society, with Habermas's contribution at its core.

Lying in the background of this task is another view of the relationship between normative theory and the theory of society. Habermas's attempt to communicatively reorient political philosophy in a manner consistent with his social theory has inspired some critical sociologists to develop a normative sociology that would go beyond the kind of empirically oriented normative analysis dominant in the discipline (see Miller, 1986, for an early example; Strydom, 2011). Normative theory should, in this view, recover some of the ground of the macro-sociological contributions of classical and neo-classical sociology. It should therefore be concerned with the overall direction of society, for which inspiration already exists in social practices. These social practices enable the reconstructive identification of normative potentials that could lead to morally justifiable social change. This sociology would therefore add disclosing critique concerned with imaginative leaps beyond contemporary actuality to the unmaking or negative critique dominant in the discipline. Less emphasized in its work, it also adds conserving 'critique', that is, defence of what has been historically achieved in cultural and institutional structures from unjustified attack.

Such a revitalized critical macro-sociology is built upon the epistemological constructivism inspired by the micro-sociological renaissance of the latter part of the twentieth century. It therefore operates with a communicative-constructivist epistemology that takes the cognitive form that will be elaborated in Part III. Such a cognitive sociology incorporates a focus on the communicative-constructive and reconstructive capacities to engage in collective learning that point to new developmental options for society that exceed what has been already institutionalized. Within this communicative-, cognitive-, and learning-theoretical framework, the various kinds of critique, negative, disclosing, and conserving, acquire a fundamental role.

The theory of discourse ethics is intrinsic to the revitalization of critical normative sociology. The current chapter initially addresses the project of discourse ethics that Habermas has jointly developed with Karl-Otto Apel. The chapter starts with an account, following Apel, of the philosophical foundations of discourse ethics, which proposes a transformative communicative epistemology, before turning to explore how Habermas traces a relationship between a discourse ethics founded on this basis and the theory of democracy. Here, the distinctive epistemological foundations of discourse ethics that inform its key democratic principles are related to epistemologies of other democratic traditions. The second main theme of the chapter relates discourse ethics to social theory, exploring how both Apel and Habermas attempt to relate the theory to the actual conditions of political life. Habermas's contribution in this regard is fragmentary and spread out over the second half of his career. It remains, nonetheless, extremely important as a rare attempt to connect democratic theory with the theory of society, an attempt that moreover seeks to absorb insights from other democratic traditions with their implicit theories of society.

In the following chapter, Chapter 9, some constructive criticisms are offered of Habermas's theory of democracy with respect to the strength of its deontological commitments and associated pure proceduralism. It is argued that these emphases, notwithstanding the efforts documented in this chapter to build a combined democratic and social theory, take the theory in an idealized transcendent direction that leads to difficulties with the immanent analysis of actual practices. The intention in doing this is not to diminish the normative claims of Habermas's theory, emerging from discourse ethics and grounded in the appropriate institutionalization of communicative claims to validity, but to show how this theory has to adopt a more realistic position on the contemporary circumstances of democratic communication in order to better integrate immanent and transcendent planes.

The criticisms offered of Habermas's project in Chapter 9 connect to the review of the communicative constructs of political philosophies in Part I, especially with regard to the need to build in to a communication theory of society some of the basic insights of these philosophies differently from Habermas's own approach. Nonetheless, modified theoretical orientations arising from his own work allow a relation to be drawn between deliberative and other political philosophies. The outcome is a reorientation of Habermas's discourse theory of norm formation that opens the way to a new foundation for the relationship between immanent and transcendent planes. It does this by integrating the varied normative proposals of political philosophies into a societal theoretical framework, the focus of Chapter 10, which works simultaneously on sociological and philosophical levels. These discursive-normative foundations, in turn, point the way to the task of developing a cognitive sociological account of the communication theory of democracy that retains normative intentions, a task shared between Parts III and IV.

Discourse Ethics: Communicative Epistemology and Democratic Justification

Forty years or so ago, Apel laid out a programme for the transformation of philosophy that provides a rationale for the discourse ethics that he has jointly developed with Habermas (Apel, 1980). Such a transformation takes leave from the communication-independent, monological orientation of 'traditional' philosophy, whether empiricist, rationalist, or transcendentally oriented. Traditional philosophy saw itself as context independent in its focus on the formal truth conditions of statements and monological in that perception was reduced to individual acts of understanding and knowing the world, without relating such perception to the intersubjective context of communication with others.

According to Apel, this radical freedom of the individual was taken in various philosophical lineages – Descartes via Kant to Husserl, on the one side, Hume to Locke and the empiricist tradition on the other – to ground the capacity for autonomous judgement free from prejudice and external authority (Apel, 1978, p. 89; Böhler, 2003, p. 15). Apel claims that this philosophical inheritance goes in two directions which, notwithstanding their apparent mutual competition, actually ideologically complement one another: the rationalist and empiricist tradition moves in the direction of an objective and value-free foundation for science as the privileged rationality of western civilization and the transcendental tradition ends up in a self-consciously irrationalist existentialism concerned with subjective decisions of conscience. The value-free scientific rationality grounds the ethically neutral ideal of 'publicly valid rationality'. The subjectivization of conscience consigns morality to the sphere of private decision. Apel describes this as the western 'complementarity system', specifying value-free public rationality and subjective moral freedom.

In Apel's view, this complementarity system is epistemologically and ethically problematic. Epistemologically, the single, knowing subject is unable to perceive the further consequences of any given action in the complex action systems of modern society and is therefore incapable of ethically responsible action. Apel's claim has a reconstructive intent: the western complementarity system has a non-obsolete core in that the freedom and responsibility of individuals as behavioural agents must be rescued from the domain of irrational decision, and its potential mobilized for *collective responsibility* that is built upon the post-conventional outcomes of socialization.

Apel proposes a communication-theoretic reformulation of epistemology and ethics to rescue the possibility of responsible action in modern social conditions. For this purpose, he develops the idea of a communication community following C. S. Peirce's reformulation of Kant. Instead of monological presuppositions of cognitive qualities inherent in individuals that work outwards to the world, the individual *a priori*, Apel proposes an intersubjective *a priori* of communication that has two related components (Apel, 1980). First of all, in the real communication community, following Peirce and his pragmatist successor, G. H. Mead, meaning is conceived as a fundamentally social accomplishment (Mead, 1934). One can only judge what is meaningful and communicatively significant by learning the cultural codes and the linguistic, logical, and numerical rules of a real communication community. Such a communication community in this sense temporally precedes individual actions, whose horizons can only be formed in the light of its existence.[1]

Secondly, claims about the meaningfulness and validity of statements raised in the real communication community point beyond it to the *argumentation a priori* of the unlimited communication community. Beyond prejudice, power, and individual judgement, the claim to *validity* of statements in the real communication community presupposes the will to argue this validity within an unlimited communication community. Practical argumentation processes within the presupposed context of the unlimited communication community can only ever generate provisional agreement – and often don't get this far. Nonetheless, common normative principles can only be sustained if certain basic epistemic principles, moral norms, and cultural values are tested and agreed upon against the open horizons of the unlimited communication community and, on this basis, built into the moral, legal, and ethical frameworks of real communication communities. The contemporary period, by contrast, shows evidence of a crisis of the real communication community, unable to find a way forward through productive exploration of the counterfactual horizons of the unlimited communication community.[2]

---

1   Habermas's phenomenologically derived account of the communicatively structured lifeworld is analogous to the idea of a communication community, by which it is of course influenced.
2   This remark anticipates a sociological account of the relationship between the real and unlimited communication communities developed in Chapter 12.

The unlimited community of argumentation is at the heart of discourse ethics. In modern conditions, where ethical ideals are pluralist and often opposing, the validity of moral norms can no longer be claimed from within what now stand as particular *ethical* standpoints. Instead, moral-practical disputes can only be resolved according to the basic Kantian insight by designing procedures for conflict resolution that respect the substantive conviction that all individuals are free and equal (Bohman, 2013). These individuals have correspondingly equal chances to advance their particular point of view, while respecting the right of others to do the same and committing to reciprocal acts of speaking and listening. Identifying transcendental standards of validity implies that argumentation should only end when the rightness of a norm is universally agreed.

Discourse ethics breaks with Kant's idea of moral individualism that underlies the liberal idea of substantive pre-political rights. In this account, morally acting individuals are separated from one another by what Honneth, following Habermas's critique of Kant, describes as an 'abyss of speechlessness' (Honneth, 2007, p. 105). Instead, following discourse ethics, the validity of norms arises not from the self-reflection of an individual subject, but from intersubjective procedures of argumentation that include all affected parties. Moreover, such procedures must take place in appropriate conditions of publicity, participative opportunity, and information adequacy. Discourse ethics understands itself in transcendental-pragmatic terms, in the sense of the a priori necessity of a discourse free from domination and the intersubjective assent to a norm by all those affected.

As Böhler points out, the transcendental possibility of a discourse free from domination marks out discourse ethics as a moral theory (Böhler, 2003). It has indirect and direct application to social integration: indirectly, the transcendental-pragmatic conditions of the unlimited communication community opens up the continuous possibility of intersubjectively grounding moral norms; directly, any form of social integration that can be said to conform to moral standards of justice and responsibility must contain moral norms that could satisfy the justification condition of the assent of all in the real communication community.

The conditions of universalization illustrate these dimensions. The standard of universalization (U), which becomes fully revealed in the experience of application, stipulates that all affected in a process of justification accept the consequences of a norm for themselves and for others. The principle of universalization depends on the fact that the norm was justified in circumstances where the principle of discursivity (D) was in operation, that is, where only those norms are valid that are approved by all affected in full practical discourse.

Universalization operates as a counterfactual basic standard of modernity that can always be applied to new normative issues. Its potential for further application is never fully exhausted and it therefore triggers new experiences of denied recognition by social groups. They in turn seek the realization, in the here and now of the real communication community, of counterfactual potentials available in the unlimited communication community. In immanent social practice, something is claimed to be true, right, lawful, or beautiful with reasons that, if challenged, would be justified by all affected by the claim on the basis of the relevant counterfactual standard of truth, rightness, legality, or beauty. The claim could be proven wrong, inappropriate, incomprehensible, or insincere, but the essential point is that it is constantly subject to communicative testing of validity claims. The counterfactual idea of the need for redemption of validity claims through communicative testing within the horizon of the unlimited communication community structures real and present communication.

The fundamental idea of the responsibility or ethical-ladenness of all communication arises in the requirement for the communicative testing of validity claims. Apel and Habermas locate such standards in four formal-pragmatic validity claims; statements should be comprehensible, truthful, appropriate, and sincere, and each of these relate to distinct normative world relations. The validity claims associated with any and all of these world relations can be brought to bear in communication practices. When Apel speaks of the macro-ethical challenges facing humanity today – global justice, ecological reorientation, capacity for species destruction – he conceives of these challenges as necessitating a new kind of co-responsibility between interacting agents (Apel, 1975, 1987). Such co-responsibility is an example of the primacy of communicative reason over the factual results of opaque or merely interest-driven social processes.

The primacy of communicative reason is not intended to imply the status of a moral commandment whose validity lies beyond the social world. On the contrary, it signifies intra-mundane co-ordination of actions through the communicative interplay of multiple validity claims. The co-ordination of action in this way must also be societally organized. Cultural values are, as Habermas puts it, at best 'candidates' for embodiment in norms designed to give expression to a general interest; social actors can only acquire the necessary distance 'from norms or normative systems that have been set off from the totality of social life' (Habermas, 1990, p. 104).

Socially effective communicative reason depends on the interweaving of epistemic, ethical, moral and legal discourses guided by distinctive validity claims. Hence, from the standpoint of the action-orienting implications of communication practices, discourses interpenetrate one another and form cultural structures that relate validity claims together within the forms set by orienting cultural models.[3] The *interweaving* of validity claims to form these action-orienting cultural models is critical from a constructivist and applied perspective, though Apel and Habermas on the whole do not give it emphasis.[4] It nevertheless stands as a clear concomitant of the theory, essential to its sociological application.

Discourse Ethics and Political Epistemologies

According to the procedural conception of morality of discourse ethics, all affected by a given norm should have an equal chance to fully participate in its establishment. Such a basic participatory-moral presupposition depends on appropriate societal conditions to make fair participation possible. Habermas describes these conditions in democratic theoretical terms as the result of the 'equiprimordiality' of, on the one hand, the rights of the ancients, communication and participation rights and, on the other, modern

---

3 The concept of cultural model is further developed in Part III, where it is understood as the cultural template for making collective action possible amidst a spectrum of discursively generated commonalities and differences. It is there situated within a wider cognitive theory.

4 It must be noted that Habermas in *Communicative Action* analyses in some detail the interplay of validity claims in various kinds of communication. This *social* theoretical exercise is, however, never fully developed or applied *societal* theoretically.

private rights (Habermas, 1996). Hence discourse ethics depends on the complementarity of autonomy-securing private rights with an institutional order that secures the public conditions for the exercise of such autonomy. In keeping with the procedural foundations of the theory, this institutional order should be composed of a comprehensive system of communicative rights that would allow publics to fully justify and apply the framework of private rights (Habermas, 2006; Johnson, 2006). Habermas's position is based upon the idea that once comprehensive provision for full communicative participation in democratic life is established, then establishing the substantive forms of a domination-free social life should lie with the participants themselves. Anything other than this would reverse the modernity-long tendency towards the proceduralization of morality and run the danger of a new dogmatism.

Habermas therefore retains the deontological core of Kant's categorical imperative, but it is now reoriented from a monological ethics of duty to a discourse ethics of communication. He differentiates himself from Rawls in this way too, distinguishing comprehensive intersubjective processes from the 'egological' constraints of the original position (Habermas, 1995). The deontological legacy of Kantian constructivism is retained in the concept of universalization, which precludes a monological justification of basic moral norms. Universalization defines the conditions of communicative exchange between plural perspectives. Habermas thereby reinterprets moral-practical reasoning in communicative terms, but the deontological claim to categorical rightness persists in this altered understanding. Rightness is, though, not to be considered as something any individual could by herself achieve. It is the outcome of a communicative procedure in which all affected can participate, fully assert their distinctive point of view, and come to an agreement to which all can subscribe. Hence, rightness depends on universalization.

The commitment to non-arbitrary standards of rightness as the basis of moral order is coupled by Habermas to a continuing faith in the enlightenment idea of the autonomy of the individual, freed from the shackles of traditional authority. Autonomy for Habermas comes not before but through communicative action, though he does transcendentally assume a capacity for moral intuition. It is the ability to reason in common that is the expression of autonomous will. Individuals use this will impartially in a comprehensive dialogical process to establish norms they can uphold. Deontological commitments of this kind, coupled with the primacy of the right over the good in legal-political affairs, give Habermas's version of discourse ethics a marked liberal dimension.

The deontological cast of the theory is strengthened by the manner in which Habermas associates morality with political justice. The moral-procedural core of discourse ethics asserts the primacy of democratic justice. Democratic justice is based on realizing facilitating conditions of communication such as publicity and inclusiveness, equal rights to engage in communication, exclusion of deception and illusion, and the absence of coercion. In essence, democratic justice of this kind is as far as justice can *formally* be stretched in Habermas's account. As Cohen and Arato put it, discourse ethics asks us to refrain from judging forms of life as such, an activity that is left to participants themselves (Cohen and Arato, 1994). Discourse ethical constructivism therefore maintains moral neutrality and thus separates itself from the content of practical discourse, a position that brings it into tension, amongst others, with communitarian republican interpretations of ethical life.

Discourse ethics therefore outlines how morally grounded inclusive and unhindered argumentation can generate agreement. Such moral agreement based on context-transcending validity claims in turn generates moral and legal norms that are basic to social integration.[5] Morally grounded discursive procedures are intrinsic to a just social order and designed to adjudicate amongst conflicting positions (Rehg, 1994). Consistent with much liberal political philosophy, Habermas proposes a clear separation of the spheres of morality and ethics (Forst, 2002). Moral rules shape inclusive and comprehensive justification and embody a deontological commitment to the primacy of the right in legal-political affairs.[6]

---

5   The issue of the 'realness' of substantive moral norms in Habermas's schema is taken up in Chapter 9.
6   The relationship between norms and values is a lively area for critical reflections on Habermas, as for example in both Putnam's and Cooke's critique of his sharp separation of norms and values (Cooke, 2006; Putnam, 2002). Nonetheless, Cooke is

Another reading of the status of the moral is also present in Habermas. The only substantive moral norms that could really stand the test of universalistic justification are those basic human and political rights that have constitutional standing. These liberal rights can be justified before the unlimited community of communication and are thus consistent with full public autonomy. By contrast, the ethical involves ideas of the good that are embodied in the concrete projects of different communities and groups. Such ideas cannot stand the test of universalization. They are justified through context-dependent rather than context-independent validity claims. Moral norms – as basic rights – operationalized through legal norms, on the one side, substantively shape ethical ideas of the good and moral standards of socialization and, on the other – as norms of fair procedure – they make possible a co-ordinated social life given different and often opposing ethical projects. While the procedure of justification is different, this account of the problem of morally based co-ordination of the legal-political order is similar to that of Rawls, and shows the extent of Habermas's association with deontological liberalism.

Nonetheless, while they share common roots in Kantian universalism, Habermas is more distant from Kant than Rawls and this distance indicates quite far-reaching differences with the broader liberal project. The break with monological accounts of moral reasoning is one indication of this difference and it draws attention to Habermas's far-reaching project of the detranscendentalization of Kant. Habermas sees Kant's theory as one-sidedly transcendental. Its basic framework attempts to separate the transcendent from the immanent. What in Rawls is the quasi-transcendental sense of justice that drives deliberation in the original position, in Kant is the mental apriorism of the faculty of judgement. Habermas moves the transcendental emphasis of both authors in an immanent-transcendent direction by conceiving of concrete subjects, capable of speech and action, embedded in the socio-cultural lifeworld in which justifications used in

at one with Habermas in stressing the importance of context-transcending validity claims, that is, validity claims that surpass any single cultural context and apply to humanity as a whole. By contrast with Habermas, she would see such validity claims as taking a macro-ethical and not just moral form.

argumentation must ultimately be grounded. Such justifications are ultimately dependent on validity claims that have to be capable of being immanently defended when tested.

The justificatory structure of validity claims draws attention back to Peirce's concept of the unlimited communication community. Actors deploying reasons in speech acts have to be able to demonstrate their 'warranted assertability' against basic validity standards such as those of truth or normative rightness. Habermas shows how the over-emphasis in the empiricist tradition on the truth of assertoric statements neglects the action-co-ordinating validity claim of moral rightness contained in regulative speech acts (Habermas, 2003). Regulative speech acts are based on the standard, different from propositional truth, of what all can accept as just by means of domination-free discursive procedures. This distinction is directed against the imposition of a propositional semantics of truth as the only evaluative standard for social and political life. Normative structures are not simply a teleological product of the human accommodation with nature, or the result of the permanence of a domination that can never be assuaged. They are also the product of human co-operation achieved through various kinds of linguistically achieved intersubjectivity. The rationality that guides normative argumentation is therefore different from propositional truth and ultimately undergirds the possibility of a morally justifiable social order that is not superordinate to claims associated with social or natural facts.[7]

Rehg points out that there is an inextricable link between the way Habermas conceives of the process of moral universalization and his theory of social order (Rehg, 1994). At an evolutionary level, discourse ethics rests

---

7   Habermas's distinction between the different validity claims associated with assertoric and regulative speech acts is highly significant for the assumption of value-freedom, the credo of letting the empirically revealed world speak, which has been a key part of sociological epistemology throughout the twentieth century. Sociology has shown great reluctance, even in its critical manifestations, to *argue* normatively as distinct from criticizing existing norms. It may be noted that Apel offers a reflexive methodology of inquiry that offers a means of normative argumentation that is consistent with the requirements of empirical-theoretical, as well as normative, disciplines like sociology (Böhler, 2003).

on the idea that human sociation cannot be understood as the product of force and fraud. Force and fraud must instead be understood against the background of the necessity of co-operation. The regulative idea and co-ordinating mechanism of such co-operation is intersubjective communication. In modern pluralistic and complex societies, social order comes to depend fundamentally on the morally structured communicative procedures that guarantee both equality and autonomy and lead to well-justified substantive norms.

It is easier to conceive of discourse ethics through the prism of those procedures needed to resolve social conflicts and differences; in other words, where the moral dimensions associated with disputes are made apparent. However, discourse ethics ranges more widely. In Habermas's account, it extends on the basis of Kant's idea of technical-practical, moral-practical, and aesthetic kinds of reason to the 'wider spectrum of reasons used in communicative action' such as 'epistemic reasons for the truth of statements, ethical orientations and modes of actions as indicators for the authenticity of life choices or the sincerity of confessions, and, depending on the issue, aesthetic experiences, narrative declarations, cultural standards of value, legal claims, conventions and so on' (Habermas, 2008, p. 38). He goes on to say that accountability involves more than the moral register of practical reason, in other words, the deployment of unconditional moral principles. It also depends on 'the general ability of an agent to orientate her action by validity claims' (ibid.). Habermas signals here the importance of the interpenetration of validity claims, an insight that is translated into a macro-sociological framework in Part III.

Drawing from the discussion so far, Habermas respectively distinguishes not just between normativity and truth, but also between morality and ethics. In making these distinctions, drawing from Kant, he nonetheless establishes post-Kantian *communicative* foundations for these validity claims. The account of the interpenetration of validity claims, which Habermas never fully develops, may be understood from a Kantian standpoint as the mediation of Kant's three value spheres that Habermas in the neo-Kantian tradition sees as basic to modern life. But understanding this as a process of mediation of cultural spheres on the 'horizontal' plane is not sufficient to grasp the significance of Habermas's reworking of Kant. He also brings to bear a communicative reconstruction of Kant on the 'vertical' plane with regard to the mediation of societal levels that join meso-communicative with macro- and micro-levels. He outlines how Kant conceives of an agent's self-understanding as a person's knowledge of herself and how he abstractly opposes such self-understanding to an observer's third-person knowledge. The observer cannot know the subjective state of another person. In establishing this divide, Kant creates a transcendental gap between these two forms of knowledge so that agents' self-understanding cannot be corrected by empirical knowledge generated in the third-person perspective. Habermas contrasts this with the situation of speakers and addressees in communication in which actors take on first- and second-person roles against the backdrop of an intersubjectively shared lifeworld that enables them to make sense of one another's utterances. The addition of communicative intersubjectivity between first- and third-person perspectives delineates a mediated position between third-, second- and first-person knowledge that is both reproduced and potentially transformed in communication (Habermas, 2000).

Various epistemological distinctions separate discourse ethics from the political philosophies outlined in Part I, with the exception of the deliberative. Already, in this part of the book, a basic distinction was drawn between Habermas and Rawls with respect to the detranscendentalization of Kant and the capacity of publics to reason in common; a further distinction made between truth and rightness epistemologically separates discourse ethics from political realism; while the distinction made between morality and ethics separates Habermas from republican ideas of the good. A further distinction, that between formality and context, separates discourse ethics from radical epistemologies. This last distinction also overlaps that between discourse ethics and republican conceptions of the good.

The balance that Habermas strikes between formality and context has generated controversy. Contextualist arguments about the diminution of the good in discourse ethics converge with ethics of care arguments that claim that the theory lacks the capacity to grasp embodied situations (Benhabib, 1987; Cooke, 2006; Gilligan, 1982). Universalist arguments are claimed to represent dominant positions that under the guise of impartiality can specify what discourses count as moral. This universalism is presented as a contradiction in terms. Both by virtue of the norms it has historically generated, and even more by the manner in which these norms are interpreted and applied, it is claimed that it excludes critical dimensions of power and injustice whose victims remain without influence.

Two related points are at the heart of this ethics of care argument. The first relates to the standing and comprehensiveness of the idealizations that Habermas claims must underpin the communicative procedures of discourse ethics. The second questions the procedures used in justifying norms and how they are applied. For present purposes, it is not proposed to take up these points in depth, merely highlighting below how discourse ethics develops its own arguments in the context of these debates.

In certain respects, discourse ethics offers a merely formal account of which social positions and which arguments should be presented in communicative procedures. As long as conditions for democratic justice are sustained by public and private autonomy, including conditions of full publicity, respectful reciprocity, and openness of the agenda, in addition to a spectrum of other rights that guarantee status equality, then it is up to participants themselves to fully justify norms. In the republican formulation often used by Habermas, the subjects of laws are the authors of the laws that bind them. Discourse ethics can respond to arguments that no communication process can ever fully do justice to positional differences, that there will always be a significant dimension of domination by the powerful, by suggesting that its goal is the clarification of the necessary counterfactual conditions of domination-free discourse.

These counterfactual conditions may not be capable of being perfectly realized in the contingent circumstances of real communication processes. They nonetheless remain present as standards of ethical responsibility in the form of universal pragmatic presuppositions that give form to this communication. The considerations that should be properly included in such processes remain open to advances in human understanding, emotional re-orientation, and the revision of ethical systems. Issues previously excluded from political debate, such as the rights of women and minorities could be better, if far from perfectly, represented today due to collective learning processes and associated institutionalization. To put it in more colloquial terms, discourse ethics is not committed to the perfect realization of ideal conditions of discourse for all societal problems any time soon. It is merely committed in that sense to establishing the conditions to which such ideal discourse should aspire.

With respect to the relationship between justification and applications, discourse ethics, as Rehg makes clear, is not committed to the idea that participants in justification processes have an omniscient capacity to foresee all present and future problems of application (Rehg, 1994). Even fully justified norms need appropriate kinds of application that can address either unforeseen complexity in the application of the norm, or circumstances where contradictions become apparent between norms that are individually but not relationally justified in the context offered by other justified norms. The application of norms in other words follows relational logics of appropriateness and consequences, which are not fully determined by the prior logic of justification.[8] Learning initiated by application problems of a justified norm will require a renewal of the justificatory process and the possible correction or replacement of the norm. Universalization of norms provides the normative standard for their democratic acceptability.

The communicative epistemology of discourse ethics is based upon identifying conditions of intersubjective discursive learning that can address the various challenges presented by alternative political epistemologies. It does this by retaining a transcendental position in positing unavoidable, formal presuppositions of rational argumentation. Discourse ethics – here with reference to Habermas in particular – has been engaged in a protracted debate with other traditions to advance the epistemological and practical significance of its viewpoint. It tries to incorporate Rawls's transcendental idea of principles of justice achieved by the normative use of reason; it distinguishes the moral and the ethical, but allows a significant place for

---

8   Norms affect other norms in application in that agents have to balance out their respective implications, hence the term 'relational'. In modern society, such relational balancing of norms, or normative integration, is often extremely complex. How does an agent, for example, desiring to buy a car with an ethically clear conscience distinguish between those components that generate ethical problems, for example, environmental, from other components that do not do so, or at least not in the same way.

ethical values in contexts of application; it seeks to establish the distinctive nature of normative argumentation, while retaining insight into the facticity of states of affairs; and it tries to incorporate fundamental learning processes arising from new experiences and the articulations of needs claims. By virtue of its basic epistemology, and through these exchanges, discourse ethics opens up the conditions and mechanisms of rational intersubjective communication and discursive learning on the meso-level, generating a mediating epistemological position between the different cultural spheres of modernity and between the different levels of social organization and experience that range from macro, through meso, to micro.

Discourse Ethics, Democratic Practice and the Theory of Society

Moral Foundations and Political Conditions

Discourse ethics lies in the interstices of democratic and social theory, yet it has frequently been criticized for its lack of realism. The criticisms offered by systems theory and post-structuralism serve as examples. Systems theory criticizes discourse ethics for its continuing adherence to the enlightenment ideal of a society that in spite of growing complexity can still be epistemically organized on the basis of normative principles. Post-structuralism criticizes it for neglect of the language game of power that infiltrates rational argumentation and disables it. Partly in response to these kinds of criticism and partly for intrinsic reasons, Apel and Habermas seek to add realism to the theory by addressing how discursive co-ordination can proceed in the actual conditions of political life.

Apel distinguishes between Part A and Part B of the theory. Part A applies to benign circumstances for democracy in which its counterfactual validity claims can be institutionally realized. Part B, by contrast, applies to circumstances where the institutional facilitating conditions of discourse ethics are absent. Rather than a consensual communicative rationality, as in Part A, a strategic rationality is institutionally dominant (Apel, 2001). Even in circumstances characterized by Part B, Apel argues that ethically grounded discourse is still possible. Such discourse, in the right circumstances, might facilitate a shift from strategic to consensual forms of communicative rationality as soon as conditions allow. Consequently, certain kinds of strategic action are justified in Part B type scenarios. The criterion for such justification is based upon the possible future realization of discourse ethics, Part A. In the Part B scenario, full conditions for the realization of discourse ethics would then be 'anticipated' in that strategic communication would be informed by what is absent and should be present.

What Apel describes as Part B, designed primarily to address non-democratic societies, may also be applied in some respects to the normal situation of 'fully functioning' modern democracies in which social freedom substantially operates. Such societies are far from completely characterized by conditions approximating to Part A. Indeed, when Apel describes the nature of contemporary international relations he sketches a 'realistic' institutional translation of the self-organizing and independent logic of discursive procedures of the kind envisaged in Part A (ibid.). That is to say, democratic discourses occur in institutional environments characterized by a mixed kind of rationality. In these circumstances, not everything is open to be thought through anew. The results of prior processes cannot be continuously re-examined, nor can future possibilities due to epistemic limitations always be adequately anticipated. The degree to which conditions of discursivity and universalization prescribed in the theory can be realized is variable. The justification of norms operates in a mixed mode form, with Part A and Part B kinds of rationality commingling. In the real conditions of democratic life, procedures have limited autonomy, which forces participants to make extra-procedural judgements about epistemic and moral matters.

The mixed mode scenario is more plausible and constitutes the 'reality model' of the theory, though it is not fully carried through in the theory. In line with such a reality model, Habermas's earlier *The Theory of Communication Action*, written before his deliberative democratic turn, actually envisaged political communication as being powerfully influenced by the symbolically generalized medium of power that operates as a relief mechanism for an overburdened lifeworld. This left his normative theory relatively weak. Norms were understood as one of three cultural components of the everyday lifeworld, along with epistemic culture and expressive identity. He did not demonstrate how overarching norms regulated both system and lifeworld and, accordingly, assumed systems to operate beyond intersubjective norms. Another normative meta-perspective, drawing from the Marxist theory of reification, was introduced that drew attention to the dangers of the 'colonization of the lifeworld' by de-normatized systems.

The theory of democracy and with it the renewal of his earlier theory of the public sphere that had almost no role in *Communicative Action*, re-emerges in his later work, operating as a third term between system and lifeworld. The extent to which democracy has been realized on the basis of true public autonomy illustrates discourse ethical progress, even if actual democracy falls far short of the counterfactual ideal. In *Between Facts and Norms* (Habermas, 1996, pp. 55–56), Habermas returns to the relationship between system and lifeworld by means of a critique of Teubner's theory of law. He shows how Teubner is forced for empirical reasons to introduce the concept of lifeworld to describe the encompassing communication of society beyond the specialized and closed codes of social systems. The lifeworld is a kind of reflexive structure that allows for translations between all the system codes.

Habermas then claims that Teubner can only mean, even if he doesn't say so, that the lifeworld is reproduced by means of ordinary language communication. Habermas places this observation in the context created by the distinction he himself draws between the internal differentiation of the lifeworld and the differentiation of the media-steered systems of power and money from this lifeworld. A democratically constructed law now becomes the normative translation mechanism between the lifeworld and social systems that was absent in *Communicative Action*. With respect to the system of public administration, law translates the communicative power generated by public sovereignty into administrative programming. In this way, Habermas introduces a mediated and 'realist' account of the communicative presuppositions of discourse ethics into his theory of democracy.

Between Facts and Norms completes the project of the *Theory of Communicative Action*. In *Communicative Action*, the relative rigidity of the distinction between system and lifeworld allowed a political system, steered via the medium of power, to remain too autonomous from civil society and the public sphere. Indeed, the latter terms played an extremely limited role in this earlier theoretical synthesis. *Between Facts and Norms* corrects for this and gives the public sphere, as the carrier of currents of opinion arising in the civil societal periphery, a much stronger role in democratizing the space between system and lifeworld. The debate with systems theory appears then as a debate with a form of political realism. In spite of many differences, such a version of political realism has strong compatibilities with Habermas's project in operating with a communicative theory of society with a strong phenomenologically grounded counterfactual dimension. The difference between Habermas and systems theory is ultimately about whether the counterfactual standpoint should give primacy to functionally understood systems or normatively understood institutions.

The discursive and deliberative theory of democracy, conjoined with a revisiting of his theory of society, allowed Habermas in *Between Facts and Norms* to extend the framework of discourse ethics to the reproduction of society as a whole. The moral framework of discourse ethics, equality of rights to participate and equal responsibility for outcomes, procedurally structures deliberation and allows the fullest possible argumentation on the respective status of different validity claims so as to generate just material norms in the democratic constitutional state. This moral framework is designed to address the complex co-ordination problems of modern life, arising from the proliferation of collective identities and autonomy-seeking social spheres. Discourse ethics, taking effect within the legal-political contexts of deliberation and discursive will formation, offers an account of how society in the right circumstances could be morally integrated in a manner that is respectful of social plurality and functional differentiation.

Not just Habermas, but also Rawls and other liberal and deliberative theorists of democracy, have grappled with the challenge to democracy offered by social plurality and functional differentiation. Habermas and Rawls are perhaps notable for the extent to which they do so by means of the theory of society, even if the latter does so only implicitly. As explored above, Rawls separates public reason, the means of developing and sustaining a political conception of justice, from the plurality of comprehensive conceptions of justice in social life generally. He examines how the development and sustaining of a political conception of justice in public reason should lead to justifiable standards for the organization of society's basic institutional structure. Public reason has a stabilizing effect on society's basic structure by supporting widely accepted principles of justice (Rawls, 1993).

Habermas develops a more emphatic society-wide conception of public discourse that, unlike Rawls, he does not want to separate from institutionally located public reason. Habermas holds against Rawls that a comprehensive idea of public discourse should give more room to the discourses of citizens (Habermas, 1995). In Habermas's account, discourses of political justification comprehensively reach from the civil societal 'periphery' to the decision-making 'core' of the legal-political order. He understands this process as the discursive formation of political will. Will formation is achieved by a public that is at least potentially active and influential and not diminished in importance, as with Rawls, by the hold of specialized, elite deliberation in the 'higher order' of public reason (Habermas, 1996; Rawls, 1993).

Public will formation is achieved by means of the unfolding logic in the public sphere of a series of differentiated discourses, pragmatic, ethical, moral, and legal. The discursive manner in which political will is formed reaches into the political administrative core as a conditioning influence on deliberation and legal programming. Overall, in Rawls's terminology but differently from him, the implication is that public reason and public discourse mutually and regularly condition one another. This gives substance to two foundational principles of discourse ethics, the principles of Discursivity (D) and Universalization (U). These principles, specifying the conditions of a fully informed, fully inclusive, and fully responsible process of justification, contrast with the third party, restricted quality of Rawls's account. This observation is not sufficient to show that Rawls's emphasis on public reason over public discourse is empirically wrong. If it is empirically right, and is all that could reasonably be expected of modern democratic forms, normative consequences may follow from it. The difference rather expresses a more fundamental disagreement on the nature of those deontological normative commitments that should be regarded as necessary presuppositions of a just and responsible democratic order.

Complexity, Democracy, and Public Participation

From his earlier work on the theory of society in *Communicative Action* onwards, Habermas broadly accepts the notion of a differentiated, polycentric society, but with one essential difference to that of systems theory, the primacy accorded to the moral level of social integration orchestrated through public discourse. The polycentric theory of society, best associated with Niklas Luhmann, understands society as composed of a series of differentiated, operatively closed systems that function autonomously as zones of specialized action-organizing communication (Luhmann, 1982; Willke, 1992). Habermas accepts the autonomy of certain social systems and their communication codes (Habermas, 1984, Habermas, 1987). However, especially as clarified in *Between Facts and Norms*, moral-legal discourses should be regarded as circulating around such systems qualifying their autonomy – or operative closure – in critical respects. The public sphere is the mechanism whereby discursive and deliberative processes come into play in these systems, asserting the primacy of democratic politics over them. The discursively and deliberative structured political system is specialized in the goal of achieving social integration, achieved through the discursive construction and institutional application of normative culture. Such a culture should in the end prevail over functional considerations of strategy and success. It should do so without denying the autonomy of spheres of action where such considerations are dominant, such as the economy and science, or others, like the political system itself, where they are important but are not dominant – or at least should not be.

Habermas combines a theory of functional differentiation, both of social systems and between system and lifeworld, with a theory of modern quasi-segmentary differentiation arising from the core-periphery architecture of what he terms the constitutional circuit of power, a term he takes from Bernhard Peters (Habermas, 1996; Peters, 1993). In this second kind of differentiation, perception of normative problems, to take a few examples, unacceptable levels of inequality, disrespect, and alienation, first arise in civil society, which is assumed to constitute the societal periphery. Over time, in cases of successful mobilization, these normative problem perceptions become converted into communicative power by means of the discursive process of public will formation in the public sphere, penetrate the core and become normatively binding through law. A third kind of differentiation, stratificatory differentiation, increasingly disconnected from the theory of class, takes the form of structurally conditioned differentials of access to the public sphere. The later Habermas assumes that such power differentials, at least potentially, can be transposed into the consensual form of communicative power in a fairly organized public sphere, which, over time, enables normative inequalities to be resolved. It is therefore essential that the public sphere is participatively open, epistemically comprehensive, and interactively adequate so that something like what Nancy Fraser calls 'participatory parity' can prevail (Forst, 2007a; Fraser and Honneth, 2003).

Overall, this theoretical architecture depends on the capacity of 'wild' public and deliberatively organized discourses to pick up and normatively address societal problems. To the extent that it can do so, differentials of social power can be processed and minimized. The societal instantiation of discourse ethics thereby assumes that deliberative-discursive processes should – ideally – prevail over imbalances of social power. In an essay, 'Political Communication in Media Society: Does Democracy still Enjoy an Epistemic Function?', Habermas illustrates this understanding of power (Habermas, 2006). Problems in the functioning of the public sphere relate less to differentials of power in civil society or to the status and capacities of publics in communication and more to structural factors in the organization of communication. He instances in the latter regard the lack of differentiation of the media from the economic system in Italy and, more generally, the inadequate feedback between civil society and mediated political communication that he attributes to problems in the structure of political communication itself.

In this essay, Habermas claims that the public sphere is not itself deliberative, because it is characterized 'at the bottom' by the non-procedural, face-to-face nature of everyday or associational interaction. Moreover, the space in between the deliberative top, located in the political core, and the conversational bottom is characterized by mediated communication, which also follows a non-deliberative logic. The core-periphery architecture therefore allows the separation of the discursive public sphere from the deliberative political core. The idea that the public sphere is not itself deliberative raises the question of how its discursive forms relate to deliberation. Habermas describes political communication in terms of a directional complex that operates as a mode of eliminating pathological differentials of social power on the one side, and yet is compatible with the universalistic procedures of deliberative democracy on the other. Initially 'wild' public discourse gives way to organized, 'anonymous' discourses and then to inclusive deliberation. He thereby develops a notion of communicative power, that when functioning correctly, that is, non-pathologically, aligns discursively organized public will formation and deliberative procedures.

In *Between Facts and Norms*, Habermas both shows faith in the democratic competence of civil societal associations, while expressing reservations that the public sphere is moving in the right direction to take full advantage of the partly realized but still extensively subdued normative potentials of democracy. On the plus side, associational life in civil society retains the capacity to generate collective identities and construct publics so as to pursue new needs claims. It was the periphery, in his view, that had generated the big 'responsibility' issues of the early 1990s, ecological, global justice, and the arms race, and not big organizations, social systems, or governments. Civil societal associations play a critical role in mobilizing the public sphere, a role that can lead to a new political agenda and potential political and wider social change. If they are to succeed in this, they require both that their messages resonate in the mass media and hence gain wider public support, and show the capacity to make normative arguments that can be translated into a deliberatively constructed law.

More pessimistically, Habermas reiterates his older argument from *Communicative Action* that civil society remains in danger of systemic colonization by means of economic and administrative power. These power complexes, for example, through the paternalism of the clientelist welfare state or through the undue political influence of economic power have the capacity to block the formulation of effective need claims. Publics operating at the informal end of the public sphere, even with its sophisticated channels of communication, may be unable to translate ideal innovations on the periphery into norms at the institutional core. This is not always the case and, for Habermas, the feminist movement provides one successful counter-example that exploits the normative potentials of liberal democratic institutions (Habermas, 1996; Johnson, 2006).

Changes in discourses and procedures constantly reconstruct the relationship between democratic institutions and their societal environment. The requirement of translating peripheral discursive innovation into legitimate, just, and effective norms entails that political discourses must be able to handle the complexity of modern societies. Such complexity leads to the fundamental contemporary democratic problem raised by Claus Offe: how may just and responsible action be democratically instituted in conditions of complex interdependencies and destructive potentials (Offe, 1987, 1992)? The manner in which Offe addresses this question, along with Habermas's long-running exchange with Luhmann, indicates the significance of the debate with systems theory for critical theory.

According to systems theory, there is no longer any privileged standpoint from which the rationality of society as a whole can be gauged. This is both a descriptive and a normative stance. On the basis of a description of the organizational logic of modern societies, the normative conclusion is reached that action that fails to recognize the boundaries of social systems risks an evolutionarily reversal of the rationalities necessary for modern society that have been differentiated in a long learning process. Luhmann prioritizes, therefore, societal differentiation processes that constrain social action into system conforming patterns (Luhmann, 1982).

While recognizing the explanatory value of the differentiation model of systems theory, Habermas descriptively understands and normatively evaluates the development of modern society differently. In the account given in *Between Facts and Norms*, actors in society are not simply helpless in the face of systemic rationality but *to some degree* interrogate it, choose it, and change it in processes of deliberation. They do this within the discursive framework of the democratic order. This discursive framework is composed of networks of communication that range from procedurally well-ordered 'parliamentary' public spheres to procedurally diffuse but culturally innovative 'mass' public spheres. Political communication in these spheres both subjects the outcomes of politics to discursive testing and formulates new political agendas. Deliberatively justified norms, formed under pressure from the communicative power generated by discursively formed will, constrain the autonomy of systems.

In *Communicative Action*, Habermas operates with a two-track model of societal reproduction emphasizing social and system integration respectively. Though much has evolved in his theoretical writing since, he has never gone back on this distinction. His account of the interrelationship between the two types of integration allows significant autonomy for the functioning of 'formally organized' social systems, such as the economy and administration, from the constraints of normative culture, even if ultimately a democratically formed normative culture must have primacy. Moving between the different imperatives of system and life world, Habermas has sought over time a satisfactory middle between the unmasking critique of social pathologies and 'disclosing' critique of immanent institutional and discursive potentials (Strydom, 2011).

He views society as consisting of overlapping and competing rationalities consisting of a functional orientation to technical and economic rationality, a moral-normative orientation to social order and the reconciliation of conflict, and an ethical orientation to expressive community-building, incorporating designs for the good life and the interpretation of needs. The core of deliberative politics, in a descriptive sense, is how society's problem-solving capacities in each of these dimensions may be discursively mobilized so as to maintain a social and system integration that is not closed to further learning. From a normative perspective, in part realized in contemporary societies, it involves the further assumption that *all* citizens have participated in producing the given outcomes, even if they do not absolutely agree on the final form.

The functional, normative, and expressive dimensions of culture have to be communicatively balanced so as to make possible the continuation of a democratically ordered society in conditions of polycentric differentiation. Rational responsibility depends on 'strong', deliberatively responsive, democracy, which is substantively and procedurally constantly evolving. New kinds of needs articulated by actors on the periphery gradually enter into democratic discourses and then, through norm building, penetrate democratic and other functional arrangements that regulate the pace and direction of social change.

From the standpoint of Habermas's discursive-deliberative model of politics, Offe's call for complexity reduction by reducing interdependencies between action spheres depends on the capacity of publics to clarify what counts as responsible action that would not burden its environments with unmanageable externalities. Deliberative politics, in principle, offers the possibility of dealing with the problem of inter-system co-ordination and of reducing unmanageable complexity, not necessarily only by confining the issue of responsibility within specific systems, but potentially also by improving the efficacy of the communicative mechanisms that exchange meaning between them. The deliberative model, in Habermas's formulation, leaves open Offe's options of managing increased complexity or reducing overall complexity. It depends on the practical rationality of deliberating publics whether higher or lower levels of interdependency can in fact be managed.

In *Between Facts and Norms*, Habermas illustrates this approach by bringing together discursive democratic and system-theoretical considerations. This arises from his critique of Willke's systems-theoretical model with its neo-Hegelian and neo-corporatist undertones (Willke, 1992). According to Habermas, Willke ascribes the role of supervision to the grey zones between state and society, where entities such as round tables, concerted actions, and co-ordination mechanisms of all kinds are located. Willke calls these phenomena symptomatic action systems. He regards their capacity to solve problems to be constrained by the autonomous rationalities of the different social systems, which they must either respect or suffer the fate of irrelevance. They are therefore disconnected from the discursive and normative logics of public spheres – whose efficacy Willke in any case doubts. He can therefore follow Luhmann in postulating the disappearance of the primacy of the political system, while bringing the state back in through the backdoor as the guarantor of social integration. Social integration is thereby achieved by means of an account of state and societal power that does not include a clear moral-normative function for the public sphere, about whose capacity to resonate across differentiated social systems the theory remains pessimistic. This theoretical stance makes peripheral demands for just and responsible action hard to conceive, as opposed to technical adjustments to the non-normative logics of social systems.

Habermas, by contrast, on the basis of a three-fold criticism of Willke's model, reasserts the centrality of the public sphere as the medium through which norms of responsibility are defended or extended by a variety of communicating publics. He claims, firstly, that Willke's model illustrates how systems theory has lost the idea of a common world that was at the heart of Hobbes's idea as to why individual interests should be co-ordinated. Systems theory is unable to escape from the multi-sided non-transparency of the relations between self-referencing, autopoietic social systems, that is, social systems that are autonomous, normatively closed, and self-transforming under environmental stimulus. Such social systems need rules to integrate how they relate to one another. Systems theory is unable to provide such rules because of its limiting assumption of the reciprocal observation of semantically closed systems disconnected from public discourse. This leans too much to understanding social integration as system integration and fails to account for the power of the ethical and moral-normative dimensions of social integration that become influential through public discourse.

Secondly, Habermas considers as merely contingent the normative idea advanced by Willke that individual rights are somehow served by the requisite level of differentiation between function systems. While the relation between differentiation and liberty is important, the efficiency and reproducibility of function systems has to be normatively controlled by the counter-power of individual and collective claims emanating from the periphery directed against the danger of systems paternalism. Thirdly, Habermas disputes Willke's assumption that co-ordination between function systems can be seen only as a problem of expert shaping, as this co-ordination also depends on the nature of the public sphere, where experts emanating from the function systems have to engage in discussion with counter-experts controlled by public opinion.

These criticisms of the inter-systemic co-ordination model of systems theory lead back to Habermas's belief that various kinds of discursive and deliberative communication, operating through differentiated but interconnected public spheres, are necessary to the achievement of inter-systemic rationality in complex, democratic societies. The mass public sphere offers the widest framework whereby democratic societies reflect upon themselves. In Habermas's sense, the public sphere represents the stage on which societal actors in the political community – individuals, collectives, organizations, and associations – can call systemic complexes to order.

The institutionalization of communicative power in public spheres and parliamentary bodies provides a responsibility-demanding society with the means of influencing administrative and political decisions. This may vary widely depending on the system in question. Habermas notes the difference between the market system, which is only indirectly connected to the lifeworld, the spheres of law, education, and science that stand between system and lifeworld, and the private, intimate milieus that are closest to the lifeworld (Habermas, 1996). The degree of public influence will also depend, though less stressed by Habermas, on the character of political mobilization on the periphery, the structural conditions that feed into the mobilization, its organization, its goals, and the context supplied by social, cultural, and political opportunity structures (Kitschelt, 1986).

The manner in which Habermas connects the inter-systemic co-ordination model of systems theory with the normative theory of the public sphere establishes the grounds for a mediated relationship between them. It also allows for a corresponding relationship between the thus strengthened theory of society and democratic theory that could together be made consistent with a discourse ethics that in this way acquires greater realism. In this account, the model of stratificatory differentiation linked to the capitalist generation of class differences is relegated to a lesser position and a combined theory of quasi-segmentary differentiation embracing the core-periphery model and functional differentiation as part of a polycentric theory of society given more prominence.

Discourse ethics is extended in Habermas to offer a theory of modern democracy that is grounded in an equivalent social theory, combining deliberative proceduralism with the discursive formation of public will. The combined political and social theory constructively engages with other democratic traditions. It addresses the claims of political realism through its engagement with systems theory's non-normative account of political activity. Here, Habermas seeks to balance a theory of functional and communicative power. With respect to Rawls and liberalism generally, Habermas accepts the idea of a system of basic human rights that have 'equiprimordial' origins with the right to make rights that characterizes public autonomy. He further accepts, most emphasized in communitarian republican theories, the importance of practices specific to a way of life that are given shape and meaning by a political culture. Within normative theory, Habermas attempts to reconcile liberal and republican standpoints. He grounds the moral foundations of public autonomy in the basic telos of human communication revealed in discourse ethics. A public autonomy thus conceived recognizes the equiprimordiality of liberal private rights. It would also, as a communicative practice, accept the contextual foundations of justification by allowing society-specific values to shape the multiple paths for realizing both discursivity and universalization.

This is a bold attempt to link democratic theory with the theory of society. Discourse ethics provides a standard for the reconstruction of the intersubjective foundations of democratic communication and thereby compels critical consideration of its performance and identifies potentials for its improvement. These transcendental normative standards that lie beyond the facticity of existing communication can nonetheless be brought to bear upon it as presuppositions of a communicative rationality that may, in these practices, be met or violated. From Habermas's point of view, not just formal political communication in deliberative forums can be assessed according to the standard of communicative rationality. Beyond, this, as part of a communicative theory of society, all kinds of politically relevant communication can be assessed from this standard. This encompassing account of communicative rationality incorporates liberal, republican, radical, and realist motifs within a deliberative framework.

CHAPTER 9

Deontology and Democracy: Limits to the Primacy of the Right

Discourse ethics has a two-fold relation to immanent social practices. On the one hand, it operates as an idealization, gesturing towards a *future* state of justification that could, on the basis of the social realization of formal pragmatic presuppositions of communication, be fully transparent, inclusive, and reciprocal. On the other hand, the operation of societal discourse within *actual* deliberative procedures is already a kind of imperfect, but real, discourse ethics in practice. This discourse ethics in practice represents a moral achievement of democracy, realized above all in the framework of rights, modern and ancient. From the discourse ethical perspective, this moral progress may be interpreted as the social realization of the formal pragmatic presuppositions of communication. The moral diagnosis of discourse ethics, therefore, relies on the manner in which formal pragmatic validity claims are immanently realized in social practice. Discourse ethics as a normative theory, developed after the fact of such historical realization, serves to retrospectively reconstruct such achievements. But, as a critical theory, the counterfactual, reconstructive standards it proposes are also used, by demonstrating their non- or only partial realization, to identify the pathologies and blockages that have impeded the full realization of available potentials.

Discourse ethics thus works with both a constructivist and reconstructive methodology. It is constructivist in the radical sense of accepting that publics, both historically and currently, are capable of reconstructive rationality. Academics do not do it on their behalf, as the academic habitus tends to assume; rather, academics are part of the process of socio-cultural innovation, which is of many different kinds. Discourse ethics in this sense adds to the reconstructive rationality that publics are already performing, revealing the consequences of choices such publics may make in their world-constructing activity. Publics, through theoretically assisted collective learning, can in turn deviate from embedded or follow new paths.

The category of 'publics' has a wide range of reference, spanning institutional and extra-institutional contexts, and allows for great variety in the focus of normative theories. In the range of normative traditions developed in Part I, distinctions may be made between institutional public actors and societal publics of different kinds that correspond to the various theories. Discourse ethics, as explored in the previous chapter, brings to bear a strong version of democratic justice whose aim is to create a power balance between various publics. If this can be achieved, communicative power, the power that publics through public discourse confer on legitimate political authorities, can fully function. This concept of communicative power entails that discourse ethics is committed to a strong theory of democratic justice in which all affected have full opportunity to shape the public agenda and contribute to norm building.

The commitment to the primacy of democratic justice reveals discourse ethics as a procedural theory of justice. While the procedural core of the theory is foundational, discourse ethics in several important respects tends towards the kind of normative idealization that separates it from actual processes and mechanisms of political change. This is not necessarily a weakness in itself. The term 'normative idealization' refers in this context to the idea that procedural mechanisms may be instituted that fully decide important questions of justice in some possible world. The world as it is should, as far as possible, tend in that direction. The essence of the idea is that where full access to democratic justice is made possible, substantive questions of justice become theoretically and practically secondary. The normative challenge for political theories is to provide arguments in favour of comprehensive, inclusive, civil, and fully reciprocal procedural justice.

The universalistic, discursive ideal of discourse ethics conforms to the deep heartbeat of the democratic principles of modernity. The culture and institutional orders of modernity are infused with the idea that all should be equally treated, and should have a right to assert their opinion, though the condition of *equal* voice is heavily disputed. There is a reason why equal treatment and equality of voice are regarded differently. Given the complexity, plurality, and volatility of modern society, the *normative-procedural* ideal as represented in discourse ethics appears unrealizable.

So, circumstances obtain where the normative ideal is defensible, but the normative model cannot institutionally provide for it.

Yet, the apparent contradiction is allowed to continue. Habermas often writes as if the discursive-deliberative ideal of discourse ethics was realized in existing democratic procedures, though at another level he is aware that moral principles and legal norms did not come into being in that way. They emerged through real societal argumentation processes that over time, by means of social struggle and *combined* deliberative, discursive, and legal elaboration in multiple arenas, acquired a universalistic quality. Habermas's theory does not contain a full and consistent sense of these struggles and their outcomes. His version of discourse ethics, counterfactually grounding validity claims beyond the real communication community in the idealized forum of the unlimited communication community, tends to privilege transcendental ideality over present actuality. The manner and the extent to which actual democratic practices may generate a substantive moral-legal framework – the formal or informal constitution – do not receive sustained examination.

Neither does Habermas make clear what for him would constitute substantive moral principles and how they are actually generated by social actors combining immanent and transcendent horizons, as opposed to how they might be ideally justified by other grounding, transcendental principles. Substantive principles have a shadowy existence in his work in that they appear to only be immanently realized through law. It is thus to law in *Between Facts and Norms* that Habermas extends his efforts, showing how social integration depends on deliberatively achieved, legitimate legal norms. Following Niquet, this solution, transferring the challenge of applying moral norms to law, cannot be regarded as satisfactory (Niquet, 2003); it does not address what is moral action in its own right. To address this, Niquet proposes that a concept of situated moral experience is essential. Moral action should be understood as taking place in contexts that are also characterized by non-moral or un-moral action, and to be informed by the interests, preferences, and worldviews of morally competent subjects. It should not be assumed to take place in an ideal, deliberative forum rising above such contexts.

The relationship between morality and procedure is weakened in Niquet's formulation. As understood by discourse ethics, the relationship absorbs immanent practices into transcendent idealizations. The contexts of experience that Niquet sees as generative of moral action, in conjunction with other kinds of action, extend beyond those that are procedurally regulated to multiple non-procedural or weakly procedural arenas of public discourse (Hilgartner and Bosk, 1988). These contexts are not mainly concerned with making decisions; they are concerned with building agendas and specifying moral and ethical principles. In short, they are shaped by, reproduce, and build a normative culture.

The building of a normative culture, addressed in more detail in Part III, is a communicative achievement and far from only a procedural one. It is what allows the public to see itself as what Dewey called it, the most general of all associations (Dewey, 1927). The question of democratic justice should not therefore be seen as only a normative-procedural accomplishment; it is to be regarded more broadly as a cognitive achievement arising from the communicative construction of the 'mind of society', especially that part of it that frames its normative culture. This is the second sense of democratic justice that complements the normative-procedural version and it calls for the democratization of the production of non-procedural discourses in the communication arenas of the public sphere. The democratization of the means of communication is central to public participation in democracy.

Public participation in this cultural-communicative sense does not oppose the normative-procedural extension of democratic justice. But it is unrealistic to suppose that normative-procedural innovation will solve the problem of democratic justice on its own, even with a significant extension of deliberatively based public participation. Insofar as its counterfactual value is over-stretched in order to make up the gap to the recalcitrant reality of existing democratic structure, the emphasis on normative-procedural innovation is one-sided. Habermas's two-track model of the discursive formation of public will and procedurally regulated deliberation is on the same path as that being explored here. But this two-track model still operates with the assumption that society generally can be organized to serve the political core of normatively regulated procedures. By contrast, the emphasis here is on an idea of society that generates conflict and innovation on a constant basis and that thereby challenges its democratic structure to evolve; and where the more fundamental work of justification is done through the medium of public communication rather than through public deliberation.

Deontology and Democracy

The debate is a complex one. The conclusion is not easily reached and the steps towards it have to be properly explicated. It is made all the more complicated because Habermas covers so much ground in both sociology and philosophy that he always manages to cover some of the space of possible criticism. Yet, while Habermas's deliberative democratic theory opens a new way of viewing the foundations of democracy in public sovereignty, it cannot be easily applied. Such an application deficit follows from its confidence that the counterfactual standards of democracy are, to a great extent, already adequate and can be used to establish a just society. In the following sections, this chapter will offer some criticisms of Habermas that are ultimately intended to build on the innovations of discourse ethics with a view to greater empirical-theoretical relevance in its application.

In the first section below, discourse ethics is set within the broader context of the procedural turn in both philosophy and sociology. While accepting the importance of the turn to procedural thinking as part of the broader constructivist transformation of epistemology in the last half-century, it is argued that this procedural turn as it applies to democratic theory has the effect of excessively diminishing the significance of extra-procedural processes of public justification. While Habermas's two-track model appears to address how procedural and non-procedural processes can be productively reconciled, it is suggested that, notwithstanding the importance of the attempt, its account of the non-procedural context is designed to preserve unrealizable counterfactual premises of deliberative procedures to the detriment of grasping the true significance of the public's democratic contribution. This contribution lies in the capacity of publics to cognitively build a normative culture. The emphasis on normative culture is intended to introduce a substantive corrective to the theory's procedural emphasis, a corrective that better connects a deliberatively conceived formal politics with the discourses, learning processes, and cultural structures its societal environments generate. In this way, the broad movement towards a more applied form of democratic theory may be advanced without conceding the term 'realism' to the non-normative, classical liberal realism outlined in Part I.

Three further theoretical moves are made in subsequent sections to consolidate this broad impetus towards critical reconstruction of Habermas's version of discourse ethics. Firstly, the importance of theorizing from injustice, following Forst here, qualifies ideal theoretical tendencies in

Habermas's formal pragmatically derived counterfactual assumptions. The fact of injustice, both substantive in the sense of an unjust social structure and procedural in the sense of bad justification, forces democratic theory to balance empirical-theoretical realism, including concern for the facticity of normativity, with normative idealism. It also forces it to incorporate a greater concern for injustices in social power. Secondly, Axel Honneth is introduced to show the value of a societally extended normative theory that has echoes of Habermas's work on the normative content of modernity in *Communicative Action*. Honneth opens the door to a substantive dimension in critically oriented democratic and social theory that would argue for context-transcending standards of the good and, correspondingly, not inhibit the substantive intentions of critique as critique of actual social arrangements, but would indeed start from it. Honneth, through his reassessment of Hegel's contribution, places normative theory in a close relation to the theory of society, as his recent work makes explicit (Honneth, 2011). In the last section, continuing a theme of Honneth that aligns itself with a radical democratic motif, the issue of collective agency is considered. Here, the constitutive role of collective agency and the collective learning such agency animates is contrasted to the consensual assumptions of moral proceduralism. This last section, on this basis, opens up the issue of how organized collective action can be considered if strong counterfactual assumptions about the moral role of procedures are weakened and this role is partly dispersed into general public discourse.

Democratic Theory, Social Theory, and Limits to Proceduralization

The shift in social theory from a structuralist emphasis to a dynamic, open-ended, and process-oriented one was already anticipated in Parsons's late theory. Wenzel documents how Parsons moves from a theory of universalistic moral consensus guided by overarching values as the telos of modern society to the procedural view where consensus is reached through the *communication* of trust (Parsons, 1963; Wenzel, 2005). Such a procedural view of consensus breaks from the idea of a transcending value consensus that characterizes society as a whole. It is instead to be understood as a continually revised network of partial solidarities. Wenzel views this as an evolutionary shift from a normative to a non-normative account of social order, whereby the movement from ascription to achievement as a social standard makes it increasingly possible to co-ordinate action through symbolic media of interchange such as money, power, and influence.[1] He describes it as a shift to a *systems functional* paradigm.

Viewing action and social relations as increasingly guided by symbolic media addressed the problem of the rigidity that had been built into Parsons's earlier theory in both its action-theoretical and structural-functional variants. In the light of the problem of the empirical fact of increasing levels of individuation in modern life, a communication theory that emphasizes the construction of value commitments supplanted a structural theory that assumed their functional emergence. Parsons's turn to the significance of communication organized according to symbolic media anticipated Luhmann's more radically constructivist systems theory of societal communication (Luhmann, 1982, 1989, 2002).

The normative critical social theory developed by Habermas in *Communicative Action* crosses over both Parsons's late communicative turn and Luhmann's systemic theory of self-organizing communication. It also retains elements of the Marxist critique of modern society while transforming its theoretical and methodological foundations. The theory of society advanced in *Communicative Action* recasts his earlier emphasis on the twin categories of work and interaction into system theoretical and social phenomenological terms, communicatively reproduced through symbolic media and communicative action respectively. The Marxist moment

---

[1] Influence as a steering medium operates according to a continuing normative logic that may run along with or challenge societal co-ordination achieved through money and power. This distinction cannot be followed further here, but see Warren who follows Parsons in viewing the growth of influence as a steering medium that gains ground against money and power as part of the logic of modern associative forms of organization (Warren, 2001).

is retained in his treatment of the concept of reification that he locates in the potential colonization of the lifeworld by social systems, that he accepts should be allowed to function at least relatively autonomously. As outlined in Chapter 8, the normative moment, restrained in *Communicative Action* by its confinement to one of three structural components of the lifeworld along with the other components of culture and personality, emerges as central in Habermas's next major work, *Between Facts and Norms* (Habermas, 1996). Here, the moral-procedural standard of discourse ethics, increasingly articulated as a theory of inclusive deliberation, institutionally mediates system and lifeworld. This mediating moment is achieved by means of communicatively legitimated political power, symbiotically realized through legal-political deliberation and the discursive formation of public will.

Habermas therefore emphasizes the social centrality of communicative procedures and processes. Moral principles should no longer be substantively specified by normative theories, as this must be left as the responsibility of democratic agents themselves operating in deliberative procedures characterized by principles of discursivity (D) and universalization (U). Normative theories should confine themselves to clarifying the principles and impediments to deliberative procedures. The most important impediment to deliberative procedures is the existence of inadequate structures of participation in the political public sphere. Such an impediment can be traced to a pathology that can be explained from a differentiation-theoretical perspective (Habermas, 2006). Inadequate differentiation between the media and political systems of some societies, leading to the colonization of the media by politics, inhibits fully discursive will formation with downstream implications for deliberative procedures.

Along with Habermas and Parsons, Rawls and Luhmann also emphasize communicative procedures as the basis of societal co-ordination, though their respective normative and non-normative theories are very different (Luhmann, 1993; Rawls, 2005). Rawls's account of procedures is based on acting in conformity with public reason in the context of overarching principles of justice. Luhmann takes over Weber's theory of legitimacy and views procedures as based on a clear distinction between what is law and what is not. Procedures enable agents, who learn through disappointment from the experience of a systemic logic they encounter in procedures, to co-ordinate, that is, reduce their expectations. Procedures within the legal-political system are thereby reproduced by their own success in reaching decisions in spite of the presence of different social positions. Without this procedural remedy, modern society would simply spiral out of control into permanent antagonism.

All four theorists in one way or another are responding to the challenge of social co-ordination generated by multiple and frequently conflicting action orientations that follow from the modern differentiation of cultures, institutions, and systems. The idea of co-ordinating action orientations through procedures responds to fundamental norms of equality and freedom, which accompanies such differentiation and the modern form of association generally. Whatever the internal differences between accounts of procedures, Klaus Eder offers an insight that can be used to reach across them. He claims that modern communication societies utilize superordinate cognitive meta-rules to restore practical rules for the co-ordination of social action (Eder, 2007). Social and political theories aspire to reconstructing society's practical capacity to bring about social co-ordination through communication, even if the different theories emphasize different essential functions and modalities of communication. They all view procedures as the locus of cognitive meta-rules that facilitate the immanent co-ordination of action, though the procedures they emphasize are built upon such varying cognitive meta-rules as the communication of trust, deliberation, public reason, and systemic logics.

This procedural turn unquestionably provides a theoretical description that matches many of the characteristic features of modern societies, captured in such current theoretical terms as pluralism, difference, complexity, fragility, and contingency. Its moments fatefully divide insofar as normatively oriented theories in the manner of Rawls and Habermas go in the direction of reconciling the moral quality of social integration with the social facts of cultural pluralization and institutional differentiation, whereas non-normative theories like the later Parsons and Luhmann explain societal stability as an outcome of non-normative communication codes. However, even the later Parsons remains concerned with the relationship between non-normative communication codes and value consensus, whereas Luhmann wishes to dispense with the paradigm of morally anchored social integration altogether (Parsons, 1967). For Luhmann, any kind of social stability accomplished through the formation of communication systems that continually draw contingent distinctions is an evolutionary improbability; it is merely an evolving formula to reduce contingency.

Normative and non-normative standpoints, the distinction partly mirroring disciplinary differences between philosophy and sociology, are not entirely insulated from one another. Within political theory, study of the gap between normative and aggregative dimensions of voting systems – the fact that voting systems use an aggregate logic that imperfectly reflects the intentions of voters – is one example of work in progress that spans the difference (Goodin, 2003). The interplay between systems theory and critical theory, arising from the Habermas-Luhmann debate, is another (Kjaer, 2006). Proper consideration of the respective merits of normative and non-normative theories requires a return to a concern of Parsons and the sociological tradition before him, establishing the proper balance between utilitarian and normative kinds and spheres of action, a concern continued in Habermas's theory of communicative action. This challenge is directly relevant to the theme of the interpenetration of validity claims in action-orienting cultural models, which will be addressed in Part III.

While acknowledging that the procedural turn theoretically contributes to understanding the process of reaching legitimate agreement across multiple perspectives, it comes at a cost. Faced with the challenge of accommodating the dynamism of society, procedural theories reduce the moral creativity of agents. Either, as is respectively the case with Habermas and Rawls, moral norms are restricted to being conditions or outcomes of procedures or, with Luhmann, such issues are simply excluded as irrelevant. Proceduralism, while in one way vitally contributing to it, also in another way limits the scope of constructivist analysis of moral processes.

In this light, the normative proceduralism of Rawls and Habermas, the central concern of this chapter, diminish non-procedural processes, such as the contribution of publics, who are mostly influential beyond procedures, to the genesis and institutionalization of moral innovation.[2]

---

2   Rawls's principles of justice are derived in such a way that they clearly represent a preemptive decision by him of the principles that those in the original position

This is not to deny that distinguishing institutional and extra-institutional loci of democratic communication is difficult, whether it is attempted through Habermas's distinction between the context of application and the context of discovery, or Rawls's distinction between public reason and public discourse (Rawls 2005; Habermas, 1994). Yet, legislative actors must always bear in mind, beyond their own interests and preferences, the normative realist dimension of a public opinion that is only virtually present. This addresses what the public regards as important, but cannot *directly* represent in procedures (Niquet, 2003).

The triple contingent perspective offered by Strydom may be understood within this normative realist dimension of democratic politics. In the triple contingent perspective, the public is a bodily absent, but virtually present, third party in all deliberation – the third term that informs all democratic activity. Strydom suggests that Habermas, along with Parsons and Luhmann, operate with the simplifying assumption of a double contingent perspective on communication between 'ego' and 'alter' (Strydom, 1999). Translating this into the terms of the present argument, it suggests that, confronted with pluralism and complexity, deliberating actors operate with substantive *assumptions* about matters they cannot fully know, such as the views of others and the secondary consequences of action.[3] In these circumstances, they draw from epistemic constructions of the world – ideologies – that cannot be easily deliberatively revised.

Ideologies thus generate epistemic clarity about similarities and differences. But such clarity mostly does not lead to consensus. The differences built into competing ideological positions preclude it and more often lead to strategic and normative competition that conditions deliberation

---

would be bound to produce. On sober reflection, the epistemic claims built into such a perspective are remarkable in their catholicity.

[3] Jonas's theory of responsibility, applied to the conditions of complex societies, emphasizes the unforeseeable consequences of individual actions. Whereas the emphasis in Jonas is on the secondary consequences of individual action, revising Kant's categorical imperative as it affects individual action, it is also the case that dialogical processes are confronted by the non-transparency of the consequences of the actions that might ensue from them (Jonas, 1979).

than it does to consensus within it (Miller, 2002; O'Mahony, 2010). For example, social actors can agree on the nature of the stake, the problem of political apathy or the negative influence of capitalism on social equality, but still contend over what direction society should follow – more or less participation, acceptable degrees of inequality. It is not that theories of deliberation are merely consensus theories that do not address conflict (Mansbridge et al., 2010). Nor is it the case that the universalistic assumptions of Habermas and Rawls are wrong. Rather, counterfactual assumptions feed into discourses and thus become socially immanent. The methodologies of discourse ethics or public reason do not satisfactorily show the mechanisms and consequences of such a process. They instead show the signs of a reconstructively dominated constructivism.

Adequate consideration of non-procedural contexts and processes should therefore be seen as an important corrective to the excessive procedural emphasis of modern political philosophy and social theory. These non-procedural discursive contexts are key to moral innovation. Moral innovation is not settled in ideal forums hovering above society as with Habermas's version of discourse ethics, or at a remove from contentious politics in Rawls's account of public reason (Habermas, 1990). Morally relevant processes are not confined to those who actually deliberate. The 'third party' of the public always occupies the virtual gallery. It observes and evaluates what is going on and has views imputed to it by those who deliberate. There is a never-ending dialectic interchange between those present and those absent from deliberation. Consequently, epistemic uncertainty always arises between deliberative processes and societal contexts, precluding the claim that deliberative processes can be *autonomously* right. Such processes have to provide reasons for actions and decisions that are not just procedurally justified, but stand as good reasons from the viewpoint of observing publics (Peters, 2008, pp. 232–233).

Political legitimacy is thus not only about conformance with moral rules governing procedures; it is also about making reasonable substantive assumptions both about the viewpoints of non-present publics and the good of society as a whole. Comprehension of the multiple societal contexts and associated discourses – moral, ethical, pragmatic, and legal – and how they interact are not always, or even perhaps seldom, fully available to deliberating actors, because of epistemic constraints arising from present complexity and the non-transparency of the future. The interplay of moral, ethical, pragmatic, and legal issues can only be revealed, if at all, by elaborate, multi-faceted *societal* discourse and by observation of consequences over time.

Participatory deficits of existing forms of democracy cannot easily be deliberatively 'corrected'. The actors in wider societal discourses are structurally locked in and have to understand themselves, others, and the general public good through complex and changing contexts. Moral norms are shaped in these complex contexts and, even if under constant pressure to adapt, must nonetheless acquire a degree of substantive fixity to regulate complex, multi-faceted action sequences. The model of co-present, rule-based deliberation is not adequate for the complexity entailed in generating *both* variation and stability on the societal plane. Procedurally 'pure', deontological versions of democratic justice are too limited in their reach and scope faced with the contemporary historical situation, including the need for co-responsibility in non-transparent circumstances in the light of the challenges facing human society on technological and distributive planes (Apel, 1993).

In both the sociological projects of the later Parsons and Luhmann and the philosophical projects of Habermas and Rawls, a transcendent position that goes *beyond* possible agency trumps immanent moral learning *within* society. In the disillusioned progression from the early and middle to the late Parsons and on to Luhmann, the relationship between morality and social action becomes weakened to vanishing point. By Luhmann, the possibility disappears that society could morally organize itself. Belief in moral organization appears as an illusion. Moral orientations to justice and responsibility appear only to form part of the theory negatively – generating disappointed expectations as social systems are forced to reject moral claims with socially integrative intentions that are no longer feasible (Bora, 1999).

By contrast with Luhmann, Habermas and Rawls still hold to the idea of a morally regulated society. In their case, the deliberative core of democratic procedures is given too much weight over the agency of society itself and counterfactual ideals interact confusingly with real socio-historical processes (O'Mahony, 2010). While there are significant differences between them, they both nonetheless depend on the idea of a counterfactually constructed capacity for reasoning, developed in such a way as to diminish the significance of actual, immanent reasoning in real communication communities. The observing and participating public loses importance over and against idealized deliberation procedures taking place in the political 'core'. Habermas and Rawls in their different ways do not of course deny the existence of substantive norms, but the mechanisms they envisage for their initiation and continuation are overly procedural. This restricts the scope of collective learning processes to formal deliberative procedures and leads to the neglect of learning processes that are independently initiated by publics enmeshed in wider social structures. So restricted, these authors tend to privilege formal democracy over far-reaching democratization, which reduces their ability to address moral issues such as *social* justice and ecological responsibility (Niquet, 2003; O'Mahony, 2010).

A renewed emphasis on the mode of generation of substantive moral-political norms would help to balance different theoretical perspectives. Substantive complexes of norms, and the cultural models that orient them, potentially remain stable for a period, even if they never escape transformation pressures. On one level, they operate on the immanent social plane of practically realized rationality that 'realistically' combines the various normative commitments, moral, legal, ethical and functional, in plural and differentiated contexts of action. On another level, they embody quasi-transcendent regulative ideals, Kant's ideals of reason, which specify standards for a tolerable and just social order. Regulative ideals should neither mirror the normative facticity of existing institutions, nor postulate an ideal state of society completely different from foreseeable potential transformation.

Principles of justice serve as a good example of regulative ideals. They rest on certain cultural – socio-cognitive – foundations. Principles of fairness, of desert, of opportunity for participation, and of certain rights and entitlements derive from the settlement of ideological disputes. Sometimes these disputes are settled consensually – the post-war welfare state – and sometimes more through power – the more recent neo-liberal ideology. Both examples nonetheless depend on the promulgation and public acceptance of broad cognitive assumptions about how society should be organized, what Strydom has referred to as moral master-frames that succeed one another temporally, that is, rights, justice, and responsibility (O'Mahony and Delanty, 2001; Strydom, 2000). These moral master frames are regulative ideals, partly realized in social practice and partly not yet exhausted ways of thinking beyond such existing practices. The idea of justice extends beyond what is institutionalized as justice.

The well-being of society is not simply a matter of establishing the right formal democratic procedures, but of creating a society as a whole capable of rational reflection and learning. Rational reflection and learning on a societal plane forces attention beyond formal democratic procedures. Normative standards that guide critique are discursively elaborated in society as a whole. The public is present, from normative innovation to public justification and on to critical evaluation, in recursive waves. Critical theory should not only, as Habermas states, be concerned with the procedural conditions that allow the public to decide what's best; in so doing, it separates itself from actual publics *in* society who constantly offer evaluations *of* society. Critical theory, too, should offer evaluation of society for critical testing. It should not therefore be only about the conditions and mechanisms of collective learning, but should also be about the direction of that learning.

Communicative, Functional, and Social Power

A concept that has been intermittently important in Habermas's work is that of communicative power. Communicative power, a concept taken from Arendt, is the mechanism whereby legitimacy is conferred on legal-administrative actions though their consonance with discursively formed public will. By contrast, he understands social power as tied to positions in function systems. In Habermas's understanding of the relationship, communicative power should smoothly absorb social power that has not bypassed will formation in the public sphere. In that sense, social power is subordinate to democratic justice, which is founded on communicative power.

Or, at least, that would logically seem to be the relationship. For, in an empirical-theoretical intervention with normative intent, Habermas outlines the question of power in the public sphere but, surprisingly, he does not refer to the concept of communicative power as such (Habermas, 2006). He speaks instead of political power that by definition requires legitimation and that, in the deliberative model, must pass through a public sphere capable of fostering considered public opinion. Neither does he use the idea of functional power in this essay, though this would be consistent with his systemic account of power in *Communicative Action*. In addition he refers to economic power not in the functional terms of his account of money as a steering medium in *Communicative Action* but, instead, as a dominant form of social power. He also refers to media power as the selection and processing of politically relevant content by media professionals. Economic and media power, at least in part, may be interpreted as forms of functional power, of the kind that Habermas theorized so intensively in *Communicative Action*, as well as forms of social power.

These kinds of power, political or communicative, social, and functional, are interdependent. Communicative power should reflect the balance of social power, and functional power should be qualified by the requirements of a properly working formation of communicative power. Habermas (2006) – implicitly – asks the question as to what pathologies of social power prevent communicative power from properly operating. Two possibilities are offered: inadequate differentiation of the media and political system and lack of competence of civil societal actors. Leaving aside the empirical accuracy of how possibilities are addressed, they indicate that he has a restricted understanding of the relationship between deliberation and public discourse that makes the realization of full democratic justice appear beguilingly possible. If certain pathological de-differentiations were corrected and general public competence assured, then problems of differentials of social power could be overcome by the reflexive operation of the public sphere itself. Reflexive operations of this kind would force the reciprocal cross-examination of validity claims that would expose the illegitimate influence of social power.

There are problems with this account that should be systematically addressed and, though this cannot be done here, one central issue may be highlighted (O'Mahony, 2010). While Habermas is unusual amongst democratic theorists by virtue of his attempt to actively build the perspective

Deontology and Democracy

of the theory of society into democratic theory, he remains restricted by the manner in which he understands the counterfactual ideal of deliberative inclusion. To match this ideal, the public sphere is organized to serve deliberative procedures, not to generate the normative culture of society, including the concerns associated with the informal as well as formal constitution – for example, actual ethnic, gendered, racial and social experiences and justice claims that go beyond formal-legal norms. The point raised, following Niquet above, must be reiterated. The moral foundations of communication cannot be separated out from non-moral and immoral contexts of action. Purified arenas for the morally regulated consideration of public issues cannot be realistically expected. The best that can be expected is that the generation of moral principles and the setting of moral norms will occur in the best possible deliberative and discursive conditions. But there are no guarantees of discourse unimpeded by domination. Nor can the effect of the social positioning of agents in the basic structure of society be always made fully open in discursive interaction. The challenge is rather, therefore, to understand how the counterfactual ideals of discourse ethics operate in real contexts of justification, which are underpinned by complex basic social structures. And, on this basis, a reconstructive critique of present actuality may be offered that points to how public justification can be improved.

For this task, it is of value to place the concept of communicative power in the wider context of a diagnostic-evaluative structure of justification, a concept developed by Forst in his response to the Fraser-Honneth debate on justice (Forst, 2007a). This concept clarifies both the *creativity* and pathologies of social power and its relationship to communicative power. Forst outlines the theoretical requirements of a discursive-evaluative structure of justification as follows (Forst, 2007a). Firstly, he claims, critical analysis should be directed at unjustifiable social relations that are based on 'justificatory power', political, economic or cultural. He understands such relations as institutionalized arrangements that fall short of the standard of reciprocal and general justification and that are marked by forms of exclusion and domination. Secondly, he claims that such unjust relations should be subject to discourse theoretical critique that exposes asymmetrical power relations and traditions of exclusion. And, thirdly, he claims that an account is needed of the failure of social and political structures of justification to (a) unveil and (b) change unjustifiable social relations.

Forst envisages that the critical analyst will start from the presumption of injustice. Such a presumption can emerge from the manifest social-political mobilizations of civil society and/or might also take the form of a diagnosis of the hidden operations of power. He describes Honneth's account of modes of recognition as a potential 'sensorium' for detecting unjustifiable social relations for these manifestations of power. For this activity, he describes power as the most important good of justice, for it is the good that allows relations of (in)justice to be set up in the first place. Forst thus identifies the importance of repressive social power. Yet he opens up the possibility that such repressive power can be overturned in favour of good justification and good justice. The latter occurs when justification is general and reciprocal in a way consistent with the idea of communicative power as used by Habermas.

Following Forst's account, though he does not explicitly consider the relationship between communicative and social power, these kinds of power may be related to one another differently from Habermas.[4] Social power is simultaneously the expression of injustice arising from problematic power-based justification and from the state of social relations generally *and* the creative potential to construct morally defensible forms of justification that expose and correct domination. Communicative power may then be regarded as the kind of power that legitimates legal-political action within given substantive parameters. These substantive parameters emerge through fair *public* justification in which differences of social positions and differential social power attaching to these positions may be addressed.

---

4   It is not along the main line of the argument to draw this out but Forst, in his wider work, reveals a commitment to the normative paradigm of democratic justice and ideal justification (Forst, 2007b). This commitment is in tension with the realization of what he describes as a justified basic structure – substantive justice. This is so because Forst does not develop an account of *public* justification in the public sphere that circulates around social institutions and acts to reciprocally align, if never fully – here heeding the radical democratic insight – substantive and democratic justice. A framework for understanding public justification is offered in Part III.

For democracy to operate justly, principles of societal organization have to be established that make the granting of communicative power morally meaningful. Communicative power cannot only be understood formally as the granting of legitimacy to legal-political power holders. Such formal legitimacy must continually be led back to the collective self-understanding of society. And the state of civil society is not conditioned only by formal democracy. Nor is it even fully conditioned by the non-formal kinds of democracy that are spread across social institutions. It is also conditioned by the dynamic of forces that are not democratic in nature, but which generate issues that democracy must handle. This is the consequence of differentiation in society and, to that extent, Luhmann is right.

These observations highlight the general problem with Habermas's account of the relationship between justification and power. It depends too much on the analysis of structural configurations – inadequate differentiation, the form of political communication – that impede good justification and do not allow sufficient room for analysing the wider range of pathologies built into bad relations of justification – ascriptive non-recognition, authoritarianism, repressive hegemony, majoritarian dogmatism, and so on. It also does not attend enough to the impact on democratic arrangements of those social spheres that have powerful non-democratic impulses.[5] And it does not give sufficient attention to those publics that act as social carriers of innovation, including repressive innovation, whose interplay, in conditions of adequate public autonomy, decides whether good or bad justification prevails.

Such publics are the social carriers of collective learning. Max Miller has outlined in recent work some pathologies of social power that block learning processes (Miller, 2002). These take the form of consensus pathologies, for example, unwarranted and unexamined assumptions of agreement with a dominant position or dissensus pathologies, for example, ad hominem attacks directed at those who argue against dominant positions.

---

5   This is precisely what Habermas began to do systematically in *Communicative Action*. He then switched to a stronger democratic theoretic paradigm and the project of how democratic and primarily non-democratic institutional spheres can be aligned has never been completed.

They serve as examples of how the discursive structure of justification can be subject to misrecognition, denial, and authoritarianism for protracted periods. The existence of structural pathologies such as those identified by Habermas, or culturally borne pathologies as documented by Miller, may indicate embedded deficiencies of modern society as much as certain dimensions of democracy represent embedded achievements.

There is good reason to suspect that democratic institutions are malfunctioning and inadequate to the challenges they face, a state of affairs that calls for democratic innovation. This has given rise to a sustained interest in the potentials for the expansion of public participation, bringing to attention another problem arising from Habermas's problematic separation of social and communicative power. The contemporary form of communicative power may be regarded as tied into institutionally inadequate and, to that extent, arbitrary legal-political authority. The restructuring of democratic institutions must generate the capacity to get beyond malfunctions and blockages that inhibit justifiable collective learning. The analysis of the diagnostic-evaluative structure of justification does not simply specify the formal legitimacy of communicative power in existing institutional conditions. Such analysis may also indicate institutional problems of democracy and potentials for democratic innovation that may remedy them. And this analysis will partly have to read the possible direction of such innovation from the balance of social power. Social power is not only repressive but also creative and its cultural organization is the key to the manner in which communicative power is realized.

Honneth: Society and Plural Contexts of Justice

The cultural organization of social power cannot be understood on procedural assumptions alone; it requires a wider focus on social processes and cultural structures. Such processes and structures are communicatively generated. Procedural democratic communication is one important part of this process, but far from the whole. In the tradition of critical philosophy, a Axel Honneth extensively advances a wider reading of the tasks of normative theory (Honneth, 2007, 2011). Honneth's normative theory adds a stronger substantive dimension to democratic theory, now powerfully influenced by the procedural turn. His approach is not substantive in the communitarian sense of historically embedded values, which are assumed to provide comprehensive moral and emotional foundations for a just and satisfying social order. Instead, anthropologically grounded cultural needs are shown to take on a universalistic quality in modern society (Honneth, 2007). The universalistic recognition of these needs potentially enables modern society to achieve moral socialization on the individual level and higher moral levels of social integration on the collective level.

This potential for moral socialization and moral integration, following the moral claims built into each of three standards of recognition, may be either more or less realized. The extent of its non- or only partial realization shapes the depth and direction of moral critique. Honneth understands forms of recognition as pertaining to the three 'structured complexes' of modernity, respectively comprising of intimacy, legal equality, and achievement, with the corresponding standards of love, respect and esteem (Honneth, 2007). The ethical content of forms of life can then be assessed according to these context-transcending standards, rather than being located within the context immanence of specific forms of life. The recognition standards are both context transcending, in which case they serve as cultural orientations, and also immanently realized as norms. Individuals and groups may seek the remedying of denied recognition with regard to these standards and further seek to change deficient normative arrangements that led to such denial.

Honneth thus identifies universalistic ideals of the good life to which societal critique might direct itself. In this sense, his work both involves a specification of the formal, normative content of these ideals and the socio-historical conditions for their concrete realization. While such ideals are subject to changing interpretations, they nonetheless presuppose that the state of society can in the end be normatively judged, as a whole or in particular dimensions. Such an approach assumes the capacity to evaluate social organization, distinguishing communication and its normative outcomes. Normative structures for Honneth are presuppositions of further communication. He thereby relates cultural ideals, institutional norms, and democratic communication to one another.

Honneth's work opens towards a sociological approach that would complement his normative framework, in particular, drawing attention to social pathologies that block the realization of recognition standards (Honneth, 2004; Strydom, 2011). His approach overcomes the idealization of procedure – discourse ethics or the original position – in Habermas and Rawls. It extends the scope of critique to spheres beyond the formal political sphere, raising issues about the boundaries of the political, the different kinds of societal good associated with widening these boundaries, and the diversity of the mechanisms that interrelate these goods. It also has the value over non-normative theories, such as Luhmann's, of addressing ethical, moral and emotional communication in multiple social spheres – work and intimate life as well as public politics – and not leaving these wider spheres to functional rationality as Habermas did in *Communicative Action*.

Honneth seeks to locate the origins of social conflicts and the challenges they pose to established norms in forms of contestation that reach beyond organized discourses in the public sphere. The social structures of modern society are never stable, but nonetheless they can be institutionally organized over significant time periods by particular configurations of recognition standards. The denial of recognition impels public contestation, which is articulated by socio-political movements and forces its way into public discourse. Cumulatively, these movements over time seek to actualize in social arrangements the full, universalistic implications of recognition standards. The relationship to the universal-pragmatic validity claims of discourse ethics is apparent, but Honneth's standards are more sensitive to socio-historical variation in states of society.

Honneth's recognition theory provides a fruitful starting point for empirical-theoretical analysis, clarifying the relationship between quasi-transcendent ideals of reason and the capacity of immanent social forces to realize them, or non-capacity due to structural blockages and pathologies. Nonetheless, the theory presents some difficulties for possible empirical-theoretical extension. The first difficulty lies in the dominant action-theoretical framework that does not address institutional and systemic levels of sociological analysis (Strydom, 2011).[6] In Honneth, recognition standards

---

6   This deficit is partly corrected in Honneth's later work on freedom (Honneth, 2011).

operate as learning horizons for social agents concerned with their specific denial to particular groups, rather than to explain overall, macro-social normative deficits. Even if these deficits always remain at issue in his work, he has no mechanisms with which to fully explore them. The second difficulty is that his spheres of recognition are an uneasy mix of anthropological constants and socio-historically varying standards. This inhibits their value for concrete analysis, as the mechanisms that determine how they vary historically are not made apparent. This limitation is compounded in that they are generally understood as distinct recognition spheres and not as simultaneously distinct *and* interdependent at cultural, institutional, and practical levels.[7]

These problems, respectively the macro-sociological deficit and the lack of clarity of the mechanisms and interdependent configurations of standards of recognition, can be converted into classical sociological challenges. The first may be related to mediation on micro and macro levels, on the vertical plane. And the second, on the horizontal plane, is related to action that leads to the reciprocal mediation of cultural spheres. To the first, Honneth's acknowledgement of the importance of the theory of society to critique, thereby drawing a relation between macro- and micro-levels, offers foundations from which to build (Honneth, 2011); to the second, his plural concept of justice, extending beyond the legal political sphere to that of work and private life, already acknowledges the wider societal environment beyond the legal-political order. Here, too, he explicitly addresses the issue of the interpenetration of the spheres of justice that he associates with each of his recognition standards, even if this analysis is not taken very far (Honneth 2004). The issue of interpenetration is taken up in some detail in Parts III and IV of this book.

Honneth's approach, in line with the methodological intentions of critical theory, addresses how critical normative analysis might be extended

---

7   In the 1997 essay, 'Recognition and Moral Obligation', Honneth speaks of the lack of a harmonious relationship between these three modes of recognition, asserting that their respective moral claims exist in a relationship of constant tension. This is not the same thing as what is referred to below as interpenetration and mediation, where the modes of recognition – or validity claims – are understood as combining to structure social practices (Honneth, 1997).

beyond political philosophy, political theory, and law to the empirically oriented social sciences. His approach to grounding normative standards is focused on the general good of society, its overall level of moral integration, as opposed to concentrating only on democratic justice (Honneth, 2011). Further, if the action-orienting micro-social assumptions of the theory are to be associated with macro-social consequences, the structures of recognition must take effect within relatively stable and temporally extended social arrangements.[8] Only by drawing such a relation between structure and process, macro and micro, is explanatory normative critique possible.

Honneth connects the two orientations of critique, the one bound up with general social critique of the conditions of the bad actuality of society, the source of injustice, and the other with the relation between critique and democracy that Habermas connects with procedural justice. This double orientation allows critique to take on the tasks of respectively explaining the substantive, structural foundations of injustice and irresponsibility, and also to elucidate the discursive and procedural mechanisms whereby such injustice is created or sustained by bad justification or remedied through good justification.

Difference, Agency, and Learning

Critical reflections on Habermas's democratic theory thus far have focused on the consequences of the strong counterfactual assumptions that guide his understanding of deliberation as morally regulated procedure. While the universalistic intentions of the counterfactual idea are defensible, the actual mechanisms whereby such a counterfactual order could actually enter social arrangements are unclear. To clarify these mechanisms requires the capacity to theorize from injustice as well as the other way round. And such injustice must not be assumed to inhere only in structural arrangements, but to be present in forms of justification itself, that is, in what Forst calls bad justification. An important step towards bringing in counterfactuals,

---

8   For example, as he puts it, 'the liberal capitalist social order is to be described as a process of differentiation by three spheres of recognition' (Honneth, 2004, p. 352).

in some respects to be understood as a move towards republican theory, is Honneth's specification of recognition standards that provide a moral framework for social institutions.

Honneth is also clear, and here he accommodates the central thrust of radical democracy, that recognition standards do not make their way into social life by themselves, but are carried by social agents. The idea of agents carrying moral standards is compatible with what Touraine calls subject formation, outlined in Part I (Honneth, 2004; Touraine, 1991, 1997). The important implication is that moral subjects are formed in institutional spheres beyond the formal political arena, acquiring standards of moral socialization and general moral judgement. Moral capacities, especially critical moral capacities, are also developed in non-institutional contexts of association, for example, in social movements.

Moral capacities formed in these contexts of experience feed into political positions. It matters for moral-political outcomes what quantities of people adhere to certain moral positions and how influentially they can deploy these positions in societal discourses. In principle, on the one hand, all possible opportunities could be offered for inclusive and reciprocal justification, but the outcomes in the real, situated context of political argumentation might still not be just or responsible. On the other hand, subjects undergo moral formation processes in social struggles and the outcomes of such processes have moral relevance whether they are legally institutionalized or not, or whether all affected parties agree or not.

Honneth's identification of three moral standards associated with the modes of recognition, which extend beyond the formal political sphere to work and intimate life, illustrates morality in action. These moral standards have a substantive quality that cannot be restricted to the moral ground rules of procedures. In fact, the standpoint of discourse ethics allows, or at least within its framework could allow, for the existence of moral norms that all do not currently agree on, but on which all could in time come to agree. The implication is that democratic reasoning relies on the formation of moral norms – and subjects – in societal contexts beyond formal democracy.

Public discourse rarely leads to consensual moral outcomes. Rather, societal argumentation reaches a higher level of rationality by generating a range of perspectives claiming moral validity (Peters, 2001). Insofar as these are opposed, not all can be 'right' in the ultimate sense of discourse ethics. In certain cases, some first have a real but disputed moral force and *may* then acquire universal institutional validity. Examples are minority rights in a democracy or some basic precepts of social or gendered justice. The discourse ethical condition of morality is retained in the sense that positions claiming moral validity must survive certain kinds of basic scrutiny. If a position is clearly shown neither to be potentially universal or responsible, it quickly loses moral force. But rebutting clearly unmoral perspectives claiming to be moral is different from adjudicating between positions that plausibly claim moral standing before the hypothetical standard of an unlimited argumentation process. In the real conditions of public discourse, moral claims are raised without the possibility of an exhaustive procedure of validity testing that would satisfy the adequacy conditions of moral argumentation. As Niquet suggests, morality becomes problematically idealized by its narrowing to the effect of a procedure whose prerequisites cannot be satisfactorily realized in the complex conditions of modern life (Niquet, 2003).

This problem may be taken up in two directions. In the first case, within philosophical discourse, and indeed within discourse ethics, Apel suggests that Habermas's attempts to ground the principle of democracy as popular sovereignty on the same moral foundations as the principle of law realized in human rights cannot be sustained (Apel, 2001). This is so because the principle of democracy, realized in the discourse principle, is not fully possible in actual conditions characterized by social injustice. Apel illustrates his argument through the non-constitutional realpolitik of an international system of states. The same argument can be extended to injustice within constitutionally regulated democratic societies. Apel here strikes a blow for normative realism in democratic justification and reinforces the emerging contemporary sentiment about the necessity of starting from injustice. Not to do so generates the kind of methodological complications that are the subject of this chapter.

While conditions of social injustice and non-responsibility prevail, democratic discourse can at best only partly vindicate the universalistic assumptions of discourse ethics. Habermas exhibits the danger of a counterfactual idealism that obscures the actual capacity of public discourse to generate moral and ethical variation. The heterogeneous, differentiated, and pluralist manifestations of modern publics shape such discourse. Peters describes learning by publics as coming about through a rise in the rationality level of public discourse, achieved through the distributed production of meaning (Peters, 2001). Miller's concept of rational dissensus, the principled agreement to disagree, may be employed to express how such distributed meaning can generate resources for collective action across perspectival differences. Rational dissensus, explored further in Part III, adds to the suite of concepts that explain collective action orientations, including also interest-based compromises and consensus (Miller, 1986, 2002). Deliberatively achieved narrowing towards consensus on certain principles is complemented by, in the case of many issues, the continuance of distributed discourses, belief systems, and normative commitments. Democracy is as much a process of finding a way through persisting differences by means of public discourse as it is about deliberative procedures.[9]

The second dimension of the critique of Habermas's emphasis on deliberative procedures goes in a social theoretical direction. Moral subject formation and the generation of a moral framework from differentiated social positions may be tied in to the concept of collective learning, as developed by Eder, Miller, and Strydom over the past thirty years (Eder, 1985, 1999; Miller, 2002; Strydom, 1987; Trenz and Eder, 2004). Moral-political collective learning can be envisaged as, firstly, the construction of institutions and procedures that enable reciprocal and inclusive consideration of issues so that all affected can effectively engage in discursive justification. Secondly, such learning also entails the capacity to bind into a substantive moral framework the range of differing conceptions of the good. Thirdly, it entails the capacity to effectively adjust this framework in the light of emergent social positions. Fourthly, such learning should be capable of relating moral norms to the identities and codes of other social spheres so that morality, constructs of the collective good, and the functional organization of society are rendered compatible. Finally, moral

---

9   Trenz and Eder provide an excellent illustration of this in the EU case (Trenz and Eder, 2004).

innovation taking the form of extra-institutional learning processes carried on in the societal periphery, often carried by new kinds of subjects, should be capable of being thematized and, thereby, enter processes of public justification and deliberation.

Though a theory of societal learning is implicit in his account of the constitutional circuit of power, the mechanism whereby peripheral demands translate into institutional action, Habermas does not operate with a strong theory of collective learning. Strydom shows how the learning Habermas envisages in his early and middle work is individual rather than collective (Strydom, 1987). Individuals develop innovative standpoints that open the way to structure formation and social evolution. Strydom finds this insufficient as it fails to explore the relationship between the intersubjective, experiential context and collective social learning. Habermas's focus on learning, even individual learning, is de-emphasized in his later work, where no clear agential carriers of learning are apparent.

In *Between Facts and Norms*, the public is represented as responsibility demanding, but the category public is not further broken down into the agents that compose it. It is claimed that anonymous discourses emerge from the initially wild discourse of the public sphere and become converted through communicative power into a form suitable for political influence. While innovative discourses do lose some of their associations with particular groups as they gain wider acceptance and approach institutionalization, all significant socio-political ideas are 'carried' by sponsoring actors for long historical periods, for example, individual rights, social justice, environmentalism, and feminism. The deontological quality of Habermas's formal pragmatics makes it difficult to recognize teleological standards that collective actors, experiencing social life in the manifold, bring on to the historical stage. Eder's work on environmentalism as a collective learning process, spanning several centuries, serves as a good illustration of this process (Eder, 1996). Collective learning generates potentialities forged by the combination of associations and discourses. In the political context, it generates potentials for the further development of normative culture.

In the later Habermas, the synchronic emphasis of the combined democratic theory and theory of society increasingly replaces the diachronic emphasis on the social change wrought by innovating actors, who extend and reinvigorate the cognitive structures of modernity. For Habermas, discursive structures mediate between periphery and core and these structures appear to order an otherwise contingent spectrum of voices. What is absent is the social logic of groups who carry non-contingent moral learning processes that endure over temporally extended periods, and that translate collectively shared experiences into consistent discourses. These may be described as publics that shape the historicity of an epoch (Emirbayer and Sheller, 1998; Touraine, 1977).

The criticisms offered of Habermas in this chapter are intended as reconstructive. Reconstruction, in this sense, involves the task of indicating how the theory can be productively developed through revising and extending elements already present in it. In the spectrum of his work addressed here, Habermas performs two important and related tasks. Firstly, he shows that the counterfactual foundations of communication structure actual discourses that must operate by raising and testing claims to validity. This opens the way for social inquiry with normative intentions to address the mechanisms whereby individual and combined validity claims become socially immanent.[10] Secondly, he demonstrates that extra-procedural and procedural discursive contexts should be aligned and, in so doing, connects the social sciences and philosophy within the common horizons of normative theory. This normative theory has the intention of contributing to a constructivist understanding of public sovereignty. On this basis, the public may be understood as equipped to establish a constitutional normative framework by its own efforts and according to its own designs.

No issue is raised with regard to these theoretical and normative intentions in this chapter. The criticisms focus on how such a theory can *realize* its intentions in the context of actually existing or foreseeable normative orders. These criticisms are ultimately united by a different societal theoretical description that has significant normative implications. This description variously draws attention to the continuous reality of injustice;

---

10 For this to be achieved, the formal pragmatic notion of validity has to be radically extended. This extension of validity claims is considered below by means of the idea of a cognitive order that is social pragmatically realized.

the realness of moral action and its dispersion through social contexts; the constitutive role of collective agents; the societal dispersion and structural embedding of justice regimes; and the role of publics in collective learning and building normative cultures. The principal normative implication of these descriptive differences is that the discursive construction of normativity is a more extended, diffuse, and complex process than Habermas allows. The discursive construction of normativity leads in the direction of a cognitive-constructivist theory of mechanisms. As a further preparatory task for this, the normative implications of this description also make more room, within the enlarged significance of the theory of society thus envisaged, for the continuing contribution of the political philosophies outlined in Part I. This is the concern of the next chapter.

CHAPTER 10

Democratic Theories and the Theory of Society

The current chapter applies the insights of Parts I and II, thus far, to further address the relationship between democratic theories and the theory of society as part of the general aim of advancing a discursive theory of public sovereignty. In pursuit of this goal, the chapter continues to follow the discourse ethical foundations put in place by Habermas but with critical elaboration and reconstruction. The principal goal of the chapter is to develop a relational framework that leads to the positioning of the five theories of democracy, outlined in Part I, within the framework of the communication theory of society. This framework then continues into Parts III and IV of the book, where it is further developed as part of a cognitive-, communicative-, and learning-theoretical sociological approach to public communication.

Taking up again, in summary, the themes of Chapters 8 and 9, the balance in Habermas's work shifts away from the theory of society towards democratic theory from the late 1980s onwards. From that point, he has given sustained attention to political philosophy, especially focusing on deliberative democracy, which springs from the joint foundations of the philosophical project of discourse ethics and the social theory of communicative action. Yet it is not the case, even if his project was mainly a philosophical one, that he turned his attention completely away from the theory of society. The latter received continued, though not systematic, attention in keeping with his concern for the alignment of empirical-theoretical knowledge with the normative concerns of political philosophy and legal and political theory.

Habermas develops his theory of deliberative democracy through an extended exchange with other theories of democracy, chiefly liberal and republican. While the relationship of these theories to the theory of society is mostly indirect, it remains an indispensable context for normative theories that offer wide-ranging prescriptions. Drawing off the conceptual vocabulary of critical theory, normative theories of democracy operate with both transcendent and immanent conceptions of the democracy-society relationship. The transcendent dimension specifies a normative 'ought' that is at some remove from the actual state of society and, instead, projects a desirable state of the relationship. Even this transcendent ought, nonetheless, must carry some indication of its achievability. These theories therefore also incorporate an immanent description, nearly always implicit, addressing how the actual state of society corresponds with normative preferences of the theory.

Habermas sets out in his deliberative theory to correct the limited, and mostly implicit, treatment of the democracy-society relation in these theories. A deliberative complex set within political institutions is related to discursive processes that 'represent' society, a framework that bridges the divide between normative and empirical-theoretical knowledge. Habermas not alone pursues this task, but also the equally difficult one of relating political philosophies, which emphasize different but in some respects complementary dimensions of democracy, to one another.

His essay on three normative models of democracy, already referred to in Chapter 1, represents two of these other traditions, namely, the classical liberal and republican traditions (Habermas, 1994). The liberal model, accomplishing the task of programming the government on behalf of society, is based on a negative conception of freedom and rights and a corresponding aggregation of pre-political interests. The state-society relationship in this model is conceived in terms of a coercive state that protects the freedom of a market society. The overall perspective of this tradition may be represented as emphasizing autonomy as the individual liberty to pursue rational self-interest. It corresponds to the realist position outlined in Part I. According to Habermas, in the republican view, politics has more than a mediating function between society and state. It is instead constitutive of society as a whole, constructing full and equal associates under law. Political authority should then be mobilized to serve this collective political will, which is ultimately founded on a common conception of ethical values.

At this time, Habermas also began to formulate liberalism in terms of the social and intersubjective liberalism chiefly associated with Rawls. He views Rawls as a 'fellow traveler', given their common interest in the normative core of the public use of reason (Habermas, 1995). Rawls does not view the state as a mere programming instrument for a free society, as does classical liberalism. For Rawls, by contrast, politics and political authority vitally matter as the institutional centre of a political conception of justice.

Finally, direct references to a radical tradition appear infrequently in Habermas's writings, though feminism is prominent. The general infrequency probably owes something to the fact that Habermas sees himself as in the radical tradition, or at least within the broad heritage of republican radical democracy. His core-periphery model, for example, makes room for the effect on politics of the associations of civil society and his concept of deliberation is fully inclusive. He also generally utilizes the radical language contained in ideas such as need interpretations and demands for responsibility on the part of civil society.

In *Between Facts and Norms*, Habermas, reaching beyond his account of three normative models of democracy, now works from the assumption that Rawlsian social liberalism is more the dominant representation of the tradition than classical liberalism's market metaphors and theory of aggregative effects. Habermas associates an emphasis on rights, the rule of law, and democratic procedures with this liberalism, which he sums up through the concept of *private autonomy*. This emphasis on private autonomy is counterposed to the *public autonomy* emphasized by the republican tradition. But these traditions are ultimately complementary; the necessary foundations of private autonomy are sustained by a public autonomy that makes use of participatory rights and communicative freedom.

The liberal tradition emphasizes formal and relatively minimal political procedures within a constitutional order primarily understood to sustain private liberty, whereas the republican tradition stresses the active, ongoing, public task of establishing normative foundations. While Habermas agrees with this dynamic aspect of the republican tradition, in his view it over-substantializes the idea of ethical community, correspondingly subordinating deliberative and discursive processes, in spite of apparently requiring them to realize the republican ideal of full public autonomy (Habermas, 1996).

Habermas's deliberative and discursive theory of democracy is designed to counter what he perceives as the respective weaknesses of liberalism and republicanism. As deliberative, it adds needed dynamism to the deontological liberal account of political procedures; and, as discursive, it extends the spectrum of political will formation in a universalistic direction. This extension of will formation is meant to provide a channel for the voices of the periphery, which introduce, in line with the radical tradition, new needs claims into politics.

Figure 1, Democratic Theory and the Theory of Society (p. 229), builds from and develops how Habermas relationally understands these democratic traditions from the perspective of his deliberative-discursive democratic theory. The figure attempts to make explicit the manner in which he implicitly positions other democratic traditions with respect to the democracy-society relationship. But the figure can also be used to stretch the relationship between Habermas's version of deliberative democracy and other democratic theories beyond what he himself undertakes. In this way, Figure 1 may be used to close the gap between his work on the normative foundations of social theory of the early 1980s, and the normative theory of democracy that he fully developed in the 1990s.

In later chapters, the framework offered in Figure 1 for relating political philosophies to one another and to the theory of society, at present accomplished in terms of the latent potentials of Habermas's own work, will be further developed beyond Habermas. In a sense, though, building from the critical remarks of the last chapter, that further project is already in play in this chapter. For Figure 1 is, at the same time, responding to themes that have already arisen in earlier chapters of the book while anticipating their later development. These include such themes as the *relation* between immanence and transcendence, the nature and significance of *collective* learning, the status of the *socio-historical*, the related derivation of the *situated subject*, and the issue of *communicative power*. These themes are intended to contribute to the development of a theory of discursive-deliberative democracy that could claim to be feasible as well as democratically innovative.

Democratic Theories and the Theory of Society

Figure 1 positions various normative theories within a societal theoretical framework. The figure is organized around two binary conceptual relations that characterize distinct eras in Habermas's work, and which come together in *Between Facts and Norms*. The early Habermas of *Structural Transformation* distinguished between state and civil society, with the public sphere emerging as an intermediate category that differentiated itself out of civil society. The later Habermas of the *Theory of Communicative Action*, heavily influenced in the meantime both by systems theory and social phenomenology, emphasized the relationship between the socio-cultural lifeworld and media steered systems, in particular, the political-administrative system steered through power and the economic system steered through money. Hence, in Figure 1, the distinction between the *Public Complex* and *Civil Society* parallels that between state and civil society; while the distinction between *Formally Organized Spheres* and *Private Life* parallels that between system and lifeworld.

In the way of diagrams, these distinctions and relations are far from perfect. The category of private life, used in Figure 1, does not exactly correspond with Habermas's phenomenological understanding of the lifeworld, but it does refer to a significant part of what he regards as being colonized when he speaks of the systemic colonization of the lifeworld by social systems. Private life, as represented in the diagram, in any case incorporates those kinds of milieu that underpin extra-institutional associational life in civil society. The category of private life is, therefore, more understood in the political sense of feminism than in the non-political sense of liberalism. But, as will be seen in the account below, using private life to refer to a significant part of the lifeworld allows more general use of the term lifeworld to refer to the cultural foundations of society *as a whole*.

Neither is the term 'formally organized spheres' entirely consistent with Habermas's use of the category *social systems* in *Communicative Action*. This is largely because, from the standpoint of his general normative framework as it later developed, the combined theories of differentiation and reification that connected system and lifeworld in that book gave systems too much autonomy. The use of the term 'formally organized spheres' also opens the way to ideas about the interweaving of validity claims later in this book that denies that there can be spheres of systemic autonomy entirely free from norms and values. The reach of formally organized spheres, in Figure 1, extends upwards to the public complex where it partly covers public administration.[11]

The lifeworld, underpinning society as a socio-cultural reality, is structured into the three distinct components of culture, society, and personality, which are reproduced through communicative validity claims.[12] The emphasis on validity separates Habermas from hermeneutic traditions with their emphasis on conventions of meaning. The emphasis on validity by no means excludes meaning; indeed, meaning is the central category of social life. But it asserts that modern life is characterized by mutable, cognitively structured action contexts, including individual human agents understood as contexts of action, contexts where meaning is not culturally-historically determined but intersubjectively constructed through the raising and testing of validity claims. For social life to be co-ordinated on such a basis, what Honneth describes as reflective freedom, that is, freedom based upon the discursive capacity to make sense of institutionally generated contexts of life, has to be possible (Honneth, 2011).

Habermas's emphasis on validity claims emanates from this discourse ethical reconstruction of the phenomenological theory of the lifeworld. This emphasis is pivotal to how he understands the relationship between the deliberative and other democratic traditions. Deliberation is the forum for post-conventional agreement on validity claims that are raised in the other

---

11   Habermas has two significantly different account of public administration in *Communicative Action* and in *Between Facts and Norms*, in the earlier book drawing off a theory of functional power and, in the later, off a theory of communicative power.
12   In *Communicative Action*, as earlier observed, norms are confined to the internal reproduction of the lifeworld, associated with the societal component, whereas by *Between Facts and Norms* they are extended to the relationship *between* system and lifeworld by means of Habermas's discursive and deliberative treatment of the law-democracy complex.

Democratic Theories and the Theory of Society

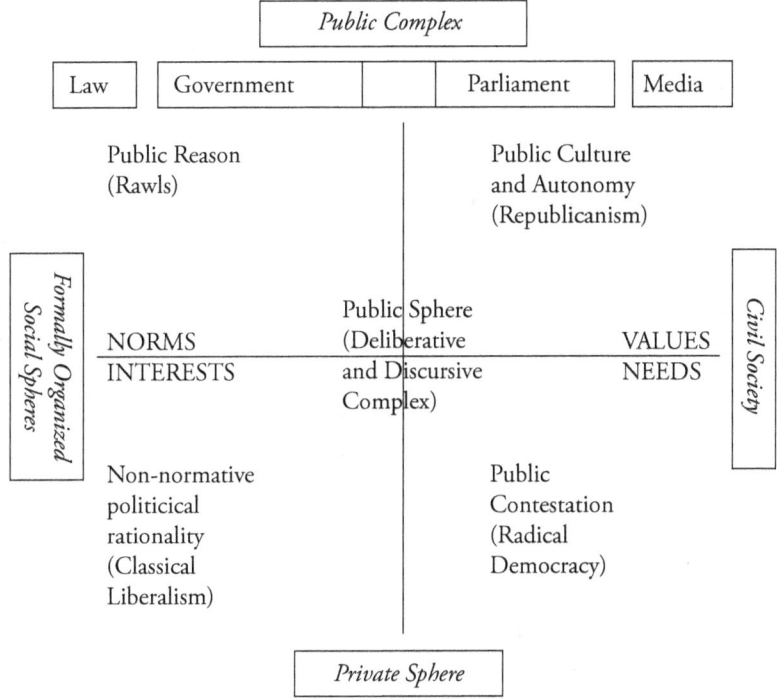

Figure 1: Democratic Theory and the Theory of Society

democratic traditions, though they cannot be universalistically resolved from within these standpoints, because they lack a standard of communication that utilizes the full range of its formal pragmatic presuppositions. Beyond methodological deficiencies in their communication theories, some of the other traditions struggle to match Habermas's exacting deliberative standard of acting for the good of all. Classical liberalism, with its instrumental assumptions, cannot conform to such a standard. Even Rawls's original position must be purged of its 'egological' formula. Deliberative procedures should therefore address normative and evaluative principles from a moral perspective delineated by the overarching principles of Discursivity (D) and Universality (U). These pivotal insights, both for Habermas's own deliberative theory and for the wider theory of communicative politics addressed in this book, may be illustrated by more detailed treatment of Figure 1.

The four sides of Figure 1 are loosely derived from these double complexes of state/civil society and system/lifeworld. The top of the figure and the right hand side, *public complex* and *civil society* respectively, are more or less consistent with the first binary distinction, state/civil society. As outlined above, more significant modifications to Habermas's categories of *system* and *lifeworld* are made to the bottom and left hand sides. The bottom is described as the *private sphere* and this sphere is in part a primary locus of the non-systemic, communicative reproduction of the lifeworld. The whole of what Habermas understands by the lifeworld extends to all dimensions of social life, but the primary locus of its non-pathological reproduction or innovation lies in those spheres of private life that are intrinsically communicatively organized. This dimension of private life articulates with civil society. The sphere of private life also reflects the type of rationalized conduct that is consistent with the role competences required for participation in formally organized spheres of which, for Talcott Parsons, the economy was exemplary.

Formally organized spheres are co-ordinated by what Luhmann calls symbolically generalized media of communication – steering media – such as *money* in the economy or administrative *power* (Luhmann, 1982). The most salient for political purposes is the system of administrative power but, in recent decades, the medium of money has increasingly been used as a supplement to legally grounded power. For the Habermas of *Between Facts and Norms*, at some distance from the Habermas of *Communicative Action*, the steering medium of administrative power is qualified by communicative power. The implementation of legal norms and administrative decisions is legitimated by the communicative power that emerges from collective will formation in the discursive complex of the public sphere. It is this latter sense of an administrative complex of power, operating in the context of communicative power, which is taken to be characteristic of formally organized spheres in Figure 1.

Two directions of force are attached to the polar axes of the figure. The first is of *structuration* that moves from top to bottom on the vertical axis. Structuration is high on the top of the vertical axis and agency is corresponding high at the bottom. The spheres involving the articulation of (material) interests and needs are characterized by low structure and high agency, whereas the spheres of norms and values have high levels of structuration and less capacity for innovative agency, though are subject to innovation over time through collective learning processes. The second is that of *formalization* that moves from the right to the left of the figure. Formal kinds of action, such as action with high moral definiteness or material predictability will therefore tend to lie on the left side of the diagram; actions with greater cultural or material contingency will lie towards the right.

Each of the four quadrants represented in the diagram correspond to political philosophies reviewed in the previous chapter. Deliberative democracy is positioned at the centre, because of its intrinsic significance for communicative politics. In the top left-hand section, at the heart of the legal-political system, is located the central communicative construct of Rawls's political philosophy, that of public reason. Both Habermas and Rawls establish a strong connection between morality and legality. Both also believe that the moral shaping of law becomes *finally* specified in exacting deliberative procedures. For Habermas, the legitimacy of the deliberative core is based on the communicative power that issues from discursively formed public will. Because morality must be legitimated society wide according to the universalistic presuppositions of discourse ethics, he does not accept Rawls's categorical restriction of public reason to a political and judicial elite. Rawls can argue in return that his account of public reason, enabled by the methodology of reflective equilibrium, depends on a *political* conception of the *construction* of reason arising from the fact of reasonable pluralism. In that sense, it can also be said to be society wide though, apart from the counterfactual device of the original position, Rawls advances no mechanisms other than public reason for realizing the moral significance of reasonable pluralism. Leaving the issue of mechanisms to one side, both approaches concur in accepting that the political core should be responsive to peripheral issues and cultures. In other words, they both employ a two-track core and periphery model, Habermas strongly and explicitly and Rawls latently and indirectly.

All feasible theories of modern democracy presume competence at the core; theories based on the normative use of reason assume deliberative competence, even if its forms widely vary. Core actors are charged with a special kind of procedurally formal and legally bounded deliberation, even in those cases where direct public participation is also envisaged as part of a wider process of democratic innovation. This suggests that, from the perspective of adequately describing real institutional mechanisms, the communicative concept of public reason should be retained though, contra Rawls, no firewalls should be erected between it and public discourse. Following the theory of triple contingency, the public must be regarded as always *virtually* present. To the degree that structures of public participation are extended, the public may be increasingly *really* present in formal procedures (Cohen and Fung, 2004; Peters, 2008; Strydom, 1999).

The communicative concept of public reason is used by Rawls to mediate between his two principles of justice. The second principle, generally known as the difference principle, is a substantive principle of social justice. In keeping with aspects of the critique of Habermas in the last chapter, this top left-hand quadrant involves linking public reason with not just the formal constitution of communicative or subjective rights but also with the informal constitution – that in some cases makes its way into the formal constitution – of substantive social, cultural, and environmental rights. Rawls's principle of justice may therefore be regarded as a restricted subset of possible principles that could be justified at the core. Public reason is a normatively bounded and empirically manifested type of communication that is specialized in the justification and application of these principles.

The top right hand quadrant, framed by the interplay between organized political civil society, the discursive complex of the media, and the deliberative complex of parliament, is the locus of public culture. This sphere is primarily composed of what Habermas describes as ethical discourse in his account of the various discourses implicated in public will formation. In this sphere, context-transcending validity claims of a moral-legal kind encounter validity claims of an ethical kind.[13] While this sphere

13 Maeve Cooke, who believes that ethical validity claims can also be context-transcendent, disputes the distinction drawn by Habermas between moral and ethical validity claims in which the first are regarded as context-transcendent and the second context-immanent (Cooke, 2006). Generally, from the vantage point of the communitarian republican tradition, using the language of critical theory, context-immanence does not present a problem. The situation is different, as outlined in Part I, and in this

is most strongly associated with ethical discourse, both in the sense of the reproduction of consensual values and in the sense of structured kind of collective value disputation – ideological cleavages – moral, pragmatic, and expressive discourses also characterize it. The assumption that profound value differences characterize pluralistic modern societies has grown over the last four decades and not, as was anticipated by ideas of cultural assimilation, declined.

This sphere should therefore be understood as comprising constellations of values, some enjoying widespread support, some expressing latent differences, and some expressing manifest differences. It is a sphere characterized by plurality. It is also the predominant sphere of general public argumentation. By and large, it can be associated with the republican tradition described above. This applies both in respect of the more recent emphasis on non-domination in the republican literature, as well as well as the substantive-ethical emphasis of the communitarian republicanism.

With respect to the substantive-ethical emphasis of communitarian republicanism, the focus is, as discussed above in Part I, on substantive normative cultures that are significant – or should be more so – for the realization of just and motivating democratic organization. In certain circumstances such normative cultures take on action orienting cultural forms, though also excluding ones such as racism and xenophobia that raise issues of minority and individual safeguards. With respect to the contrary republican emphasis on cosmopolitan plurality and non-domination – contrary, that is, to exclusionary ideas associated with some, though very far from all statements of communitarianism – diagnostic-evaluative structures, identified in different ways by Peters and Forst, and the theory of rational dissensus offered by Miller, may be brought into play as concepts of action co-ordination that show how difference can be fully accommodated (Forst, 2007a, 2007b; Miller, 2002; Peters, 2001).

The two versions of republicanism, and the evaluative orders they specify, do not have to be in tension. Relatively enduring, socially articulated value constellations – what Rawls understands by reasonable comprehensive

---

chapter below, with non-communitarian republican theories, especially those with a deliberative orientation.

doctrines – can, in some cases, constitute a reciprocally accepted structure of dissensual positions that, in turn, create a legitimate, substantive set of generally held cultural commitments. The moral procedures of discourse ethics can be extended to the acceptance of legitimate differences within such a framework of rational dissensus, thereby not isolating the moral, but rather seeing it as effective in social practices (Niquet, 2003). In terms of Figure 1, this would mean not rigidly separating pragmatic, ethical, moral, and expressive discourses by singularly identifying them with the various quadrants, though accepting that each discourse is dominant in one of quadrants. For example, the ethical has a dominant standing in the top right quadrant of public culture. But it is significant also for the other three quadrants. In the bottom right-hand quadrant, ethicization is an expression of value innovation; it has strong standing in the bottom left-hand quadrant as an ethics of purposive rationality in the sense of Weber's Protestant ethic; and it operates as an ethic of the reasonable, in Rawls's sense, in the top left-hand quadrant.

The bottom right-hand quadrant is understood as the sphere of *public contestation*. This sphere is framed by the less organized, cultural-political contexts of civil society and by the associative and intimate dimensions of the private sphere. In *Between Facts and Norms*, Habermas documents how social movements seek to generate a societally resonant collective identity and, on this basis, how they also seek to constitute publics. These movements actually account for the transformative potentials of the public sphere as it moves from a state of rest to a mobilized state. For Habermas, the release of transformative potentials is critical to the vitality of democracy. He is therefore far from insensitive to the periphery of civil society and its capacity to generate the new political agendas to which the political core should respond.[14]

---

14   Though Habermas's two-track model is broadly going in the right direction, it nonetheless is, as argued above, excessively constrained in two ways. The first is the dimension of subject formation and the new ethical and moral agendas they bring to the table. Habermas's procedural concept of morality is too limited to capture the associational collective learning of movements that result in these new agendas. The second is that these peripheral forces are too restricted by his two-track distinction

This sphere is specialized in the exploration and communication of new needs, that is to say, needs that respond to dissatisfaction with established norms. As emphasized both by Habermas himself against Rawls, and the non-Habermasian strain of radical democratic theory, need formation reflects the constantly changing nature of the relationship between politics and other social spheres. Radical need interpretations generate constant pressure to change formal and informal constitutions. Touraine's concept of subject formation, understood in the sense of the formation of new kinds of subject with innovative balances of ethical, moral, and emotional components in their make-up, captures this aspect well (Touraine, 1997). The formation of such subjects may have significant institutional implications, depending on logics of identity formation, public resonance, the constitution of publics, and the outcomes of social struggles.

Distinguishing between the sphere of public culture as that of politically relevant values and public contestation as the sphere of politically articulated needs may make for difficulties of understanding. The crucial point of differentiation is that radical constructions of needs generate *candidate values* that have not yet acquired institutional leverage. Collective actors in this sphere try to construct innovative collective identities and publics, which seek to acquire movement-internal evaluative stability that may, in the course of struggle, be transferred into more widely held political values that may, in turn, become binding norms.

The bottom left hand quadrant is constituted by non-normative political rationality. The term non-normative, while it is sufficiently accurate to be employed to define this sphere, is not entirely satisfactory. The term is based upon Habermas's systems theoretical derived account of steering media in *Communicative Action*. While Luhmann does not generally use the term 'norm', his concept of expectation that applies to what

---

between discursive will formation and deliberation. If the periphery is to become genuinely influential, democratic innovations towards wider participation will be needed that go beyond diffuse and unpredictable kinds of discursive influence on political agendas, This is a point stressed both by Cohen and Sabel with their concept of directly deliberative polyarchy and by Bohman (Bohman, 2004b; Cohen and Sabel, 2004).

systems impose on social action cannot be understood in any other way. Expectations as norms are compatible with his cognitive concept of system coding – expectations translate such codes into action orientations. The crux of Luhmann's distance from the term 'norm' lies in a double objection to Parsons's norm concept. Firstly, the internalization of norms has no place in Luhmann's theory, since he strictly separates psychic and social systems (Luhmann, 1982). And, secondly, expectations are not of a moral and ethical nature in his theory. Such moral and ethical expectations exist, but only misleadingly; social agents experience disappointment, as they discover their moral arguments have no cash value in the face of social system codes that do not recognize them.

This idea of norms as expectations associated with system codes is adopted to describe this last quadrant, albeit with qualifications.[15] The dominant frame in the sphere is assumed to be the codes of social systems and their associated expectations, which promote what Habermas in *Communicative Action* calls success-oriented action (Gould, 2005). The sphere of private life in which purposive rationalized conduct is dominant, and which generates suitable mentalities and labour power, supports this complex. It is consistent with market liberalism and is closely associated with rational choice theories and also with pluralist concepts of interest bargaining (Habermas, 1994). It is thus generally consistent with the account of political realism outlined in Chapter 5 above.

From a political standpoint, the sphere is therefore concerned primarily with how established interests are articulated. In various strands of political realism, these interests are generally assumed to exist without considering their formative mechanisms. This does not change the fact that movements carrying values associated with this sphere have been successful in generating the currently dominant political ideology of neo-liberalism. On this basis, they have penetrated into and to some degree colonized other spheres by imposing system codes based on money and power on

---

15 Hereafter, the term expectation will be used to describe this kind of 'non-normative' rationality to avoid confusion.

normatively structured domains of life.[16] With Luhmann in particular, this sphere becomes associated with a communicative concept, systemic communication, though in its liberal philosophical home terrain it predominantly does not represent itself by means of a communicative rationality.

Habermas, as outlined earlier, envisages his discursive-deliberative democratic theory as drawing off each of these philosophies. Each of them represents a communicative construct that attaches to an important dimension of, using Luhmann's formulation, the politics of society, namely the constitutionally regulated legal-political core characterized by formalized public reason; the public cultural sphere of institutionalized political values and dominant forms of ideological cleavage; the contestatory articulation of new needs; and, finally, the communication of non-normative rationality. The two-track deliberative-discursive theory of democratic politics involves two complementary theories in the form of a deliberative theory of democracy and a discursive theory of the formation of public will. This deliberative-discursive complex lies at the centre of Figure 1, and it is assumed to have input-output relations to the democratic complexes represented in each of the other quadrants.

Habermas's combined discourse ethical and discursive theories explicitly and implicitly utilize the various dimensions of the political philosophies associated with each of the quadrants of Figure 1, and also implicitly his earlier theory of social action, to generate a unified communicative theory of politics. In the next steps below, a few remarks will, firstly, be offered on the social theoretical foundations associated with each of these philosophical perspectives, before, secondly, turning to a short outline of

---

16 The university is a case in point, where expectations associated with the system codes of power and money have substantially displaced normatively embedded collegial models. The dissolution of enabling and constraining moral and ethical normative complexes may have pathological consequences to which some of the contemporary difficulties of the university may be traced. The evidence of such dissolution in the economic sphere and the significant degree to which it is responsible for the current dysfunctional relationship between the economy, society, and politics offers a further example.

Habermas's model of discursive will formation, which shows how they enter into political communication.

Normative Theory, Communicative Action, and Social Integration

The framework elaborated in Figure 1 extends Habermas's work on the two communicative planes of social integration and the reorientation of normative theories of democracy. Though the social theoretical dimension is less prominent in the last few decades, it remains latently present, nonetheless, in the symmetry between the theory of communicative action and discourse ethics.

The theory of communicative action attempts to represent three accounts of action, each with distinctive validity claims, as components of an overall theory in which all the validity claims can be put into play together. The three forms of social action that Habermas identifies and that raise distinctive validity claims are, respectively, teleological action based on egocentric calculations of utility associated with the validity claim of truth; normatively regulated action taking place with reference to the intersubjective, social world and associated with the validity claim of rightness; and dramaturgical action that is directed at the inner, subjective world to which an individual has privileged access and which is associated with the validity claims of truthfulness. Interaction within the framework of communicative action puts all three validity claims into play together, truth, rightness, and truthfulness, thereby constituting an illocutionary framework oriented to mutual understanding.

Habermas counterposes such communicative action oriented to mutual understanding to strategic action, in which purposive orientation to the effectiveness of means takes place through egocentric calculations of utility. Communicative action should not be characterized by strategies mobilized through differentials of power, but through reasons that justify claims to validity. Such reasons supersede not just strategically mobilized power but also, in the conditions of a fully secularized society, substantive norms that might otherwise be put forward without warrant as grounds for action. It would also exclude the use of subjective claims that impede public rationality. But it would include that aspect of teleological action that is oriented to the validity claim of truth as the expression of an intellectually rationalized culture.

The distinction between action oriented to success and action oriented to mutual understanding overlaps Habermas's distinction between system and lifeworld. The delinguistified and denormatized media of money and power that operate in systemic contexts are consistent with success-oriented action. While this separation of rationalities has the positive function of relieving the lifeworld from becoming over-burdened by the costs of communicative co-ordination, by colonizing that lifeworld it runs the risk of impeding communicative rationality from playing its normatively necessary role. Partly because of the way in which he formulated the original theory, partly because of the general legacy of the critique of instrumental reason in critical theory, and partly because of his concern to advance the claim to normative rightness in practical discourse as lying on the same level as the claim to truth in theoretical discourse, Habermas's account is generally interpreted as viewing success-oriented rationality as a threat to communicatively integrated forms of life. The practical utilization of theoretical discourse in social technologies, for example, scientization or juridification, threatens the integrity of those areas of life that depend on free and open practical discourse.

At least things appear that way from a critical standpoint. As indicated, where theoretical discourse is appropriately pursuing the goal of truth or where purposive rationalization or media steering makes a positive contribution, they may help to establish benign conditions for communicative action. This latter position is illustrated in Habermas's later understanding of interrelated dimensions of facticity and validity in modern law, where validity achieved through communicative action within the general institutional and public discourse of law secures the legitimacy of law beyond its mere social effects as a system of norms. But to have action co-ordinating social effects, nonetheless, is intrinsic to law.

Validity claims have both real and counterfactual status. They have *real* status when validity testing processes ultimately lead to the consolidation in the here and now of justified truths, normative standards, and subjective self-understandings to which the status of the social realization of reason can be ascribed. Collective learning comes into play when, by contrast, unreason exists that violates true, just, and authentic foundations of social life. Collective learning, thus unleashed, involves the interplay, consistent with the normative ideals of communicative action, of *critical counterfactual* validity claims that seek to reshape immanent facticity – including the facticity of normativity (Brunkhorst, 2007).

The theory of communicative action is Habermas's social theoretical account of the co-ordination of action through mutual understanding. Discourse ethics is its philosophical equivalent. The theory of communicative action invites a *societal* theoretical account of how counterfactual conditions of reason can be socially realized, whereas discourse ethics, though it has compatible foundations, ultimately heads towards counterfactually identifying normative premises of deliberative democracy. In *Between Facts and Norms*, Habermas attempts to bring together both paradigms in the integrated account of discursive public will formation and deliberatively generated law.

The argument here does not follow the ontological, epistemological, and methodological foundations of the respective approaches. Instead, it addresses the implicit social theoretical foundations of his attempt to incorporate other political philosophies into his deliberative theory of democracy. To assist with this process, and without doing violence to Habermas's intentions in the theory of communicative action, a compatible schema of his former collaborator, Bernhard Peters, may be introduced (Peters, 1993). This is a schema directly deriving from Peters's theory of social integration. It allows the perspective of the theory of society to become more visible, as distinct from Habermas's account of the communicative foundations of action categories, while still remaining consistent with Habermas's specification of validity claims.

Peters sociologically depicts the action-co-ordinating dimensions of the dominant institutional and cultural spheres of social life as functional co-ordination, moral integrity, and expressive community. They may, respectively, be described as follows:

Functional co-ordination may be understood as the goal-oriented co-ordination of activities and co-orientation in the objective world. It has the evaluation standard of goal attainment and efficiency whether in the form of economic or cognitive-instrumental rationality. An exemplary negative characteristic is disorganization.

Moral integrity involves the even-handed balancing of different claims, solidaristic commitments, maintaining the integrity of persons and social relations, and establishing conditions of trust. Its evaluation standards are justice, solidarity, and moral recognition by means of moral rationality. Characteristic negative syndromes are anomie, anomic conflicts, violence, injustice, and de-solidarization.

Expressive community involves need interpretation and satisfaction, individual and collective identity, and self-realization. Evaluation standards are good fortune and successful identity building achieved by means of evaluative and expressive rationality. Exemplary negative characteristics are alienation, indifference, deprivation, disturbance of identity, loss of meaning, disorientation, and lack of authenticity.

According to Peters these complexes interpenetrate or mediate each other in social practice. For example, he argues that moral and expressive elements are involved in many social conventions, such as those of appropriate levels of personal nearness and distance in different cultures. Moral conventions of how one should relate to others are complemented by symbolic conventions of how to give expressive form to these rules (Peters, 1993, pp. 112 et seq.). A further example might be added; certain moral and expressive rules are present in economic activity contained for instance in moral rules involving trust, morally founded legal rules with respect to honesty, and expressive rules with respect to the appropriate use of financial or economic power in social relations.

With this schema of dimensions of action co-ordination, Peters does not typologically distinguish social and system integration, as does Habermas in *Communicative Action*. Peters views them as forms of action co-ordination that frequently *occur together*. This does not mean that the standard of universalization associated with discourse ethics, which asserts certain overarching moral imperatives, is to be set aside. Rather, their applicability is restricted to delimited contexts and situations – for example, basic rights in constitutional law or certain kinds of personal relationship. In many other situations – for example, balancing economic efficiency and social justice – they only apply in a mediated and restricted fashion, taking account of other considerations.

Functional co-ordination must allow for the non-intentional consequences of action arising from the aggregated effects of interdependencies. Such aggregated effects can be seen as critical to social change in Marx, Durkheim, and Parsons and, more emphatically still, in Luhmann. Success-oriented action, which routinely generates unintended consequences, is better aligned with symbolic media than moral, ethical, or expressive action, with their respective validity claims of rightness, appropriateness, and truthfulness. While the latter kinds of action can be pursued with a strategic intention – a variation on Apel's Part B of discourse ethics outlined above – such strategies are ultimately not consistent with the grounding idea of these validity claims, but only 'justified' in circumstances characterized by asymmetries of power and unjust conditions.

In actual democratic societies, though, such circumstances are commonplace and require differentiated theoretical assessment of hybrid contexts. To Habermas's diagnosis of the colonization of spheres of action, therefore, must be added the reverse diagnosis of the extent to which functional contexts of action can be normatively regulated and thus curtailed. This reversal of perspective has remained a weakness in Habermas's work. It extends from *Communicative Action*, where norms that bridged lifeworld and system were not theorized – as distinct from norms within the societal component of the lifeworld – continuing right through to the later emphasis on morally grounded proceduralization. The emphasis on proceduralization left substantive questions to participants and thus elided the question of the degree they could be expected, in the actual discursive-deliberative circumstances of modern democracies, to realize justice by appropriately harnessing social systems. Strong proceduralism in this sense, designed to solve normative issues of full inclusion, makes social scientific analysis of real communication communities difficult.

Not everything can be comprehensively problematized, and accordingly justified, to satisfy exacting formal-democratic counterfactual standards, given challenges such as that posed by the difficulty in consistently applying multiple, overlapping norms, and epistemic limits with regard to anticipating the future. The unpalatable choice arises between, on the one hand, insisting on a fully inclusive justification process for all moral and legal norms that, for all its claims to moral rightness, could never be sufficiently comprehensive and timely; and, on the other, realistically accepting that legal norms could be only narrowly justified *within* the legal system but not publicly justified, as Luhmann proposes according to the model of functional co-ordination. The only way out, in the societal conditions of modern democracies, is to extend *public* justification by giving collective learning, achieved through the medium of public discourse, a wider theoretical and practical role, not least for the task of understanding of what further democratization should consist.

Given that the conditions of justification in legislative law making can be highly populist and 'reactionary', intellectual inquiry, if it is to make a normative intervention, has to consider substantive moral principles that in various ways respond to the socio-historical conjuncture, as well as procedural arrangements that improve the comprehensiveness of justification processes. Rawls's difference principle illustrates a substantive moral principle for which intellectuals may choose to argue. As outlined above, though, Rawls arrives at justice principles by objectively short-circuiting actual justification processes. The intermediate perspective between the Scylla of fully comprehensive public deliberation and the Charybdis of Rawls's objectivist interpretation of what principles intersubjective processes *should* decide upon, lies in a social scientifically assisted objectivating attitude that engages with intersubjective discursive processes, including deliberative procedures. Discourse and deliberation are what participants themselves must do but, in this activity, they can draw from academic knowledge, including the normative arguments of social science and philosophy. Reciprocally, the constructivist turn in social science, democratically interpreted, means that the knowledge and perspectives of social agents must, in return, inform the social sciences and philosophy.

Functional co-ordination as a means of achieving social integration may therefore be understood in the old Marxist phrase, an oxymoron but a useful one, as relatively autonomous. Separating the world of functional co-ordination from democratic processes that work towards moral integration may have methodological value, but as soon as the object is the social investigation of complex issues, this value is limited. Another approach is required that enables moral considerations to become embedded in functional contexts, as restraints that can also enable success-oriented action not to destroy its own ongoing conditions of realization.

Similar conditions of complex interaction also apply to the relationship between morality and ethics. In *Communicative Action*, normatively regulated action is not just morally guided. It is guided also by values that correspond with the ethos of a way of life. To have standing independent from morality, the role of an ethos must be understood in either of two ways; as something arbitrary but influential, corresponding, for example, to groups that assert social power based on ascriptive identity markers; or, alternatively, as something that necessarily sustains the reproduction of social life by providing people *generally* with orientations they need, but which remain specific to contexts of experience that cannot be universalized. From the standpoint of the boundaries of public discourse, the first reading of ethos could only be strategically justified, whereas the second could support the *necessary* contextualization of moral principles, Habermas's rationalized lifeworld that meets universalistic morality halfway.

Operating, then, from the second understanding of ethos, morality may be regarded both as presuppositions of procedural justice and as a set of substantive principles that endure over time in imperfect conditions of social organization. A supportive ethos becomes a means of binding together the otherwise fragmented orientations of social life, enabling moral orientations to gain social traction. For example, such an ethos might secure the integrity and the will to struggle for justice of a marginalized social group. The ethos of a social group may thus carry a proto-morality with wider claims, already real in its effects and fully justifiable, even if it has not actually been generally and reciprocally justified in Forst's sense, due to incomplete and power-saturated relations of justification. And the existence of such a moral force, though not fully recognized or even trenchantly opposed, potentially acts to reduce the level of domination experienced by such a group.

Ethos can be understood in a sociological sense as being in a permanent tension, of either a constructive or contradictory nature, with morality, legality, and the will to succeed. The idea that a single ethos should dominate in a society has proved to be dangerously essentialist. One expression of this is national identity whose values, when too readily assimilated to the order of institutionalized social norms, may generate the repressive hegemony of one group over others on social, ethnic or racial lines (O'Mahony and Delanty, 2001). Ethos can express the domination of a social or political group, and here lurks danger, but it can also result from the relatively stable interplay of group identities within a pluralistic order and, in that case, it can support moral principles.

Figure 1 operates with four quadrants that correspond with normative philosophical orientations. Peters operates with three dimensions of social integration. This difference may be explained by the manner in which values and counter-values are differentiated in Figure 1.[17] In Peters' formulation of three dimensions of social integration, values are absorbed into what he calls expressive community. The crucial distinction is that, in Figure 1, institutionalized values and expressive identity are distinguished; it is assumed that the bottom right-hand quadrant indicates the source of countercultural values or not yet institutionalized needs. While values compose the sphere of expressive community, institutionalized ethical values and non-institutionalized identities that propose alternative values should be distinguished.

This quadrant, associated in Figure 1 with radical political philosophies, generates counter-values or counter-reasons. These are articulated through forms of subjectivity that lead to norm-reconstructing expressive action, which has affinities with what Habermas, following Goffman, calls dramaturgical action. Expressive action, which contains a strong aesthetic element, articulates dissatisfaction at denied recognition. The culture of this sphere operates, following Forst's description of Honneth's recognition theory, as a 'sensorium' for the experience of injustice. A sense of injustice at denied recognition is expressed, depending on time, place, social position, and circumstance, either through the private rejection of

---

17 In Part III of this book, in ways complementary to Peters, various operations are operated on the four quadrants that both expand them to eight and reduce them to three.

institutionalized values, or through socio-political mobilization directed at their public rejection.

Towards a Communicative Theory of Democracy: An Intermediate Assessment

The focus of the discourse ethically grounded theory of deliberative democracy is on the moral foundations of democracy, while that of the social theory of communicative action is on communicatively co-ordinated social integration. Alone amongst normative theorists, Habermas thus offers a theoretical framework, built on the social centrality of communication, that allows normative theories to be located within the theory of society. In this way, the constructivist dimension of the methodology of critical theory becomes fully manifest. A deliberative-discursively conceived democracy becomes the 'third term' that interposes between system and lifeworld and acts to give the lifeworld 'positive' influence on social systems. The general public becomes the critical agent in 'doing democracy', not elites, compromising interests, and extra-democratic ascriptive identities. While, from a descriptive realist perspective, elites, interested parties, and forms of identity have undeniable roles, democracy is only a façade if the communicating public is not at its core.

Nonetheless, the project is incomplete. Most obviously, Habermas has never sought to closely link the theory of communicative action to the theory of deliberative democracy through the prism of normative theories of democracy. The communicative reorientation of social theories of action completed in *Communication Action* is never extended to the relationship between deliberation and other normative theories. The symmetries between the two projects are partly made apparent by Habermas himself through his process model of discursive will formation. This process model is intended to clarify how discursively structured opinion and will formation operate in the public sphere. The process model starts with pragmatic issues, advances along what he calls the branches of compromise formation (bargaining) and ethical discourse to the clarification of moral questions, and ends with a 'judicial review of norms', understood as well in the wider sense of legislative norm specification.[18]

In pragmatic discourse, an 'ought' is directed towards the free choice of actors who can make intelligent decisions on the basis of hypothetically presupposed interests and value preferences. In ethical-political discourse, a 'ought' is relative to the maintenance or alteration of a community or group specific conception of the authentic, good life. He claims that entry into moral discourse requires a step back from all 'contingently existing normative contexts' and that 'the categorical "ought" of moral norms is directed towards the autonomous will of actors who are prepared to be rationally bound by insight into what all could will' (Habermas, 1996, p. 164).

This process model with its identification of pragmatic, ethical, moral, and legal discourses has distinct affinities with Figure 1, It would be a Herculean, and perhaps ultimately self-defeating exercise, to take the affinities between the various dimensions of Habermas's project and on that basis to show, on his theoretical foundations, how the social theoretical and normative theoretical projects could be joined up. This is actually the task of Parts III and IV of this book, but there it will be attempted on reconstructed theoretical premises. Nonetheless, the task that calls for such a reconstructed theoretical project only becomes apparent on the basis of the communicative premises of Habermas's dual project of communicative action and deliberative democracy. The review of this project in this part of the book therefore supplies indispensable orientations for the task to come. Such orientations can be grouped into several key dimensions.

The first dimension relates to the components of the discursive will formation model. This indicates the different kinds of discourse that are present in democracy, which are reflected in the kinds of communication present in Figure 1. These, in turn, draw from the action theoretical framework of *Communicative Action*. Without now engaging in fine comparison between these architectures, Figure 1 may be said to work with a model of success-oriented communication in the realist tradition; of normatively regulated communication shared between the Rawlsian (top

---

18 See Arjomand on the contemporary intertwining of legislature and judiciary (Arjomand, 2003).

left) and republican (top right) quadrants; and of expressive, contestatory communication characterizing the radical quadrant. And, on this basis, it operates with the same intentions as the theory of communicative action in assuming that the deliberative-discursive core of democracy processes these different kinds of communication, interweaving the different validity claims, and coming to agreement on what kinds of collective action are appropriate to the situation.

If the above dimension is 'affirmatively' built on modified Habermasian foundations, the second dimension is built on a constructive critique of these foundations. Speaking across the various issues arising in Part II, the most unifying critical observation is that Habermas idealizes the contexts and social carriers of communication. Communication is embedded in the identified kinds of political rationality associated with the normative theories but these, in turn, are embedded in cultural and social structures. Hence, the plural rationalities and their multiple structural contexts ensures that the nature of democratic communication is temporally, socially, and spatially uneven, even fragmented, and therefore cannot flow to a secure centre that can deliberatively process all peripheral inputs in the manner proposed in *Between Facts and Norms*.

Beyond Habermas's account of the flow between periphery and centre lies an immensely complex communicative infrastructure composed of processes of initiation, thematization, discursive structuration, and learning. These processes do not simply go in the direction of law making at the core, but go into democratized social practices in different social spheres. Even where they do go in the direction of law making, any deliberative practices there are qualified by the complexity of the context, a condition that makes the agreement of all difficult. Indeed, the only way the agreement of all may in any sense be approximated for *some* fundamental issues is through the communicative alignment of this cultural structure. But, as will be addressed in Part III of the book, the agreement of all is not the only means of legitimate action co-ordination in democratic societies.

From the transcendental pragmatic perspective, the public sphere, operating in the fullest sense of the term with fair conditions of participation, *has* to generate sufficient universalistic agreement on basic matters of justice. But, from a sociological standpoint, this vantage point of the unlimited communication community has to be qualified by considerations of what is actually possible in the socio-historical conditions of real communication communities, often characterized by what Forst calls bad relations of justification (Forst, 2007a, 2007b). For real public spheres operate in conditions of power asymmetries that vitally affect the degree of democracy they can internally attain in the organization of democratic communication, or can externally bring about in the world by means of this communication. In spite of the power asymmetries that attend public spheres to varying degrees, they represent the key site of *public* democratic participation. The public sphere is the only place in contemporary democracies where rival argumentative positions can meet one another in anything like equal terms, even if full equality is scarcely ever realized.

PART III

Cognitive Sociology, Collective Learning, and the Public Sphere

CHAPTER 11

Cognitive Sociology, Communication, and Social Theory

Part III will outline the essential elements of a communicative theory of politics that builds from recent developments in cognitive sociology and sociological learning theory. This theoretical approach will show how the democratic core of the public sphere consists of discursively achieved collective learning that is guided by the cognitive foundations of normative culture. Normative theories of democracy short-circuit this process, failing to properly grasp the importance of the wider cognitive foundations of normative practices. The public sphere, understood broadly to incorporate multiple communicative arenas, is a cognitive construct in the sense that it is not focused on justifying or applying particular norms. It is, instead, focused on argumentation across competing standpoints and ideologies, a process that reaches beyond existing normative frameworks to their cognitive foundations. Public argumentation is conducted not through the normative process of finding agreement on a precise legally framed norm given convergent epistemic horizons, but through the discursive process of collective cognitive learning in conditions of uncertainty and conflict. Discursively, the public sphere does not concur with the dominant deliberative model of co-present reasoning. Co-present argumentation is a component, but only one component of the wide variety of arenas, themes, and modalities of discourse that are variously designed to repair the breakdown of normative rules, introduce new themes, and clarify latent cognitively stored generative potentialities.

The theoretical orientation of Part III of the book continues the debate with Habermas and discourse ethics and other normative theories of democracy but here that exploration mostly takes on a latent status. The challenge arising for Part III from Parts I and II may be briefly put. The normative theories of democracy that were in Chapter 10 placed within a communication theoretical framework demonstrated a comprehensive normative reach to which a sociological approach with normative intentions operating at the level of the theory of society must do justice.

Part III contains three chapters. The current chapter, drawing from micro- and macro-sociological theory, outlines the prerequisites of a version of cognitive sociology that would be suited to the above challenge. The next chapter, continuing the task of building a communication theory of democracy and the public sphere, introduces the sociological theory of collective learning and ties it into an account of the cognitive structures and communicative mechanisms underlying normative reproduction and change. The outcomes of these two chapters then feed into the concluding chapter of Part III, focused on the analytic and synthetic aim of outlining a cognitive framework that underpins the communicative understanding of democratic politics.

Cognitive Sociology and Social Theory

As a political regime, democracy rests on communicatively generated normative validity claims such as moral rightness, epistemic reliability, and ethical inclusion. The process of the communicative generation of valid norms takes place in the factual context of society composed of a multiplicity of spheres of action characterized both by normative and non-normative orientations. These various social spheres may be guided by democratically relevant validity claims – for example, legitimacy, freedom, rightness, truth – but it may also resist them. Such resistance may be for the good reason of rejecting inappropriate kinds of normativity or the inappropriate colonization of non-normative rationalities by normative rationality. But it may also work the other way, in line with the theory of reification, in which the degree of autonomy of non-normative rationalities inappropriately excludes normative considerations, generating phenomena such as inappropriate rationalization, contradictory institutionalization, and potentially crises of legitimacy or symptoms of social pathology (Habermas, 1984, 1987; Honneth et al., 2008).

The public sphere as the set of arenas that sustain normatively relevant public discourse translates between the various social spheres of modern society. The very idea of a public sphere reflects the necessity of communicatively co-ordinating multiple normative and non-normative viewpoints and standards. Through public discourse, it helps to construct and sustain the cognitive-cultural context for realizing normative rules or, alternatively, for delegitimating these rules. In communicatively evaluating normative rules against wider cognitively grounded pragmatic, moral, legal, evaluative, and expressive criteria, the public sphere enables society to reflect on the normative implications of what Touraine calls its cultural model (Ballantyne, 2007; Touraine, 1977).

The political public sphere is a discursive medium in which society reflects on its existing and potential normative rationality. Its macro-sociological standing requires that discourse in the public sphere should be relevant to the normative structuring of multiple social spheres, for example, private life or the economy. Normative arrangements are generally not decided on by public discourse with the exception of democratic rules, including those affecting the public discourse itself. But these arrangements must be shaped by a context established in public discourse if a society is to remain democratic. Public discourse sets the agenda for normative structures and establishes the range of democratic perspectives and, by extension, social standpoints that should be recognized in normative innovation in various institutional spheres.

The account offered in Parts I and II of normative theories of democracy, and especially as synthesized in Figure 1, Chapter 10, indicates the characteristic dimensions of society from which they originate. It also outlines the social rationalities – success-oriented, moral, legal, ethical, and expressive – they bring into public discourse. Taking a cue from Ferree et al., normative theories of democracy, implicitly or explicitly, narrowly or broadly, positively or negatively, offer an account of the public sphere (Ferree et al., 2002). Historically, these theories generate contrasting operative models of the public sphere, in large part derived from the different social spheres from which the philosophies originate. Different social origins lead to differing characteristic emphases such as, for example, the private autonomy stressed by liberals or the public autonomy stressed by republicans. These emphases are combined in different measures in various country specific models of the public sphere. The power of these theories to normatively specify public spheres is far from complete, given the influence of many other factors. Nonetheless, normative theories are highly influential in shaping the socially effective normative principles that condition the operation of public discourse. These theories acquire practical force in public cultures, normative structures, and procedural arrangements. The concrete import of normative theories does not emerge straightforwardly from canonical 'texts', but from complex interplay in formal and informal justification processes between texts and their social appropriation.

Normative structures do not determine general social organization on their own; they coexist with non-normative symbolically generalized media of communication, counter-normative expressive identities, and ideal innovation. The macro-sociological role of public discourse requires it to be flexible enough to translate between these varied modalities of coding culture that arise in differentiated social spheres such, as the economy, health, law, science, and private life. It is not just the structural differentiation of modern societies that makes the idea of the unqualified normative structuring of social reality implausible. Modern societies are also interpretively dynamic and contradictory, generating opacity as well as clarity, and frequently not knowing for a long time, and only by means of complicated and sometimes painful learning processes, which is to prevail. This interpretive dynamism generates ideal innovation beyond institutionalized practical rationality, and it poses an ever-present pressure for normative change. Normative structures cannot foreclose on the potential for innovation arising from the play of different discursive rationalities. They must, therefore, be both self-limiting and, as reflecting societal learning, amenable to change.

The public sphere is a set of discursive arenas that is organized according to the principle of publicity. It is characterized, at least in principle, by egalitarian conditions of access that make possible normative, democratic collective learning. Cognitive sociology, applying itself to the interplay of cognitive structures, collective learning, and discursive processes, is essential to understanding how normative order is generated, sustained, and transformed. The concept of 'cognitive structures' is at the core of the cognitive approach developed here. Such generative structures, to be dealt with in more detail in Chapter 13, are composed of four elements, cognitive principles, cognitive cultural models, socio-cultural models, and collective learning (Strydom, 2012, 2013).

The first element, and at the heart of the approach, is that of cognitive principles. These are second order reflexive properties, located on a quasi-transcendent plane, which make possible first order rules, such as norms, values, pragmatic maxims, and emotional judgements. The latter directly guide immanent social practices, though these practices may over time exceed the structuring effect of these rules systems and lead to their transformation. The quasi-transcendent status of cognitive principles accordingly refers to the capacity of society, animated by the discursive competences of social agents, to 'think' in registers that extend beyond the existing, applied rationality of first order rules. So, for example, the reflexive discourse of justice is more than the existing, immanent application of justice principles. Such 'thinking' on the level of cognitive principles involves the capacity to reframe reality into new patterns of collective meaning. Shared collective meaning allows co-ordinated communication, but it does not necessarily entail agreement on validity. The very essence of the cognitive approach is that reflexive capacities enable differences to be reciprocally comprehended so as to make possible the co-ordination of social practices in the multiple registers of modernity. Differences are socially more fundamental than agreement. Agreement is to be understood as a special case of the co-ordination of difference and non-coercive consensus is the rare, if important, outcome of differences fading away.

Cognitive cultural models, the second element of that which is intended by the term cognitive structures, lie on the horizon between transcendence, reflected in cognitive principles, and immanence, reflected in socio-cultural models and in first order rule systems at the institutional and other social levels. This means that the term cultural model has two references, the first being to cognitive cultural models and the second being to socio-cultural ones. Both kinds of cultural model bridge immanence and transcendence. Both involve agreed upon frameworks that orient social practices. Cognitive cultural models lie closer to the transcendent plane in that they 'package' cognitive principles to establish foundational integrated master frames and rule systems of modern life. Put simply, cognitive cultural models take the discrete cognitive principles of modern societies, and combine them into orienting master frames and rules. Examples of cognitive cultural models are democracy, self-determination, environmental responsibility, and social justice. These are historically mutable complexes, but they structure what is assumed to be possible and, for a significant time, establish templates for legitimate agreement and disagreement. In this role, they bear some relation to Kuhn's concept of paradigm.

The third element of cognitive structures, socio-cultural models, is closer than the previous two to the immanent plane of social practice. Socio-cultural models constitute macro-cultural orientation systems that bring into immanent play various dimensions of cognitive principles and cognitive cultural models. It is this dimension of 'immanent play' that distinguishes socio-cultural models from cognitive cultural models; socio-cultural models construct paradigms for various kinds of normative action rules through aligning different and competing selections made from cognitive principles arising from different vantage points. Such models delineate the spectrum of relevant considerations and the hierarchy of values that *actual* societies consider legitimate for norm-building practices. The cognitive cultural model of democracy claims context-transcending status; socio-cultural models belong context-immanently to actual societies. Of great sociological interest is the manner whereby cognitive cultural models enable the emergence of socio-cultural models, for example, the relationship between democracy as a cognitive cultural model and democracy as a socio-cultural model that takes account of beliefs, norms, identities, and power relations in a given society. Also important is how the form of existing socio-cultural models block innovations in cognitive cultural models, or the generation or adoption of new cognitive cultural models, within a given society or more generally. The multiple difficulties associated with building a transnational cognitive cultural model of democracy in the European Union empirically attests to this difficulty, a theme that is further developed in Chapter 18.

A fourth and final element of cognitive structures is that of collective learning. Collective learning, described in more detailed in Chapter 12, consists of the discursive production of potential cultural models – cognitive cultural or socio-cultural – or potential variations to existing cultural models. The content of collective learning takes the form of the temporally extended packaging of discursive structures, which do not vanish after an episode of discursive exploration. They can remain as latent sources of learning stored in the collective memory of society or they may lead to the generation of *emergent* cultural models. In liminal periods of social change, collective learning may even lead to the generation of new presuppositional cognitive principles, as in the contemporary case of ecological responsibility (Strydom, 2013). These elements, cultural principles, cognitive cultural models, socio-cultural models, and collective learning are intrinsic to the cognitive-approach to grasping the democratic nature of the public sphere, with public discourse understood as the critical animating force that mobilizes their reproduction and change.

In this chapter, some recent intellectual developments will be reviewed that assist with the project of building a cognitive sociology of the above kind. It first proposes a foundation for cognitive sociology in the relation between 'mental' structures and social practices, This opens the way to transpose the structure/agency relationship, explicated in various theories of 'structuration' that stress the reciprocal constitution of structure and agency, into cognitive terms. Further, theoretical moves that introduce systems theory, cognitive micro-sociology, and the theory of communicative action supplement the cognitive value of the structuration model. On these foundations, and drawing from macro-sociological theory, Chapter 12 will explore how the discursive construction of normative order may be understood in cognitive sociological terms. This will help to set up the foundations of a sociological framework, completed in Chapter 13, which will build on the relational positioning of political normative theories in Chapter 10, and allow their distinctive contribution to normative order and innovation to be made sociologically evident.

The Emergence of a Cognitive Sociology

As outlined by Strydom in several recent papers (Strydom, 2006; Strydom, 2007; Strydom, 2011), cognitive sociology is emerging as a distinctive approach to sociological theory. It is easier to say what generally animates this emergence than it is to outline what specifically constitutes it. Cognitive sociology derives from two related processes, one the cognitive revolution, primarily in philosophy, linguistics, and psychology, inspired by the synthetic discipline of cognitive science; the other is the broad cultural turn in the social sciences (Bonnell, Hunt, and White, 1999). At least initially, these currents pointed in opposing direction. Cognitive science was mainly concerned with the computational modelling of human mental functions that concentrated on inductive and deductive reasoning processes, while the cultural turn generally sought to develop a more encompassing sense of the relation between cultural orders and human practices, in general emphasizing the unplanned creativity of interaction and interpretation processes as against any kind of structural or formal determinism.

Cognitive sociology partly derives from each of these traditions. With some notable exceptions, such as the work of Boudon and Bouvier (Boudon, 1986, 2007; Bouvier, 2007), cognitive sociology does not follow a strict analytic programme that would tie it closely to existing cognitive science. Its focus is on an analytically differentiated specification, in the terms outlined above, of the relationship between cognitive cultural structures and practices, where cognitive structures are to be understood as the quasi-transcendent principles and immanent cultural models that orient all kinds of practice. The analytical differentiation and application-oriented recombination of culture and practice distinguish cognitive sociology from the generally dominant symbolic or representational idea of culture dominant. Cognitive sociology – following the use of the term 'cognitive' to signify intra-mental processes in cognitive science, philosophy, and cognitive psychology – emphasizes instead generative competences such as perceiving, classifying, justifying, deciding, and interacting, which operate on collective, intersubjective, and subjective levels (Zerubavel, 1997).

The concept of 'mental' operates both in the normal sense of the specification of individual mental capacities and also as an analogy to what makes a collective mind. Developing the latter, some versions of cognitive sociology address 'quasi-mental', supra-individual cultural forms. Such quasi-mental cognitive principles are trans-subjective, presuppositional cultural structures taking the form of reflexively operating schemata that shape the actuality and potentiality of social organization. These quasi-transcendent cognitive schemata may securely support institutionalized norms, values, and habits, or they may open horizons for their criticism and change. The remit of a critical cognitive sociology is therefore oriented to two characteristic cases; the case where institutionalized knowledge and normative commitments, securely embedded in immanent cultural structures, routinely shape practices; and the case where innovations in such structures through discourse and collective learning challenge epistemic, ethical, legal, expressive, and moral norms and, depending on circumstances, may transform them.

While the 'mental' and 'practice' elements and their relation to one another are understood very differently from theory to theory, the essence of the cognitive turn lies in establishing a relationship between these elements. In terms of the cognitive-communicative theory proposed here, meta-cognitive structures emerge from communication practices and these structures then become practically effective, including effective in reflexively structuring communication. This cognitive approach depends on the creativity of discourse, showing how available cultural potentialities are pressed in new directions as part of discursively carried learning processes.

Cognitive Sociology and the Circuit of Structure and Action

Variation in macro-cultural structures generated by social practice, vital to the cognitive sociological perspective advanced here, is well-charted ground in the structure-agency debate with different versions proposed by Bourdieu, Giddens, and Archer (Archer, 1988; Bourdieu, 1977; Giddens, 1984). This debate has emphasized how agency is intrinsic to social reproduction and change (Emirbayer and Mische, 1998). Such a reformulation of agency also leads to a transformed understanding of structure. Bourdieu's account of habitus, for example, represents it as a 'structuring structure' composed of mostly latent dispositions that condition practices. Over time, the practical rule competence of actors potentially allows them to reflexively adapt the form of the habitus itself, weakening the hold of engrained socialization. The relationship between habitus and practice, as developed by Bourdieu, is a good illustration of the cognitive underpinnings of structure/agency theory. The habitus as a socio-cultural model shared by a particular social group is composed of dispositional perceptual structures that shape practice. The habitus may therefore be regarded cognitively as a classification system and conflict between different forms of habitus, occurring within various social fields, takes the form of classification struggles (Bourdieu, 1984). And classification struggles may also take place within an individual's habitus, a process that is at the core of a micro-cognitive understanding of the self that is broadly consistent with pragmatist ideas. As illustrated by habitus theory, structure/agency theories draw attention to the mediation of macro and micro, with the micro providing the dynamic impetus to structural transformation, whether through Giddens' idea of reflexive monitoring conducted by knowledgeable agents or Bourdieu's reflexive practices.

The concept of reflexivity in both Bourdieu and Giddens offers a corrective to Durkheim's idea that the moral glue of social integration is found in social structures that are external to individuals. Nonetheless, the concept of reflexivity appears to carry too much cognitive weight without its precise role and modus operandi being explained, generating a number of limitations that ultimately require a widening of theoretical perspectives. The first limitation is the problem generated by the predominant emphasis on implicit reasoning and routine practices that results in the diminution of explicit reasoning, however much this emphasis is qualified by the notion of knowledgeable agents in Giddens or embodied reflexivity in Bourdieu. This has made this paradigm of limited value to the construction of a cognitive-constructivist sociology addressed towards agents that are capable, in the right circumstances, of sophisticated ethical and moral reasoning and learning. On a wider plane, the emphasis on implicit reasoning may, somewhat paradoxically, also be traced to Durkheim; if, on one side, Bourdieu rejects the societal 'externality' of morality, he also diminishes almost to vanishing point the capability of individuals for moral reflection that is stressed in the philosophical tradition and rejected by Durkheim. This latter rejection of an explicit moral competence is precisely what leads to the over-extension of the concept of reflexivity in Bourdieu. For without an adequate theory of discursively elaborated intersubjectivity and trans-subjective culture in the tradition stemming from G. H. Mead, it cannot properly bear the weight placed on it as a mechanism for changing dispositions (Habermas, 1987; Mead, 1934).

The second limitation lies with the lack of capacity to address sources of variation generated by either highly contingent outcomes of human activities such as, of one kind, improbable sequences of events or non-human natural and technical 'actants' that interpenetrate human systems or, of another, abductive leaps that reconfigure knowledge in unanticipated ways. Outcomes from events, unpredictable technical and natural processes, and abduction generate challenges to the circuit of structurally conditioned agency. The latter ontologically privileges the social structural embedding of agents as carriers of cultural forms and cognitively restricts their capacity for learning beyond this structure. Two versions of sociology of science that adopt a contrasting 'methodological situationism' in which the emphasis is both on the presence and reconfiguration of structures are the predominantly non-cognitivist, ethnomethodological 'self-organizational' route taken by Latour and Lynch, while Cicourel and Knorr-Cetina, by contrast, follow a cognitive interactionist route that is of greater interest in this context (Latour, 1997; Cicourel, 1981; Knorr-Cetina, 1981; Lynch, 1997).

The third limitation arises from insights arising with the modern system theoretical emphasis on a non-dualistic, non-normative, and actor-less systems constructivism that emphasizes the agency of systems in a variant of self-organizing theory (Luhmann, 1982). The connection to agency in this view is indirect. Systems themselves do the ongoing boundary work of drawing distinctions and hence do the fundamental 'learning'. Agents are reduced to later discovering the 'realistic' system-conforming expectations, which they should have had at the outset, through experiences of learning through 'disappointment'. This insight, translated into the distinction between structure and practice, means that the structures themselves are reflexively capable of organizing practice and this second-order activity conditions first-order practices. While Luhmann and Bourdieu share a common phenomenological influence, systems theory beyond structure/action theory stresses the cognitive capacity of systems that operates autonomously from human action. Even without going all the way with systems theory to an actor-less sociology, and to a disillusioned political realism,

Luhmann's theory captures the capacity of systems to reach beyond existing practices. They do this by weaving together semantic elements into configurations of expectation generating meaning that, in the language of structuration theory, both enable and constrain practice.

The import of these three critical comments is to break the conditioned cycle of structure and action. The limitation of structure/action theory is not that it fails to throw light on practice, but that practice is restricted to conditioned action. Consequently, the contexts and mechanisms that link cultural models – too closely integrated into social structure – and practices are never satisfactorily elaborated, notwithstanding the imputation of reflexive, cognitive capacities to agents. It remains, nonetheless, an extremely valuable contribution to cognitive theory, notably for the analysis of reproductive action in the line of the pragmatist concept of habit or what Emirbayer and Mische more recently call iterative agency, and especially here via Bourdieu's elucidation of the relationship between social and mental structures (Emirbayer and Mische, 1998).[1]

Filling in the Cognitive Picture: Systems, Interaction, and Explicit Action

The points of critique raised above generate three other kinds of sociological cognitive perspective. Taken up below in reverse order to their appearance in the last section, these are the systems theory of Niklas Luhmann, the interactionist cognitivism of Cicourel and Knorr-Cetina,

---

1   Bourdieu's theory is an attempt to overcome, by means of emphasizing the *ethos* carried by social groups, the externalist account of the relationship between values and action that had come down from Durkheim and Parsons, whose concern was with the functionally understood foundations of social order. In Parsons's account, the individual internalized the value requirements of differentiated social systems. And insofar as Rawls relies on an ethically particular, territorially bound sense of justice, he too shows some affinity with the problematique of this tradition, in this case more in line with Parsons's ultimately liberal presuppositions – his a priori of transcending cultural values more matching Rawls's 'sense of justice' than the critical presuppositions of Bourdieu.

and the respective theories of morally guided explicit action provided by Boltanski and Thévenot and by Habermas (Boltanski and Thévenot, 2006; Cicourel, 1981; Habermas, 1996; Knorr-Cetina, 1981; Luhmann, 1982). These are developed below in order to establish foundations for understanding how the cognitive order is intrinsic to the communicative construction of social order.

For Luhmann, social systems develop domain-specific rule systems based on binary codes – for example, legal/illegal, government/opposition – that condition the expectation of agents and thus determine social practice. Though Luhmann does not explicitly use the concept, systems are repositories of learning that operate on a plane above social practices. Individuals don't learn, systems – or the discourses of systems – do (Miller, 2002). They do so not in line with the older concept of norms, at least not in the sense of generally binding ethical, moral, and legal norms as distinct from epistemic expectations, but by means of semantic codes that organize communication. Semantic codes prescribe what belongs to a system and what does not, and what such orders of belonging entail or do not entail. In this latter sense, norms understood only as epistemic expectations are countenanced in the theory. Systems form and reform by drawing ongoing distinctions out of the basic binary codes that give them meaning, hence truth/non-truth in the case of science, legality/illegality in the case of law or government/opposition in the case of politics. Luhmann's constructivism is a systems constructivism. Systems change their cognitive form through adapting their communicative coding, that is to say, distinctions within the basic binary forms, a process that is without any teleological presuppositions about its ultimate direction, as opposed to Parsons's idea of ultimate reality-shaping religiously originating cultural values.

The semantics of systems have a transcending cognitive import on social communication and they recursively decide the direction of further semantic distinctions. Luhmann entirely separates psychical systems from social systems. Actors are not supposed to directly influence social systems, only to conform to them. Practice in this reading can then take two possible forms. The first kind is practice that tries to ignore the realities of systems, which have improbably but decisively formed, and this is doomed to recurrent 'disappointment'. The second kind is practice that conforms to systemic expectations, which can be understood as weak agency. Actors cannot knowingly influence how the system should evolve, but they do act in ways that excite further autopoiesis or system self-development. The later Luhmann added some strength to this weak agency with his idea of social movements as second-order function systems of modernity. Movements generate problem-driven semantics that reshape the environment of primary systems, forcing them to draw different distinctions than they otherwise would have done (Luhmann, 1997).

Luhmann's theory offers am important framework for cognitive sociology. System logics impose complex preconditions for collective learning. For a cognitive sociology that goes beyond Luhmann's intentions to be productive, ethical and moral learning processes must prove capable of regulating the codes of social systems. But they should do this without denying them necessary levels of autonomy. Yet this autonomy always threatens to exceed reasoning capacities, a theme long explored in the theory of reification (see Honneth et al., for a recent contribution). Strydom describes the cognitive presuppositions of the systems paradigm as being strongly naturalistic or meta-biological as it assumes that evolutionary processes can be connected to life experiences without the mediation of reasoning processes (Strydom, 2007). The *degree* to which social experience can be directed by social systems without such mediation needs empirical assessment, but it is extensive. Collective learning, which depends upon advances in the reasoning capacities of subjects, must also reckon with the capacity of social systems to autonomously 'learn' (Miller, 2002). Systemic learning changes the cognitive framework by specifying functional imperatives above the heads of general social agents. In some respects, contra Luhmann, it is not so important whether such learning is entirely autonomous from conscious social action or not – it could be planned by agents with functional power, or the wider impact of cognitive change wrought by systems could be a by-product of such actions and not consciously planned. The essential point, whatever the mechanism, is the extent to which such cognitive reorientation is able to escape appropriate democratic controls. At the cognitive level, escaping such controls would entail the capacity to specify goals for social organization that have not been examined by means of thorough processes of public discourse.

While ontological dimensions of the theories do have common features – fields as a correlate of systems for example – systems theory is very different to Bourdieu's theory. Bourdieu's theory is emphatically pragmatic and 'vertical' in connecting structures to action, thereby relating context and subject in a conditioned relationship. This is combined with a theory of ideology that is based upon agents' misrecognition of their own domination – though the idea is retained, at least in principle, that agents can cognitively break free and reshape dominating cultural and social structures through reflexive practices. As a theory of pragmatic capacity, which can be inhibited or blocked by ideologically mobilized social power, it has distinct affinities with Sen and Nussbaum's capability theories (Nussbaum, 2000; Sen, 2009).

Systems theory is by contrast a 'horizontal' theory of functional differentiation. The emphasis is on 'learning' by social systems. Structure is not understood as bound up with the pragmatic capacity of social agents, but as built upon a social semantics that operates independently of them. Since semantics have primacy over structures, systems theory operates with assumptions of cultural autonomy, but only in the restricted sense of the transcendent cognitive ordering capacities of systems. In both Bourdieu and Luhmann, the concept of culture that is respectively understood as habitus and code, underpins social reproduction through the respective theses of power; social power in Bourdieu 'negatively' sustains social order; functional power in Luhmann 'positively' sustains it in the form of simultaneously constraining and enabling social systems (O'Mahony, 2009, 2010).

The impulses of both theories contribute to the development of cognitive sociology. Bourdieu's theory captures the idea of *vertical mediation* between the 'objective' level of social structure and the habitus. Social structure, articulated through the concept of social field understood as both a social arena and a cultural preference structure, is intertwined with the subjective level of the different kinds of habitus carried by agents operating in the field. Bourdieu's concentration is on categories of agents, their domination, their misrecognition, and their reflexive, cognitive capacities to assert themselves. Systems theory illuminates the process of *horizontal mediation*. Semantically organized communication systems both assert their operative autonomy and yet interpenetrate one another by reciprocally constructing external environments that further system-internal autopoiesis.

Though the methodological value of systems theory to a cognitive theory of society is considerable, it operates with pessimistic assumptions about collective learning capacities in a normative register, so pessimistic, in fact, that it completely denies the social immanence of ethical or moral validity claims. In this respect, it has some affinities with Bourdieu. In Bourdieu, the exclusive use of 'negative' critique obscures normative grounding. He therefore misses the process whereby normative learning is cognitively generated in public discourse (Strydom, 2011). Both observations demand greater attention should be given to clarifying the cognitive preconditions of the capacity for normative agency, a task that micro-sociology in the pragmatist tradition has for long set itself.

The cognitive micro-sociology of Cicourel and Knorr-Cetina takes over the pragmatist emphasis on the situation as a basis for understanding the construction of action-co-ordinating norms (Cicourel, 1974). This kind of 'local' sociological perspective accords well with contemporary conditions of political de-alignment and ubiquitous controversy and value contestation that appears to make the prospect of macro-social order unfeasible. Another micro-sociological tradition, influenced by ethnomethodology, is located both within the fields of sociology of science and discursive psychology. This tradition highlights the local and contingent nature of sense making and weakens the status of 'mind' (Edwards and Potter, 1992). This latter tradition is sometimes aligned with Luhmann's systems constructivism in that system formation is assumed to work behind the backs of actors in linguistic interaction, whose restriction by systemic framing processes is stronger than their perceptual capacities (Bora and Hausendorf, 2006).

Writers such as Cicourel and Knorr-Cetina are, by contrast, explicitly cognitivist. Cicourel breaks with the Parsonian idea of socially structured roles, where expectations associated with such roles can be led back to the presumed existence of external common values (Cicourel, 1981). He asks how Parsons can account for the existence of these values in the first place in modern circumstances of interpretive openness. With this question, he indicates the need to shift from a normative to a cognitive account of social order. Interactive competence, which now replaces role theory as the carrier of social structure, is manifested in normative accounting practices that actors use to justify the validity of their claims to knowledge. These accounting processes in turn depend on socio-cognitive processes of thought, socially organized memory, selective attention, and sensory modalities. The accounting practices that structure interactive situations together account for 'contextual emergence', the structure-building capacity of micro-level interaction.[2]

A similar picture emerges in Knorr-Cetina's account of the cognitive order (Knorr-Cetina, 1981). Knorr-Cetina describes the 'cognitive order' as activities of sense making and describing, to be contrasted with the normative order of shared rule-embedded social practices. The idea of cognitive order frees itself from the idea of structure as normative obligation and turns instead to the negotiated, contingent, and dynamic interaction procedures that generate local order in given situations. Order is therefore situationally specific. While social reality is to be found in micro-social situations, 'macro-social constructions' are endogenous to these situations. The cognitive should be understood as various kinds of competences that make possible interactive practices. This account of the cognitive dispenses with the idea of macro-level cognitive structures altogether. To illustrate this point by taking the example of one of those elements of cognitive structure outlined earlier, nothing like cognitive cultural models that could generate practice-ordering schemata feature in this account. For her, cognitive order lies on the meso-level of the organization of social interaction (ibid., p. 2).

Knorr-Cetina, consistent with certain kinds of micro-sociology, works with a single model of social causation rather than a necessary double model, only working upwards from interactive practices, but not downwards

---

2   The terminology used here and in the book generally requires some clarification. The term 'micro' as used with regard to Knorr-Cetina's ideas in this paragraph is normally rendered as 'meso' in the book generally. Micro sociology characteristically blends together meso and micro levels. To explicate why this is so is a bigger question than can be addressed here. What may be shortly noted is that the introduction of a much broader macro-sociological framework in this book influences the distinction between meso and micro levels. In general, the meso-sociological level of discourse and learning is essential to the approach.

from – cognitive – structures, a version of what Margaret Archer calls upwards conflation (Archer, 1984). Addressing, for example, the *individual-level cognitive models* that interlocutors construct of bureaucratic records, she draws attention to the necessity of understanding the way in which these records are produced rather than also considering the consequences for further action and interaction of them *having been produced* at some antecedent time (Knorr-Cetina, 1981, pp. 13–15). For Knorr-Cetina, these micro-level cognitive models construct the necessary cultural context in the course of interaction and recurrently generate a provisional macro-social order. But micro-social interactions of this kind do not control all contextual conditions, neither those established by other similar interactions at others times and places, nor the capacity of macro-cultural structures to exert unintended influence. If the latter perspective of the external shaping of social life may be regarded as too strong in Bourdieu and in systems theory for very different reasons, it is too weak in cognitive micro-sociology (Celikates, 2006).

These reflections raise the pressing issue of the cognitive status of the individual in contemporary micro-sociology. Some versions of ethnomethodology as, for example, that offered by Michael Lynch, question the usefulness of the category of mind (Lynch, 1997). For Lynch, what we understand by mind is really only the patterns of judgements used by individuals in interaction who enact a 'social mind'. Knorr-Cetina, by contrast, follows G. H. Mead in viewing the self as relationally constructed – referring to Mead's concepts of the mind as a parliament of selves and multiple interior audiences – and also follows him in taking seriously the idea of ego identity that offers, so to speak, a point of resistance to social forces (Knorr-Cetina, 1981). Developmental social psychology after Mead also emphasized self-formation as comprised of relatively stable stage-bound cognitive structures. For both Mead and Piaget, rules guide practices, but the rules are elaborated and ultimately superseded by learning from these practices that leads to replacement rule systems. Structured outcomes of learning form the independent ground of further learning processes. The same can be understood with respect to supra-individual cultural forms. Interaction never begins with either a social or an individual tabula rasa.

The nature of the relationship between interaction and both intra-mental and social structure formation is contested ground in modern sociology.

Contra movements in micro-sociology that diminish its significance, intra-mental structure formation, taking the form both of cognitive competences and substantive meaning schemata and values, is critical to understanding the relationship between individuals and the social. Structure formation at both individual and supra-individual levels is related, with the ontogenesis of subjects closely bound up with collective normative structures (Habermas, 1987; Miller, 1986). Mead shows how individuals inherit a socialized world as well as contributing to remaking it. The pragmatist concept of habit is related to the concept of habitus used by Elias and Bourdieu to signify the related and mutually constitutive symbolic structures of self and society, a point of view consistent with Mead, the genetic structuralist social psychology emanating from Piaget, and the phenomenological social constructionism that followed from Schutz (Bourdieu, 1977; Elias, 1992; Piaget, 1972; Schutz, 1932). This notion of the self is also consistent with the political understanding of the subject in the work of Touraine, who views the manner in which subjective capacities are crystallized and socially distributed as normatively significant (Touraine, 1997).

A cognitive sociology that has normative intentions must pay close attention to micro-level cognitive structures. Without assuming that actors have cognitive capacities and stored knowledge that enable them to act consistently, neither morally creative nor purposive goal-oriented actions can be understood. Actors acting in situations without such a priori endowments could only derive them each time anew from the immediate situation, an implausible assumption. The refinement that actors acquire such competence in previous interaction and bring them to new situations is more plausible, but it presumes learning mechanisms such as recognition, transferability of knowledge, and memory. In other words, it depends on intra-mental cognitive structures that make learning possible.

Societies develop social rule and symbol systems, which, though they are revisable in interaction processes, have to be temporally enduring if a common social life, showing a sufficient measure of reliability and reproducibility, is to be possible. In contemporary social theory, a shift may be observed from the primacy of the normative paradigm in a line from Durkheim to Parsons towards a cognitive-interactive paradigm. What Knorr-Cetina and others describe as methodological situationism is best realized if social theory adopts a multifaceted approach in which norms, cognitive structures, collective learning, and interactive and individual competences all have a role. This is far different from following Parsons along the one-way path from transcendent cultural values that institutions should normatively specify as role expectations and that rationally acting individuals should internalize. The alternative is to leave open many possibilities: that individuals might come to social situations with well formed or very diffuse sets of values, preferences, and strategies; that interaction may have far-reaching consequences on many levels or that it may be blocked by wider structural constellations; that cognitive classification systems that underpin normative justification and application converge sufficiently to allow the formation of stable norms or that norms have merely nominal force in a sea of classificatory and interactive turbulence. From this vantage point, the major contribution of the contemporary micro-sociological concern for the situation is to refashion the relationship between micro- and macro-sociology so as to give greater importance to the mediating role of interaction.

The relationship between macro-cognitive structures and cognitively relevant practices is pivotal to cognitive sociology. From the standpoint of developing a cognitive sociology that can properly underpin a normative sociology, two of three indicated limitations of structure/agency theory have been outlined: firstly, the inattention to the autonomous capacity of social systems or, more generally, cognitive structures, to independently shape social life; and, secondly, according insufficient attention to the cognitive mechanisms that shape interaction processes and underpin their action-co-ordinating capacities. A third limitation that is raised above, with regard to lack of attention to explicit action as opposed to implicit practical rule following, will be developed next (Brandom, 1998).

One of the paradoxes of contemporary social theory is the extensive theorization of agency accompanied by relatively little attention to its explicit ethical or moral dimensions. This is a very striking lacuna with regard to the kind of agency that involves creative acts of elaboration or transformation of existing norms or interpretive repertoires. Social theory, trying to balance a concern for structural foundations with dynamic impulses, has largely relegated to a secondary status what Peirce describes as abductive kinds of reasoning, which frequently take the form of moral critique, or what Joas calls the creativity of action that is aimed at the democratization of differentiation (Joas, 1996). In everyday, professional, and political worlds, for example, ethical and moral justification is commonplace, on the one hand, addressing what are deemed to be unacceptable or immoral situations and, on the other, grounding regulative norms. From a cognitive standpoint, the question that emerges is how may explicit ethical and moral agency be theorized from within a multilevel cognitive approach. While this problem is taken up in an analytical register in Chapter 13, the following paragraphs open up some theoretical avenues that lead towards better understanding of its nature.

Treatment of morality and ethics in contemporary sociology frequently brings in its train a pragmatic theory of action. The two most sustained recent attempts to address this question, in both cases operating with a combined philosophical-sociological framework, are those of Boltanski and Thévenot, initially at least influenced by Bourdieu, and Habermas (Boltanski and Thévenot, 2006; Habermas, 1984, 1993, 1996). Boltanski and Thévenot are committed to the re-moralization of sociology in the form of a pragmatic sociology and identify what they variously call pragmatic repertoires, modes of justification, and orders of worth that are derived from different philosophical lineages. These orders of worth are cognitive orientations that guide social agents in justifying their standpoints. Such orders of worth are frequently distributed according to institutional role. For example, policy officials use the 'industrial' order of worth and economic actors use the 'market' order of worth. The authors describe their sociological approach, like that of Knorr-Cetina, as a situational one. They therefore look to situations rather than pre-existing structures to identify social positions, in this sense differing also from Bourdieu. However, the orders of worth follow established modes of justification that are embedded in situation-transcending macro-structures analogous to the structural differentiation of the common socio-cultural lifeworld traced by Habermas (Habermas, 1994). For example, the industrial and economic orders of worth appear analogous to success-oriented action, the civic order of work to normatively regulated action, and the inspirational order of worth to expressive action. Moreover, the fact that these different orders of worth contend with one another in controversies, making sense of one another and sometimes reaching agreement, indicates that there is a shared integrating framework in the form of a cognitive order lying behind them.

The extent to which Boltanski and Thévenot's framework is fully pragmatic in the intersubjective sense is restricted. For a start, in their concrete analysis, actors' positions are held fixed within a single order of worth (Moody and Thévenot, 2000; Thévenot, Moody, and Lafaye, 2000). Actors thus appear restricted in their capacity to engage in justification using multiple orders of worth and to generate complex, mediated positions out of them. Identifying actors with a single order of worth, though sometimes empirically demonstrable in the consistency of their behaviour, leaves out of the picture the interpenetrating consequences of discursive argumentation. The approach *is* pragmatic in that communicating actors are vertically embedded in multiple cultural forms. Actors do not simply perform in a horizontal relationship to one another as in some versions of micro-sociological interactionism and systems theory; instead, they are actively guided by historically established cultural forms, both cognitive and normative and, on this basis, seek to shape their situation.

Beyond this commitment to pragmatism, though, it is difficult to see how the approach of Boltanski and Thévenot is a *moral* sociology, unless in the sense of addressing the modalities of resolving conflicts between orders of worth. Their accounts of actors' justifications are not *morally immanent* in the sense of moral positions that can be justified by actors themselves. But their account of pragmatic repertoires that guide action contributes to understanding the cognitive foundations of social action, including moral action. Moral action does not stand beyond but is infused with morally relevant knowledge and rule competence. The epistemic foundations of moral action lie not in the autonomous convictions of the individual arising before social experience, a viewpoint Kant bequeathed to liberalism, but in the grounding of such action in the communicative and intersubjective flow of cognitively organized, sense-making practices. By contrast with some kinds of ethical action that may involve conventionally reproducing an ethos, moral action must be conscious and explicit. The morally acting agent must be able to identify and defend her actions as moral if challenged. To that extent the subject must internalize moral action, though such internalized morality is constructed from cognitive principles and schemata. Orders of worth do not address the grounding of moral action directly, but the basic idea of multiple orders of worth gives a clue as to how it might be done.

The problem sociology confronts in advancing moral arguments is that its complicated inheritance of commitment to value-free inquiry, which survives as a latent methodological norm in spite of constant criticism, makes it unable to argue affirmatively for an alternative moral-political order, as opposed to morally criticizing established orders. Its comfort zone is to be found, therefore, in forms of latent, moral critique of 'bad' identity projects or institutional arrangements rather than the affirmation of good ones that either actually exist or should exist. The sociology of moral justification therefore remains obscure. By contrast, a cognitive approach can clarify how principles of moral action are formed from sense-making practices in the context of other forces that shape action. Such an approach opens the space of available societal potentials for sociological analysis; matters, including appropriate ethical values and moral principles, can always be *cognized* differently by means of sense-making practices.

By contrast with Boltanski and Thévenot, Habermas emphatically understands democracy as a morally willed state. He takes over Dewey's pragmatist understanding of democracy as a pervasive kind of social organization that extends from formal institutions to the self-constitution of the public in communities and associations, locating the democratic impulse in the telos of communicative action oriented to mutual understanding. From an early stage, he developed a moral cognitivism in the sense of the evolutionary significance of individuals capable of post-conventional reasoning that initiate learning processes and generate social change. In this sense, Habermas understands explicit moral action as intrinsic to the construction of the good common world, and that social evolution cannot be understood without it.

Still following Habermas, moral action cannot be reduced to the moralization of society. It is only one kind of social action set within the context of a culturally differentiated lifeworld and functionally co-ordinated social systems that separate out from that lifeworld. The theory of the lifeworld allows for the identification of cognitive interests in truth and objectivity, moral-practical understanding, and expressive identity. By means of the pragmatically conceived theory of communicative action that incorporates all three cognitive interests, social integration proceeds and the lifeworld is reproduced. Habermas conceives of social integration as brought about by the generation of normative legitimacy through the communicative process of raising, testing, and redeeming validity claims in practical discourse. In other words, cognitive sense-making practices oriented to validity claims make possible normative integration.

For Strydom, Habermas's account of normative co-ordination has to be cognitively reconstructed (Strydom, 2006). While he considers that Habermas operates with an underlying cognitive paradigm in his account of a lifeworld that is reproduced and transformed through communicatively co-ordinated validity claims, he fails to follow through with this cognitive paradigm. Instead, he consistently falls back on the normative paradigm of shared action-guiding norms that is the target of both Cicourel's and Knorr-Cetina's critique of Parsons. He does not attend sufficiently to the more fluid and socio-historically responsive cognitive rules that, through combined processes of communicative practices and collective learning by means of discourse synthesis, shape the context through which normative rules are understood and applied. From this basic insight follows another. Habermas's attachment to the normative paradigm means that his theoretical focus is more on normative order than on idea-generating, communicative mechanisms that result in collective cognitive learning and potential, downstream normative innovation.

To Strydom's point it may be added, presenting the issue from a different vantage point, that Habermas favours the normative circuit of social integration over the generation of variation through learning to such an extent that he underplays the impulses towards and the mechanisms of social change. This, as explored in Part II, generates problems both with the status of the public and his treatment of public discourse. Strydom also analyses the problem of the conceptualization of the public in Habermas (Strydom, 1999; Trenz and Eder, 2004). Habermas's double contingent, ego-alter account of the achievement of mutual understanding in communication neglects to address the role of the public as a third, observing party in all democratic communication. Interlocutors in democratic communication always must anticipate the public's response, and thus the public is always virtually present. This insight can be extended. Interlocutors in co-present communication, or spatially distant 'speakers' in mass media communication, constantly engage in the social positioning of third parties. In the wider circuit of public communication in the public sphere, this activity generates a different kind of virtual pragmatics to non-mediated communication. It forces actors to take up a different kind of relation to themselves as speakers and to others as hearers than they would in co-present communication. The virtual pragmatics of public communication radically changes ideas about pragmatic capacity in a collective direction and about the illocutionary force of utterances in a mediated direction.

A further problem has to do with the epistemic foundations of public discourse. The ideal limits of Habermas's theory implies the possibility of full consensus over the justification of a norm once certain conditions are met such as inclusivity, equal chances to participate, and the absence of distorting ideologies (see Bohman and Rehg, 2001). While this provides an ultimate standard for defending the normative status of public deliberation, from a sociological standpoint, it abstracts too far from the actual conditions of public deliberation and discourse. Habermas's version of the operation of the public sphere in *Between Facts and Norms* is a sociological political translation of his strong epistemic principle, but it is still characterized by an idealized structure where, for example, the public mainly appears as a unified, singular entity. Rehg and Bohman propose a formulation that is more amenable to political and sociological analysis (Bohman and Rehg, 2002). Habermas's strong epistemic principle should be replaced with the weaker epistemic principle of a model of deliberative democracy in which participants should co-operate on not unreasonable principles. This is close to the insight of Max Miller that political co-operation often takes the form of rational dissensus rather than consensus (Miller, 2002).

The epistemic problem in Habermas is derived from his formal pragmatic account of communication as already discussed in Part II. He extends a normative, idealized model of communicative action onto the more unruly terrain of actual political discourse. Ultimately, the social integration model for which the formal pragmatic presuppositions of intersubjective communication furnish species-level principles of co-operation cannot be easily transposed into empirical-pragmatic and semantic levels of societally open argumentation and learning processes. The latter take place in conditions of uncertainty and contingency that are shaped by the past and radically open to the future. This consideration leads to the insight that a formal pragmatics must be complemented by a *social* pragmatics, a perspective explored in more detail in Chapter 12. Such a social pragmatics involves the communicative capacity to co-ordinate different, and even opposing, social positions. Ultimately, this holds the key to understanding explicit moral action from a sociological standpoint. Discursive argumentation is retained as the mechanism of moral capacity, but it becomes transposed from a normatively determined ideal to that of the socio-pragmatic capacity to make socially effective the moral content of cognitive principles.

Towards a Conclusion: Eder's Synthesis, Cognitive Sociology, and the Public Sphere

Klaus Eder has made some suggestions about the relationship between the cognitive and the normative that resonates with the account given in this chapter (Eder, 2007). He links the cognitive and the normative by means of Goffman's idea of an 'interaction order' (Goffman, 1983). The concept of an interaction order is similar to the manner in which Cicourel envisages the interplay between cognitive structures and normative accounting practices.[3] Eder claims that it is not norms that create order as Parsons thought, but rather the cognitive rules that in the first place govern the construction of norms. The cognitive world is a rule-governed world that lies behind the normative world and takes the form of a cognitive capacity for interpreting and validating norms. Even when normative order malfunctions or breaks down, communication on the basis of cognitive rules is still possible. These cognitive rules are predicated on a fit between the reasoning competence of human beings and the communicative structures they have historically created in the form of an interaction order.

---

3   On the subject of normative accounting practices, see also Brandom's normative pragmatic theory (Brandom, 1998).

In the first instance, cognitive rules are competences that are made possible by cognitive structures in individual minds. But this raises the further question of how they got there in the first place. In line with Goffman's pragmatism, Eder sees such structures as individually anchored but socially produced through interaction. Cognitive structures are also to be found on the macro-level. Eder examines what kinds of supra-subjective 'mental' entities could carry these structures and concludes that Luhmann's notion of 'autopoietically' self-organizing social systems offers the answer. Eder's turn to Luhmann to illustrate how cognitive rules could operate on a supra-subjective level is supported by the linguistic conception of a 'grammar'.

The idea of grammatically structured social systems as trans-subjective structures of cognitive rules does describe an important dimension of the cognitive order, though it also presents some problems. For Luhmann, the transcendental phenomenology of systems is conceptualized above the level of agents, which are left with roles of mere compliance with systemically specified 'expectations'. Luhmann's account of systems denies a role for individual or collective perceptions and interventions on the supra-subjective level. Bora, for example, denies that action can ever be an element of a system; these are categorically distinct entities (Bora, 1999). Schimank, by contrast with Luhmann and Bora, introduces actors' perspectives into systems' operations in three dimensions: the most general level of preference formation in social subsystems that reduces the complexity of such systems; the middle-level of rule systems that have the function of guiding action; and the most specific level of the interactive co-ordination of actors' intentions (Schimank, 1996).

Schimank here outlines a mediated epistemology that is consistent with the kind of cognitive framework that will be developed in Chapter 13. The assumptions underlying this framework provide a means of linking macro-level cognitive structures both with actors' preferences on the micro-level and with the meso-level of the interaction order. Discourse and collective learning complete the picture and enable the various horizontal spheres (functional, moral-legal, and ethical-evaluative) and vertical (macro-, meso-, and micro-) levels to become reciprocally active in collective sense-making practices.

On the horizontal level, the cognitive dimension emphasizing the generative requirements of normative practices coexists with paradigms that emphasize other cognitive dimensions. These other dimensions include, on the one hand, functional coding that specifies the requirements of success-oriented action and, on the other, evaluative-expressive coding that specifies the requirements of self- and group-understanding. These three dimensions together delineate the range of available macro-cognitive principles and the spheres of societal meaning to which the rules apply. Following Eder, these are what actors look to when normative rules, which were themselves the outcome of previous cognitive processes, break down. From the perspective of justice, it is imperative that the first dimension of the macro-cognitive order that emphasizes democratic meaning, standards, and rules should have primacy. If a democratically organized social order is to survive, even to prosper, a cognitively well-authorized form of normative practice must ultimately direct social systems. Such systems should be designed to answer discursively specified human needs, rather than to define what needs humans should have (Rosenfeld, 1998).

On the vertical level, the interaction order is based upon meso-cognitive rule competences that interpose between micro- and macro-cognitive levels. These three cognitive levels are not isolated from one another. They continuously circulate around one another, though each enjoying a significant degree of operative autonomy. The cognitive foundations of democratic communication lie on all these levels and on the kind of collective learning processes that are associated with each of them. In one way, the cognitive paradigm turns the claims to primacy of the normative paradigm on its head but, in another way, it offers the prospect of securing that primacy by different means. It turns it on its head because it disputes the assumption that action co-ordination is predominantly achieved on the basis of shared values. But its primacy may still be asserted if communicatively achieved cognitive ordering leads to well-justified norm building. The cognitive paradigm, nonetheless, means that the recent procedural emphasis of normative theories of democracy should be rethought. Norm justification procedures should be placed in the general context of discursive structures that extend throughout society carried by multiple social networks. The next chapter will address the collective learning processes achieved through networked forms of public communication, showing how such learning contributes to the cognitive foundations of the public sphere and of democracy.

CHAPTER 12

Discourse, Learning, and Social Integration

This chapter, building on the overview of relevant literature in Chapter 11, outlines further considerations that bear on the theoretical development of a cognitive-communicative-learning framework. The framework, systematically assembled in Chapter 13, offers a means for analysing and evaluating reproduction and change in both cognitive structures and normative culture. It thus sociologically clarifies pivotal dimensions of the democratic process that have received little systematic attention.

The first goal of the current chapter is to overview the theory of collective learning. Collective learning occurs by means of the discursive exploration of the cognitive foundations of normative culture. Macro-social learning consolidates itself through discursively enabled cognitive innovation and takes hold as a structural potentiality. The structural form of collective learning is that of discourse structures, in other words patterns of meaning that have been constructed in the process of public discourse. These discursive structures are in turn emergent cultural models that have yet to – often may never – move on to become established cultural models. The relationship between discourse, learning, and the cognitive order is fundamental to the prospects for innovation – including regressive innovation – in normative culture. The term normative culture embraces the cognitive foundations of that culture, but exists in another register also, what is commonly called normative order. Normative order results from the stabilization of the outcomes of the discursive construction of the cognitive foundations of normative culture.

The second goal of this chapter is to describe this normative order in terms of the cognitive-normative complexes that constitute it. These complexes, which are combined in various patterns in institutional spheres, form the substantive content of the normative order. They constitute patterns of normative rationality that are shaped by the cognitive meta-rationality of democratic procedures and others societal communication processes.

These normative complexes should not be artificially separated from the cognitive order; norms take the form of obligatory rules for the achievement of social outcomes suspended in a cognitive web of meaning that they succeed in stabilizing enough – the process of rationalization – to reliably structure types of action and interaction. The categories of norms identified in this chapter are basic to modern social experience, but the form of their individual articulation and relational combination varies significantly.

From the cognitive perspective concerned with how the normative order is constituted, Peirce's distinction and interrelation of the concepts of limited and unlimited communication communities, already outlined in Part II, is here sociologized within a collective learning framework. The third goal, therefore, combining the insights into collective learning provided by the first and the account of normative complexes of the second, is to show how normative potentials are anticipated in a cognitive medium. Such anticipated potentials have to be transposed into a cultural framework, taking the form of cultural models, which sufficiently overcome conflicts to allow normative practices to continue. This process leads to the question of how such cultural models are 'composed'. It is argued that this occurs through a range of modalities of communicative organization that bridge the cognitive and normative levels. But composition is not always positive as pathological learning can steer this process in an adverse direction.

The Sociological Theory of Collective Learning

To those interested in a sociological theory of learning, it seems evident that there is a tradition to draw off, albeit mostly a heterodox one. Some years ago, Max Miller instanced Durkheim, Mead, the early Piaget, and Vygotsky as evidence for the presence of a theory of collective social learning that was concerned with ontogenetic and socio-organizational potentialities (Miller, 1986, 2002; Piaget, 1932). For many social scientists, learning is mistakenly understood as synonymous with social progress and neglected. When learning is actually conceptually foregrounded, it is, in one approach, conceived instrumentally and narrowly as in the policy-theoretical concept of 'social' or 'policy' learning (Sabatier and Jenkins-Smith, 1993). Or, in another, it is conceived as primarily driven by individual learning, as in Mead and Habermas, even though the intention of both is ultimately to comprehend society as a mediated supraindividual, intersubjective, and intrasubjective reality.

Some twenty-five years ago, Piet Strydom, taking a lead from and closely interacting with other sociologists working in the tradition of critical theory, Klaus Eder and Max Miller, began the task of reformulating an explicit sociological learning theory. This first phase followed two related directions; firstly, the critique of Habermas's ontogenetic account of learning and, secondly, a broadly sympathetic reception of the work of Miller and Eder, who had already developed a sociological theory of collective learning (Eder, 1985; Miller, 1986; Strydom, 1987). This was followed by a second phase that built on the first, in which Strydom has developed a cognitive sociology that is both reconstructivist and constructivist (Strydom, 2000; Strydom, 2006; Strydom, 2007).

This first part of Chapter 12 closely follows Strydom's outline of a theory of collective learning that is compatible with the general cognitive theory of the public sphere whose main lines will be schematically outlined in Chapter 13. The first part of the chapter will therefore follow how Strydom engaged with the theory of collective learning theory of Eder and Miller in two steps. The first step addresses critical dimensions of Strydom's theory of collective learning comprising of, firstly, the constructivist-inspired reassessment of reconstructivism; secondly, the shift in emphasis from moral development to the social evolution of practical reason; and, thirdly, the shift in emphasis from double to triple contingency in accounting for the role of the public in a communication society. The second step will move on to Strydom's later cognitive emphasis that closely articulates with the general theory of collective learning.

Towards a Social Pragmatic Theory of Collective Learning

Strydom's social pragmatics is a sociological variation on Habermas's formal pragmatics and the transcendent/immanent epistemology of discourse ethics. Social pragmatics retains the normative intentions of formal pragmatics, while retaining both the explanatory advantages of evolutionary theory and concern with socially generated contingencies. It differs from Habermas by virtue of seeking to realize its normative intentions by means of a theory of public discourse that is fully aware of its socio-cognitive foundations.

A reconstructive methodology is central to the transcendental epistemology of discourse ethics. Terrence Kelly nicely describes reconstructivism in a paper primarily concerned with Rawls (Kelly, 2001). Reconstructivism is a project shared between philosophy and the social sciences that identifies the various competences and commitments embedded in a particular practice, or necessary presupposition of 'good' social interaction, so as to make explicit the implicit formal aspects of the practice.[1] It then 'idealizes' the commitments and competences associated with justifiable practices, and proposes their more extended social realization. This includes, in the case of a critical approach, identifying blockages that should be removed. This approach has been present in the work of Habermas since the early 1970s (Alford, 1985; Habermas, 1973). Following Alford's account, Habermas uses the term 'reconstruction' to characterize philosophical reflection on such transcendental questions as what cognitive abilities are necessary for science or morality to exist (Alford, 1985, p. 330).

Discourse ethical reconstructivism involves the transfer of the 'moving spirit' of the transcendental regulative idea from Kant's a priori of moral intuitions to the formal presuppositions of linguistic communication. This post-Kantian reconstructive transcendentalism focuses on the intersubjective presuppositions of language use. These presuppositions contain a communicative rationality based on principles of discursivity and universalization. The direction of communicatively realized moral universalization proceeding against the backdrop of social problems in need of a solution – for example, violence, inequality, non-recognition, loss of meaning, and global endangerment – takes the form of a communicative a priori that is progressively institutionalized in modernity. This process can be

---

[1] Robert Brandom, in *Making it Explicit*, systematically follows similar intentions (Brandom, 1998).

reconstructed and made explicit as an immanent, but not yet fully realized, communicative rationality, with the reconstructive method providing the twin theoretical advantages of normative grounding and anticipation.

While reconstructivism in this sense remains in a qualified form integral to Strydom's later cognitive turn, he also criticizes it for over-anticipating and hence subsuming social practices. A *social* pragmatics would rather give social practices a clearer generative and creative role than in Habermas's formal pragmatics. The revaluation of the constitutive role of social practices, and the accompanying recognition of contingency and non-linear dynamics, would open the path to a constructivist approach that would have communicative practices in socio-historical situations as its generative core. This constructivist approach would still be reconstructively shaped by the potentials that make their way into innovative micro-cognitive models and from there into social practices and public discourse.

The theory of collective learning emerges from a social pragmatic reformulation of Habermas's ontogenetic account of the relationship between moral learning and normative innovation. Strydom criticizes Habermas's individualist account of learning in which the individual subject is assumed to do the learning, so generating rational potentialities that can subsequently be practically applied (Strydom, 1987). Building from the early Piaget, Miller, and Eder, he proposes a shift from Habermas's genetic individualism to a genetic interactionism in which a 'collectivity or intersubjective experiential context serves, on the one hand, as the objective condition of individual learning and, on the other, is simultaneously the outcome of collective learning which is able to transpose the collective effect of individual actions not only into the object but also into the medium of learning' (Strydom, 1987, p. 269). He claims that the individualist understanding of learning used by Habermas cannot grasp the constitutive role of collective action.

Following Eder, Strydom not alone emphasizes learning as a collective achievement but also decouples learning from practice, an association that is prevalent in the ontogenetic model where practice is regarded as the external sign of internal learning. He claims instead that collective learning processes make available collectively utilizable knowledge, but cannot guarantee that such knowledge will be practically utilized. The extent to which collective learning becomes available for practical utilization in normative structures determines the social evolution of practical reason. Collective learning processes themselves do not guarantee a gain in practical evolutionary rationality; only transformations of such learning into collective practices do that. These insights are important for critical normative sociology. Instead of criticizing normative structures from ideal standards derived from the formal pragmatic presuppositions of communication, social criticism should instead focus on communicatively mobilized collective learning that generates potentials located in macro-cognitive structures whose realization potentials are blocked.

In the late 1990s, Strydom developed some of the implications of the above paradigm shift by addressing the democratic status of publics through the theory of triple contingency as part of a general cognitive sociology of critical publicity (Strydom, 1999). The idea of triple contingency critically extends Habermas's model of double contingency in which ego and alter are assumed to form communicative relations geared to the exchange of validity claims against the backdrop of a situation-defining social order and in the context of text-generating practices. In the model of triple contingency, ego and alter relate not just to one another, but, in the case of democratic communication, they must also relate to the validity standards and factual beliefs held by the general, observing public. As Strydom observes, Habermas's account does not alone confine attention to contingency generated in intersubjective communication to the relative neglect of the observer but, in the general model of the co-present exchange of validity claims, it also privileges normative reconstruction over empirical description. The validity standards and fact interpretations held by the observing public in the model of triple contingency permeate *all* democratic communication as political actors must recognize the omnipresent necessity of legitimacy before a public.

The core-periphery model taken over by Habermas from Bernhard Peters in *Between Facts and Norms* is a doubly, doubly contingent one; first, the public representing the political periphery is predominantly represented as a single, unified entity engaged in a relation with the political core through the medium of public discourse (Habermas, 1996; Peters, 1993). Then, once issues are transferred from the realm of discursive will formation in the weak public of the mass public sphere, they again become conceived, double contingently, in the deliberative communication of strong publics at the core including parliament, administration, government, and law (see Fraser, 1992, on strong and weak publics). Habermas is ambivalent on this issue in that both the agenda-setting role of public discourse and answerability before a public is at the core of his theory, hence pointing in a triple contingent direction, yet his theory of communication does not adequately incorporate the continuously active role of the public. This leads into the problematic 'normativism' of his account of deliberative democracy in which the category of public is transcendentally incorporated into normative procedures.

The theory of triple contingency is a logical concomitant of the constructivist and collectivist emphasis of Strydom's sociological reformulation of critical theory. The expansion in the range of contingency does not identity the public as only a unified collective or as only a diffuse carrier of 'subjectless communication' (Habermas, 1996), though it can be partially conceived in both these ways. Rather, it pragmatically expands the notion of 'public' so that publics in the plural are regarded as carriers of multiple identities and issue positions, some of which can never be fully reconciled, and the public sphere is correspondingly understood as a conflict-based, discursive medium of collective learning.[2] The public, both generally in the sense of the public of publics and as multiple partial publics, does not fade away with the onset of deliberation; the public is always present whether in the 'gallery' as observers or as external interlocutors of deliberative activities in which it does not have a formal role. The concept of triple contingency, thereby, radically changes the understanding of the context of the double contingent communication between ego and alter

---

2   This formulation raises a wide range of issues for Habermas's account of the public sphere and the public sphere generally. These relate to issues of multiple kinds of resonance (Strydom, 2003), the relationship between cognitive structures, normative structures, public discourse and social positions; the nature of resolution of issues to do with the situation-relative co-ordination of validity claims and fact interpretations within and between multiple publics and multiple power-holders; and the macro-sociological architecture within which the public sphere is located.

that Habermas assumes to be characteristic of deliberative procedures. It conforms to the kinds of temporal and spatial dislocations characteristic of actual democratic discourse and the fuzzy, serpentine quality of achieving good justification in a mediated public sphere.

Collective Learning and the Cognitive Turn

Strydom's constructivist cognitive approach regards cognitive rules as means, devices, and tools for categorizing, classifying, and ordering the world. This cognitive constructivism builds on his social pragmatism – constructivist reconstructivism, collective learning, contingency, and situation responsiveness – and has two pivotal theoretical implications. These are, firstly, the ongoing negotiability and reflexivity of norms and, secondly, that normative innovation depends on its cognitive context. These implications in turn have a pivotal ramification; they necessitate changed assumptions about the scope of public discursive processes that now take on the greater role of aligning the cognitive and normative orders.

The implication of Strydom's position is that deliberation cannot be regarded as self-organizing and self-contained in the manner that Habermas and other deliberative theories tend to view it. It should instead be seen as part of a wider process of discursive action co-ordination, taking place in and across multiple arenas and generating the multiple kinds of resonance that will be explored in Chapter 17. The combined effect of the theories of triple contingency and of the cognitive order is to reduce in importance the special kind of intersubjective communication represented by deliberation. Deliberation remains important, but existing forms of deliberation cannot by themselves satisfy basic normative-procedural criteria such as full inclusion, impartiality, parity of esteem, openness, and responsiveness, because such criteria are dependent on interpretation within a cognitive order that forms a wide context for democratic communication of which deliberation is only one part. These criteria can and must operate normatively guided by the further cognitive standard of universalization, but their normative authority is continuously reinterpreted and its range extended through collective cognitive learning processes.

Deliberation exists amidst a wide range of partially deliberative or non-deliberative mechanisms of generation of political meaning. Moreover, it is also shaped by cultural constructions and processes, such as ideologies, interest articulations, patterns of resonance, and collective identities, which are cognitively structured. The manner in which the observing public is discursively constructed in political deliberation, for example, especially within representative systems, will depend on how the cognitive context illuminating the various dimensions of *public* is discursively mobilized; beyond this, deliberation by the public themselves in direct acts of public participation remains a pressing but largely unrealized demand. Its relative absence from the spectrum of important democratic institutions indicates the relative weakness of *public* deliberation (Cohen and Sabel, 1997).[3]

Strydom criticizes the over-extended counterfactual, consensual foundations of Habermas's deliberative proceduralism as opposed to a concept of discourse synthesis understood as the varied, possible social outcomes of argumentation processes. Habermas therefore considers the outcomes of deliberative procedures as universally accepted norms emerging from unlimited and unconstrained interaction, rather than the multiple standpoints that actually shape cognitive cultural models. Max Miller and Bernhard Peters have productively raised questions about the outcomes of episodes of public argumentation that, especially in Peters's account, points beyond consensus as the only possible outcome to other possible outcomes such as shifts in the spectrum of meaning and levels of argumentative rationality (Miller, 1992; Peters, 2001). The latter kind of outcome is not consensual, but represents a form of rational dissensus or, alternatively, the persistence of misunderstanding and regressive conflict. In some circumstances, such shifts in the spectrum of meaning lead to a rethinking of socio-cognitive foundations. In a similar manner, Strydom's cognitive approach emphasizes

---

3   Direct public participation serves as a good example of both an emergent cognitive rule system and cultural model. As a rule system, direct public participation has a mostly latent status; as a cognitive cultural model, it is currently emerging as a framework idea for the discursive organization of politics; as a socio-cultural model, it has greater and lesser importance in different societies (see O'Mahony, 2009, on the cognitive construction of participation).

the openness and variability of both discursive mechanisms – beyond but incorporating deliberative procedures – and *substantive* outcomes manifested in shifts in meaning and normative commitments that may induce change in both cognitive cultural and socio-cultural models.

Habermas's process model of discursive political will-formation addresses how public discourse and deliberative procedures might be aligned. While this two-track approach is extremely important, it nonetheless involves an unrealistic account of the capacity of deliberative procedures to incorporate the outcomes of discursive processes. In proposing that final agreement on the validity of norms is necessary, Habermas operates with a counterfactual standard against which reality will nearly always problematically fall down. The concept of reality is here understood not in the sense of disillusioned political realism, but with regard to how public sovereignty is actually realized through contemporary democratic communication or through foreseeable institutional innovations in such communication.

Realism in the above sense means that key dimensions of actual democratic communication must be reflected in democratic theory. It is troubling that, at least in the later Habermas, a pivotal idea such as ideology has little role, whether the concept is understood as applying to the *description of* political belief systems or in the critical theoretical sense of *criticizing* hegemonic ideological projects that lead to bad justification and unjust social relations (Freeden, 1996; Mannheim, 1935). Nor, generally, has he given much prominence to the fact that political systems are predominantly majoritarian and representative, even if it is true that these arrangements do ultimately depend on communicatively achieved meaning and legitimacy in the manner he emphasizes (McCarthy, 1995).

The cognitive and learning theoretical approach outlined here is meant to compensate for these limitations. A multi-level concept of the cognitive order is proposed that identifies macro, meso, and micro levels in the forms of, firstly, the macro level of cognitive structures that encapsulate learning potentials in society; and, secondly, suggests that, at the meso level, these cognitive structures are produced, reproduced, and transformed by discursive processes of a particular kind that are animated by subjects with appropriate interactive cognitive capacities; and, finally, the micro-level is characterized by subjects with cognitive capacities to either reproduce existing practical rationality or, through learning processes, individually and collectively develop innovative micro-level cognitive models that point beyond it.

Following Miller, critical to the communication theoretical point of view is that meso-level discursive structures are related to what he, following Durkheim, describes as the system of co-operation in society (Miller, 1986). These discursive structures reflect different perspectives, above all, on the moral principles that should guide the system of co-operation. This discursive structure is itself structured by the most abstract and fundamental structures of meaning available, that which is located in cognitive principles, operating as transcendental presuppositions, that specify how to collectively think matters of legality, sovereignty, legitimacy, and many others. And these principles, in turn, are selectively combined in cognitive cultural models through discourse and learning. These models shape the spectrum of relevance within which the building of normative structures takes place. According to Miller, democratic institutions of public decision-making will have to undergo institutional innovation to remain relevant to society's evolutionary differentiation and the underlying logic of dissent expressed in its discursive structure (Miller, 1986). Theorizing democracy in this way yields a different vantage point on the relationship between democracy and wider society than that of a political philosophical perspective that abstracts too far from cognitive learning processes, and the multiple communicative mechanisms that animate them.

Like Habermas's two-track discursive theory of democracy, Miller envisages two related processes, discursive exploration of dissensus in the public sphere and democratic procedures, but beyond that there is a significant difference. For Miller, as for Strydom, Habermas's theory remains too consensus-oriented and, by implication, the gap between idealized consensus and the other agreement oriented co-ordination option that Habermas's offers, interest-based compromise, is too wide. Miller fills this gap with his theory of rational dissensus (Miller, 1992). Democracy and the real organizational principles of society should be brought into closer relation and different discursive perspectives stemming from social positions in the system of co-operation should not be ideally denied. Miller follows Durkheim in proposing that the system of social co-operation is regulated by moral norms whose types and configuration will vary with the different systems of such co-operation. This suggests also a double orientation for morality, instantiated both in substantive norms that adequately address the system of co-operation and in procedural norms of democratic discourse. Accepting this also entails that it is not enough to imagine that democracy should only be guided by the communicative presuppositions of discourse ethics; democracy is only formal and empty if it cannot be related, through the discursive mobilization of cognitive structures, to the system of co-operation.

The most significant change that follows from the above is the need to break with the idea of an immediate correspondence between individual democratic participation and consent to norms. In complex, modern societies it is not thinkable that such a comprehensive standard could ever be followed. Trying to follow it leads to such a minimal, procedural specification of moral norms that the actual extent and modality of moral action in society is left unclear. Habermas's discourse theory of democracy requires to be reconceptualized. Such a task should go beyond the a priori transcendental standards of formal pragmatics to adequately address both the collective cognitive principles and the related cultural models that societies actually produce and that underpin *social pragmatic* presuppositions of communication. It should be shown further how these cognitive structures establish a spectrum of relevance for institution building, drawing from mechanisms of dissensual argumentation and collective learning by means of which cognitive structures are formed in the first place.

The needed reconstruction is addressed in what follows by, firstly, strengthening the substantive grounding of Habermas's typology of discourses by introducing a corresponding typology of political norms. The norms represented in this typology are institutionally combined in the system of co-operation. The normative order is pivotal to the organization of social life, even if it must be situated in the broader context of the cognitive order. Secondly, the cognitive, cultural contexts that thus condition the normative order are shown to be grounded in Peirce's concept of communication community, with its blending of immanence and transcendence. The pivotal kind of norm relevant to radical change in the system of co-operation – moral norms, de-emphasized in much of twentieth-century sociology – is then placed in the context of the communication community. Thirdly, the relationship established between the communication community and the typology of norms leads to a specification of mechanisms of achieving normatively regulated social order. Finally, the pathological mechanisms that impede morally organized but also feasible social integration, that is to say, horizontally and vertically mediated or 'equilibrated', are outlined following some ideas of Max Miller (Miller, 2002).

Collective Learning, Cognitive Order, and Social Integration

The typology of norms, set out in Table 1, both mirror and are complementary to the discourses that Habermas identifies in his account of public will formation. Table 1 is designed to capture the normative complexes that these discourses – pragmatic, bargaining ethical, moral, and legal – reproduce or challenge. These normative complexes structure the institutional contexts from which discourses emerge or, at least partly do, for they also emerge from non-institutional contexts. The normative complexes, specified separately in Table 1, are combined in various configurations for the purpose of institution building. Combined normative configurations temporally endure for long periods in institutional settings, though they are subject to potential adaptation or transformation on an ongoing basis.

Table 1: A Typology of Political Norms

Norm type	Pragmatic	Bargaining	Ethical	Moral	Legal
Process	Decision	Compromise	Evaluation	Justification	Application
Standard	Control	Equilibrium	Appropriate	Right	Coherence

In Table 1, *pragmatic* norms specify what consequences predictably follow from certain actions, leaving aside ethical and moral considerations. Such norms result from the interplay of rational collective or individual action and the aggregated logic of the consequences of such actions. They typically take the form of action guiding maxims like 'do this to achieve that'. They are decision-oriented in the sense of the predictability of the relationship between action and aggregated consequences. They are at the core of Luhmann's sociology, where this relationship is given the term 'expectation'. The technologically conceived standard is that of control, where aggregated systemic logics compensate for the opacity of disaggregated contexts of action.

Bargaining norms fall between ethical and moral norms, on one side, and pragmatic norms on the other. On the ethical and moral plane, Habermas (1996) draws attention to the legal institutionalization of fairness codes in the design of bargaining procedures so that all affected interests can come into play and have an equal chance of prevailing. The normative standard in bargaining shifts from that of control in the case of pragmatic norms to that of equilibrium. Representative, legitimate interests seek to advance their positions, but they do this within a framework that should respect other interests and the viability of underlying common concerns, such as productivity/wage trade-offs or environmental sustainability (Elster, 1989).

Ethical norms or values constitute individual and collective identities. They represent commitments that underpin shared forms of life, specifying membership criteria and terms of esteem and solidarity within small- or large-scale communities. Ethical norms thereby establish common bonds between members of a community who are prepared to make sacrifices for the common good or the good of disadvantaged members (Habermas, 2001; Honneth, 2007). The nation-state is the prototypical modern ethical community, though ethical allegiances exist below and above the nation-state in groups of all kinds, from families, to organizations, to place-based communities. Beyond group membership, individuals and sub-groups bring to bear ethical differences, in the public sphere generally, in multiple contexts of association, and in various kinds of procedures such as, for example, ethics committees. The standard for ethical norms is appropriateness, implying, on the one hand, the social validity of what is right by 'us' in this time and place and, on the other, the recognition in conditions of post-metaphysical pluralism that 'our' commitments must take proper account of the differing commitments of others.

In the tradition of discourse ethics, *moral norms* take on an unconditional quality; they are agreed by all and, correspondingly, are binding on all. They are not therefore situation or group relative. Nonetheless, moral *ideas* are open to imagination and argument (Fesmire, 2003). Moral norms emerge from argumentation on moral ideas and acquire institutional force. In discourse ethics, the most fundamental moral norm is that of universal inclusion in fair deliberative procedures. This norm is realized through the establishment of a comprehensive and legitimate structure of public autonomy that is equiprimordial with the framework of individual private rights. In modern conditions of ethical pluralism and the contingency of contexts of experience, moral norms increasingly depend on procedural justification. Hence, intersubjective agreement on what is unconditionally right – the standard of moral norms – depends on procedures and discursive processes – public, legal, parliamentary – that specify the relationship between universalistic criteria and specific situations, for example, fair treatment for women depends on women's situations and experiences and does not only consist of the extension of existing individual rights to women in the name of formal equality.

Nonetheless, it is not adequate to only admit to moral status those norms that pass the exacting universalistic justification standard of discourse ethics. For to do so would effectively exclude from moral standing those commitments that, though they may be well supported, are not universally agreed. A more inclusive standard of moral justification would therefore be what all *could possibly* agree as opposed to what all *should* agree. It is a fine difference that squarely faces the fact that fully comprehensive justification procedures cannot foreseeably happen. Moral norms, whether as procedural norms or material outcomes, depend on less comprehensive justification procedures, wider public argumentation, and ongoing management of moral disagreement than is classically allowed for in discourse ethics. This is precisely why the theory of rational dissensus is so fundamental to understanding moral processes.

Legal norms take on a double character. On the one hand, they have an enacted quality in the sense of legal statutes that are factually observed, since they emanate from a recognized legal procedure and are backed by coercive power. On the other hand, the legitimacy of legal norms depends on normative justification processes that reach beyond the legal system, narrowly defined, to include the counterfactual foundations of moral, ethical, and pragmatic discourses that enter legal discourses (Habermas, 1996, p. 30). This double character emphasizes, then, on the one side, the need to understand legal norms in application as both enabling and coercive and, on the other, the shaping of these legal rules by legally relevant pragmatic, ethical, and moral discourses. In the latter case of the discursive construction of law, it is not simply the de facto acceptability of law that is at issue, but the overall legitimacy and symbolic standing of the legal system itself. Today, there is an increasing interpenetration of legal and political norm setting, described by Arjomand as the judicialization of politics and the politicization of the judiciary, comprising of judicial-type legislation by parliaments and administrative organs and legislative jurisprudence by the constitutional courts and supra-national judiciary organs (Arjomand, 2003, pp. 3–9). These processes demonstrate the strains on the legal system in its dual normative roles of social regulation and political steering. At bottom, though, legal norms have to translate the heterogeneity of ethical and pragmatic positions into applied rules that do not contravene basic moral norms.

The normative complexes outlined in Table 1 are reproduced and elaborated by norm-building practices that are special cases of cognitive practices. Macro-cognitive structures specify the constitutive cognitive principles for how society or specific groups 'think' and interact in various ways and elaborate these principles for relevant cognitive domains. Norm-building practices, whether they take place in democratic or other institutions, are modes of action co-ordination that are shaped by cognitive structures and discursive processes. But they organize these practices in a specifically normative way, that is to say, with a view to utilizing communication procedures and processes of various kinds to meet substantive normative goals. Such substantive normative goals have high consequences and are therefore partly immunized against rapid cognitive rethinking.

The distinction between horizontal and vertical mediation processes, drawn in Chapter 11, clarifies this relationship. In horizontal view, that is to say, mediation between different cultural spheres, the norm complexes of Table 1 are subject to a cognitive logic of disjunction and combination to create normative configurations as institutional structures. Cognitive cultural models specify how norm complexes may be combined. Ideologies are important to understanding such specification. From a cognitive standpoint, ideologies are enduring discursive perspectives whose mediation leads to characteristic emphases in cognitive cultural models. The cognitive cultural model of capitalist class society, for example, generates right and left ideologies, which discursively contend for primacy in respect of the predominant direction of the model. But their common existence and logic of competition shape the model. Collective learning processes both generate ideologies and cultural models, the first as outcomes of associational learning by movements in conjunction with specific kinds of institutional learning, and the second as a result of rational dissensus and compromises between ideological standpoints.

Discursive perspectives, associational collective learning, and various kinds of outcome are also embedded in the terrain of vertical mediation, ranging from the macro to the micro. In this view, the range of social positions present in a society and how they contend or align is fundamental. The key to such patterns is what Miller calls the discursive structure, or what Forst describes as the diagnostic-evaluative structure (Forst, 2007a; Miller, 2002). It is this structure that underpins alignments of social positions that arise on the micro- and meso-levels of society as forces of reproduction or change.

Cognitive structures may harbour surplus capacities that are not fully visible until society encounters new kinds of challenge that call for their further development. Cognitive principles may then be pushed further. In other words, by means of pressures exerted by discursively carried learning processes, further dimensions of cognitive principles are elaborated and immanent cognitive cultural models incorporate these latent dimensions. For example, neo-liberalism cognitively respecified the relationship between efficiency, as a functional cognitive principle oriented to the standard of control, and moral and ethical principles such as equality, legitimacy, and legality. This process led to the generation of a dominant cognitive cultural model and gradually, if still inconclusively, a new socio-cultural model. In this process of re-elaborating macro-level cognitive structures, further potentials harboured within cognitive principles become socially available. Social transformation is often socially triggered by hitherto unrecognized, socially immanent minority insight whose perceptions, if successfully diffused, change what is thought to be possible or desirable.

The Cognitive Construction of Normativity and the Communication Community

Peirce's original idea of a distinction between real and unlimited communication community was built upon a consensus theory of truth. Truth would emerge through eventual convergence of opinion if communication could be imagined to continue for a sufficiently long period. As taken over into discourse ethics, the unlimited communication extends beyond the real communication community as an idealized horizon that could confirm or deny the validity of utterances. Utterances in the real communication community always have the associated claim that they would be valid if subjected to testing, according to criteria of truth, rightness, and sincerity, in the unlimited communication community. Both Apel and Habermas apply this counterfactual mechanism of testing validity, through the device of the hypothetical unlimited community, to actual discourses of real communication communities. As already developed above, discourse ethics does not see itself as a normative guide to the substantive norms the real communication community should produce, but rather it is focused on the ideal communicative conditions that would enable participants themselves to produce well-justified norms.

Discourse ethics therefore blends the real and the unlimited communication communities. Counterfactually operating cognitive principles located as cognitive presuppositions underpin the validity of actual communicative action, because real utterances are always subject to being called to normative account. Speakers operate with the assumption that the claims to validity in their statement might be tested and that therefore following implicit formal pragmatic rules is necessary in the long run.

Moving from co-present context of interaction to multiform, complex, structurally embedded interaction, leads to the insight that this way of viewing the relationship between real and counterfactual horizons of communication does not capture the full social import of counterfactuals. The real communication community constantly reaches beyond its existing self-understanding and its associated practical rationality. But from a societal standpoint, the further question arises as to how such real discourses might incorporate the structural outcomes of learning processes that point beyond existing knowledge and normative arrangements. Thinking in this 'structural' register involves thinking of the real communication community as exploring systematic and interrelated functional, moral, legal and ethical horizons that point beyond its existing normative rationality. The concomitant of 'going beyond' would then involve the actual building of an already cognitively anticipated new normative order.

Constant processes of ideal innovation and argumentation hence characterize real communication communities. These processes generate knowledge that exceeds existing practical rationality. The stake of this conflict is over the direction of societal learning processes that are either adaptations of or challenges to established practical rationality. Three gradations of the real communication community may be specified that indicate shifts in the state of knowledge that begins to institute in the real communication community that which hitherto only existed counterfactually as potential. The first gradation is closely related to existing practical rationality, while the other two depart progressively further from it. As they do so, the relationship between the cognitive order and the dynamics of public discourse becomes more apparent.

The first gradation of the real communication community, then, will be called the 'normal' communication community in which the interpretation of the cognitive order is closely related to an existing practical rationality. Such a practical rationality is sustained by a specific, temporally enduring organization of the normative order that has public legitimacy, variously involving stable translation arrangements between normative complexes, legitimated power relations between social groups lying within and between these complexes, and the availability of epistemic and social resources to sustain the social model. Such a communication community achieves a practical equilibrium between society-specific patterns of historically established need interpretations, on the one hand, and its 'horizontal spatial' distinctiveness from other communication communities on the other. But normal communication communities may not be normal across all social fields. Some social fields, perhaps gender, for example, may be in a mobilized, transitional state while others, for example, the economy, may be relatively stable. But no communication community is completely stable because structural conditions and their discursive interpretation vary constantly. Brief reflection on the extent of cultural and social change in any modern society over a thirty-year period makes this observation self-evident.

The spatial relation to other communication communities brings into play a second gradation of the real communication community, the degree to which a given community engages with the cultural models of other real communication communities, opening up learning potentials that elsewhere (that is, in these other communities) have been already transposed into a practical social rationality. What appears in *this* communication community as an innovation that merits consideration has already been implemented in *that other* communication community. The prospects of the innovation being adopted frequently depend on whether collective learning needs to be fundamental, which would entail challenging ethical and moral reorientation. In this second gradation of the real communication community, societies on the whole do not simply take over a normative template from other societies, for example, innovation systems or industrial relations structures, but engage in complex discursive respecification of their own cognitive cultural and normative models in the light of external stimulus. Such respecification takes on an almost permanent quality in the context of transnational pluralistic and multi-demotic arrangements such as the European Union.

The third gradation of communication community is the furthest from practical social rationality and the nearest to the counterfactual horizons of the unlimited communication community. At this third level, fundamental ideas are at issue that have major implications for existing practical rationality, but run counter to its existing logic. It can be conceptualized as a moral, ethical, and epistemic 'diagnostic' critique of the normative content of existing social arrangements, a diagnostics that can, in the right circumstances, transpose into a prognostic demand for moral innovation. History is replete with many examples of these kinds of constitutive, actor-borne learning processes, such as the ethic of capitalism, minority rights in majoritarian democracies, the status of rights frameworks affecting women, and the call for an ecological ethic that would take the form of a transformed foundation for human relations with external nature (Strydom, 2013).

As Klaus Eder points out, history is also replete with examples of collective learning processes that cannot find an evolutionary pathway at a given point in time (Eder, 1996). The example he gives is of the new nature relation that emerged in European societies with the Romantic Movement, including its vegetarian eating culture. This culture could not, in the conditions obtaining in the early nineteenth century, find a social evolutionary path into general practical rationality. It was forced to give way in this period to the more powerful force of an anthropomorphic and nature-dominating scientific rationality and its mechanistic relation to nature. According to Eder, it went underground to emerge again in changed circumstances, and with new social carriers, in the modern environmental movement. From a cognitive perspective, the cognitive standard of a different relation to nature was retained, but was socially only very weakly held until circumstances arose when, through diffuse learning processes, it became anchored in a collective micro-level cognitive model of sufficient size and intensity. At that stage, it became part of the second wave environmental movement, taking off in the 1960s, and began to have significant implications for the cultural models and normative order of modern societies.

The role played by cognitive cultural models is consistently present across these historical, spatial, and counterfactually creative collective learning processes that bridge real and unlimited communication communities. Cognitive cultural models reflect agreement on what is collectively possible and what should be done, given the plurality of cognitive principles and the different perspectives associated with each of them. Such an agreement can remain stable for a time, but is always subject to change. And at certain periods within the lifespan of all cognitive cultural models, innovative collective learning processes vie with more strongly established cognitive patterns and sometimes succeed in fully transforming the model. Just as cognitive cultural models are related 'upwards' to macro-cognitive principles, they are related 'downwards' to socio-cultural models. Such socio-cultural models further concretize cognitive orientation systems by building in the perspective offered by the normative and institutional orders of actual societies.

From a democratic theoretical point of view, out of the variety of types of norms, moral norms have a foundational status. The traditions associated with critical theory, both in the discourse ethics of Apel and Habermas and the collective learning theory of Eder, Miller, and Strydom, are unusual in the degree of emphasis they place on moral learning (Eder, 1985; Miller, 1986; Strydom, 1987). Elster, by contrast, excludes moral and legal norms from the domain of sociologically relevant norms (Elster, 1989). In Durkheim and Marx, moral learning processes appear as the ineluctable outcome of other social forces such as the dynamics of interests, technological change, and the rise of certain social classes (Pharo, 2004). While these and other factors can by no means be excluded as critical contextual conditions of moral learning, they do not explain how such moral learning operates as an indispensable condition of radical social change or, indeed, how such change must be conceptualized through the standard of achieved moral learning.

Moral learning and moral norm formation are pivotal to social change. Moral norms specify rules of democratic interaction – discourse ethics identifies the standards of discursivity and universalization – that make possible the establishment of legitimate, morally informed, substantive norms. Moral learning processes variously involve the generation of moral claims that take the form of proposals for substantive moral norms, such as rights or social justice, the assertion of moral influence on other norms, and the assertion of procedural and processual principles for democratic discourses of various kinds. Moral learning may also be impeded, sometimes with disastrous consequences. In one of his other major works, for example, Eder characterizes the pathological history of moral-legal learning in nineteenth-century Germany, manifested in the failure to build a democratic institutional framework out of the interplay of ethical-political associations (Eder, 1985).

In further work of Eder (Eder, 1996, 2007), in Strydom's cognitive sociology, and in Honneth's recognition theory, the medium of collective moral learning is located in the classificatory struggles between social groups over the specification of the kind of rational-critical, intersubjective *meaning* out of which moral norms can be forged. The classificatory practices of social groups in such discursive struggles do not take place in a rarefied 'moral' space; moral norms are forged from collective learning that is conditioned by pragmatic, bargaining, ethical, and legal discourses. But moral ideas are also generated that cannot find an evolutionary path; hence Eder separates collective moral learning from social evolution and this is used to distinguish his approach from that of Habermas who, working from the normative paradigm, puts learning and evolution together.

In real communication communities, moral innovation may not actually emerge from successful outcomes of classificatory struggles; such learning does not guarantee translation into normative structures. This depends on a political process and legitimation struggles. In cases of non-existent or poor translation, moral learning may be real, but too diffuse and motivationally weak; 'we' know what we should do but can find ways not to do it. This is precisely where the circuit of *social construction* of morality comes into play, whether inside the individual, in groups, and in society at large. Within the moral and constitutional frameworks of actual societies, moral norms do not usually emerge from deliberative and discursive practices that are practical equivalents of Habermas's counterfactual universality condition (U); they mostly emerge from dislocated discursive and deliberative processes that nonetheless succeed in gaining universal assent, frequently only *after* the relevant moral norm is actually instituted in legal norms. Partially achieved moral learning may also simply be by-passed. Discursive and deliberative processes in many cases address social problems in need of a solution via pragmatic, bargaining, ethical, and legal innovations. In such cases, the influence of power differentials is likely to be far higher than if moral learning processes are strongly present in societal communication. The cost of non-moral learning such as, for example, significantly diminished commitment to egalitarian principles in hard times, is experienced differentially across advantaged and disadvantaged groups or, in the case of regressive and/or authoritarian learning, it can be felt by the society as a whole.

As analysed above, moral learning processes sometimes result in the formation of moral norms associated with rights, justice, and responsibility.

Such moral norms are interpreted and become effective in concrete forms of life, that is, in real communication communities that are structured by ethical, bargaining, legal, and pragmatic norms and associated discursive practices. Moral norms always coexist with non-moral norms and practices; they offer a set of unconditional standards and rules, in the sense that all could ideally assent to them as individual norms, but they are in most cases conditionally applied in real contexts of application. To give a 'negative' example, the process of jury selection or judicial prejudice may compromise the right to a fair trial or, to take a contrasting 'positive' one, the right to freedom of speech may, in certain restricted circumstances, be justifiably curtailed in, for example, the case of curbs on race hate speech (Günther, 1993; Alexy, 1993).

From a macro-sociological standpoint, it is important to grasp what determines the capacity to innovate in or successfully resist moral norm formation. Such innovation or resistance will take place in real communication communities that cognitively position themselves in relation to their context in the three ways described above, namely, incrementally, comparatively and imaginatively. All modern societies in one way or another sustain ongoing communicatively achieved reflection on their own historical and comparative situations. Whether, and the extent to which, collective learning takes place across groups or the whole society and becomes transposed into practical social rationality depends on how discursive perspectives are aligned within their socio-cultural models. These cultural models are formed from 'below' by existing patterns of social integration and from 'above' by selectively appropriating available cognitive principles. These relations and mechanisms are outlined in more detail below.

The Cognitive Organization of Social Integration

The normative structure of a society has a facticity of its own and cannot be changed all at once. Potential change is constrained by material systems such as the economy and technology, by established practices sustained by latent dispositions in the sense of Bourdieu, and by orders of power, functional, social, and communicative. The normative order, no less than the cognitive order, may be regarded as horizontally and vertically mediated. The typology of norms outlined above captures the normative complexes that become horizontally mediated in the design of institutional normative configurations. Vertical mediation operates from macro to micro by means of meso level communicative structures. Communicative structures and processes that are *internal* to the reproduction of norms – represented as *processes* in Table 1 – whether these norms are understood in the horizontal, cultural sense of Table 1 or in the social sense of the distribution of norms across groups, are more institutionally bound than public justification of the overall *societal* validity of norms. A fundamental distinction may be drawn on this basis between norm-reproducing communication, which can also include some degree of intrinsic normative elaboration, and norm-transforming communication that enters into the discursively carried cognitive-learning circuit. From the point of view of understanding the public sphere, the latter is fundamental, though equally so is the resistance provided by embedded normative structures, often sustained by cultural, psychical, and communicative pathologies.

Normative integration must first be cognitively articulated. Key modalities of the communicative organization of social integration are outlined below that, following the last remarks above, facilitate social integration by linking the institutional structures of the system of co-operation with the cognitive-learning circuit of public communication. This means that these organizational modalities operate on two planes. As will be explored further in Chapter 13, they are, firstly, fundamental to the organization of cultural models, while, secondly, they also offer a suite of co-ordination mechanisms for normative practices. At least this is true of four of these modalities. The fifth, permanent conflict, indicates the failure of social integration on a relevant issue or across an entire society.

Permanent Conflict: This is essentially a state of societal *disintegration* or integration that is only sustained by non-normative means, that is, by domination potentially backed by violence. Examples include the case of extreme ethnic conflict where groups carrying irreconcilable ethnic identities are forced to live together within territorial jurisdictions or the case where, for various possible reasons, there is no functioning state and anarchy is let loose. In contemporary democracies, this kind of societal 'integration' is prominent on issues such as genetically modified crops and abortion. Communication carries on in these cases, but it is extremely polarized with institutional law-based 'solutions' sure to offend one of the contending parties. Insofar as such solutions are attempted and gain some kind of de facto traction, permanent conflict in these cases shades over into repressive hegemony. True cases of permanent conflict are probably to be distinguished from these intermediate cases by the impossibility of any collective action of general scope. The situation of permanent conflict is consistent with the idea of a *dissensus* pathology, which is outlined below following Max Miller (Miller, 2002).

Repressive Hegemony: Repressive hegemony involves circumstances in which the ethos and interests of a particular social group come to dominate over the – actual or potential – ethos and interests of other social groups. This can occur across society as a whole – the domination of a particular class for example – or can be differentially present in various social spheres. In the latter case, for example, economic relations might be conducted on a basis of – relatively – fair bargaining while, for example, the gendered domestic sphere or the environmental sphere may be based on strongly asymmetrical and symbolically latent power. Repressive hegemony may be achieved, on the one hand, by ideological distortion and subterfuge or, on the other, by the unchallenged belief, even by the dominated, that the values of a particular group serve the good of all.

Situations of repressive hegemony characteristically bring to the fore certain kinds of ethical norm, for example, that strong national identity makes for a just society that are either not tested, or only weakly tested, in public discourse. Ethical norms of this kind have an extensive influence on the selection of available moral norms – on rules of distributive justice or conceptions of autonomy, for example. They also influence agendas for bargaining. From the standpoint of innovation, they structure what can be thematized, that is, what is allowed to come on the public agenda and the initial form it takes. The emphasis on ethical hierarchy often involves restrictions both on compromise seeking, for example, recognition of ecological values in environmental negotiation, and on moral norm formation, for example, asserting moral standards such as animal and information rights.

Compromise: If structures of repressive hegemony operate largely *latent*ly through the symbolic concealment of social power, the communicative organization of social integration achieved through compromise operates *manifestly* as the outcome of bargaining or, more diffusely, societal argumentation processes. This kind of communicative organization presumes a high degree of symmetry in the distribution of social power, including the epistemic and communicative capacity to effectively understand and present social positions. It therefore represents a filtration process in which issues characterized by power symmetry move from being addressed within conditions of hegemonic domination to become explicitly thematized and practically considered within bargaining or argumentation processes. The ideal of compromise is relatively well understood as a process of the rational aggregation and reconciliation of interests (Nine, 2013). This kind of compromise-based integration is conditioned by moral norms; the play of interests occurs within a morally regulated constitutional framework (Apel, 1978). The underlying constitutional framework cannot, however, itself be constructed from the play of rational interests, since such interests can only issue in contract type arrangements between consenting parties and do not include all those potentially affected by the norm that are not parties to the contract. Nor does compromise-based modes of co-ordination allow sufficiently for those who put the interests of others and the general good before their own.

Rational Dissensus: Rational dissensus lies somewhere between compromise and consensus. The term refers to the identification of differences arising in argumentation that nonetheless leads not to conflict but to agreement on rules for managing disagreements (Miller, 1992). It is different from compromise – which is founded on interest-based bargaining on the distributive model – in that arguing parties fundamentally disagree and yet are able to understand why they disagree. A state of rational dissensus frequently entails the construction of co-ordinating schemata of a partly moral, partly ethical, and partly pragmatic kind. This concept has wide application. Many of the social preconditions of democracy, for example, the balance between economy and equality, depend on it. The last example shows how rational dissensus can be related to compromise while also distinguished from it. The ability to even enter discussions that might eventuate in compromises depends on prior rational dissensus. In that sense, rational dissensus might be understood as a means of rationally co-ordinating disagreement that could in the end result in compromise or consensus. But rational dissensus also operates as an outcome in that it is intrinsic to a liberal vision of agreeing to differ. In these circumstances, it might take the form of mutual non-interference or of accepting the right of others to introduce innovations to which one is opposed. In the latter sense, rational dissensus is intrinsic to majority rule.

Consensus: Consensual kinds of communicative organization are characteristic of circumstances where moral justification processes determine norm formation. Where morally structured justification relates to consensus over norms with high moral content, deliberative processes, especially those that bear on constitutional legal issues, have a big, and sometimes decisive, role to play. Consensus is not only of a moral kind. It is also characterized by shared epistemic and wider symbolic assumptions on what should be valued in factual, social, and emotional worlds. Such shared background assumptions operate within the horizon of a common lifeworld and might either support or inhibit the achievement of moral consensus. Moral norms derive from morally grounded procedures for realizing consensus. They are possible consensual outcomes of such procedures. They take the form of fundamental moral norms or other norms – or general principles – with high moral content such as Rawls's difference principle. This kind of *substantive*, consensual outcome is stressed, over against the procedural moral formulations of discourse ethics, because of the importance attached to the actual social realization of democratic standards, for example, blending standards of social justice, ecological responsibility, and various other kinds of rights and responsibilities. Innovation in moral norms frequently emerges at the end of a phase of collective learning characterized by category struggle between disputed ideas of what counts as moral in a given case or situation. In these circumstances, rational dissensus may express a crucial breakthrough that opens the door towards consensus on fundamental moral norms or, alternately, 'going on' by means of institutionalized rational dissent arising from the combination of moral norms and admixtures of legal, technical, and functional norms.

Apel's idea of a macro-ethic of responsibility also corresponds with the consensus mode of societal integration; since it has the status of a macro-ethic, it exhibits a consensual quality that does not reflect the ethos of a particular group and, depending on processes of social selection, could result in the generation of collective moral commitments that are institutionalized through legal norms (Apel, 1987). The idea of *social* justice is another example of a macro-ethic with moral implications. Democratic moral principles are conditioned by consideration of the good of all, whether this is understood with regard to liberal private rights emphasizing autonomy and freedom or with regard to collective principles of responsibility and social justice. Moral norms specify foundational procedural rules or substantive standards that should not be transgressed. Nonetheless, there is considerable historical contingency and variability in collective, public conceptions of morality, partly because many kinds of rights, including human rights, are weakly institutionalized.

In concrete societies, all the above types of communicative organization tend to find a place in various combinations. Certain social issues, for example, may be subject to bargaining; others to rational dissensus; some issues are prone to indivisible type conflict; moral norms underlie consensus formation; repressive hegemony excludes or minimizes the impact of certain innovative ideals. They offer different possibilities for the communicative organization of the system of co-operation. The moral dimension, critical to democracy, is present in each of the five integration models; more obviously in the latter three in the very principle of consensus, as agreement to disagree, and as fair compromise. Even communicative organization through repressive hegemony may entail moral learning processes as, for example, in conditions of majority rule where a moral idea is institutionalized against strong opposition, but later comes to be universally accepted. And, even in these conditions, the majority must still respect minority rights.

Learning pathologies only become apparent when just procedures and justified moral norms are by-passed and non-moral norms become dominant. These circumstances lead to repressive and authoritarian kinds of imbalanced integration in which pragmatic and ethical norms in particular can be combined to serve the hegemony of particular interests. In this case, which characterizes primarily either authoritarianism associated with permanent conflict or certain forms of repressive hegemony, counterfactual appeals to validity beyond the existing normative rationality are shut down in favour of a normative facticity orchestrated by repressive social power.

Learning Pathologies and Discursive Co-ordination

The communicative organization of social integration represented by compromise, rational dissensus, and consensus, provide non-pathological avenues for the social realization of collective learning. Each of these operates through characteristic mechanisms. These are the deliberatively formed constitutional order and others forms of fully inclusive and reciprocal deliberation in the case of consensus; public argumentation in multiple arenas in the case of rational dissensus, ranging from the diffuse publics of the public sphere to parliamentary debate and discursive institutions; and bargaining institutions in the case of compromise. These arenas may be characteristic of the different modalities, but their purity should not be overstressed. The different modalities of communicative organization interpenetrate in the three arenas.

The case of repressive hegemony is consistent with the realist account of politics described in Part I and, accordingly, with widely held assumptions about the actual modus operandi of formal democratic politics. The preferred modality of democratic communication is predominantly formal and elitist. Co-ordination based on repressive hegemony, nonetheless, substantially depends upon other more exacting modes of communicative organization, that is, compromise, rational dissensus, and consensus, even if it deviates from their underlying principles in its actual practices. In other words, action consistent with repressive hegemony purports to act in a moral fashion, but in actuality does not do so.

These communicative modalities organize discursive processes of the generation, elaboration, and transformation of normative rules. Most fundamental to this process is not fundamental agreement, only one possible outcome, but common horizons of meaning to allow for various of the possible outcomes. For this, cognitive principles such as legitimacy, legality, solidarity, and equality make possible substantive as well as procedural normative ideas to be advanced, and potentially to become socially effective, even where there is no universal agreement. In given discursive conditions, the cognitive principles, firstly, stipulate horizons of relevance that, secondly, enable immanent, communicative organization through the modalities or rule systems, including the balance to be struck between them.

In fact, the essence of the communicative modalities lies in their capacity to organize differences, not always for the good of course. The historically long-established construct of unacceptable exploitation of labour is a case in point, arising from the orienting cognitive principle of equality. The realization of such an immanent standard arose through a long collective learning process utilizing cognitive principles of dignity, esteem, and legality as well as equality, eventually resulting in a *normatively justified* standard of non-exploitation. While this standard is far from universally applied, in certain conditions it acquires institutional force through the operation of the various communicative rule systems, albeit with significant variation between possible realizations.

The idea of a society free from domination provides a moral standard against which communicative pathologies can be diagnosed. Such pathologies are above all those that block moral learning and generate action and interaction that leads to the consolidation of non-moral, pathological learning inconsistent with the idea of a society free from domination. Illustrating how such pathologies might concretely be understood, Max Miller provides an account of interaction pathologies that can be related to the communicatively organized forms of social integration. The manner in which interaction pathologies of this kind are closely connected to and sustained by macro-cultural pathologies embedded in the cognitive cultural models, and in individual pathologies that become collectively manifested on a sub-societal level can only be mentioned in passing here, but will be taken up again in the next chapter.

Miller identifies types of conflict and associated potential collective learning processes that might lead out of it, which are blocked by social pathologies (Miller, 2002). The three kinds of social conflict identified by Miller are infinite conflicts, finite conflicts, and conflicts that result in consensus. These correspond to the various modes of societal co-ordination sketched above. The first corresponds to the irreconcilable disagreement characteristic of permanent conflict; the second to finite conflicts that are characterized by rational dissensus; and the third to consensual processes of the kind outlined.

In its essentials, then, Miller's framework of conflict corresponds to three of the integration types identified above, namely, permanent conflict, compromise, and rational dissensus. Even repressive hegemony can be seen as lying somewhere between infinite and finite conflict and compromise can be seen as a variant of finite conflict. The import of Miller's approach is to attach considerable importance to infinite conflicts as a common form of conflict in modern societies; he outlines four kinds of blocked learning process that he claims prevent infinite conflict from becoming finite conflicts or, more unusually, finite conflicts from producing a consensual outcome. The first of these is *authoritarian learning* that involves the assumed right and capacity to be dogmatic and hence to enforce a pre-defined consensus; the second is *defensive learning* that is based on a defensive avoidance of dissensus and thus represents a more subtle kind of pre-defined consensus; the third is *ideological learning* that actually entrenches conflict by promoting the belief that whatever can be learned must respect the permanence of certain kinds of antagonism and falsely presumes that particular interests have the status of general ones; finally, *regressive learning* involves the use of *ad hominem* arguments and an a priori commitment to the dissensual exclusion of certain groups and individuals. Miller classes the first two of these kinds of blocked learning operate as consensus pathologies in that dogmatism and exclusion ground a false kind of consensus, which should not be equated with the above consensual model of social integration. The second two he classes as dissensus pathologies, given the conviction that antagonism cannot be overcome and the willingness to engage in *ad hominem* arguments.

These four learning types and associated consensus and dissensus pathologies help to explain why problematic forms of the communicative organization of social integration in the forms of infinite conflict and repressive hegemony may take hold. Repressive hegemony differs from infinite conflict in that it involves a form of conflict resolution – either by the exercise of coercive power or by symbolic artifice or both – that ends constructive conflicts or prevents recognition of the need for such constructive conflicts from forming. The very idea of consensus pathologies intrinsically includes the avoidance of conflict as both those in hegemonic positions and the dominated may not see the value of conflict. In particular, the dominated may see the given state of affairs as normal or, at least, be willing to accept it as normal rather than incur the risk of trying to change it. As Honneth has continuously emphasized, conflicts only become manifest when perceptual categories related to the denial of recognition are activated (Honneth, 2007). Infinite conflicts are more characteristic of dissensus pathologies in that they involve not alone denial of the validity of others' arguments but also of their public standing.

Infinite conflicts and repressive hegemony represent power-saturated modes of social 'integration' that entails, in the case of repressive hegemony, unjustified domination by the ethos of one social group. Such domination might be associated with the hegemony of a particular class habitus, a misguided general ethos that leads to bad societal goals, a non-moral or power-shaped utilization of pragmatic norms in conjunction with such an ethos, and the employment of law as a de-moralized, positivized medium that serves a particular ethos (Bourdieu, 1986).[4] In the case of infinite conflicts, any kind of agreement that would allow norm building to take place is absent. Yet, the existence of infinite conflicts can indicate a balance of power, sustained by dissensus pathologies, that prevents hegemony from forming and, in that sense, allow for an uneasy 'truce'. These conflicts could also indicate a dangerous state of normlessness, where distrust and suspicion impede the emergence of the kind of reciprocity that might bring about more constructive forms of conflict. Such constructive conflict, if they were to happen, could open the way to more justifiable kinds of the communicative organization of social integration, namely compromise, rational dissensus, and consensus.

The five modalities of the communicative organization of social integration are intrinsic to the construction of both cognitive cultural models and socio-cultural models. Discursive learning leads to the appropriation and combination of cognitive principles, through complex processes of selection within these models. Such models establish agendas for norm-building practices. Innovative discourses, first advanced by social carriers groups, 'agitate' cognitive principles and shape how they are combined in cultural models. Such cultural models don't simply pertain to possible future

---

4   It may be noted, in the light of the discussion of communal ethos in communitarian theory in Part I, that these remarks show the dangers of a politically repressive ethos that serves domination.

normative innovation; as the neo-institutionalists emphasize, the interpretation of established norms that conditions how they become effective in social life depends on their cultural foundations (Powell and DiMaggio, 1991; Scott, 2001). From a processual standpoint, therefore, cultural models, which shape both the substantive agendas and mechanisms of norm building, are built on the foundations of the collective learning that potentially emerges from the interplay of discourses and cognitive structures.

The possible mechanisms for organizing such cultural models are intrinsically related to the cognitive-communicative organization of social integration – or repression, domination, and other negative syndromes sustained by learning pathologies. Before these forms of social integration can operate on the normative level, they have first to be aligned cognitively. Cognitive alignment in cultural models generates distinctive patterns of normative orientation. The normative complexes outlined in Table 1 are at the core of this process of cognitive/normative alignment. For example, on the level of socio-cultural models, environmental issues in the Republic of Ireland are organized according to the modality of repressive hegemony in a manner that blocks eco-*moral* learning (O'Mahony, 2011a). This organization is based on the dominance of pragmatic and legal norms accompanied by very restricted democratic justification. The operation of repressive hegemony in such cases also intrinsically depends on certain kinds of ethical norm that validate powerful habituses over weaker ones.[5] Such normative practices depend on the cognitive alignment of the relevant socio-cultural model – what is collectively validated as societal goals or as acceptable contention within a legitimated spectrum of relevance. When oppositional voices reach beyond this spectrum, they face the challenge of discursively shifting the relevance spectrum legitimated in the cultural model, a challenge that indicates how fundamental collective learning must first be discursively achieved through cognitive reorientation rather than through norm-building practices.

---

5   Chapter 13, and also Part IV, address the structural foundations of cultural models, including the significance of differences in social power.

CHAPTER 13

Cognitive Sociology and the Public Sphere: Towards a Theoretical Framework

This chapter proposes to synthesize insights deriving from the two previous chapters of Part III and, on that basis, establish a framework for a communicative-cognitive-learning oriented approach to the analysis of public culture and communication. It therefore draws from the key themes of the last two chapters, as well as Parts I and II of the book. In Chapter 11, the basic elements of a cognitive sociological theory were outlined. The advent of the structure-action paradigm has opened up insights into mediation processes between structure, culture, and action. This paradigm has significantly contributed to the constructivist transformation of the foundations of social theory. Constructivist epistemology denies that an independently evolving social structure effectively determines agency. Or, at least, such a determining force of structure can now only be asserted on constructivist premises, as is the case with Luhmann's systems constructivism that offers an account of how systems 'construct' structures from semantic distinctions. The period in which structure-action thinking emerged coincided with the renaissance of micro-sociology and, correspondingly, gave rise to concern for the exploration of micro-macro relations (Alexander et al., 1984). One important expression of the rise of constructivist epistemology in the social sciences was growing interest in a mediated epistemology linking macro structures to micro processes. With respect to such a mediated epistemology, the constructivist structuralism of Bourdieu has become the most influential.

Chapter 11 developed a mediated epistemology utilizing the structure-action paradigm as a base. Such an epistemology, intrinsic to understanding the dynamics of public discourse, was employed as an important way station for developing a communicative-cognitive sociology.

Bourdieu has a distinctive cognitive position of his own, owing much to his earlier anthropological fieldwork, in the form of his account of the classificatory schemes used by social agents and the classificatory struggles that occurred between these schemes. In Chapter 11, the mediated cognitive foundations of structure-action theory were supplemented in important dimensions.

Firstly, Bourdieu does not theorize the counterfactual use of rules and so tends to attach cognitive classificatory schemes directly to immanent social positions. Luhmann's account of systemic rule systems offers an insight into how the counterfactual foundations of discourse ethics, contrasting with Bourdieu's immanent cognitive approach, may be extended in a cognitive sociological direction. For this purpose, whereas for Luhmann discourses follow from an action orienting, transcendent system semantics, the impulse towards sociologizing discourse ethics leads in a different direction. Quasi-transcendent principles are 'agitated' by the discourses of agents resulting in patterns of collective learning that in turn shape cultural models. This does not deny, in line with Luhmann, the other possibility of potentials for the autopoietic *self-transformation* of these quasi-transcendent reflexive principles. But such autopoiesis cannot be completely decoupled from intentional action in the way that Luhmann proposes. Above all, it cannot be decoupled from the moral foundations of democracy, whether understood with respect to its procedures or its substantive prerequisites, or democracy will not survive. Autopoiesis is possible with respect to those functional codes that have high potential for autonomy, but not with respect to other codes where explicit moral discourse comes into play.[1]

---

[1] Hans-Georg Moeller provides a valuable overview of Luhmann's account of morality. Luhmann observes on the necessary passing of older substantive forms of dogmatic morality, for him explained through the emergence of a non-stratified functionally organized society in early modernity. In modernity, the moral coding of good and bad is to be regarded as a special code that does not have a social system of its own but is distributed throughout other systems and contrasts with the strictly functional codes of these systems. The contrast arises in that moral communication is a polarizing communication that carries potential symbolic violence in its wake. Morality therefore appears in Luhmann as resulting in pathological social communication. Methodologically, one dimension of Luhmann's theory of morality is consistent with

Secondly, Bourdieu's structure-action theory lacks a strong processual dimension located on the meso-level. The meso-level is narrowly conceptualized in Bourdieu through his account of strategic interaction in social fields. The meso-level is pivotal to the cognitive-communicative sociology. Communication at this level mediates the micro- and macro-cognitive levels. Following Cicourel and Knorr-Cetina, pragmatic-argumentative and memory storing cognitive capacities come into play at this level. These cognitive-interactive presuppositions on the meso-level can also be understood through theories of formal pragmatic and social pragmatic competences. The meso-level, as developed in this book, draws inspiration from and yet differs from the way it is developed in much interactionist theory, including that of Knorr-Cetina, where it is presented as the sole location of socio-cognitive capacities. Such a viewpoint sees cognitive capacities as shaped by the experience of interaction and dedicated only to its furtherance. The presumed absence of structural conditioning of interaction is implausible, and excludes consideration of those enduring micro- and macro-level cognitive structures that impact on, even if they do not determine, the meso-level. It further tends to exclude non-cognitive social structures, such as the structuration of the public sphere and other communicatively relevant social structures.

Thirdly, the relationship between cognitive categories and explicit moral action, under-theorized in Bourdieu, is fundamental to a normative sociology. Reaching beyond the naturalistic focus on structurally determined expectations, and the phenomenological focus on implicit practices, the capacity for explicit moral reasoning by social agents is essential to a responsible democratic society. This does not entail that cognitive demands

---

the arguments raised in this book; morality is not only concentrated in constitutional fundamentals, nor in the ethics of procedures, but dispersed across cultural models and action spheres. While there is much to recommend in Luhmann's account of the history of morality, and also with respect to his suggestions about contemporary dangers of moral dogmatism, this should not deny the moral-constitutional foundations of democracy in formal and informal constitutions and in structures of democratic justice. While elements of this Luhmann-critical argument appear in this book, to fully argue it out with such an original and powerful diagnostician of modernity would take much more attention than can be granted here (Moeller, 2009).

that are epistemically impossible to satisfy should be placed on individual agents, such as comprehensive knowledge of the far-reaching consequences of actions. Rather, it presupposes a society that is able to communicatively comprehend and represent its options so that individuals and collectivities can co-responsibly reason. The capacity for morally responsible action on the micro-level of both individuals and collective agents is not naturally inherent; it is a socially constructed capacity that shapes socio-centric dispositions that in turn support higher-level reasoning.[2]

For the purposes of elaborating a cognitive-communicative theory of public discourse, Chapter 12 added essential elements. The first, following Eder, Miller, and Strydom, is the theory of collective learning. This is a fundamental socio-cognitive accomplishment or, depending on its forms, a pathology. Collective learning arises from interplay between public discourse and cognitive structures that involves the societal reconceptualization of the validity foundations of the normative order. Such reconceptualization takes the form of a cognitively grounded anticipation of a changed normative order. The formal pragmatic understanding of the relationship between the limited and unlimited communication community is thereby social pragmatically extended and given an appropriate degree of structural durability as a collective counterfactual anticipation of possible social change. Such anticipation, which is a collective learning process, is expressed through the form of emergent cultural models and possible options are, in some cases, filled in by the example of other societies or sub-societal experimentation and, in other cases, involve radical innovation for which no template exists. The five modalities of the communication organization of social integration, outlined in that chapter, provide a means of understanding both mechanisms and outcomes of collective learning processes. They are mechanisms when they are part of the process of counterfactually driven learning, whether radical in the form of generating emergent cultural models or ongoing in the co-ordination

---

2   Axel Honneth offers support for such a position in his argument for the primacy of capacities for recognition over cognition in the socialization process (Honneth, 1996).

of established cultural models. And they are outcomes in that they play a role in stabilizing cultural models that guide norm-building practices.

This chapter moves forward in two steps. The first step is to systematically represent the various dimensions of the cognitive order, including the various dimensions of its discursive reproduction and transformation, and show how it is related to the normative order. In a second step, this account of the cognitive order of modernity, using Strydom's term, will then be brought into relation to the diagram at the end of Part II, which laid out a societal theoretical representation of the review of political philosophies of Part I. These two steps are closely interrelated; the first step provides an abstract account of the components of the cognitive order and the second how this abstract account may be related to the dynamic, cognitive-communicative production of normative order.

The Modern Cognitive Order and Public Discourse

In Table 2, Discourse, Learning, and the Cognitive Order (see pp. 324–5), the various dimensions of the cognitive-communicative construction of normative culture are outlined. Later on in this chapter, in Figure 2, these dimensions are presented in a more dynamic manner to give a sense of the flow between these dimensions. The table and the figure are based upon a number of key theoretical distinctions developed in the text so far that will first be summarized before describing the contents of Table 2. These distinctions take effect between transcendent and immanent, cognitive and normative, vertical and horizontal, and external and internal.

The distinction between immanent and transcendent has become central to the self-understanding of critical theory in recent years, but it can also be applied to other theories, as Strydom does in applying it to Rawls, who emphasizes transcendence, and to Bourdieu, who emphasizes immanence (Strydom, 2011). The application of the distinction to both a philosopher and a sociologist indicates that the problematic is shared between both disciplines. While the divided emphasis on immanence and transcendence in the above example may appear to be utterly consistent with the self-understanding of the two disciplines, common to the recent philosophy and sociology emanating from critical theory is the pursuit of a framework that tries to break down this distinction. The renewed focus on injustice in political philosophy, together with the critique of transcendental theories of justice such as that of Rawls, shows that the shifting ground affects more than critical theory narrowly defined.

These attempts to bridge immanence and transcendence implicate complex considerations that cannot be fully followed here. A few key dimensions of the approach adopted may nonetheless be highlighted. Transcendence is understood as the existence of specific kinds of reflexive principles such as efficiency, sovereignty, legality, and legitimacy. These reflexive principles are expressions of cognitive rationality standards and rule-following and rule-elaborating competences that are diffused across the key domains of modernity. They are therefore domain specific and clearly defined, though they are constantly being 'thought into' afresh as agents confront problems and seek orientation. 'Transcendence' implies the existence of 'surplus' capacity in a principle that has not yet been translated into instituted practices. These surplus capacities, which enter into social life when triggered, are precisely what constitute the specifically transcendent level. These principles are 'pushed' in the direction of rule evolution – Luhmann would say autopoietically – by discursive learning processes that provide a sense of what is desirable and possible.

The cognitive principle of publicity, for example, has public participation at its core, but the idea of participation reaches beyond the current, limited form of democratic participation that stands in tension with the ideal of public sovereignty. Whether the ideal can be stretched to overcome this tension is first contemplated as a transcendent potential, perhaps animated by small-scale experimental practices such as, often cited in deliberative theorizing, the British Columbia experiment that delegated to ordinary citizens the redesign of the electoral system. Understanding transcendence in this way is a sociological translation of the formal pragmatic presuppositions of communication. Transcendence has a *social pragmatic* core that goes beyond normatively framed proceduralism. This social pragmatic core is manifested in two senses. Firstly, cognitive principles are not consensually agreed rules; they are rules that emerge from the synthesis of different discursively articulated perspectives. Over time, these perspectives lose some of their conflictual quality and the principle becomes generalized across them as taken for granted world-orienting presuppositions. But the surplus potentials latent in such principles – for example, alternative rationalities for realizing public participation may be anticipated – can still be discursively activated within episodes of collective learning, leading to potential evolution of the principle itself. Secondly, assuming transcendental *social* pragmatic presuppositions add a stronger teleological or ends-oriented dimension to cognitive analysis, enabling the reconstructive identification of better ways of dealing with problems or taking opportunities that arise in social practice.

The idea of immanence, contrasting with that of transcendence, refers to that which is already practically operative in social life. Cognitive principles make their way into immanent social practices through cognitive cultural models. Cognitive cultural models, lie on the horizon between immanence and transcendence. Responding to thematization, discourse, learning processes, and 'lower-level' socio-cultural models and normative models they construct cultural orientation systems that offer principles for social organization. Quasi-transcendent cognitive principles do not simply flow into cultural models from above. Discourses stimulated by collective action induce various kinds of collective learning that agitate these principles into further operations that are then sifted into cognitive cultural models, into socio-cultural models, and into social life generally as group and individual level cognitive models and as meso-cognitive interactive capacities. It is at the interface of micro and meso-levels that radical change is first discursively formulated. This frequently takes place in milieus and associational contexts that are distant from mainstream public culture in, for example, techno-scientific, moral, and ethical contexts of innovation. Not just academics, but also social actors in these contexts, develop reconstructive ideas about how relevant cognitive principles could become differently operative in social life and initiate learning processes. The emphasis on the immanent reconstructive capacities of publics in the pragmatist tradition is what a sociologically revitalized critical theory offers as a challenge to 'objectivist' philosophical reconstructivism.

A further distinction, important to Table 2, is that between the cognitive and the normative (Strydom, 2012). The normative import of public communication is central to the idea of the public sphere. The empirical-theoretical application of the concept of public sphere has suffered because it has been fused with idealized, consensus-oriented, social and political theories. The problem is only partly with the goal of consensus that, with regard to certain basic norms, is a basic prerequisite of any justifiable, democratic order. The problem becomes fully apparent when the idea of the normative is based on assumptions about the necessity of strong epistemic and value consensus. Not alone is the full range of communicative mechanisms for the production of possible consensus not adequately taken into account, but the over-emphasis on consensus leads to the neglect of dissensual and other integrative mechanisms. A cognitive sociological account of the construction of normative culture operates differently. The social institution of normative rule systems, which lead to the actual justification and application of norms, depends upon a selective appropriation of cognitive potentials. Normative rule systems, including deliberative rule systems, are conditioned by these macro-level cognitive principles. The generation of cognitive structures, and the logic of their normative appropriation, takes place under the influence of power, and available time, energy, opportunity, and knowledge. A creative tension is maintained between cognitively specified normative potentials and available norm-building processes.

The distinction between vertical and horizontal has already been addressed as the separate and interrelated processes of the mediation of horizontal cultural spheres and vertical levels. In brief recapitulation, and as applied in Table 2, the horizontal dimension covers the differentiation of the socio-cultural spheres of modern life, which retains the distinction drawn in Part II between functional, moral-legal, and ethical-expressive world concepts, ultimately springing from, but also modifying, Kant (Peters, 1993) As will be clarified below, these three master concepts may be used to encompass the full range of cognitive principles. Horizontal mediation arises through the manner in which they are combined in cultural models and institutional rule systems. The vertical level refers to the by now classical, if not everywhere agreed, distinction between macro-, meso-, and micro-levels of social life. No less than the mediation of cultural spheres, this form of mediation is intrinsic to the schematization offered in Table 2.

The distinction between external and internal is also a key distinction in sociological analysis. It separates ontological standpoints that respectively emphasize, on the one hand, reproduction and change in social life by virtue of external, law-like, causal, and non-intentional forces, which arise beyond and determine agency – though also these forces may also be understood as the unintended consequences of agency – and, on the other hand, reproduction and change through interactively generated meaning. From Weber to Habermas, there have also been many attempts to link explanation in the first sense to interpretive understanding in the second. Table 2 follows in this latter tradition by assuming that the macro organization of social life may evolve relatively independently of the action and interaction of agents, but at the same time it must be emphasized *only* relatively independently. Whether understood as the unintended consequences of action or the self-unfolding of systemic logics, quasi-autonomous modalities of macro-social organization are constantly in tension with discursively carried moral and ethical norms that restrain their autonomy. It nonetheless remains possible that institutional and systemic structures can causally influence 'lower level' social processes in ways not legitimated at these lower levels, or only pathologically 'legitimated'.

Outlining these distinctions already completes some of the task of describing Table 2. The structure and rationale of that table is now addressed in more detail.

Cognitive principles are transcendent in the sense that they constitute regulative ideas of reason that become immanent through reflexively structuring social processes. The top two rows in Table 2 are internally related. Cognitive principles (row 1), consistent with their core rationalities, may be placed in the 'containers' constituted by the three basic rationality structures of modernity, functional, moral and evaluative (row 2). These cultural rationality structures encompass the various cognitive principles of modernity: the functional structure addressing empirical truth, the achievement orientation, economic efficiency, and technological effectiveness; the moral structure encompassing rightness, procedure, publicity, freedom, plurality, responsibility legitimacy, legality, and autonomy; the evaluative

Table 2: Discourse, Learning, and the Cognitive Order

1 Quasi-transcendent Cognitive Order	Presuppositional cognitive principles, taking variously the form of rules of reasoning, rational properties, formal principles (organized according to the cultural structures outlined in (2) below)		
2 Cognitive-cultural Structures	Functional, e.g. Truth, Achievement, Efficiency, Mastery, Control	Moral, e.g. Legitimacy, Publicity, Legality, Respect, Plurality, Equality, Responsibility, Autonomy	Evaluative, e.g. Appropriateness, Sincerity, Good Intimacy, Good Social Bonds
3 Associated Forms of Power	Functional	Communicative	Social
4 Dominant Institutional Spheres	Science, Economy, Administration, Formal organization generally	Political institutions, Law, Civil Society	Civil Society, Everyday Life
5 Learning/Learning Pathology	Systemic learning, purposive rationality, hierarchy, functional coding/ disorganization, opacity, selective rationalization	Moral Learning in dimensions of justice, responsibility, legitimacy, equality/ authoritarian, defensive, ideological, regressive learning	Ethical-Expressive learning in dimensions of values, needs, esteem, intimacy, social bonds/ alienation, reification, repression

Cognitive Sociology and the Public Sphere

6 Cultural Models (established and emergent)	(a) Cognitive cultural models as master orienting complexes of modernity, e.g. democracy, cosmopolitanism, environmental responsibility; (b) Socio-cultural models as functional, moral, evaluative and combined institutionally orienting meaning complexes and value hierarchies composed from consensual, dissensual, compromising, excluding, and repressing rationalities	
7 Normative Models	Composed from deliberative and co-ordinative procedures (based upon compositional rationalities of (6) above) producing as outputs substantive legal and other norms – and linked to social systems and expressive complexes	
8 Meso-level: Discursive Learning/ Learning Pathologies	Discursive Justification (discursive structure formation; triple contingent learning); Argumentative cognitive capacities enable 'progressive' collective learning/Consensus and dissensus pathologies sustain pathological learning	
9 Micro-level Learning: Cognitive models (Individual and Collective Agents)/Pathologies	Micro-level cognitive models (Interpretive Schemes) composed of factual beliefs, normative commitments and ethical identities (combined application to self, concrete and generalized others/states of affairs); constructed through cognitive rule competences/ innovation capacities blocked, non-reciprocity (ideologization, authoritarianism, ad hominem critique, denial, exclusion)	Cognitive Rule competence: Representing, Strategizing, Justifying, Evaluating, Emoting *in different registers of cognitive order*/self-defeating reasoning (performative contradiction), imbalanced absorption of cognitive order, weak ego identity (blocking cognitive competences)

structure encompassing appropriateness, truthfulness, authenticity, self-determination, ego identity, well-being, and motivating social bonds.[3]

Moving on to the immanent plane, each of these cultural structures is characteristically associated with institutional spheres as distinguished in row 4, functional organization is associated with formal organization, moral integration with the public complex and civil society, and ethical orientations with civil society and private life. Nonetheless, as stressed through the text, the validity standards associated with each of the structures should be understood not only as standing on their own, but also as combined in cultural and normative-institutional models. The law, for example, is in part a moral-normative institution, in part a functional system, and in part an ethos of conduct, even if, from a discourse ethical standpoint, the moral dimension is the most fundamental. They are also stabilized by distinctive kinds of power (row 3); functional power is associated with symbolically generalized non-normative media of communication such as money or administrative power that generate pragmatic norms, or what Luhmann calls expectations; communicative power involves the necessity of generally and reciprocally justifying political norms with and before a public; and social power involves the capacity of a social collectivity to develop an identity and to project it onto others. Once again, the distinctions between these kinds of power should not be over-emphasized, as they interpenetrate in practice. Further, unity is not assumed internally assumed in any of these forms of power; for example, different sources of functional and social power may lead to internal conflict, and even to a recurrent conflict structure. Such a conflict structure – and a corresponding alliance structure – also extends across these forms of power.

Each of these cultural structures is also associated with particular kinds of learning (row 5): functional learning is associated with the production of logically coherent techno-scientific and socio-institutional complexes and the application of purposive rationality that is achieved through denormatized symbolic media by means of processes of technicization, scientification, and monetization; moral learning is associated with

---

[3] See Part IV for a fuller development of the spectrum of cognitive rule systems.

the development of a basic structure of justification from reciprocal and general principles together with the substantive goal of improving the moral level of social integration with the ultimate – counterfactual – horizon of bringing about a justified basic structure of society to be achieved through legitimate authority, fair co-operation, impartial legality, and respectful plurality (Forst, 2007); and evaluative learning is associated with achieving the good life, well-being, and a capacity for need identification and articulation. By contrast, the kinds of pathologies that these rationalities may bring in their train include respectively, disorganization, opacity, and contradiction in the functional sphere, intractable conflict and symbolic and material domination in the moral sphere, and alienation, reification, and repression in the evaluative sphere.

Cognitive principles permeate and structure all the social levels of discourse and reflection on the organization of society. They reach from transcendent ideals, through cultural and social models, to public communication and collective and individual identities. Each principle exhibits a degree of purity that has some consistency with Luhmann's conception of autonomous social systems. Cognitive principles represent distinct areas of modern society that are built upon semantic universes of meaning and associated pragmatic competences. But contra Luhmann, if the theory of society is to have moral and ethical foundations, cognitive principles exhibit more than functional meaning and competences; they also exhibit moral and evaluative meaning and competences. Furthermore, still contra Luhmann, such extended rule systems must be shown to interpenetrate or mediate one another as they continually, and necessarily, do in practice.

The extended canvas thus generated by the concept of horizontal mediation is captured in Table 2 by the idea of a *cognitive cultural model* (row 6). These models are generated from the collective learning processes that may accompany discursive argumentation. These discursive practices reflect different social positions and cultural perspectives, some of them completely opposed to one another, but these positions and perspectives are nonetheless related to one another by at least agreeing to argue on a common theme according to the communicative modality of rational dissensus. Collective argumentation takes place on the foundations of both transcendent cognitive principles and the historical patterns generated by their institutional application. Such argumentation may, over time, result in collective learning, if it results in discourse structures and schemata that minimally interrelate perspectival differences so as to generate discursive and action-orienting coherence.

Cultural models are, on the one hand, composed from constitutive codes associated with the various cultures of modernity, functional, moral-normative, and evaluative. Luhmann's emphasis is on a non-normative descriptive semantics; Habermas's on prescriptive moral-legal coding; communitarian philosophy's is on evaluative ethical coding. For Touraine, cultural models reference society as a whole, for example, industrial or post-industrial. But unlike his idea of a singular dominant societal cultural model, cultural models might instead be better understood as constituted in plural forms that are derived both from transcendent principles of the cognitive order and from immanent social rule systems.

In pursuit of this plural goal, row 6 draws a basic distinction between cognitive cultural models and socio-cultural models.[4] Cognitive cultural models lie on the boundary between immanent and transcendent. In the phenomenological sense, they constitute a horizon. Two examples of such cognitive cultural models are the cultural complexes of cosmopolitanism and ecological responsibility. Cognitive cultural models, thus understood, are orienting master frameworks that integrate multiple perspectival differences, including differences that are grounded in fundamental differences of social position. Even though agreement on their elements is not complete, they have a context-transcending status. Cosmopolitanism, for example, driven by its various interpretations, now begins to compete with national self-determination as, using Giddens's word, a 'container' for social organization (Giddens, 1987).

The second dimension of the category 'cultural model' is positioned more emphatically on the immanent plane. In Table 2, these are designated as socio-cultural models. Such models delineate the spectrum of relevance and the hierarchy of values that societies consider legitimate for

---

4   Remarks on the difference between cognitive cultural models and socio-cultural models are present in Chapter 11. They are extended here.

norm-building practices. Norm building takes place under these conditions and it is therefore highly constrained. Touraine's macro-sociological idea of a socio-cultural model indicates how they may be conceptualized. He distinguishes two such socio-cultural models, conflict and mediation between capitalists and workers in industrial societies and between technocrats and new social movements in post-industrial societies. These socio-cultural models constitute in Touraine's view the stake – or common theme – that results both in contention but also in social organization.

This is a rather simplified example. Socio-cultural models are present in all dimensions of society. For example, each of the areas in brackets below generates a cultural model:

Functional (Science, Economy, Public and Private Bureaucracy);

Moral-legal (Constitution, Justice, Democracy);

Ethical-Evaluative (Family, Class, Ethnicity, Gender, Race, Religion, Subjectivity, Friendship).

While each of these socio-cultural models is positioned within one of the three cultural spheres of modernity, in actuality they are discursively constituted and reconstituted from both transcendent cognitive principles and immanent social rule systems that cross these spheres. Socio-cultural models are therefore intrinsically culturally mediated. These models should be distinguished from cognitive principles. Their overall place is different. Socio-cultural models guide how societies immanently construct epistemic orientation for their modes of functioning, moralizing, and identifying.

Cultural models may be contextualized by three additional factors:

Spatial reach of societal units: From national-territorial to transnational, e.g. what is the reach of functional interdependencies?; what is the reach of territory?; and what is the reach of common identity?

Social orientation: The role of ideological differences and compromises for each of the models, e.g. socialism, liberalism, conservatism, environmentalism, feminism, and general post-essentialism;

Temporal sequencing: The temporal evolution of elements of the models, e.g. economic templates, moral constructs, and ethical orientations.

Socio-cultural models are constructed through the discursive mediation of transcendent cognitive principles and immanent social rule systems. This discursive process is guided by logics of space, sociality, and temporality and by the available compositional elements of consensus, rational dissensus, compromise, repression, and exclusion. Through such a process, socio-cultural models create a framework of meaning and value hierarchy for norm-building practices. The cognitive order composing of cognitive principles keeps apart basic elements of how society constitutes itself that are irreducible to one another, though also continuously contested components of modernity; socio-cultural models selectively combine them and reduce contestation by means of integrating mechanisms that allows norm-building practices to proceed.

Mediation in cultural models is therefore the outcome of multi-faceted discourses of different range and kinds. Some of these discourses experience significant public elaboration in the public sphere and others gain influence, at least partly, through other non- or quasi-public channels, such as elite networks that operate through institutional channels. Even in the latter case, fundamental changes in cultural models require public elaboration and legitimation, though this process may be heavily loaded in one direction through the effects of repressive hegemony.

Discursive processes lead to change in various kinds of cultural structures – comprising of discourse structures, collective learning, cognitive principles, cognitive cultural models, and socio-cultural models. With respect to socio-cultural models, radical changes should be distinguished from comparatively small changes that minimally affect its orientation. Ideal typically, radical change operates via a three-fold process: (a) discursively generated ideal innovation at the micro-level leading to new kinds of public thematization; (b) discursive interaction, distributed resonance, and public appropriation of the new ideas, leading to the formation of discursive structures and collective learning; and (c) structure formation within cultural models through a selective recombination of various elements of cognitive and social rule systems that reorient the socio-cultural model. The latter dimension, (c), may take time, since the process may lead to initially weak 'emergent' socio-cultural models that may best be regarded as collective learning potentials that may not find their way into fully developed socio-cultural models that have extensive normative implications. As the title of one of Klaus Eder's papers observes, 'Societies learn yet the world is hard to change' (Eder, 1999).

The outline of a plural and varied order of cognitive principles that are variably mediated in socio-cultural models breaks with Luhmann's idea of binary functional coding that he confines to autonomous social systems. It replaces it with a conception of cognitively and institutionally organized social spheres that process multiple kinds of coding – as well as functional, moral and evaluative in various ways and in various combinations. It also takes seriously the concept of an institutionally unbound public sphere that incorporates the full range of coding possibilities and communicatively combines them. This dimension is even more significant in the light of potentials for further democratization of the public sphere. And finally, it differs from Luhmann too in identifying an extra-institutional associational sphere from which critical communication emanates and penetrates into the public sphere proper. It also identifies another extra-institutional cultural form, ideologies, which enter into the composition of socio-cultural models. Such ideologies may acquire sufficient stability so as to influence the construction of the 'good world'. Ideologies that succeed in becoming institutionally resonant are in various ways 'reconciled' in cultural models, both creatively and pathologically.

The normative theories of democracy, outlined in Part I, contribute significantly to the generation of ideologies. Ideologies engage in political cultural struggles for the power to define cultural models, especially the politically critical moral-legal model. When influenced by social projects of various kinds, for example, social liberalism, social democratic republicanism, neo-liberalism, conservative communitarianism, left libertarianism, political philosophies trace preferred paths from the available cognitive principles of a society into its cognitive cultural models and then into its socio-cultural models. But before they can play this role, important dimensions of such philosophies have to lie deep within the cultural structures of a society. These dimensions can become discursively reactivated and pressed into new social projects by social movements. Margaret Somers's analysis of the deep historical roots of Anglo-American liberal citizenship theory provides a telling example. She shows how liberal political ideas and social values have been retained and yet reoriented to fulfil the contemporary social project of neo-liberalism (Somers, 2008).

Both cognitive cultural models and socio-cultural models, lying between the real and unlimited communication communities, are concretizations of the mediation of validity claims. They can be influenced by the historical experiences of a society, by its comparative relationship to other societies, and by the social logic of argumentation. As specific to societies, both kinds of cultural model may, in certain circumstances, give rise to distinctive idea systems that even if they acquire the term 'ideal' may in fact be pathological distortions of defensible ideals. Such pathological ideals may inhibit or block a society's capacity to correct itself, that is to say, prevent it from learning through its discourses. Cultural models, especially socio-cultural models, then operate as means of learning not to learn. On the other hand, pathological ideals may be corrected through discourses that feed off bad experiences and generate new kinds of collective learning potentials that ultimately lead to change in these socio-cultural models.

Touraine stresses how cultural models are formed through struggles. These struggles, which have the underlying unity of a common thematic focus, are transposed into competing perspectives on the normative structures of society that nonetheless allow institutionalization to proceed (Ballantyne, 2007; Touraine, 1977). This marks a decisive break with the consensual normativism of Parsons's social theory where norms followed from overarching cultural values and were assumed to have a functional significance for the directed evolution of modern societies. For Touraine, both the structures of relevance and value hierarchy provided by cultural models and normative arrangements are the product of the defining social struggles of an epoch. Touraine's later work on democracy continues the theme (Touraine, 1997). Here, he recognizes the importance of universal principles of freedom, rights, and autonomy, plus a public sphere held in common, but he fundamentally anchors all of this in the capacities of social subjects to struggle against domination and for further democratization. With this additional insight, the differing modes of the communicative co-ordination of social order outlined in the previous chapter begin to emerge into light. Touraine's approach always starts from the 'lower' forms where conflict and hegemonic domination are uppermost, but his approach is fundamentally based on rational dissensus, even if this term is not explicitly used, and it includes also what has become consensual as the grounding principles of any possible form of democracy.

Moving on to consider the relationship between cognitive structures and normative models (row 7), it becomes apparent that introducing a macro-cultural cognitive order 'above' the normative order raises fundamental challenges for social and political theory. The move to include a defined cognitive cultural level has been anticipated by the internal development of cultural theory, particularly the pivotal influence of structuralism, but it is also animated by transformation in institutional theory. The historical assumption was that once norms were formed they became socially efficacious and difficult to contest. Now, under the influence of both cultural and conflict theory, it is accepted that while in some specific institutional spheres certain norms may remain relatively uncontested, most norms are continuously contested such as, for example, norms of obedience and freedom that enter into the relationship teenagers have with their parents. The degree to which norms operate should then be understood in a more subtle way as based upon the, perhaps temporary, stabilization of differences. These differences follow from the competing interpretive schemata that are anchored in socio-cultural models. Socio-cultural models provide the parameters for delimiting the spectrum of legitimate action orientations. Hence, cultural models are meta-institutional in the sense of guiding those differences of interpretation that go into framing 'contested but still efficacious' norms at the institutional level.

At the level of socio-cultural models, by contrast with the level of specific institutions, the differentiations are more clear-cut. At the institutional level, relatively consistent behavioural sequences go on, even where there is no fundamental agreement over norms, for instance with regard to the above example, teenage withdrawal or rebellion. In such cases, social power may be used to support certain norms or compromises may be reached. Even teenage withdrawal or rebellion has a rule structure. At the level of socio-cultural models, the underlying perspectival differences that animate such disputation can and, in some instances, must be reoriented. Sometimes, on the one hand, reorientation is accomplished, often with the help of academically generated knowledge. In those cases, academic knowledge makes socio-cultural models more explicit. New fronts may be established and new priorities may even be formed. On the other hand, the structuring of socio-cultural models also has a latent quality in that agreement and difference may operate through poorly understood cultural beliefs whose genesis lies in the past, or there may be a general lack of clarity about the consequences of commitments, for example, the implications of strong ethnic commitments for multi-cultural societies.

Speaking loosely with Touraine, a society's cultural models encapsulate the way in which it culturally organizes its modes of constituting itself. Cultural models involve the reconciliation of difference by way of the composing mechanisms of exclusion, repression, compromise, rational dissensus, and consensus. Two channels lead from cultural models to the socio-institutional plane in which norms are justified and applied. The first is directly through various communication processes, and the second is through the mediation of democratic law-generating institutions. Democratic law-generating institutions specialize in fulfilling specific steering functions for other social spheres. Democratic theory's overwhelming concentration, as Honneth points out, is on formal democracy and law as a normative medium of social integration (Honneth, 2011). It is principally concerned with norms directly relevant to democratic action, how democracy should be organized, and to some degree but far less, on the implications of legal norms produced through the courts or legislatures on other institutional spheres. Informal democracy in other institutional spheres has always had a shadowy existence, operating as something like the bad conscience of democratic theory. It should be concerned with it, but somehow it rarely actually is.

The problems democratic theories have with the cognitive order and cultural models are partly corrected by Honneth (Honneth, 2011). He follows Hegel in having recourse to the normative standards generated in multiple institutional spheres, formed by their own normative practices, though indirectly shaped by legal norms. This generative activity exceeds the conceptualization of society as solely integrated by law, the view he ascribes to political philosophy. Honneth therefore wants to extend the normative theorizing of political philosophy to society at large, granting reasoning and norm-building competences to actors in these institutional spheres. Here lies the vista for the democratization of society that conventionally understood formal democracy can never accomplish. If Honneth is on strong ground here, he pays less attention to the extra-institutional competences, mechanisms, structures, and processes, in short the cognitive-communicative process that, beyond formal normative democratic processes, shapes normative orders (Strydom, 2011; O'Mahony, 2011b).

Row 7 in Table 2, *normative models*, gives rise to two *internal* kinds of normatively relevant communication. The first is formal democratic communication and the second is intrinsic institutional communication. And both forms of communication are shaped by the wider *external* context of public communication in the public sphere. Formal democratic communication, given its norm setting function, is procedurally structured. Bobbio has identified the restricted social range of formal democracy as not a triumph but a retreat. It is an expression of disappointed expectations about the influence of democratic practices in other institutional spheres (Bobbio, 1984). The heralded promise of far-reaching democratization in a line from Marx, through pragmatism, and on to the new wave of participatory democratization emerging from the 1960s, has not been delivered. Instead, a contradictory landscape has emerged, with democratization proceeding in some respects – the extension of human rights to work contexts for example – but also undercut by other technologies of governance that revitalize functional steering media of money and power (Boltanski and Chiapello, 2005).

The mechanisms of composition of socio-cultural models continue over into the norm-building process. Legal-political actors are oriented by the various possibilities of exclusion, hegemony, compromise, dissensus, and consensus, particularly as they negotiate the spaces, on the one hand, between moral, ethical, and legal discourses and, on the other, between these discourses and the functional consequences of the normative alternatives they might justify. In the normative paradigms of both Habermas and Rawls, the formal democratic sphere is at the heart of the legal-political process and the ultimate locus of the moral structuring of society. While it is argued above that this strong normative paradigm is restrictive and attaches too much significance to the power of good deliberation, it nonetheless counterfactually clarifies what a constitutionally regulated political process would look like that would be free of arbitrary power and that would hence lead to norms that are generally and reciprocally justified. From a cognitive perspective, such norms cannot be understood as isolated single norms. Instead, they should be seen as interpenetrating complexes of norms vitally shaped by overarching cognitive structures, above all, socio-cultural models. These socio-cultural models are in some vital respects decontested as consensual, constitutional principles; in other respects, they are decontested by consensual but not constitutional agreement; in yet other respects they are decontested by the cultural hegemony of some social positions; and, finally, they are contested by manifest ideological differences and ongoing argumentation. Even in instances where consensus or hegemony is the norm, this is to be understood in all cases as the product of existing or past ideological differences that, in many cases, are sublated but not eliminated and therefore may recur in changed circumstances and ideological configurations.

Norm building is not confined to democratic justification. Norms are partly independently constructed in the various institutional spheres. Such norm building is partly democratically structured and partly operates with other social logics. The historical failure to fully democratize these spheres has meant that hegemonic and excluding co-ordinative mechanisms are powerful in them, as are pragmatic, compromising, and functional-legal norms. The problem is not so much that these kinds of norm are prevalent so much as that the dominant co-ordinative mechanisms are excluding and repressive. The conditions of democratically relevant norm building in institutional spheres need to be researched and the extent to which democratic controls can be imposed on arbitrary power documented. Reciprocally, the way in which institutions contributes to the agenda of public discourse is a very powerful shaping influence on the public sphere. Discursively articulated proposals for social change arising from within institutional spheres coalesce with the activities of civil societal associations or interest groups to generate context-transcending proposals that draw down the potential of cognitive principles in a manner consistent with the given socio-institutional animus. For example, business, academic economics, think tanks, and other civil societal associations have generated in the last half-century the institutionally transformative ideology of neo-liberalism.

The meso-level (row 8) is socially realized in the arena structure of the public sphere, for example parliament, the mass and new media, public participation structures, and publicly relevant communication within associations of all kinds and in informal contexts of life.[5] This communicative infrastructure, explored in detail in Part IV, makes possible the relational formation of text-producing, text-disseminating, and text-receiving networks, associations, and milieus. Communication of this kind results in the formation of discourse structures – the term used by Miller or what Forst calls diagnostic evaluative structures – on public issues (Forst, 2007a; Miller, 2002; O'Mahony and Schäfer, 2005). Discourse structures have much in common with the ideological structures that partly constitute cultural models. Discourse structures are distinguished by having a shorter duration and a more experimental quality in their role of carrying new public agendas. O'Mahony and Schäfer, following Goffman, Gamson, and Eder, used the language of frames to capture national and international discourse structures on the human genome (Eder, 1986; Goffman, 1984; Gamson and Lasch, 1984; O'Mahony and Schäfer, 2005). Frames may be understood as topoi that are generated from different frame positions or perspectives. These frames resonate with the themes underlying what Gamson and Lasch describe as political culture (Gamson and Lasch, 2003). With respect to the theoretical description of the structures underlying contexts of resonance, the concept of socio-cultural model offers advantages over that of political culture in that it is a more flexible, plural, and social theoretically responsive concept.

Discourse structures that emerge from contested and enduring issues, for example, gender or ecological issues, and takes the form of collective

---

[5] Whereas the formal democratic order is addressed above as part of the normative integration complex, level 7 of Table 2, the formal democratic order is also a core element of the public sphere. The full implication of this for deliberative theory is increasingly recognized (Parkinson and Mansbridge, 2012).

learning may impact upon the existing structuring of cultural models and result in adaptation or even transformation of these models. These models are always situated in space and time and the propensity for change is inbuilt. If they are significantly altered, fundamental learning of one kind or another is culturally accomplished, but this generally only happens over a long period and takes place in conjunction with far-reaching innovation in normative models. Otherwise, discourse structures can be refracted through existing socio-cultural models and become directly involved in normative justification procedures.

The meso-level also sustains cognitive processes. Some of these processes are shared with the micro-level, for example, the social organization of memory or the reasoning capacity of human interlocutors. It also sustains a cognitive competence of its own in the ability to conduct collective argumentation. The normative paradigm emphasizes the counterfactual foundations of collective argumentation in the presuppositions of co-present, intersubjective communication. But in mediated societies with elaborated counterfactual cognitive foundations, collective argumentation is a much wider cognitively grounded achievement. It involves the competence to engage in the distributed production of knowledge and normative commitments and to understand the various kinds of possible outcome in forms of consensus, dissensus, compromises, hegemony, exclusion, and lack of a clear outcome. Societies develop a collective memory that is sustained by distributed and yet shared mechanisms that tell them where they are with respect to the macro-cognitive order and socio-cultural models. Beyond this structure, the capacity for collective innovations may lead to new relational cognitive mechanisms – the combined social pragmatic and semantic organization of communication – on the meso level.

Further on the question of communicative organization on the meso-cognitive plane, various kinds of collective learning may be identified. Associational learning advances or restricts innovation that is commonly first generated on the micro level, or in micro-meso borderlands where, as outlined below, 'micro' is understood as collective as well as individual in form. Institutional learning involves institutions learning from the networks in which they are embedded. But the most important kind of *democratic* collective learning at the meso-level is triple contingent learning, involving the full play of public discourse and the full involvement of publics

(Strydom, 1999; Trenz and Eder, 2004). The processual capacity to conduct discourse involving distributed publics, critically including the cognitive and normative structuring of communication media, is fundamental to the public sphere. It is unimaginable that all this complexity could be sustained without an elaborate cognitive order operating on all levels of society. But this complex achievement is frequently undone by learning pathologies that, for example, find ways to minimize or exclude the public or to include it in regressive, defensive, authoritarian, and ideological forms of collective learning. Such collective learning takes the form of the consensual and dissensual learning pathologies that were diagnosed, following Miller, in Chapter 12. Macro-societal collective learning in the form of emergent cultural models is based upon certain patterns of outcomes of collective learning on the meso-level.

The micro level is the sphere of individual subjects and groups (row 9). To some degree in line with the distinction that could be drawn between cognitive principles and socio-cultural models, the row is divided into the categories of *cognitive rule competences* and *cognitive models*. Agents use cognitive competences to construct cognitive models as interpretive schemes, individual interpretations of general cognitive principles, cognitive cultural models and socio-cultural models, which are of a factual, normative, and evaluative nature. Out of these interpretive schemes, individuals generate the will to act by combining the dimensions of modernity into a meaningful schema, or a micro-level cognitive model. The identified competences are both of a formal, underlying nature such as representing, strategizing, justifying, evaluating, and appropriately emoting and yet they are applied not just as competences in general but as competences to utilize the cognitive principles of modernity. Hence, depending on many factors and most crucially their social role, agents know – or can learn – how to justify actions in a democratic culture, how to understand the implications of legality, how to identify what they consider to be a justified political belief, and how to advance claims to recognition.

The micro level, understood within the pragmatist tradition, is composed of a semiotically constituted subject capable of forming intersubjective relations with other subjects. With Touraine, such subjects may be regarded as historically constituted and transformed. This historical constitution may, following Honneth, be traced in modernity to intersubjective structures of recognition. By following Mead, the ontological differentiation that is frequently assumed to entirely distinguish individuals from groups can be overcome. According to Mead, individuals are constituted by inner parliaments with a complex and varying inner audience for whom consistency of action can be a formidable challenge. In other words, individuals no less than groups, are multimodal infrastructures of communication that engage in complex exchange and learning relations with an external environment on social and material planes. Notwithstanding, important differences remain in assessing the reasoning competences, will-forming processes, and action consistency of groups as opposed to individuals. A communicative theory of individual as well as group agents that includes different kinds of concretization of will is nonetheless assumed to comprise the micro-level. On this basis, the complex task of constructing the varying range of motives and capacities for discursive action of these agents within the public sphere may begin.

Micro-social learning is well captured by Touraine's idea of subject formation. Of the first importance is whether subjects equipped with the range of cognitive competences and substantive judgements are formed that are adequate to the challenges of the times in which they live. Honneth's recognition theory tries to establish a bridge between forms of moral individuation and moral levels of social integration in the spheres of intimacy, equality, and achievement. In so doing, Honneth, even if not explicitly, encapsulates the cognitive order of modernity and how it becomes effective through compatible processes of socialization and individuation. But, as already identified on the macro-level, cognitive principles can be differentially absorbed into rival ideologies and hence into the variable shaping of cultural models, depending both on the balance of power between these ideologies and the willingness to form common ground on which to agree to disagree. In a similar fashion, both with regard to their own identity and that of others, individuals and groups, in part, have to sustain the infrastructure of a good common life amidst difference, and, in part, they have to make fateful choices about what ideologies, to which they might orient, contribute to the promotion of such a good common life.

Micro-level learning correspondingly should entail the formation of subjects who can respect differences of all kinds and master the interactive *cognitive rule competences* that should make these differences tractable, though the socially constituted life experiences of these individuals produce very different kind of *cognitive models* and, accordingly, preferences. Beyond individuals, the collective production of coherent classes of relationally structured commonalities and difference is also a form of learning, as Bourdieu so well analyses. As Durkheim also already saw in emphasizing morality as a collective achievement, substantive morality has to be led back to the kinds of commitment that would sustain a fair and feasible system of co-operation. For without this, modern society could only be made coherent through power and deception. Forming substantive moral commitments involve bridging the macro and the micro, as well as cognitive, normative, and material orders. It requires a continuous process of reciprocal constitution between individual minds, discourse structures, learning potentials, cognitive principles, cultural models, and norm building.

In this process, categories of subjects are formed that embody certain *substantive* beliefs, norms, and values in the form of cognitive models that profoundly affect the possibility and nature of a democratic culture. Especially critical for this process is whether learning by micro-level agents is reinforced by meso-level communication, that is, whether such agents acquire cognitive rule competences for public reasoning, balanced blending of cognitive rules of different kinds, non-authoritarianism, reciprocity across difference, and strong ego identity. The absence or perversion of these kinds of learning resulting in individual and group-level pathologies – imbalanced absorption of cognitive order, authoritarian personality, non-reciprocity, and weak ego identity – by contrast contribute to the kind of consensus and dissensus pathologies that Miller identifies and which seriously inhibit the quality of democratic culture in all social spheres.

The Cognitive Order, Communication, and Social Change

In delineating the composition of the cognitive order arising from Table 2, various mechanisms of cultural and related social change were outlined. This critical dimension requires further attention. To begin, two models of social change may be identified, the diffuse model and the directed model. The diffuse model gives rise to the paradigm of structure formation through related processes of differentiation and integration. This model is diffuse in the sense that the primary impetus of social change, consistent with the external part of the external/internal differentiation, arises from the unintended consequences of action that, following the logic of modernity, significantly contributes to the differentiation of spheres of action. Such differentiation leads to the organization of practices by means of a general evolutionary logic that exceeds the conscious grasps of human agents. With these assumptions, it is therefore possible to refer to causal laws that shape societal trajectories without reference to the category of willed, human action. This simplified account of the diffuse model is left in this way for heuristic purposes, even though differentiation theory has significantly evolved over the last three decades to include in its explanatory theories the projects of elites and other agents as drivers of both differentiation and dedifferentiation (Delanty and O'Mahony, 2002). The addition of agency in this limited sense nonetheless brings diffuse accounts of social change much closer to directed accounts, even giving rise to the common paradigm that Joas calls the democratization of differentiation (Joas, 1996).

The contrary idea of directed change is closely related to the idea of the democratization of differentiation. Socio-structural change of a diffuse kind not alone generates challenges of its own, but it also provides certain agents with the opportunities to direct change in a problematic or even pathological direction. Given the nature of modern society, social change of this kind, combining both diffuse and actor-shaped elements, can reach though the social structure with great speed and threaten its democratic mechanisms of collective co-ordination. In these circumstances, which very well correspond to contemporary conditions of enhanced globalization, societies in the singular or in concert have to develop the necessary learning to generate transformed, democratically grounded mechanisms of co-ordination that are adequate to the problem. If they succeed in doing so, and they *must* do so if they are to avoid deep-rooted pathologies, they need to engage in extensive processes of collective learning. Such collective learning potentially enables innovation in spheres other than structural and functional adaptations generated by the forward march of purposive-rational subsystems (O'Mahony, 2009). The system of co-operation in society needs renewed democratic intervention as its capacity to serve the common good becomes impaired.

This model of directed social change corresponds closely to the dialectic between the ideals of agency and the agency of ideals consistent with a democratic understanding of the cognitive order. In a given societal configuration, while some possible version of a directed model of social change might be needed, even desperately needed, there is no guarantee that one will be found. Pathologies may linger at the level of macro-societal integration, whether confined to a particular social sphere or problem, or affecting the society as a whole. These problems may be generated by processes of diffuse social change such as globalization, environmental degradation, population growth, and economic shocks that confront society's problem solving capacity with new challenges. They may also arise endogenously through social conflicts that reveal inadequacies in socio-cultural models and normative models of democratic co-ordination.

Both the critical theory of society exemplified by Habermas and democratic theory in the Kantian tradition exemplified by Rawls aim to overcome contingency by means of morally grounded deliberative governance. Over the second half of the twentieth century, the perceived challenges in some part shared by both traditions appear to have increased as diffuse and contingent social change, generated by what Giddens describes as the 'runaway world', joined with endogenous, culturally driven conflicts to threaten the capacity to democratically direct social change, to the limited extent that this was actually socially realized. The contemporary sociological tradition stemming from critical theory is not satisfied with answers based on a counterfactual, normative paradigm that would extend a kind of general public reason as a solution to society's co-ordination problems. In the cognitive and collective learning theories of this tradition, the co-ordination problem is understood as in the first instance a cognitive challenge that requires collective learning in order to clarify possible normative pathways. Through this cognitive prism, the tradition centrally explores, using Forst's terms, the twin aspirations for both democratic and social justice. These are a basic structure of justification and a justified basic structure of society (Forst, 2007b). It also explores how the cognitive foundations of both aspirations might be better realized by increasing collective learning capacity through the democratization of public communication.

Collective learning follows, firstly, a reconstructive critique of the existing social order in some respect – accomplished by social actors – and secondly, discursively achieved collective learning about potential alternatives. Collective learning follows a logic successively spanning micro, meso, and macro levels, though not necessarily always in that order. Micro level agents initiate collective learning processes by adapting their cognitive models to process various kinds of experience. Such experiences, as compelling ideal innovations, both shape public discourse, though public discourse in turn reorients the perceived status and significance of these innovative experiences. In another dimension, captured by symbolic interactionism, the intersubjective and co-ordinative meso-level penetrates into the micro-level and is there, in turn, further reshaped. In this process, micro-level cognitive competences are elaborated or extended and, through learning, new cognitive models may emerge.

Cognitive competences on the micro-level are partly constituted by 'presuppositional' macro-level collective competences that are absorbed through socialization and general social participation. As indicated in Chapter 12, through consideration of the relationship between unlimited and real communication communities, such competence formation is bound up with historically, comparatively, and imaginatively assisted 'abductive leaps'. Such innovative cognitive models are partly constituted by 'pulling down' the latent potentials of cognitive principles and cognitive cultural models residing on the 'upper' levels of cultural structure, making them immanently available to feed into discourse processes that, in turn, potentially result in collective learning on a larger scale (Strydom, 2011).

Collective learning on a larger scale begins to take off when discourses associated with micro-cognitive models become more strongly represented in society-spanning meso-level discourse structures and begin to gain some traction on the macro-level. This learning in turn can be relatively limited and fade away by gaining no traction on the macro-level, or, alternatively, it can culturally and ideologically resonate and begin to strongly influence socio-cultural models. Even then it may lose out and simply devolve to a latent status within cultural models, as with the case of early nineteenth-century vegetarianism. Alternatively, collective learning expressed as emergent socio-cultural models, that is to say, cultural models that await full incorporation into the established cultural order, may find a way of making the transition to cultural and normative legitimacy. The institutionalization of collective learning on the social level of practical rationality does not necessarily follow from the consolidation and widespread acceptance of certain kinds of discourses. Whether collective learning is actually transposed into the institutional order depends on functional considerations such as actual and perceived feasibility, moral considerations such as its fundamental acceptability, and evaluative considerations such as successful embedding in a shared narrative order that creates identification (Eder, 1999). It also depends on adequate procedural means for it to become legally justified and, even beyond this, it will continue to be discursively tested and reshaped in application.

Collective learning may by no means always be presumed to be 'progressive'. The claim that an episode of collective learning is so requires that relevant ideas of what constitutes progress should be raised and tested. This means that full justification is required of those reconstructive standards derived from macro-cognitive order that are brought to bear on the situation, for example, claims for more and different kinds of efficiency, legality, and legitimacy and the implications such claims have for cultural models. Following Miller, collective learning may actually be pathological, in relation both to the consensual and dissensual pathological mechanisms that inhibit meso-level learning, but also with regard to substantive outcomes deemed desirable, such as more or less social equality.[6] Societal evaluation of learning processes and associated institutional projects is often a long run and complicated process. But theorists may take at least intellectual heart from the fact that it happens, and that reconstructive evaluations have historical precedents. For example, there was a collective learning process in English-speaking countries that turned against the welfare state – a good

---

6   For example, the extent of inequality in contemporary China is increasingly being represented as a pathology that afflicts the institutional model of collective learning designed to achieve economic prosperity.

example of combined comparative, historical, and imaginary learning. There may well be another against the damaging neo-liberal order that followed it.

Figure 2, Cognitive-Communicative Learning, captures these dimensions of learning, in line with the general considerations arising from Table 2. It offers a simplified version of the content of Table 2 with a view to making processes of collective learning clearer. As in the text above, collective learning and associated learning pathologies and blockages are located on three levels, at micro-, meso- and macro levels, corresponding to CL1, CL2 and CL3 in the figure. These levels should be seen as distinct, but also as dynamically affecting one another. Their relationship may be envisaged in terms of Peirce's three modes of inference: deductive inference corresponding to the macro-level and corresponding to rule selection [S] in the figure; inductive inference at the meso level correction rule variation [V]; and abductive inference at the micro-level corresponding to rule innovation [I].

Discourse serves as the medium of circulation between these levels of learning. Innovative learning (I) span the micro- and meso-levels; the most prominent kind of public discourse is at the meso-level (V), and leads to variation in learning structures generated from argumentation; discourse on this meso-level leads to collective learning as selection on the macro-level (S). The macro-level also exhibits the most counter-intuitive kind of effect of the medium of discourse, non-intentional discursive learning (Miller, 2002). This kind of collective learning arises from unintended consequences as discourses circulate through complex cultural structures making connections, which agents at micro- and meso-levels cannot anticipate. The pathological dimensions represented in Figure 2 have already been discussed, as they arose, in the account given of Table 2.

A process represented in Figure 2 that has not yet been discussed in any detail is that of the formation, through learning processes, of emergent cognitive cultural models. These models are candidate cultural models that can still influence norm building, but at the margins. The cultural model of environmental responsibility serves as a good example. On one level, such a prospective cultural model has profound moral implications, for instance, with regard to climate change justice, and it penetrates into established socio-cultural models. But, at another level, where such a model encounters more established ideological forces in economic and social life,

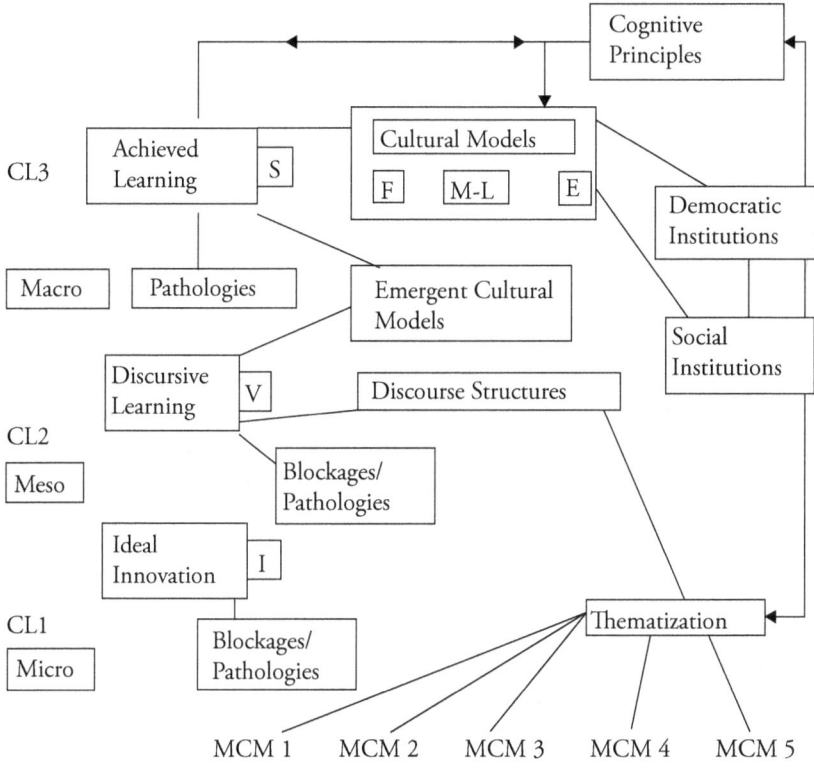

Figure 2: Cognitive-Communicative Learning

already strongly institutionalized in socio-cultural models, it may become marginalized. The debate within feminism about the degree of continued strength of patriarchy serves as another example of the relationship between achieved collective learning located in emergent cultural models and actual realization in established cultural models that influence normative rationality and content.

This is complex terrain and the theory of cultural models in all its aspects requires further work, including the introduction of empirical cases, to explicate key relevant dimensions. The wider context offered by quasi-transcendent cognitive principles must also be appreciated. Emergent cultural models may involve varying how cognitive principles are represented in established cultural models, in other words, which principles are combined and what interpretations come to be dominant. The environmental sphere provides a good example of the construction of a new cognitive cultural model, the responsibility model, which interposes between cognitive principles and socio-cultural models (Strydom, 2013). Over time, this will have radical implications for the reconstruction of socio-cultural models.

The remaining components and relations in Figure 2 have already been outlined above, but the fact that the figure is more parsimonious in its content than Table 2, along with the general advantages of the figure form, may make them clearer. Figures 3 and 4 also serve the goal of clarification, but they also advance the goal of backward integration with Figure 1 in Chapter 10. Figure 1 represented the normative implications of the communication constructs of the political philosophies that were reviewed in Part I. Figure 3, Spheres of Publicity, elaborates these normative implications still further by dividing each quadrant into two. Hence, the top left quadrant distinguishes between *moral-legal commitments* and *bureaucratic plan-making*; the top right quadrant distinguished between a *rationalized ethos* – allowing for continuing differences of emphasis within a framework of rational dissensus – and a *contested ethics* that indicates deeply structured conflicts; the bottom right distinguishes between *counter-normative reasoning* that, at least in its inception phase, lies on the margins of societal argumentation and *familiar modes of life* assumed to consist of ethicized everyday conduct that, by and large, tends to accept and work with the normative order, but which may also harbour dissent; the bottom left-hand quadrant distinguishes between the articulation of purposive-rational interests and generally rationalized life conduct, which is complementary to familiar modes of life with which it may compete. Each of these divided quadrants may be led back to the original placement of the political philosophies in Part I. The absent one, public deliberation, is consistent with the space of the *public sphere* at the centre of the diagram.

The value of Figure 3 only becomes fully apparent through Figure 4, Forms of Democratic Communication. For reason of clarity, Figure 4 leaves out the complex infrastructure of multi-level discourse, collective learning, and structure formation that lies at the core of Table 2 and Figure 2. It is nonetheless there implicitly. In the case of cultural models it is there explicitly, positioned outside of the public sphere. The elements of Figure 3, set within the broader context of Table 2 and Figure 2, represent the

Cognitive Sociology and the Public Sphere

various contexts of political communication generated by modern societies. Building from Figure 3, Figure 4 identifies three dominant kinds of political communication and locates them in the broad institutional spaces from which they arise and gain their primary resonance. These three kinds of communication correspond to the three cultural spheres of modernity, which give rise to characteristic cognitive-cultural structures that are already prominent in Table 2: deliberative communication relating to the moral legal sphere, purposive-rational communication relating to the sphere of formally organized institutions, and public communication relating to civil society. The various dimensions of Figure 4 correspondingly are arranged according to these kinds of communication. These modes of communication constitute the communicative infrastructure of the public sphere.

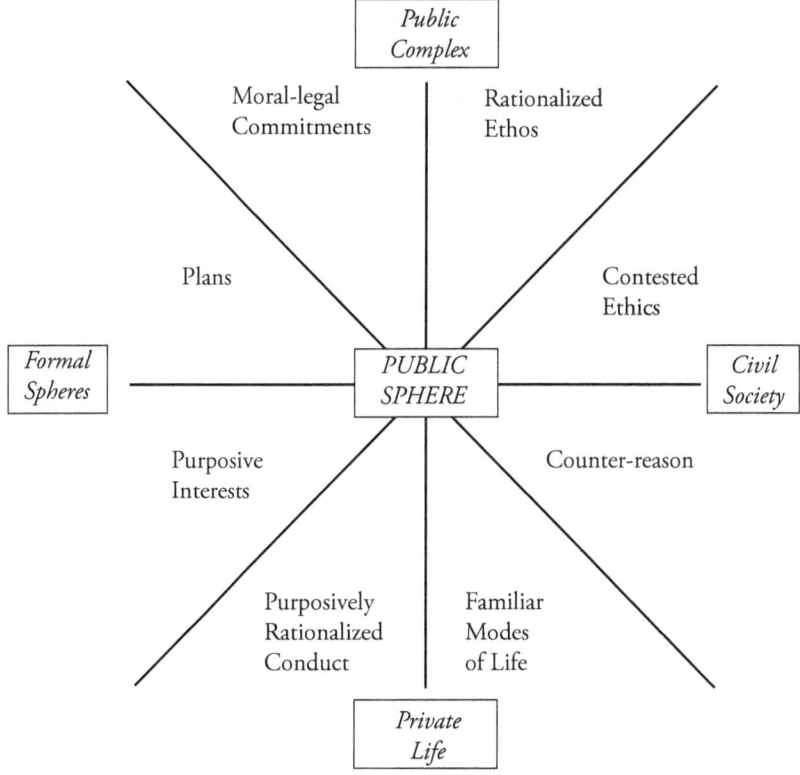

Figure 3: Spheres of Publicity

Deliberative communication, from the standpoint of the rightness of norms, is the most rationalized. It comprises the Rawlsian sphere of public reason, deliberative accounts of fundamental justification, and the republican idea of a rationalized ethos where differences are not eliminated, but, notwithstanding, may be 'productively' combined to offer stability within normative culture. Public communication is both morally and evaluatively structured, but it is 'wilder' than deliberative communication. Ethical positions may block one another or be settled through the play of power; counter-normative reason can be influential in some spheres but not in others; and familiar forms of life may in fact be antagonistically as well as co-operatively structured.[7] Purposive rational communication addresses those forms of communication that have a means-end quality. From a political standpoint, this kind of communication seeks to insert the standard of realism, control, and efficacy into political life, as outlined above in the case of realist political philosophy. This kind of communication and associated rationality is, on the contrary, frequently diagnosed as 'colonizing' other spheres of life and their non-purposive rationality standards (Habermas, 1987). The communication forms used in bureaucratic planning are associated with technocracy and social-technological steering, particularly economic, with that of liberalization. Both are associated with a kind of detached, epistemologically 'traditional' expert rationality.

Figure 4 should be flexibly interpreted. And the manner in which the three forms of political communication meet in the public sphere is the key to this, leading to the interpenetration that enters, through collective learning, into cultural models. The public sphere – and the forms of communication and structures of cultural relevance that constitute it – circulates around society and leads to ongoing collective learning at various levels that challenge cognitive and normative orders.

These are only sketchy remarks with which to capture the enormous variability of discursively achieved collective learning, both with respect to processes and outcomes. For now, it leaves such vital considerations as

---

[7] Cultural differences in the contemporary United States serve as a good example of deep-lying ethical differences that mostly relate to one another through power and disable compromise.

Cognitive Sociology and the Public Sphere

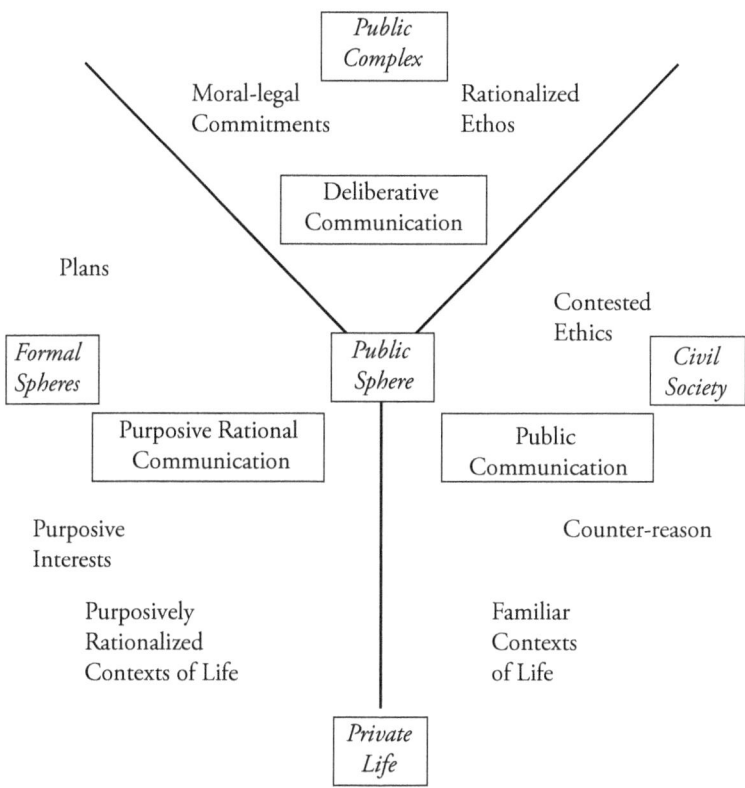

Figure 4: Forms of Democratic Communication

public formation and resonance largely out of view in order to concentrate on the cognitive-learning circuit, though these key concepts are taken up again in Part IV. This circuit is vital on a number of levels. It provides a corrective to excessively normative and procedural theories that miss the nature and significance of communicatively carried cognitive processes. Such a corrective locates theories of deliberative democracy in a wider cognitive-discursive context. In so doing, it performs the additional service, not yet fully developed in this text, of connecting democratic discourse in the formal and deliberative sense with societal discourses. Hence, as Touraine and others advocate, it connects those contexts of life that variously contribute to or inhibit democratic culture with democratic modes of deliberation and co-ordination (Touraine, 1997).

PART IV

Democratic Communication, the Cognitive Order, and the Public Sphere

CHAPTER 14

Public Communication and the Public Sphere

Earlier parts of this book have outlined the communicative constructs of democratic theories and subsequently built on them to develop a theory of communicative politics. Such a theory draws from discourse ethics, on the one hand and, on the other, from integrated accounts of communicative practices, collective learning, and the cognitive order. Such a theory is concerned with understanding the process of communicative democratization. The concept of democratization is advanced not in the normally understood sense of democratization as a historical learning process that gradually leads towards formal democracy, nor as an account of the extension of formal democracy to new areas of the world, but, instead, as a theory of the pivotal role of public communication in contemporary democracies. Democratization in this sense entails a conception of democratic processes extending far beyond the formal governance core of procedurally regulated deliberation and decision-making. It involves the twin additions of a discursive approach asserting itself against the domination of the deliberative approach and of a cognitive approach similarly asserting itself against the domination of a normative one.

Nothing in these changed emphases involves relinquishing the advantages generated by the deliberative turn, or the general theory of normative argumentation in, amongst many other theories, discourse ethics. Deliberative theory has made a signal contribution to understanding democracy as a communicative process that spans formal democracy, deliberative innovations, and society generally. Further, a large part of the ambition underlying this book is to suggest that sociology has to engage in its own kind of normative argumentation in conjunction with that of other disciplines. But the societal conditions in which such argumentation takes place have to be first clarified before the specific focus of any such normative intervention can be developed. And a first prerequisite is to recognize the historical achievement of building a communicative infrastructure for democracy, its cognitive software as well as its normative procedures and its communicative technologies.

Part IV will, then, first of all assert in the current chapter the importance of recognizing the full spectrum of this communicative infrastructure so as to preclude normative reduction in theory or in practice. Even if the normative dimension continues to be fundamental to an adequate theory of democracy, notwithstanding the claims of some kinds of realist theory, the cognitive-communicative dimension cannot be neglected if a fully modern democratic theory is to emerge. This chapter will therefore clarify how, in one direction, normative perspectives become societalized and, in another, how the evolution of society in turn shapes these perspectives. It will propose, in line with the general approach, that this can best be done within a cognitive-communicative and learning theoretical framework that shows how normative argumentation is intrinsically bound up with cultural and social structures and change, and should not be regarded as standing before or beyond them. It will be argued that only such an approach can do proper justice to the idea of the sovereignty of the public as a normative premise of democracy, both with regard to the extent to which such sovereignty is currently in place and the mechanisms whereby its further potential can be realized.

Chapter 15, the second chapter of Part IV, will examine the centrality of the mass and new media to democratic communication. The media have always been an intrinsic element of the public sphere, but the public sphere, as the chapter argues, is not to be reduced to them, an insight that somewhat paradoxically offers the best way to understand their democratic contribution. The media contribute to the cognitive foundations of normative culture, but not only on their own. For the media are inset into the complex social relations of communication, spread across multiple arenas, which constitute modern society as a communication society.

The first two chapters, respectively focusing on the theoretical analysis of democratic publicity and its mass mediation, address core elements of the public sphere. On this scaffolding, the subsequent two chapters return to the further development of a societal theoretical framework for analysing democratic communication. These chapters, developing a synchronic account of the public sphere, will draw from earlier chapters. This synchronic account, abstracting from temporal and spatial considerations, will outline in some detail how social structures and communication dynamics fully enter into the cognitive-communicative circuit described in detail in Part III.

Theoretical Foundations of Democratic Publicity

Splichal shows how, for Kant, the theory of publicity was fundamental to the idea and actualization of the normatively right (Splichal, 2006). For the right to prevail, citizens must possess the communicative freedom to express their views and to have those views be taken publicly into account. The normatively right depends on the collective capacity for public justification of norms that would oppose the secret prerogative of absolutist rulers. The necessity of *public* justification translates the moral sovereignty of reason-capable citizens into the political realm. As attested by later democratic theorists under Kantian influence, such as Habermas and Rawls, democratic rule through the public use of reason is a demanding criterion that is committed to the non-obsolete core of public sovereignty. Splichal contrasts the Benthamite account of publicness, which stands in close proximity to realist theories of democracy, with this Kantian account of the public use of reason. In Bentham's account, the public does not itself engage in the public use of reason, except to the extent of holding representative democracy accountable. The public, in this reading, is animated by mistrust and uses the mechanism of moral sanction to disapprove of inappropriate political action. Rather than the essence of publicness residing in an institutionally supported capacity for reason of citizens, these citizens may merely make use of the institutional infrastructure of freedom of the press and oversight of parliament to express disapproval. In this respect, Bentham's view is not far from Pettit's principle of contestability (Pettit, 1999).

While the general consensus in empirically informed political theory is that the Benthamite vision more closely corresponds to the actual conditions of modern democracy, evaluation of the respective influence on actual democratic practices of these rival positions is not at all easy. In Habermas's Kantian account of the public sphere and the associated theory of deliberative democracy, the reasonableness of citizens, their capacity for intersubjective reasoning, is at the very core. Public understanding of the cognitive principles and regulative ideals essential to democracy – accountability, legitimacy, freedom, legality, solidarity, publicity, tolerance, and democratic equality and their ideal combinations – are foundational, even if they frequently are only negatively expressed as defensive responses. Regulative ideas of this kind normatively structure political discourse and the manner in which they do brings out the essential truth in Habermas's counterfactual account of the public sphere. Even positions based on interests or instrumental utility according to a Benthamite logic, and still more positions based on the defence of individual rights, necessarily presuppose the backdrop of a canon of reason socially shared as cognitive foundations of democracy. Otherwise, there could be no democratic reference point for Bentham's idea of moral infringements that the public should monitor.

The superiority of a strong, procedural version of the normative use of reason is a presupposition of theories of deliberative democracy and has often been used to contrast these theories with theories based on the centrality of aggregative voting mechanisms. The argument that goes back to Dewey, and which is perhaps the very core argument of this theory, is that common deliberation best enables agents to change their positions in an uncoerced manner and to come to the best available common standpoint. This argument expresses the close relationship between theories of deliberation and the communicative theory of politics. More recently, deliberative theory has sought to demonstrate the possibility of greater compatibility between deliberation and voting, especially since the latter remains the only apparently feasible means through the principle of majority rule of establishing governments (Mansbridge et al., 2010). Notwithstanding, deliberative theory clarifies indispensable elements of the communicative foundations of politics.

From a sociological standpoint, even given the necessity of government formation by elections, a society-wide political communication system represents the only means whereby the notion of public sovereignty can have any meaning in mass democracies. Only such a communication system makes thinkable the necessary level of public involvement to sustain meaningful public sovereignty. Even public legitimacy in the most minimal sense of that gained through periodic elections still depends on an electoral process based on, at least in principle, full and fair argumentation. Few would argue that legitimacy achieved solely through electoral choice should exhaust the understanding of the concept. Even Bentham's more limited vision of publicness presupposes a public capacity and will to make its presence felt throughout the governance cycle. Theories of deliberative democracy and, even more so, those of discursive democracy, in some ways propose inversion of the priority of elections. From this standpoint, elections can be best understood as not determining, but a moment, albeit pivotal, in the overall process of political legitimation.

Even the strongest proponents of deliberative democracy would find it difficult to argue that it provides a comprehensive, realistic account of dominant contemporary forms of democratic governance, or even of available forms of communicative governance. While Bohman heralded in 1998 the 'coming of age' of deliberative democracy and recent work seeks to extend the descriptive value of the deliberative idea to wider forms of democratic process, there remains a deficit in its breadth and focus (Bohman, 1998). Mansbridge et al. circumscribe what they regard as genuinely deliberative with their conscious exclusion of bargaining and other zero sum modes of political decision, even if they also insist that self-interest should be regarded as legitimate within deliberation (Mansbridge et al., 2010). If deliberation is defined in such a normative strong manner, then it reduces radically in importance as a component of communicative politics, and the theory of communicative politics is unable to project feasible as well as normatively defensible procedural mechanisms to meet the challenge posed by the realist critique of democracy. To be fair, the most recent work of Parkinson, Mansbridge and their colleagues does propose a more radical conception of *deliberative systems* that does indeed begin to encompass an idea of a wider communicative politics (Parkinson and Mansbridge, eds, 2012). But, at that point, the very concept of deliberation starts to be stretched beyond reasonable connotations of the term.

Realist approaches pose a challenge, not just to deliberative democracy, but also to the entire case for asserting the normative significance of public communication. For Michels, Lippmann, and Schumpeter, and latterly for Luhmann, the idea that political opinion and will could be formed through genuinely public argumentation has been proven illusory. What counts for them is the more restricted ambition of realizing an elitist political rationality that can be supplemented by a range of pluralist theories that incorporate organized interests through the system of interest intermediation (Gunnell, 2004). One of the challenges for deliberative theories of democracy is how to address those kinds of political process that count for so much in governance terms – interest intermediation, electoral competition, and elite hegemony, yet predominantly lie outside its optics (McCarthy, 1995).

In his 2006 essay, Habermas does indeed address at least some of the above considerations, but only at the cost of somewhat artificially aligning wider political processes of opinion and will formation with the deliberative core of his theory (Habermas, 2006). Pathologies based on objective societal structures are identified such as the dedifferentiation of the media in Italy. If these pathologies were to be corrected, the smooth translation of discursive will into political deliberation would be enabled. While structural pathologies such as this must be recognized, this approach fails to address the core question of the pathological learning that is located in public communication itself. In other words, even if the media were sufficiently differentiated from politics, cultural blockages to non-pathological collective learning of the kind diagnosed by Miller would still remain (Miller, 2002). The differentiation of the media system from politics, while necessary, is an insufficiently radical goal for the democratization of the media.

Contemporary politics is so organized that public will can only reliably make itself heard either indirectly through the device of representation or directly through communication in the public sphere. The claim to public sovereignty is routinely redeemed not on the whole by deliberation, in which the public rarely participates, but by the public's communicatively realized influence on public culture and hence on the governance agenda. Nonetheless, *the idea* of deliberation makes it a really effective counterfactual, though mainly realized on the *cognitive* plane rather than the normative plane on which it is most often defended. The cognitive reference of the deliberative ideal marks a democratically vital shift from double contingent co-present collective learning to triple contingent learning, which is built on the basis of both the real and virtual presence of the public (Strydom, 1999).

This last point is critical if the descriptive dominance of realist political theory, indeed its ongoing institutional efficacy in some part because of that descriptive dominance, is to be contested. The communicative influence of the public on the political agenda is considerable, *though* it is not matched by its direct presence in deliberation. From the normative perspective of those animated by the desire for a fuller vindication of the principle of public sovereignty, the solution would appear to lie more in the direction of extending the possibilities for enhanced citizen participation, thus reasserting the value of *public* deliberation and necessary, associated participatory innovations that span not just norm-setting practices but all modalities and arenas of communication. This is more promising than pursuing the uneasy combination of deliberation as an encompassing counterfactual ideal with the attempt to interpret contemporary democracy as already substantially deliberative in form, precisely as Habermas attempts to do in the essay in question.

Realism, Ideology, and the Cognitive Order

What is generally left out of the picture in deliberative and participatory theorizing is the manner in which political norms are actually publicly constructed. A realist dimension needs to be added to this tradition, but it would be a realism that contrasts with the 'disillusioned realism' of classical liberalism in which the public is construed as lacking the competence, and even interest, to influence politics. The latter analysis is to some degree actually perversely justified by limitations in the quality of public will formation, limitations that realist theories actually expect and even in some cases encourage. Notwithstanding these limitations, such a position ignores the positive linkages between the public's active role in the formation of a general *public* culture and the manner in which this culture shapes the political agenda. The triple contingent position is not merely a normative standpoint; it also empirically describes the general experience of operating in a democracy. Part of the reason why classical liberal, realist theories are able to minimize the influence of the public lies in the way that political culture, linking society and politics, is assumed to be grounded in private contexts of life. Political culture is represented as a predominantly passive, historically formed repertoire of political positions whose genesis lies beyond the sphere of politics that it nonetheless is assumed to influence (Somers, 1995a, 1995b).

Not only realist theories neglect the socio-political mechanisms of the formation of normative culture and how, once formed, it becomes effective in normative arrangements. Deliberative theories procedurally incorporate these mechanisms and, ultimately, excessively diminish their autonomy. These theories in some cases do explore innovative kinds of deliberation and citizen participation, but there is no foreseeable mechanism whereby such experiments can become systematically generalized. Even if they could, they would still miss out on many of the dynamic mechanisms of public communication, out of which normative cultures on various scales and duration are formed.

Some part of the reason for the relative neglect of normative culture in deliberative theories may lie in the critique of ideology. In the heritage of critical philosophy and social science from which much of deliberative theory springs, ideology is from the outset assumed to be pathological because, informed by the Marxist heritage that represented it as an attempt to justify the unjustifiable social conditions of the ongoing exploitation of labour, it has always had negative connotations that need to be exposed. A lingering suspicion prevails in critical thinking that the cognitive mechanisms of normative culture formation requires radical normative correction, even epistemic short-circuiting in strong democratic procedures, in order to head off the dangers of an ideologically carried populism. In the realist tradition of classical liberalism, directed at populism from the other side, ideology expresses the absence of autonomous thinking and the pathological myopia of mass society, which could only be corrected by the rational rule of experts. In her critique of this latter account, Margaret Somers offers a telling argument against the standard 'anti-political' account of political culture that in its post-war, cold war form denied the political in favour of, paradoxically, identifying politically relevant values in non-political, private spheres of life (ibid.). Such ideas about the proper locus of politically binding anti-political values were assumed to operate as a bulwark against the formation of 'dangerous' entities such as political ideologies, but actually denied the *political* reality of normative culture formation.

Against both the deliberative and realist viewpoint, ideology must be reconsidered as an important concept to articulate how popular influence comes to bear on politics (Celikates, 2006; Mannheim, 1935). Ideologies should certainly be criticized if they contribute to popular ideas about politics in a manipulative or irrational manner. For critical theory, denying that ideologies can ever have a justifiable core either condemns it to a purely negative critique of the political or a restricted, procedural affirmation of democratic potentials. The latter position, developed by Habermas, concentrates its attention on those universalistic discursive conditions in which a particular norm could be rationally justified. Even when attention shifts internally within the theory from justification to application the limitation of this position already become apparent in the fact that norms have to be considered in their relational context with other norms (Alexy, 1993; Günther, 1993). To seriously address this relational dimension requires that norms should be understood as part of a normative complex, rather than justified as individual norms. But what would then govern such a normative complex? The idea favoured by many deliberative theorists is that it would be an achievement of citizens actually deliberating in common, but this is unrealistic *in current circumstances* for addressing temporal, spatial, and social complexity, and evades rather than addresses the problem. Ironically, while its counterfactual orientation clarifies the issue cognitively, at least formally, the theory conceives itself within an applied normative register.

The only alternative idea is that the shaping of a normative complex is actually more diffusely generated by general cognitive-cultural constructs that do, in some measure, spring from the complex and contradictory character of modern forms of social organization. Such an idea therefore expresses what appears to be an inevitable fact of modern society; the ideal of public sovereignty is mainly realized through the diffuse process of the cognitive elaboration of normative potentials – and dangers – in the general public sphere rather than through deliberative processes per se. Habermas's proposed two step logic, by which these diffuse public processes generate a collective will that is subsequently transferred into the comprehensive deliberative justification of norms, actually has the unintended effect of appearing to distance the public from influence (Bohman, 1994). There is no clear mechanism whereby the public can continue to influence the norm-specifying core, especially as this process is only partly deliberative and where it is deliberative it does not normally take the form of *public* deliberation. In the two-stage model of *Between Facts and Norms*, discursive capability is too firmly located in the force of the better argument of idealized deliberation, the normative-procedural endgame of democracy, and too little located in the collective cognitive construction of a normative culture.

Turning the above critical comments into a positive programme requires attesting to the frequency whereby deep-lying political agendas are formed on the political periphery. What initially takes the form of critique on the periphery may lead to the formation of new substantive 'positive' agendas that sometimes lead to political innovation. Politics reaches beyond the formal political process, even beyond the institutionalized public sphere, to any site in which are to be found cognitive innovations with normative import. This kind of communicative politics is shaped by the effect of ideologies. Much political energy goes into the constitution, diffusion, and practical implementation of these ideologies. The main directions of democratic theory, outlined in Part I, tend to sidestep them, partly because they force awkward substantively grounded moral choices on procedurally oriented normative theories, and partly because the emphasis on ideology critique, together with the procedural turn, undercuts recognition of the critical role that ideologies, and cultural forms generally, play in sustaining a communicative politics.

This is precisely where the cognitive structures, outlined in Part III, come into their own. Recognizing the importance of the cognitive level draws attention to the vital process whereby critique of existing arrangements first becomes thematized and how associations form that carry micro-cognitive learning throughout a political cycle. The complexity of modern society with its differentiated logic of functions and values deeply complicates normative integration, in part because such societies are *both* cognitively and normatively 'organized'.

The cognitive order of modern society is above all the sphere in which the reflexive rules and relevance structures of socio-political life are anchored. These principles and relevance structures, which the earlier Habermas theorized in his account of the socio-cultural lifeworld, do not determine normative procedures, but specify the generative meta-rules and 'ideal' content of modern life in general, and of political life in particular. This cognitive order clarifies possible paths of normative reproduction or innovation. It is superordinate to the normative in consisting of cognitive principles and cultural models that condition what is normatively possible. From a procedural standpoint, actors with different perspectives know how to reciprocally represent, narratively ground, and argue out these perspectives. They work from a common sense of what is relevant, derived from shared cognitive principles and cultural models, even if they contain opposed interpretations and priorities for these principles and models.

This cognitive framework can be related back to earlier observations on communicative politics. It is the collective cognitive order that is underdeveloped in contemporary normative theory, including the theory of deliberative democracy that is actually founded on the idea of a communicative politics. How difficult it is to understand contemporary politics without such a concept can easily be illustrated by reflecting on how to make sense of major transformation in the foundations of contemporary politics, such as the shift from social democratic welfarism to neo-liberalism. Such a shift is not merely the imposition of the preferences of an elite, but results from the interplay of collective preferences, popular beliefs, long-run philosophical world interpretations, embedded institutional logics, and associational carriers. New ideologies emerge from such interplay, animating collective learning processes that lead to proposals for innovation in cultural models that, if they succeed, shape the political agenda for a significant period.

Strydom argues that Habermas, though long grasping the importance of the cognitive level, consistently reduces it to a normative one in which consensus appears as the only legitimate outcome of political argumentation (Strydom, 2011). Strydom instead proposes, in line with Miller, that this approach does not do justice to the generative role of social conflicts (Miller, 2002). Conflicts are generative if they result in the formation of a structure of rational dissensus that operates as a learning structure. Such a structure could facilitate the emergence of consensus or alternatively continue as an ongoing equilibrating structure between opposed positions. Such positions are cognitively sustained since opposing ideologies do not generate normative consensus.

Habermas's blending of constructivism and reconstructivism is detached from ideological judgement. Academic evaluation of the moral, ethical, and legal standing of actual social arrangements is thereby made difficult, even though it is clear that in non-deliberative and even deliberative political arenas high consequence norms are formed on a basis that is far from perfect procedural justice. And unjust or irresponsible norms, formed in political processes that do not operate with adequate deliberative procedures, will impact further on the future of democratic justice by generating additional asymmetries in social power, further distorting the operation of communicative power. What is required is a kind of analysis that elaborates the range of generalized cognitive commitments that are at play in social situations, and which clarifies the social consequences that follow from interplay between such commitments, where interplay is understood as both discursive and deliberative in form.

While Habermas is to be applauded for linking the societal periphery to the deliberative democratic institutions, the differentiation theoretical approach he employs to supplement his deliberative model of democracy once again raises the suspicion that he wants society to simply sort itself out by somehow equalizing differences of power so that the real business of democratic justice, deliberative justification, can proceed. A cognitive approach does not envisage the periphery organizing itself to facilitate the democratic core in this way. The creative role of conflict and the structuring role of rational dissensus are not merely halfway houses to normative consensus. Conflict can be enduring and creative as much as it can be destructive. Rational dissensus is pivotal for sustaining a common orientation to problems, notwithstanding differences in preferences, and, in the end, these differences can facilitate norm building by creating a bridge between alternative perspectives. The cognitive and learning theoretical perspective of rational dissensus keeps open the possibility of a broad normative sociology that the 'consensual proceduralism' of discourse ethics simply cannot do.

These observations are far from signaling the irrelevance of discourse ethics. Discourse ethics helps to clarify a moral horizon for practical intersubjectivity that can be applied to democratic communication. As argued by Steiner et al., a rapprochement can be envisaged between approaches to deliberative democracy inspired by discourse ethics and approaches that do not work with strong consensualist presuppositions (Steiner et al., 2010). Indeed, persistent critique of normative consensualism has been widespread in the internal critical theoretical debate on the public sphere and on deliberative democracy for a long time. Nevertheless there remains a danger that one vital contribution of discourse ethics risks being diminished or ignored, its counterfactual normative dimension, a point emphasized by Klaus Eder (Eder, 2006). There is a tendency to regard such a counterfactual perspective as merely utopian, something that lies irretrievably beyond the real, empirical world as it can be experienced in the here and now (Splichal, 2006). Discourse ethics, within the heritage of critical theory, by contrast stresses the real implications of counterfactual standards. Society is always learning about the further potentialities that its own development process has opened up, a learning process that is incomplete and often obscure, even contradictory, and calls forth the work of critical scholarship to further identify.

The radical challenge opened up by the shift from a normative to a cognitive approach is precisely to identify how this counterfactual moment actually operates in modern society. This shift is predicated on the insufficiency of a deliberative proceduralism that operates with a transhistorical standard of communicative rationality. This particular reconstructive horizon provides a clear sense of how domination-free communication might be envisaged as a transcendental ultimate standard, but it is only one reconstructive horizon of normative significance. Another, as with Marx and the early Frankfurt School, is that of non-alienated, non-dominated labour; a further one is the efficiency standard of modern economics stemming from Smith; still others are ethical standards of the good life or good epistemic practices in knowledge production (Strydom, 2011). The cognitive challenge is to identify the manner in which standards of these kinds and their variable interpretation emerge and are socially co-ordinated in society. Such a challenge must identity how societal and sub-societal issues are constructed on the one hand, but also, on the other, how perceptual limitations and pathologies inhibit both cognitive and normative innovation. The reference to normative innovation indicates how a cognitive approach to social change is internally related to its normative institutionalization. Then the further challenge taken up below is not alone to clarify how the cognitive moment in political communication operates, but also to show how it is connected to normative institutionalization.

A cognitive approach as described above, while fundamentally respectful of the pragmatic, procedural, and relational emphases of contemporary social and political theory, does not neglect the study of social and cultural structures. Such structures should not be dissolved into transactions or procedures. They reflect the essential social capacity to construct entitles capable of reflexive cognitive activity in the form of systems, institutions, groups, and selves that are spatially and temporally enduring, and in these respects are recalcitrant to rapid change. Such a view does not equate to the naturalistic ontologization of the sociological imagination or, as Emirbayer and Mische style it, the focus on the self-unfolding of essences (Emirbayer and Mische, 1998). But it does emphasize the extent to which the flow of what Dewey calls transactions generates entities that regularize these flows and that are best captured by the term structure.

This approach has some affinities with Bourdieu's constructivist structuralism but, in contrast to Bourdieu, has a stronger constructivist-communicative emphasis located on the meso-level. Bourdieu's meso-level by contrast is composed of groups with culturally stabilized strategic repertoires. This underestimates the extent to which groups or individuals are constructed out of ongoing social processes and, over time, are capable of development in the form of learning of one kind or another. Bourdieu's enduring importance is to identify the 'verticality' of identity, the extent to which identities are manifested through social positions that are recurrently reproduced through social and cultural structures. Such structures are of different levels of complexity and persistence; the identity, goals and pragmatic repertoires of an embryonic social movement will be different from that of a political party, and both will be different from a bureaucratic organization or company.

These observations reinforce the cognitive perspective that the patterns of social life, expressed in structurally conditioned social positions, do not easily generate collective agreement. A considerable problem of much democratic theory is that it is better able to deal with the moral challenge of establishing what a free and autonomous individual life might consist of, than it is at dealing with the conditions of justly and responsibly co-ordinating collective life, especially from the standpoint that adequately addresses the democracy-society relationship going in both directions. Realizing such a just and responsible collective life cannot be achieved only by asserting the constitutional conditions for the exercise of individual freedom, though a just and responsible collective life is impossible to imagine without such freedom. The exercise of public autonomy is from a societal theoretical point of view more complex, uneven, and contradictory than democratic theory allows. The recent turn towards the theorization of injustice by figures such as Honneth and Sen, 'constructivistically' starting from those asserting the injustice as against abstractly theorizing justice on the basis of a priori, transcendentally derived principles, is an important step towards providing public autonomy with content. Also important are the concerns of theories that emphasize under-recognized pragmatic repertoires in democratic interactions, such as those associated with status differentials in class, gender, and race, a perspective that has more recently been taken up in bridging ethics and epistemology in philosophy (Fricker, 2007).

A cognitive perspective of the kind proposed here emphasizes the normative implications of overarching belief systems, moral claims, unexamined habits, and narratively sustained identities, as well as the potentiality for a diffuse, mediated form of rational argumentation that can generate collective learning. Such initially diffuse argumentation can sometimes translate into normative specification in the law-making core. In other cases, it will not end up in formally established laws but in ethical or moral norms, or sometimes in moral, ethical and legal norms in various combinations, including potentially contradictory ones. The cognitive perspective draws attention to the mechanisms whereby injustice – or irresponsibility – immanently reaches the threshold of recognition within social practices, or alternatively can be made recognizable through critical inquiry. It also draws attention to how disagreements about the reach and implications of justice and injustice are constructed and become practically significant. And, finally, it draws attention to how actual agreements, including constitutional provisions, are interpreted, amplified, and sustained through processes of discursive reciprocity within the parameters of socio-cultural models.

Spatial and temporal perspectives enter into this approach in characteristic ways. On one level, the task of showing how collective normative learning takes place on a wider societal plane, a breadth of perspective that is normally not given sustained attention in deliberative theories, pushes the theoretical horizon in a synchronic direction. Such a synchronic orientation takes its task as that of extending the focus of political theory to elaborating the societal theoretical context and mechanisms of communication, collective learning, and structure formation. Such a synchronic framework may diachronically evolve, an evolution that is captured by noting the progression of eras of the public sphere from liberal to mass and on to the contemporary combination of mass and post-mass elements.

Both synchronic and diachronic dimensions of the public sphere should be given due attention. This involves neither, on the one hand, neglecting the synchronic dimension by a dominant emphasis on change-inducing reconstitutive elements nor, on the other, by developing a reproductive theory that does not account for socio-historical development. This latter process is driven forward at many points in the architecture of contemporary society, for example, in discursive learning processes, systemic evolution, reorganization as a result of failure, the programmes and actions of social movements, economic development, population movement, the relation to nature, and technical change. Nevertheless, even if diachronic evolution is, in one form or another, a permanent reality of contemporary society, the structural relationship of elements has to be sufficiently synchronically stable in a given era to allow for societal reproduction processes to continue. If the diachronic rate of change of one or many elements exceeds the adaptive or learning capacity of society, then crisis is likely to ensue. The manner in which, during the first decade of the twenty-first century, the economic system, especially through financialization, outran the normative and evaluative capacities of the modern social order is a case in point (O'Mahony, 2011b). But, before a thorough going normative response can take place, a cognitive reorientation, driven by discursively generated collective learning, must undo the legacy of previous decades of learning and socio-cultural model building. Pivotal to such a reorientation is not just the will and capacity to criticize and to collectively learn, but the media forms that facilitate or inhibit these processes, the focus of the next chapter.

CHAPTER 15

Generalized Public Communication Media: Mass and New Media

Much scholarship on the public sphere has assumed that public communication is overwhelmingly shaped by the nature and performance of the mass media. In fact, as will be emphasized in Chapter 16, the mass media are only one of the arenas essential to the operation of the public sphere. Nonetheless, the mass media do have a pivotal role. The advent of a 'mass society' in the late nineteenth and early twentieth centuries was characterized by universal media readership, together with universal suffrage and universal literacy. The universalistic politics that accompanied these developments was built upon the new means of public communication, completing the long gestation of the category of publicity, originating as an idea in the bourgeois revolution, to reach the point where it structures society as a whole.

From the vantage point of public participation, the mass media are characterized by a significant disadvantage that notwithstanding their remarkable contribution mitigates their value to publicity. Their communicative form is one-to-many and does not easily allow for direct involvement of the public in producing messages and directly communicating with one another. Yet, the picture can be over-simplified. The predominant emphasis on the *agenda-setting* role of the mass media underestimates the *agenda-building* role of publics, revealed in their capacity to construct new political agendas through the kind of micro-level thematization outlined in Chapter 13, in addition to their roles as interpreters of media messages, and the ability to develop other modalities of diffusion of political ideas (Cobb and Elder, 1983; McCombs, 2004). The mass media are set within the broader cultural and communicative context, described in earlier chapters, and that context is powerful and partly organized by other communication media, for example pamphlets, books, meetings, postal, bureaucratic, even leaving the new media to one side (Zaret, 1992).

To address the very idea of a medium of democratic communication requires consideration to be given to the medium of orality, and to the medium of writing, as well as to the multiple technologies of diffusion of written content. Modern democratic institutions still depend to a great extent on institutionalized forms of the medium of orality in their deliberative practices, and also on the diffusion of printed texts, for realizing their goals.

The fact that the mass media do not constitute the public sphere in its entirety should not distract from their pivotal role in public communication. The very possibility of a democratic, communicative politics arises only because of the role and the reach of the mass media. The mass media have acquired their remarkable importance for democracy partly because other participatory mechanisms are so weak in the representative model of democracy. Nonetheless, the era of this extreme centrality of the mass media to democratic communication appears to be drawing to a close. This does not mean they will no longer have influence. Their influence will certainly continue and extend into new media, but the scale of this influence is currently being challenged by the partly related trends of decline in readership, and the rise of these new interactive media. While it is still just possible to theorize the mass media separately from the new interactive media, that era is rapidly drawing to a close and the value of persisting with the separation is not clear.

Media of Democratic Communication

In the contemporary world, spatial metaphors abound, reflecting continuous destabilization of the experience of social and material space accompanying the late modern acceleration of social change. This experience of change, constantly threatening to run out of control, continues early twentieth-century conditions of permanent disruption and dislocation, after the short hiatus of the third quarter of that century in which a certain orderliness and evolutionary gradualness was at least assumed to characterize the state of the world. The comparison with the early twentieth century can be extended to the common development of innovations in public communication. Then, it was the institutionalization of the mass media in the condition of general literacy in western societies; now, it is the challenge of the Internet as a new communication medium.[1]

One dimension of the transformation of spatial conditions associated with the Internet as a medium of communication is its implications for the constitutive conditions of public discourse established in the era of mass media hegemony. This period of hegemony saw the institutionalization of democratic publicness within the territorial space of the nation-state. The hundred or so years of the consolidation of mass-mediated forms of democratic communication were never stable but, at least for a significant portion of the globe, this form of democratic communication appeared to work within the framework of liberal-democratic institutions. At least it did for a time. Even without the advent of the Internet, the stability of this form of democratic communication appeared to be eroding with the growing presence of transnationalization and globalization. The Internet further advances the erosion of the spatial underpinning of democratic communication, contributing in no small part to the uprooting of the cultural foundations of national democratic community that is so large a part of contemporary experience, even though the expression of that experience is frequently a backward-looking reassertion of the value of such community, often taking xenophobic and fundamentalist forms.

One specific aspect of the unmooring of democratic community that has become a refrain in modern public discourse, both academic and popular, is the perceived erosion of commitments to collective goods. While this

---

[1] The reference to the Internet as a new communication medium is a shorthand for the digitization of media of communication. Though these are not explicitly discussed in this chapter, important developments such as Twitter and social media belong to that general experience of digitization. But even though not explicitly discussed, the theoretical categories that are developed to capture the implications of digitization extend to them also.

is a general worry, it is also to be found in specific studies of the assumed communicative and cultural consequences of the Internet. Writers such as Sunstein bemoan a series of related phenomena associated with the individualizing and polarizing effects of a medium of communication that allows too much choice, generating the phenomenon of the 'daily me' of the personalized tailoring of news preferences, rather than the collective experience of reading the same newspaper as many other people (Sunstein, 2002). Perhaps a case can be made that the Internet makes irremediable a tendency that was anyhow emerging and, thereby, acquires much of the blame for an intrinsic deformation of mass-mediated forms of communication (Habermas, 1989). Though changes in the form, even the very effectiveness, of democratic communication will not only be associated with changes in communication media, the potential for its revitalization may come to depend to no small degree on the practices that develop around the new digitized communication media.

Bohman makes interesting arguments in this respect (Bohman, 2004b). He argues against reducing mass and new communication media to the model of face-to-face interaction as in the strict agora model. This model did not obtain in the mass-mediated public sphere and still less can it obtain in the circumstances of digitized public communication. The spatial metaphor of the forum can be retained, but mass and new media forums are together very different from the agora model, while also being different from each other in important ways. The theoretical meaning of a medium of communication will be taken up below, for which Bohman's conclusion that there exists a systematic disconnection between contemporary potentials for mediated communication and the nature of democratic institutions is important and offers a conceptual reference point.

In what follows, no attempt is made to empirically assess the democratic contribution of the Internet – an assessment in any case that could not be other than highly tentative (DiMaggio, Hargittai, Neumann, and Robinson, 2001). Instead, the chapter proceeds via a number of steps. In a first step, it considers the Internet as a medium of communication that opens up specific possibilities for public communication. In a second step, it will distinguish between a medium and form of communication in which the latter, understood as equivalent to a public sphere, will be shown to institutionalize certain potentials of the medium in democratic arrangements.

With respect to the first step, a medium of public communication can be distinguished from a governance technology as analysed in the tradition of Foucault (Rose, 1999). A medium of public communication is not concerned with how the public is administered and classified so much as how the public is constituted as a forum with a voice. This distinction becomes clearer if the issue of administrative and public memory in modern governance arrangements is considered, where memory is to be understood as a socio-cognitive accomplishment essential to epistemic, justificatory, and identifying practices. Administrative memory is based upon formal record-keeping procedures that can be variously understood as either – or both – technologies of controlling populations or an essential means of materially reproducing social life. Public memory, by contrast, is held by the public itself and is sustained by the interpenetrating modalities of symbols, narratives, moral orientations, ethical dispositions, and recollections of states of affairs. All of these are, in turn, embedded in and activated by communication forums of various kinds, ranging from the banal communication of certain ritual symbolizations to the charged deliberation of assemblies (Billig, 1995). Memory is a kind of public knowledge, both in the sense of what the public needs to remember and actually can remember. A frequently adduced criticism of contemporary democracy claims what the public can – or chooses to – remember is not sufficient for what it needs to remember if it is to realize its capacity to sustain and revitalize democratic institutions.

Normatively relevant public memory in the period before the advent of networked electronic media depended on a fusion of the medium of writing, to a lesser but still important extent on the medium of ceremonial visual display, and on the record-keeping function of the mass media. To fully address the characteristics of public memory and their relation to new or old media in this way would be a large task indeed. It is perhaps sufficient for exemplary purposes to, firstly, sketch some important differences in medium characteristics between mass and electronic media, continuing with the theme of public memory before, secondly, moving on to consider differences in their interactive and action-co-ordinating range and, finally, differences in their temporal form.

Apart from repositories kept mainly for the journalists themselves and specialized research purposes, the mass media did not provide a specific forum for public memory. Their internal memories and record-keeping mechanisms were by and large not shared with the public. Normatively relevant public memory was sustained – and developed – by diffuse processes, such as rituals, interaction routines, and the effects of the mass media themselves. The situation is different in the case of the new electronic media. Here, the public is supplied with a comprehensive record of past events, should it choose to avail itself of it. The potential significance of such a memory is great, though the use that is made of it cannot be understood merely by the existence of this potential, but depends still more on the capacities and dispositions of relevant publics. One crucial potential effect, however, should be noted. The media characteristics of the Internet are likely to impact on the relation between time and space in the formation of political identities. Political identities in the 'high' nation-state era were formed with reference to the recollected past of the nation in the context of a bounded territorial space; political identities in the new media age are likely to be formed more by 'postnational', horizontal associations set within a wider, though not necessarily 'richer', field of cognitive constructs.

These references to different modalities of political identity formation reach beyond the repository characteristics of types of media as sites of public memory to the nature of the action horizons they implicate. Already the mass media have taken a decisive turn towards surpassing national boundaries, above all in the sphere of audio-visual content. However, the electronic media additionally allow for the *active* co-ordination of action horizons and the construction of idioscapes between actors within and across boundaries. Their interactive form is fundamentally demassified in the sense of allowing many-to-many types of communication rather than one-to-many as in the mass media. Commentators such as Sunstein illustrate the far-reaching implications in expressing disquiet that the very multiplicity of points of origin of messages and the wide discretion over consumption choices may well dissipate the collective commons (Sunstein, 2002).

Digital media are also characterized by deprofessionalization, in the sense of lower entry costs and easier usability, and thereby facilitate more complex multi-modal messages along more differentiated diffusion pathways. In this process, the role of journalists as gatekeepers of mass media is weakened, though far from entirely eroded. Epistemic authority still attaches to journalists through their high profile work in the mass media, but their role as privileged translators of the words of others will inevitably be weakened. Digital media support a plethora of networked communication forms and using the phrase of Giddens, applied to modernity as a whole, they further both time-space distanciation and compression through both the extensification and intensification of communication (Giddens, 1991). They extend into everyday life the choice-making effects of digitization that have already transformed economic production, distribution, and consumption. For better or worse, they make possible a 'personalization' revolution, in the sense of non-standard possibilities of sequencing productive, distributive, and consumptive activities in both economic and socio-cultural spheres.

One further characteristic of digital media is their radical asynchronicity understood as a temporal dislocation, in one sense, between initial diffusion and ultimate consumption and, in another, between communicative action and reaction. Mass mediated video recording technologies had already made possible asynchronous consumption on a limited scale. Digital media bring this onto a completely different plane. While the consequences of vast content banks that are gradually becoming available for personal use has been widely envisaged, less attention has been given to the possible erosion of the importance of political rituals such as terrestrial evening news, specific political broadcasts, and Hegel's realist's prayer of the morning newspaper. Asynchronous communication has advantages on the ritual level in that it allows people to engage with opinion-sharing activities at non-standard times, activities that the circumstances and dispositions generated by modern life had hitherto been weakening.

The combination of these characteristics of digital media – expansion of public memory, greater range of possible interaction, and radical asynchronicity – herald transformed conditions of public communication. Further, if a distinction is made between political public communication and communication in public, for example entertainment or cultural association building, it may also be envisaged that the communication environment as a whole, and hence cultural activity in the widest sense, is subject to transformation. Such a transformation will have very wide implications, through changed lifestyles and priorities, for democratic culture and communication. Presently, they predominantly remain media potentials, even if it is possible already to discern some apparent consequences on political behaviour and institutions. To further clarify both the possible trajectories and normative implications of these potentials, it is necessary to move from the intrinsic characteristics of communication media to their institutionalization as media of political communication, their shaping into a particular media form specialized in political communication.

Institutionalized Media of Political Communication

The idea of an institutionalized medium of political communication draws socio-political reflection beyond media theory in the narrow sense and towards a theory of the public sphere. The public sphere is an institutionalized ensemble of networked forms of political communication that is composed of both reproductive and innovative public-political discourse. It combines the technological characteristics of aggregated media of communication – for example, written, oral, visual, mass, and digital – with cognitively framed democratic practices. These cognitively framed practices are in a normative sense more basic than politically relevant media characteristics. Political speech, mass-mediated messages, political websites, anthems, and flags only acquire *normative* significance by virtue of generally shared relevance-specifying cognitive frames in cognitive cultural models. This of course applies only insofar as there actually are recognized widely shared political and democratic frames, the existence of which is increasingly called into question today.

The core components of democratic discourse became established in modernity as civil society freed itself from political domination, facilitating political socialization and political relations generally based upon the radical idea of autonomous citizenship. The definition and protection of such autonomous citizenship rapidly became bound up with constitutionally protected rights of citizenship, on the one side, and, on the other, the dynamic filtering of political discourses through the mass media. However, the democratic status of the mass media has always been ambivalent. As long as the economy could be thought of as part of an autonomous civil society in an encompassing private sphere, an assumption which as Margaret Somers points out is still part of liberal political ideology, then it was possible to conceive of a privately owned print media transcending its private base and operating in the general welfare of citizens. Undoubtedly, the mass media remain important in ensuring democratic accountability for both the creation and transmission of political will, but private media also have constitutive interests in the economic sphere that renders their role in securing democratic goods ambivalent, sometimes even dysfunctional. This ambivalent position of the private media, part of the private for-profit economy, on the one side, and a conduit for the political discourse of civil society, on the other, renders it an unstable platform for the public sphere that crucially depends on propitious conditions of communicative freedom. These conditions are worsening as private media have everywhere grown in importance.

Two other contemporary societal developments render yet more problematical the political role of the mass media. Firstly, not just the state, but also formally organized social spheres, have differentiated themselves from the socio-cultural lifeworld and, increasingly, from the normative values of civil society that the state was tasked to uphold in its legislative and regulatory functions. For example, amongst these social systems, the economy in the last twenty or so years has gained greater freedom from state control given the institutional facts of globalization and the ideological promotion of deregulation and privatization. Given the ownership and interests of private mass media organizations, media forms can be expected to lose much of their anchorage in civil society and as can already be observed to treat audiences as consumers rather than citizens or non-citizen publics.

Secondly, with the decline of the great mobilizing and institutional ideologies of the nineteenth and twentieth centuries, political civil society has become disconnected from everyday life, leading to the widespread phenomena of growing political apathy and cynicism. These developments have resulted in the political public sphere becoming weakened and fragmented. The role of the principle of publicity as the medium of collective political understanding and enlightenment has eroded. The public sphere has thus become progressively more, though far from entirely, a vehicle for the vindication of interests, articulated through professional media techniques, rather than a vehicle for the realization of the normative core of public reason (Mayhew, 1997).

Communication in the public sphere may be divided into two essential kinds of discursive communication: meta-communication on the principles and procedures of publicity, and 'normal' communication on public issues. These types of communication may respectively be regarded as self-referencing and other-referencing. Self-referencing communication relates to the cognitive rules associated with the principle of publicity, for example disinterestedness, moderation, free speech, responsibility, sincerity, regulatory frameworks and organizational structures of the media. Other-referencing communication refers to the capacity of the public sphere to contribute to discursively clarifying and resolving various social problems outside of its own communicative foundations. The distinction is far from absolute. Frequently other-referencing communication implicates self-referencing dimensions.

An air of dissatisfaction, even crisis, may be observed today on the self-referencing plane. Given that the principal mechanism of publicity in contemporary public spheres is still mass mediated, this air of crisis exists even before the anticipated radical effects of digital media are taken into account. It is possible to argue that problems in the public sphere lie beyond the formal characteristics of the mass media and relate more to the way in which they are utilized. However, some significant portion of the problem must be attributed also to the way in which a particular media form is susceptible to unsatisfactory kinds of utilization, such as poor access, populism, narrow circles of influence, high barriers to entry, and manipulation. The essential problem of the mass media is that they have never been controlled and directed by the public; rather, large public or private corporations have organized them on behalf of the public. Their very success, in Sunstein's terms, as 'general interest intermediaries', which place multiple kinds of contents emanating from multiple social positions before the public, comes at a high price in terms of expert domination and professionalization accompanied by high barriers to entry and poor access.

The traditional characteristics of the mass media contribute to this, along with the social shaping of mass public spheres.

The form of the media as a mass technology have resulted in them attaching themselves to representative democracy and transforming it into a spectacle that only the mass media themselves can properly cover (Edelman, 1988). In so doing, they have constructed a close affinity with representative democracy and some would suggest that they have an ultimately decisive role as a colonizing 'media democracy' in shaping political culture (Meyer, 2002). The problems here are twofold. The first is the lack of attention to problems of representative democracy itself that even its defenders acknowledge. Bobbio's list of the 'broken promises' of democracy is a long one (Bobbio, 1984). It includes: (a) the weakening of the content of popular sovereignty in face of large-scale public bureaucracy in part, paradoxically, resulting from democratic pressures such as the institutionalization of welfare states; (b) the superseding of the individual as actor by large groups embedded in more complex functional systems with a corresponding decline in the individual's autonomy; (c) the individual's lack of competence means that technical problems must be solved by experts; (d) the ideal of education for citizenship has failed in the face of sophisticated techniques for the organization and manipulation of consensus; (e) the general, disinterested nature of representation has been violated by corporatist and neo-corporatist bargaining structures that attribute public status to some interest groups but not to others; (f) democracy has not shaped all social relationships; it has been limited both by the power of large corporations and public bureaucracies to decide key questions and by the fact that everyday institutions such as the schools, families, and hospitals are run substantially on non-democratic lines; (g) it has failed to curb the spectre of invisible power whereby in secret and unaccountably, democratic processes are contradicted in instances such as the funding of political parties, patronage, or the denial of liberty through surveillance. On the whole, the mass media have evacuated these more radical questions in favour of technocratic – politics is about 'delivery' – and populist motifs – politics as a spectacle. Even where the above are covered – the phenomenon of invisible power has received growing levels of attention in recent years – it is not traced back to far-reaching problems of democracy and still less, in a reflexive idiom, to the contributory role of the mass media to these problems.

The second problem is that the mass media have historically had a technological propensity towards 'massified' politics. The complexity of modern life with multiple perspectives on almost every issue often presents little or no clarity on how to proceed. The media is propelled towards constructing an ideological centre for politics that it itself arbitrates. The ideological centre is at the territorial and institutional core of the representative political system that is regarded as the creative heartbeat of politics, around which the media can both organize itself and co-construct, as Evelyn Waugh in the novel *Scoop* already understood more than seventy years ago. The ideological centre is composed of technocratic and emotional criteria that progressively eviscerate the normative core of traditional political ideologies, leading the public towards either apathetic boredom or emotive over-engagement in the political spectacle. Yet a word of caution is needed. It remains true that mass mediated democracy is all we have. As Luhmann put it with characteristic provocation, everything we know comes from the mass media (Luhmann, 1996). And Sunstein's emphasis on the importance of the global information commons and the media's role as global interest intermediaries cannot be lightly dismissed. But he is also the first to admit that this global commons is on the decline as people read fewer newspapers and generally become less exposed to multiple and competing points of view. The crisis of democracy and the media taken together is a composite expression of the spiraling complexity of modern social organization, inadequate public participation in political life, and the inability to sustain a meta-communicative discourse on these problems, especially one that would point in the direction of the further democratization of the media.

The characteristics of the new media sketched above initially created a climate of optimism with respect to their capacity to revitalize the public sphere and public participation. In a second phase of greater pessimism, writers such as Sunstein perceive their potentials to be utilized in a more negative fashion, reinforcing tendencies towards atomization and polarization amongst the public. The shift between this first and second phase, at least in part, marks a shift in horizons between the emergence of a medium of public communication and its institutionalization in a public sphere. In other words, it is not that the digital media lack democratic potential, but rather that they also have the potential to further erode democratic commitments and competences. Nevertheless, mindful of that potential, it is worth engaging in some guarded utopian projections with regard to the new media and then considering how far these might be from institutional realization.

Firstly, potentially at least, it is of the first importance for the welfare and revitalization of democracy that the public has the capacity to reflexively engage with supra-individual cognitive structures and that it can, accordingly, articulate different standpoints relatively easily. To the extent that this is the case, the threshold height at which publics become culture-producing organizations in their own right is corresponding reduced. The easier ability to reach this threshold through digital media of communication and co-ordination would act against tendencies towards the alienation of public powers by large bureaucracies and the isolation of the individual as diagnosed by Bobbio.[2] The Internet with its capacity for extending public memory, its corresponding capacity to provide information, and its ability to create new interactive dynamics could make a radical difference to democratic justice. Even where the mass media could make a significant contribution in examples like local community television and civic projects, they effectively cease to be mass media and become exemplars of new communication media in which the gap between production and consumption is significantly reduced.

If the public's capacity to generate cultural production is significantly increased and tied to new democratic functions, then it might be possible

2   In a research project on the use of the Internet for communicating with the public by Irish public bureaucracies, it was apparent that these bureaucracies only envisaged the Internet as a means of facilitating client-based relations with the public. The horizon of allowing citizens real self-organizing powers via electronic media was not considered. This reluctance can be traced to unambitious conceptions of the scope of citizenship in Irish public culture and also to the limited extent to which public bureaucracies generally are willing to countenance according self-organizing rights to partial publics (O'Mahony, 2002).

to envisage alternate bases of political identity. Such developments might meaningfully change the politics and cultural construction of space. One of the consequences of the Hobbesian model of the centralized state, and the associated communicative form of the mass media, has been to generally institute circumstances of a centre-dominated periphery, on both spatial and social levels, ultimately built on the model of the centralized nation-state. This has produced a powerful territorial imaginary that operated both for good and bad, helping to build solidarity and yet also promoting exclusion and xenophobia (Anderson, 1983). The power of this entity, generally called a national imaginary – consistent with the categories used in this book it is a cognitive cultural model of self-determination – operates both as an identity code and as a filter of what is feasible. In the contemporary period its power is waning as postnational cognitive cultural models come to replace it. The in-between form of the present, between national and postnational, has so far not led to real innovation on the political periphery in the form of demands for media democratization. Nonetheless, the repository and communicative potentials of the digital media open new horizons for organizing spatial and social relations and they might help to promote smaller-scale interactive potentials, even across hitherto unmanageable distances, that might lead to the formation of political identities appropriate to the challenge of living in postnational societies. In a similar manner, Bohman describes how multiple communication networks emerging through the Internet might form the model of the global public sphere as opposed to the cultural unity and spatial congruence of the national public sphere (Bohman, 2004a). On the social plane, the proliferation of public spheres tied to particular issues and identities might also be anticipated.

The above remarks rather roughly suggest that the Internet as a medium of communication might help to forge new horizons for political organization and identity. The most compelling claim that can be made for the digital media in this register is that they contrast with the mass media due to their capacity to involve the public through direct participation. Whether this capacity is fully realized is, of course, another question.

It is easy to be pessimistic about these developments on the evidence of the contemporary political climate and the contemporary colonization of the Internet by the impulse to entertainment. Yet, counter-trends can be identified, above all lower thresholds to entry into cultural production and the corresponding empowerment of the public. The difficulty with assessing these trends is that the trajectory of the Internet as a vehicle of democratic communication cannot be simply read off the inventory of its own potentials; it has to be considered in the light of broader transformations in democratic institutions and their environments and, most centrally of all, that of the public sphere. Both the mass and new media contribute to the institutionalization of cognitive principles and cultural models of normativity. The level of democratization of the media profoundly affects democracy in its various dimensions of discursive practice, cognitive construction, and normative ordering. The project of the democratization of the media is intrinsic to the democratization of the conditions of discursive interaction that lead to cognitive selection and cultural model formation, understood in the double sense of cognitive cultural models and sociocultural models.

The transformation in the landscape of political communication wrought by the new media can be placed in the theoretical context to be further outlined below with respect to the creation and diffusion of democratically relevant, cognitively grounded knowledge. Changes in capacities for memorizing, interaction, and synchronicity radically alter the communicative rules by which knowledge frameworks are generated as well as their spatial, social, and temporal forms. The new media generate a participatory revolution of a kind, but it is not clear whether this will lead to growing political fragmentation or the elaboration of more democratically inclusive cognitive and normative models. What is clear is that the discursive rules of communicative participation have already changed and if the news media were the central mechanism of public involvement in politics, for good or bad, their role in this respect has already changed irreversibly with the advent of digital media.

CHAPTER 16

The Macro-Social Structures of the Public Sphere

The current chapter and the next propose a societal theoretical framework for the contemporary public sphere. The current chapter outlines the macro social context and the next addresses the meso-level structures and dynamics of political communication. This task follows from the development in Part III of a cognitive-communicative theory of public discourse and its implications for normative practices and culture.

The account of the macro-social context of communication in the public sphere does not start from ontological assumptions about the fixity of societal structures and then attempt to chart relations between them. It instead assumes that, far from being meta-stable, societal structures are temporally delimited outcomes of prior social processes that are constantly subject to adaptation and transformation. The assumption that underpins it is in some respects similar to Luhmann's systems constructivism in that the macro-theoretical level is regarded as itself a generative structure. What makes the account offered here different from Luhmann is that large-scale mechanisms of social creativity are not confined to this macro-social generative capacity. Other social levels, and the cultures they carry, also lead either to maintenance or change of macro-structures.

What makes the framework 'macro' is that certain structures have wider reach and a slower rate of reconfiguration than structures on other levels. They have a wider reach in that they condition these other structures. For example, the cognitive and institutional order of civil society reveals the results of collective learning that, once structurally consolidated, acts to enable and constrain lower-level social processes. And macro-structures have a slower rate of reconfiguration because they represent accumulated results of multiple temporally extended interactive processes. This formal consistency may be explained both functionally and phenomenologically. Functionally, macro-social structures acquire social functions that are stabilized both through norms and generalized steering media. And, phenomenologically, these structures culturally condition the relevance spectrum and validity basis of mental structures, action, and interaction over an extended period. The claim that macro-structures should be understood as elaborated by meso- and micro-level structures and the processes that they sustain should need no special emphasis by now. This is the essential insight arising from understanding modern society as a communication society. Communication circulates through, reproduces, elaborates, and potentially transforms all societal structures, whether cultural or social. Structures organize communication but do not determine it.

Thus far, this book has been primarily focused on cultural structures. This chapter attempts to balance that by emphasizing the social structural anchoring of these cultural structures and the social positions that come into play in public discourse. Discursive perspectives arising from social positions do not simply arise from voluntaristic choices by agents in situations; they derive, too, from the historical and spatial logics that give rise to action-orienting societal structures with different sources, functions, and cultures. This observation is consistent with disagreements between deontological liberalism and communitarianism and in the end both perspectives have social theoretical validity. Agents acting democratically have to be able to see the good of others and the general good beyond their own interests and vantage points, but neither the good of others nor the general good is *always* best served by agents trying to ignore their own interests and experiences (Mansbridge et al., 2010).

The Macro-Social Context

In Figure 5, The Macro-Social Context of Public Communication, four macro-structural complexes are positioned on the outside border. These are, respectively, the public complex, composed of integrative institution, and civil society, the private sphere, and formally organized spheres. Such positioning already reveals a theoretical ordering, which assumes that the

The Macro-Social Structures of the Public Sphere

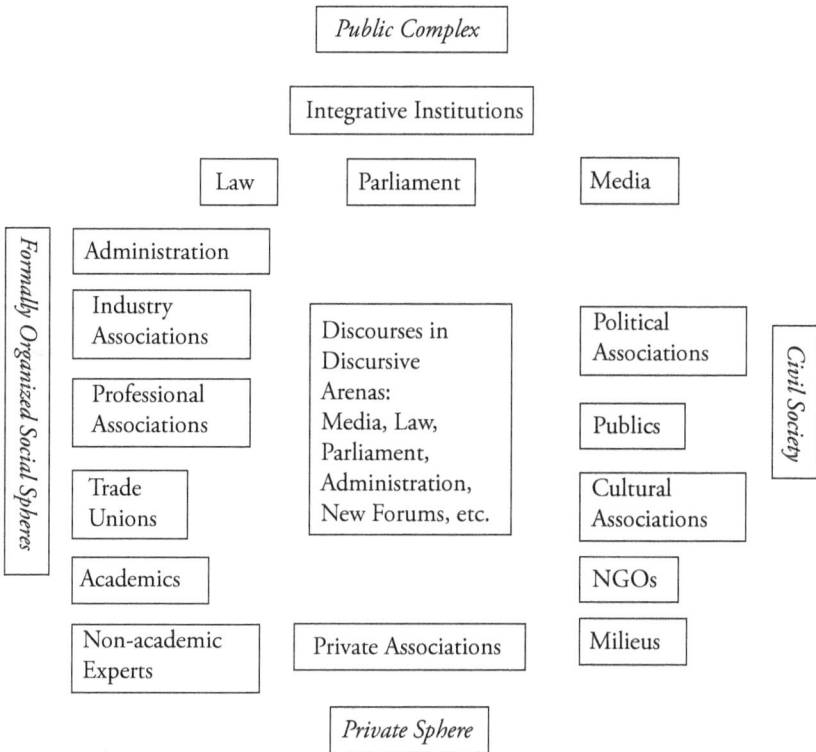

Figure 5: The Macro-Social Context of Public Communication

public sphere is located in the interstices of these four structured complexes. In Habermas's classical account in *Structural Transformation*, the public sphere historically emerged in the space between the state and civil society and represented a communicative structure for a public discourse that demanded political accountability and legitimacy. In this proto-democratic phase, located in the eighteenth and early nineteenth centuries, political civil society, as a source of autonomy and solidarity, represented the antithesis of absolutist political authority.

While some phenomena cannot be excluded from civil society without the risk of confusion, working with a narrower concept of civil society allows it still to be understood, consistent with its original ideal, as a dedicated sphere of political assertion and argumentation. This narrower conception generates the question of how those spheres that have been historically assumed to belong to civil society: the spheres of private life, the economy, even science as a form of free inquiry, are now to be understood from the point of view of political communication and normative ideals?

Deviating from the classical positioning of the public sphere between state and civil society, and instead positioning it between state, civil society, a private sphere, and spheres of formal organization, as in Figure 5, provides an answer to the question posed in the last paragraph though, in so doing, it generates new challenges for theoretical description. Such a repositioning has a vital effect on how communicative processes, such as thematization, diffusion, and resonance should be considered. The macro-structural account of the context of the public sphere is essential to understanding its contemporary role, yet generates much complexity. These macro-structures and their implications for the public sphere are taken up below in sequence, beginning with the public complex.

The Public Complex

As with a number of key ideas in this book, the relationship between the public complex and social systems both takes a cue from and yet ultimately disagrees with Luhmann. Luhmann's conception of social systems as functionally self-organized entities has affinities to the formally organized spheres represented in the figures. But his idea that functionally conceived social systems encompass the core of all social organization is disputed. In this regard, his claim that the legal-political domain, in light of the requisite autonomy of other formally organized spheres, has lost its primacy for securing social order is one dimension of the disagreement (Luhmann, 2000; Teubner and Korth, 2010). While, in the last few decades, the power of the state has notably diminished, this institutional complex does retain significant integrative power, much more than Luhmann and Teubner, whose arguments draw as much on future horizons as the present state of affairs, accept.

The continuing integrative power of the public complex is not least manifest in its regulative role with respect to the four most prominent spheres of publicity: the media, law, parliament, and administration. Only the first, *the media*, might be regarded as exclusively an institution of publicity, while the latter three have internal norm-setting functions that are conducted under public observation, even if they are, from a participative standpoint, highly restricted. In this role, they may be described as institutions of integration as well as institution of publicity. In its ideal construct, parliament is primarily an institution of publicity in the sense of facilitating authentic *public* deliberation, and many deliberative theories aspire that it actually should be so, but, in its present form, it is dominated in line with realist analysis by the programmes of government rather than by the ideals of open argumentation.

With regard to *law*, a distinction may be made between those issues that acquire the status of being publicly salient, and thus connected to issues debated more widely in public contexts, where law operates partially as an institution of publicity, and those that do not have such status. From the standpoint of the study of public communication, most interesting is the first case in which law is implicated in wider public communication. In this setting, the law is not regarded as simply autonomous and decisive in its norm-setting function, but, instead, operates as a form of specialized public communication in its own right, albeit with rationalized norms and formalized procedures. The law does not know what to do in the context of a divided society, but its inputs must still be heard. Viewing the law as an institution of publicity implies that it is responsive to other forms of societal communication. Law is absorbed into the circuit of public communication in those cases, growing in number, characterized by controversy and difference (Bora and Hausendorf, 2006; Nelkin, 1992; O'Mahony (ed.), 1999; O'Mahony and O'Sullivan, 2006).

Such circumstances of controversy are precisely where the multi-modal discourses of the public sphere interact with legal discourses and force law out of its autonomous comfort zone. The question for judicial and legislative law making in these circumstances is: how can legitimate norms be justified or applied when society is divided? Answers to this question that depend on asserting the need for consensus or semantic coherence are not sufficient, as already argued in Chapter 12. Legal argument is saturated with cognitive presuppositions and, generally for good reasons, these presuppositions must be normatively stabilized. Normative stabilization should not mean that oppositional discursive processes with legal implication should merely be seen as unrealistic, as they tend to be in the systems theory of law (Bora, 1999). Legal change first anticipated through a process of cognitive reorientation, which may well be conflict driven, is a vital part of collective learning and general social change.

The third institutional complex, jointly serving publicity and integration, is the *parliamentary complex*. The distinction between publicity and integration is as already argued somewhat awkward to sustain in this case, since the integrative functions of parliament, expressed through its role in governance, tend to predominate and colonize its deliberative role. It is an empirical matter to what extent the latter role is preserved in particular contexts, times, and places. In any case, parliament is both a public sphere in its own right, and also part of the wider public sphere. In the cases of both law and parliament, it should also be noted that secondary deliberative institutions have arisen as relief mechanisms to remedy deliberative deficits – in the context of extended controversy – in the form of public hearings, parliamentary committees, citizens' juries, and other innovations.

The fourth integrative complex is that of *the administrative bureaucracy*. This institutional complex plays an important role in the public sphere in organizing the application of norms, as well as through taking responsibility for the dissemination of public information. Democratic justification ultimately legitimates public administration, a process that at least ideally shapes its ethos and procedures. The recent tendency towards the over-burdening of 'vertical' decision-making, which has become entangled both in complexity and controversy, has led to innovations geared towards 'horizontal' steering by participatory institutions, even if public administration generally has been uncertain about its potentials and even its normative desirability.

Even a quick sketch of the public status of governance institutions indicates the extent to which they are characterized by modalities of communication that reflect high, and increasing, levels of public involvement. This renders difficult any attempt to establish a clear boundary between discursive will formation and governance norm-setting prerogative, deliberative or other. This boundary is more apparent in cases where the public sphere is not mobilized, but when the public sphere asserts itself in modern societies the boundaries become porous. Clarity as to which norms apply to which practices, required for either the justification or application of legal norms, is not readily available. The moral characteristics of disputes take on a certain prerogative, and law and politics become absorbed into argumentation in the public sphere.

Civil Society

The separation of the sphere of private life from that of civil society in the figure takes leave of the common idea that civil society and private life extend into one another. The figure also views the economy as a formally organized sphere separate from civil society, a view generally becoming more accepted (Cohen and Arato, 1992; Young, 2000). Civil society is, therefore, narrowly conceived by comparison with a view of civil society that includes the economy and private life as a whole. This idea of civil society has both an institutional dimension, in the form of a morally grounded constitutional framework, as well as a non-institutional dimension in the sense of relatively unstable, and often milieu-specific, ethical and expressive values.

Reproductive and innovative dimensions of the discourse of civil society may be distinguished. The reproductive dimension is to be found in constitutionally interpreted moral-legal norms such as freedom, solidarity, and responsibility that are part of the established culture of civil society.[1] The expressive dimension refers to the capacity for value experimentation within associations and milieus that may turn out to have moral-legal significance in the longer term (Vester et al., 1993). The distinction between these reproductive and innovative dimensions should be qualified; even reproduction of the normative framework of civil society involves recourse to counterfactual assumptions about rights, justice, and responsibility that hold the norms in place. Such exploration, then, subtly changes interpretations,

---

1   These dimensions of civil society form the bedrock of the account of constitutional values in many versions of liberal and republican political philosophies.

changes that receive further impetus from alterations in circumstances and practices. The reproduction of the constitutional culture of civil society may therefore be seen to necessarily incorporate incremental normative innovation. The point is that beyond such slow paced innovation, criticisms of the culture of civil society with regard to norms that are claimed to be unjust, irresponsible, or alienating, operate in a different, transformative register. Sometimes, such transformation processes are issue-specific and, at other times they take a wider, society-spanning form. Examples include the crisis of civilization of the 1960s and the present crisis that may, in the long view, be seen as seen as a consequence of the reaction to the 1960s crisis (Tarrow, 1998).

The proposed narrow conception of civil society may be defended more easily in relation to its role as the carrier of formal and informal 'constitutional' discourses, rather than by consideration of what kinds of agents constitute it in the form of its social membership and roles. One option is, therefore, to shift to a strong relational framework in which civil society is regarded less as a specific social space, composed of certain characteristic agents, and rather more as a culture that generates certain relevant practices. This certainly forms part of the answer in that the concept of civil society may then be extended to include some of the practices of interest groups where they advance common good discourses, or engage in fairly argued interests, though they formally lie outside it.

More generally, perhaps the core hallmark of 'belonging' to civil society is, in fact, whether its normative framework is merely engaged as a background context or as a vital context for the cognitive exploration of normative culture. Civil society is at the core reproduced by associations of various kinds that are *permanently* oriented to the exploration and vindication of key dimensions of the common good. The erosion over recent decades of the ethos of those associations, such as political parties, media associations, and universities, that should sustain the normative culture of civil society, even if they argue with different perspectives, has been a cause for concern amongst analysts of the public sphere, some of whom identify the manipulation of knowledge to serve particular interests as threatening its normative standing and, hence, its very viability (Mayhew, 1997).

The concept of civil society is easiest to apply when associated with a radical movement for the furtherance of democratic principles, such as the movement for democratization in the 1960s or those movements in Eastern Europe in the late 1980s and 1990s that were anti-communist and pro-democracy (Seligman, 1995). It becomes less identifiable and less clear once a particular dimension of democratic citizenship has been institutionalized and its functions become differentiated and less visible. New distinctions then need to be made. Are *trade unions*, for example, part of civil society or are they part of the formally organized sphere? And, by analogy, what is the status that should be accorded to *business associations*? It is hard to give a definitive answer to such questions. One possible answer clarifies a key characteristic of civil society and the public sphere; these spheres become broader, more encompassing, and more societally important in times of societal crisis.

The mass media should certainly be counted as upholders of the democratic principles of civil society. They are exclusively institutions of publicity; any integrative function they acquire derives from their role in publicity. The media are nonetheless in some ways a hybrid institutional complex in that they are integral to civil society, are variously privately and publicly owned, respond to certain distinctive readership milieus, and are society-spanning institutions through their role in the dissemination of culture. The private ownership structure of the print media, in particular, makes it difficult for it to contribute fully to the common good culture of civil society. The problem is not so much that they are private, so much as that they are subject to colonization by interests that may constrain or distort their public role. However, non-public ownership also allows dispersion of opinion and contemporary problems may lie more with the restricted options for non-public ownership. Much of this picture may change, in any case, as the new media mature.

Political associations of *all* kinds that respect democratic values, other than those that are clearly and self-consciously interest-based, should count as intrinsic to civil society. Contrary to the view of Cohen and Arato, *political parties* should be included in civil society (Cohen and Arato, 1994). Political parties may owe much of their form to governmental and parliamentary contexts, but they grow out of civil society, their parliamentary members are voted in by the public, and their broader membership convey the public mood, or part of it, to party executives. In a long-run cultural sense, they are also proponents of certain ideologies that gain currency in political culture.

Other kinds of political association intrinsic to civil society are more loosely organized, such as various socio-political movements. These movements extend to all corners of the political spectrum and often oppose each other through carrying antithetical conceptions of the common good. Such differences are reflected in issue cultures. A distinction must, however, be made between associations that respect or, through reasoned argumentation, seek to transform the normative framework of civil society and those who, like some extremist movements, oppose this framework root and branch. There is a tendency in the left-leaning literature on civil society to theorize civil society only on the basis of the 'good' movements and to ignore other less palatable movements from that standpoint but, as long as these movements respect basic democratic principles, this is inconsistent and lacks practical realism.

Beyond political associations, certain *cultural associations* that have a quasi-political function also belong within civil society. Churches, as expressions of community, are often given mention here. Others include cultural bodies of various kinds. In addition to cultural and political organizations, it is also claimed that various kinds of aid organization also belong within civil society. In the reading of civil society offered here, they only partially belong there insofar as they have a political purpose to shape relations between state institutions, systems, and the lifeworld, for example, through lobbying and intellectual work. In relation to their caring function they should be placed in the private sphere. However, since most voluntary organizations have both a caring and some kind of political mission, they may, in the end, be mainly considered as part of civil society.

Some writers on civil society place the public sphere itself within civil society, in the cases of both Cohen and Arato and Young dividing the public sphere into two components (Cohen and Arato, 1994; Young, 2000). The first is the reflexive part in which *civil societal associations*, women's groups, for example, forge identities oriented towards change in non-public as well as public practices. The second is the political public sphere proper, understood as a society-spanning network of communication. The first position – positioning reflexive publics (Emirbayer and Sheller, 1998) in civil society is defensible – but the second – placing the public sphere as a whole in civil society – elides the idea of the public sphere as a general discursive arena, open to those who wish to contribute to public culture, though without formally belonging to civil society in the restricted sense used here. The general public sphere, of which the culture of civil society is a part, is where the different institutional cultures of society discursively encounter one another as, for example, business, scientific, governmental, legal, and civil societal. Placing the public sphere in civil society elides the distinction between the associational culture of civil society that, for example, generates thematization, and the argumentative and contested character of the public sphere in which pragmatic and interest-driven dimensions of opinion and will formation have a legitimate place.

In relation to the dimension of reflexive public formation, the interaction of *milieus* and *associations* – see bottom right-hand side of Figure 5[2] – generate specific patterns of critical publicity based on publicly shared and practice-altering experiences. Critical publicity may even extend into consumption horizons in the form of specific commodity preferences, markets, and rhetorics of persuasion. It may also extend into formally organized domains such as education, research, and health. Clearly, this model of the public sphere partly already transcends the restricted conception of civil society in that the separation of milieu and association, of civil society and private life, is partly done away with. This may make it sensible to always theorize counter-cultural public spheres as involving a specific relation between civil societal associations and everyday milieus, and theorize transversal, 'dominant' public spheres as necessarily having a relationship to all four theoretical complexes of state, civil society, lifeworld, and formally organized spheres.

This latter reference to the transversal public sphere implies that this public sphere lies somewhere outside civil society proper in an interstitial

---

2   Figure 5, and Figure 6 in Chapter 17, are consistent with the earlier figures used in Parts II and III of the book, which started with the societal theoretical positioning of political philosophies in Chapter 10 and various figures in Chapter 13.

space between the four structured complexes. In fact, the degree to which this public sphere is in fact interstitial depends on the arenas in which public communication is enacted. Only mass mediated communication and, perhaps, certain kinds of horizontal bodies – legal or administrative – are in fact truly so. All other arenas, parliamentary, legal, administrative, and civil societal, are specific to particular complexes. But due to the effect of the media in amplifying the triple contingent status of the public, the public discourses of these arenas transcends their particular location in any one complex.

Placing the public sphere somewhere between the major societal complexes does not immediately evade the issue of its relation to civil society. It is, after all, constitutively supposed to carry the responsibility-demanding ethos of civil society. This problem may, perhaps, be solved through viewing the public sphere as institutionally structured according to some of the guiding principles of civil society, above all publicity, but also plurality, legitimacy, and freedom, but not to be regarded as in civil society as such. The public sphere hence expands to include participants other than those who could be regarded as native to civil society: interest groups, experts, administrators, private citizens with particular experiences, and government officials. It contracts in that the public sphere should no longer be seen as the carrier of a particular normative telos from civil society to the political core, as was the case with the early bourgeois public sphere. It continues to have this function latently – the contemporary situation in the European Union may extend this role into the transnational arena – but, predominantly, it becomes a medium of societal communication within certain normative boundaries set by civil society, though remaining normatively open to issues arising from other social spheres.

The critical import of these distinctions is that the transversal public sphere should be regarded as less normatively structured, less a good in its own right that has in various ways degenerated. It does retain this normative status as a medium for conveying civil societal public opinion to the political core of the public complex and other institutional contexts. But it also can be conceptualized more neutrally as a theatre in which those with an interest in communicating publicly have a right to enter, even though they may manifestly represent interests of state, economy, or other. But when they do enter this theatre of public discourse, they become, and must behave as, members of the public and are expected to follow the normative culture prescribed by civil society. In this way, Habermas's idea of the bracketing of status differentials, discussed in the introduction, still has currency as a counterfactual ideal.

Private Life

The relation between the public sphere and civil society, on the one side, and the everyday lifeworld on the other is often understood as a relation between public and private realms. This is a distinction strongly articulated in liberal political philosophy, and one that at least partly depends on a problematic assertion of a wide-ranging 'classical' view of civil society to include everything that is not political authority. Nonetheless, to decide how this distinction should actually be made remains one of the central issues in the study of the public sphere. Feminist accounts see gendered aspects of the 'private realm' as inherently public and the distinction between public and private as developed with the intent of relegating women to the private sphere (Landes, 1995). This problem is connected to the even more general problem of how micro-contexts – at minimum two people – might be said to constitute small-scale public spheres, a standpoint which is taken up particularly in rhetorical approaches (Hauser, 1999). This is a complicated problem also. Perhaps a gain may be made if the distinction between civil society and the private sphere is conceived as primarily relational rather than substantial. In this conception, the public sphere and civil society may be located in the realm of families, for example, insofar as gender issues are debated or contested at that level.

This leads onto consideration of the triangular relationship between the public sphere, civil society, and private life. This relationship may be addressed through a number of nodal concepts: institutionalized social identities, milieus, and selves. With regard to the first concept, institutionalized social identities, principally subsist at a latent level and consist of those identity complexes that all, or a substantial section, of the population hold, or to which they take up a relation. Examples include nation, class, gender, religion, ethnicity, and race. Such identities are continuously susceptible to reconstruction, but this process does not exclude them having a period of structural stability. The degree to which such identities are susceptible to radical, discursively induced, reorientation is a potential indicator of social change. It is noteworthy that they frequently change together; the 1960s led to substantial movement on all of them, and the contemporary period is also a period of radical reorientation through the effects of what may, loosely, be called globalization.

The second concept of *milieu*, involves the absorption of different social elements – including institutionalized social identities – into complexes of beliefs, styles, and practices, and it clarifies how agents are endowed with repertoires for acting out roles. In the work of Vester et al., it is closely connected to Bourdieu's habitus theory and also to the concept of mentality (Vester et al., 1993). The empirical-theoretical reconstruction of milieus allows individual or aggregated milieus to clarify basic social positions that agents hold, a view that strong relational accounts of the self might find problematic, preferring to regard the self as more autonomously constituted and differentiated. Nonetheless, milieus are empirically important for understanding cultural resonance, outlined further in Chapter 17, and for specifying non-arbitrary relations between everyday life contexts and the constitution of publics. Combining dimensions of social position and values, the concept of milieu is, perhaps, better suited than any other to capture those cultural contexts of life that generate association and shape the resonance of messages.

Milieus are to be distinguished from publics by the fact that publics are less stable, partly because they are likely to form across a number of milieus. Milieus are also structured by the latent identities of class, gender, race, and ethnicity. The concept of milieu softens the impact of these background forces and refracts them through cultural prisms composed of everyday and ideological elements such as, for example, success orientation, conventional, and humanistic-active. The range of socially available milieus provides a good basis for sociological analysis of the composition of publics and the resonance of messages on these publics.

And, finally, a more autonomous, active, purposeful and creative relational concept of the self can be accommodated through the pragmatist notion of the 'I' (Mead, 1934). This latter self might be understood as a carrier of new currents of meaning that crystallize into action repertoires. Such crystallizations, deeply important in generating new idea systems and in the genesis of values, eventually migrate, in favourable circumstances, into milieus, and then into associations. But the initial stimulus for the reconstruction of identity comes from supra-subjective contexts of experience.[3]

Formally Organized Spheres

In the classical understanding of civil society, drawing from the above, the economy was regarded as lying within civil society, a viewpoint that recurred in the renaissance of the theory of civil society that followed the change of regime in Eastern European countries in the 1990s. In the account given here, the economy is taken out of civil society and regarded as one important kind of formally organized social sphere. Civil societal associations may have strong views about economic development, but these views see the economy as part of an overall social project of the same standing as other formally organized spheres. The health system, education, science, elements of the legal system, and public administration also constitute formally organized spheres. The term formal organization suggests that these spheres are highly structured realms of social experience. In some cases, such as the pursuit of truth in the science system, monetary goals in the economic system, and power in the administrative system, non-normative steering media predominate. Systems theory goes too far in supposing that social life must be organized entirely non-normatively, thus free from ethical or moral norms. The very essence of the public sphere, in the light of its cognitive foundations, is firstly to establish the primacy of fully inclusive moral and ethical principles, and secondly to enable the discursive combination of the full spectrum of cognitively available meaning into normative orientations.

---

[3] All three concepts, respectively social identities, milieus and selves, regarded as key sources of social transformation, are closely related to the concepts of subject and discursive positioning in radical democratic theories (Gottweis, 1998).

The question that arises is how can the voices emanating from these formally organized spheres contribute to reproducing the normative culture of civil society that underpins the public sphere and democratic institutions? Formal organizations do contribute to the reproduction and extension of the culture of civil society by contributing to discourses of the common good but, because they pursue self-interested actions also, they cannot be said to be dedicated to the general welfare. This distinction might, perhaps, be made clearer if two conditions of membership of civil society were developed. This might consist of, firstly, commitment to a programme of the common good, and secondly possessing a transformative normative project. The second condition, in particular, allows a diachronic moment to be entered into the constitution of civil society. In the eighteenth century, proponents of key civil rights, including the principle of publicity itself, intrinsically belonged to civil society, as in the nineteenth and twentieth centuries did the various groups who fought for political rights, and trade unions, who fought for social rights. Nonetheless, the achievement of certain rights and institutional power means that the status of some of the associations has changed. Trade unions have partly become an interest group and certain political associations, though still belonging to civil society, no longer carry a radicalizing culture, mostly becoming or aspiring to become parties of government.

The implication of these remarks is that the normative culture that springs from civil society has to be permanently renovated to counter threats of erosion and to advance new claims. The constitution of civil society then bifurcates. The higher part of Figure 5 – as also are the top two quadrants of Figure 1, Chapter 10 – is concerned with the reproduction of institutionalized normative culture while another part, the lower right-band part, consistent with the bottom right-hand quadrant of Figure 1, addresses the innovative, counter-normative capacities of civil society.

Yet another problematic category in Figure 5 is the production of knowledge through research and reflection in the – broadly speaking – science system. The self-interpretation of *academics* has historically included the claim that they produce disinterested knowledge and that, in the scientific-technical sphere, that they also produce useful knowledge. The fate of the latter kind of knowledge has increasingly become bound up with commercial utility to be achieved in the shorter, rather than longer, term as the distinction between basic and applied research has become eroded. In any case, technical and natural science, from the seventeenth century on, following Bacon's prescription, self-consciously abandoned any claim to an emancipatory social role that was developed in the Puritan vision (Merton, 1936, 1938). As is well known, the idea that science is about the neutral generation of justified true beliefs became immensely important for the political system. Over the course of modernity, politics became increasingly reliant on expertise for its functioning and legitimation, even if this complex between science and politics is now weakening (Ezrahi, 1990).

The emancipatory interest, advocated in Puritan science, in the end became vested, somewhat ambivalently, in the social sciences. Yet, here, much attention has been given to knowledge that serves administrative and economic goals, on the one hand, and to the hermeneutic explication of social patterns of meaning, determinedly without political purpose, on the other. Only one category of knowledge, knowledge explicitly oriented to emancipation or to enlightenment, relates unambivalently to the normative horizons of civil society. This form of knowledge is overwhelmed by other kinds of knowledge in terms of quantity and societal influence. It therefore makes sense to identify academics as normally having relatively limited horizons when they contribute to the public sphere as specific experts in Foucault's sense. Like economic associations, this does not preclude these academics sometimes operating through the discourse of civil society but, as a category, academics are not intrinsic to civil society.

All of the above macro-social structures, and the various actors they spawn, are sustained by a multiplicity of networks. These networks are pivotal to the dissemination of information and the construction of communicative standpoints. On public issues, networks have greater importance in the production and interpretation of messages than organizations. Networks take many forms with very different topologies. At a general level, civil societal networks are loosely organized associational networks. This loose topology may be distinguished from the interest-oriented networks that spring up between governments and formally organized spheres, notably the economy, which endure over time. Networks are prolific: journalists operate many kinds of networks, and networks develop within and between formally organized spheres and within and between civil societal associations. The presence, absence, and nature of networks are important to the generation and reception of communication. Networks feature on both the input side – thematization and text production – and the output side of public communication – interpretation and resonance. Networks are contexts of learning and the formation of new or adapted networks are expressions of associational learning processes. They constitute the material membrane of the public sphere that corresponds with its cultural membrane of topically relevant communication.

The Macro-Social Order of Communication

The brief overview of the macro-social context connects in a number of ways with contemporary theorizing on the public sphere. The first is that the expansion in the range of organizations that routinely engage in public discourse has coincided with the professionalization of communication. From a normative perspective, the latter has, on one side, been interpreted as a decline in the sincerity of public utterances and, consequently, of public trust (Mayhew, 1997). It may alternately be interpreted as the wider inclusion in public discourse of organizations that previously tried to operate beyond it, and count as an indicator of the coming into being of a communication society. In either case, the expansion of the theoretical framework of the public sphere is necessary, going beyond the conventional assumption that it mediates between state and civil society.

A further major question arising is the status and boundaries of civil society. Is civil society a place or a culture? The answer suggested above is that it is something of both, but if civil society cannot be identified as a source of discourses sincerely orientated to the common good, then a critical function of the public sphere is confused and democracy itself endangered. This point articulates with the first point raised above and the answer is empirically indeterminate, partly because the contemporary formal model of democracy is in crisis, and a new model has not yet been born.

The English term of public sphere has generated a tendency to view the 'conceptual container' of public discourse as a space rather than a complex culture that permeates all social spheres. The cognitive approach is intended to correct this assumption of the spatialization of the public sphere, a problem that, as indicated above, also affects normatively 'pure' accounts of deliberative democracy (Splichal, 1999). The next chapter on the dynamics of public communication will reinforce this point.

CHAPTER 17

The Dynamics of Public Communication

The cognitive approach of this book recognizes the centrality of collectively shared knowledge for human activities, whether such knowledge is understood as discrete cognitive principles or the composite, rule-incorporating schemata of cultural models. Cultural models vary in levels of stability, but all depend on discursive processes that both generate cultural variation and guide normative selection and stabilization. This dual perspective, cognitive and normative, combines a post-positivist and constructivist-structuralist account of knowledge. This paradigm of viewing social practices as reflexively and communicatively guided by means of cognitive principles and cultural schemata entails that the relationship between structure and practice becomes transformed. A cultural structure conceives in this manner is not determining of practices, as in the older structuralist paradigm, but neither is it only vaguely related to practices as in some forms of interpretive thinking. It is somewhere between the two, exerting a power that can be the object of explanatory reconstruction and critique, and yet it is also open to constructivist analysis of volatile mechanisms of collective learning.

In the older sociology of knowledge associated with Mertonian functionalism, it was assumed that knowledge could be reconstructed according to enduring epistemic norms that specified validity standards (Merton, 1973; Lynch, 1997). Today, assumptions about the scope, endurance, and the degree to which norms may he held to determine practice have changed. Norms have come to be mainly regarded as provisionally effective complexes, ever subject to change in the light of cognitively guided interpretive and justificatory processes. The democratic theoretical challenge is to understand how structural arrangements, both socio-structural and socio-cultural – to make a necessary but never entirely satisfactory distinction – condition norm-building practices. Putting this in terms of the book as a whole, the cognitive foundation of both procedural and substantive norms *and* the material social structure that underpin these foundations are critical to normative analysis. The membrane of social structure is not independent of culture. It is substantially formed by cultural structures. Though not determining, nonetheless these culturally shaped social structures, reconstructed in Chapter 16, can exert persistent effects on discursive social positions in the manner analysed by Bourdieu. It is also the case that some issues lead to such dramatic cultural change that apparently stable, structurally anchored, social positions rapidly change.

Structurally anchored political discourse problematizes the schemata residing in socio-cultural models. Discourse in this sense is concerned with processes of justifying or opposing knowledge schemata and their associated and mutually sustaining norm complexes and practices. Public discourse is therefore both shaped by and constructs frameworks of political knowledge located in socio-cultural models and in the wider macro-cognitive order. The relationship between discourse and politically relevant knowledge leads to the building of normative cultures and institutional structures that underpin various kinds of public participation in politics.

Democratic justice in the sense of fair and inclusive public participation can only be fully achieved by means of the democratization of social arrangements generally, a view consistent with Forst's idea of a justified basic structure (Forst, 2007b). A key premise of realizing inclusive democratic justice is through the construction of a spectrum of relevance for politics that is located in socio-cultural models. The construction of such models depends on extending the concept of democratic justice to the public sphere generally. As already argued, public discourses must be able to understand and influence the cultural structures of institutional spheres. The communicative-cognitive process of public discourse clarifies how society learns through the generation of variety from which institutional stabilization emerges as a selective outcome.

One of the shortcomings of the normative paradigm in democratic theory is to simplify the cognitive process of knowledge generation. The public sphere can no more insulate itself from the generative knowledge-producing capacity of social institutions than normative democratic practices can be insulated from the cognitive-communicative process of the public sphere. Both assumptions, respectively over-stressing the autonomy of the public sphere and of formal democracy, are over-confident about what it is possible to know from within a certain institutional vantage point. Institutions of all kinds, for example, are complex culture-producing entities in their own right. Epistemically, they delineate contexts of relevance for various activities and, practically, they specify the rules and resources required for realizing them. Institutions also entail the co-ordination of practices within a relational system formed by other institutions and networks and the formulation of rules and procedures for the conduct of these co-ordinated activities (Scott, 2001). The cognitive ordering function of institutions means that they provide orientations, contexts, and rules for knowledge production and dissemination. Beyond their classifying and co-ordinating functions, institutions also have a legitimating function. They attract respect amongst the wider public – or lose it – and thereby legitimate their effects on the social world.

Social institutions, including institutionalized social identities, thereby constitute, along with the public sphere and democratic institutions, one of the three central sites for the production and reception of public knowledge. Democratic justice must be built around all three and the epistemic complexity of co-ordinating cognitive and social structures fully recognized. Full recognition of the need to resolve this complexity, animated by academic insight such as science and technology studies that lie at the epicentre of a controversy-generating society, potentially leads in the direction of democratic innovation.

Communicative Forms and the Institutionalization of Publicity

Communicative Arenas

Public communication takes place in and between institutionally structured arenas. These arenas include the legal system, the parliamentary complex, various kinds of forum that lie between state, formally organized spheres, the mass and new mediated spheres, the administrative complex, and other spheres within civil society itself that have a public inter-associational quality. The various arenas are characterized by different kinds of discourse. Viewed organically, public discourse is constructed across multiple arenas in a manner whose sequences and implications have been little studied. Discourses cognitively mature or become dissipated as they move between arenas. If they mature they may also acquire an enhanced integrative and action-co-ordinating force. Some discourses do not gain such force, and still other discourses lose some or all of the force they may have had as they move across arenas, or as they move from the periphery to the core.

Public discourse, therefore, takes place in an inter-institutional context as well as within specific institutional arenas. Each of these arenas has different membership and procedural rules. Some, for example, operate in a ratiocinative manner, while others are less structured and formal. Reflection on the plurality of these arenas throws light on a central question that divides theorists of the public sphere, whether it is to be regarded as singular or plural. If the public sphere is seen as conducted in a multiplicity of arenas that are connected, or from a normative standpoint should be connected, some of the heat departs from the debate on whether to emphasize singularity or plurality. Much of the difference of course remains concerning the relative power of the different arenas or the importance of what is excluded from any arena in the form of experiences that fail to be thematized. But the arena model allows at least for these differences to be laid out in a relative continuum and opens the possibility of some measure of theoretical integration between singular and plural concepts of the public sphere.

The model of discursive public will formation that builds on the core-periphery model was outlined, following Habermas, in Part II. This envisages 'responsibility demanding' discourses emanating on the periphery becoming successively rationalized through pragmatic, ethical, moral, and legal discourses. This model is of real value in clarifying that radical innovation begins on the civil societal periphery, but erroneous in the view that they always begin as pragmatic problems rather than as moral or ethical problems. The progress of different issues towards public salience and institutional efficacy is actually quite varied. What has become empirically apparent on a macro level is that the 'culture' of issues often exceeds the processing capacity of existing participatory arenas, often simultaneously on the discursive, deliberative, and decision-making planes.

The concept of discursive institution addresses the production of cultural commonalities and differences in cognitive cultural and socio-cultural models, while deliberative institutions specialize in the production of norms. Discursive institutions take on the organizational form of communicative arenas such as the mass media, the new media, public hearings, long-term planning committees, movements in civil society, certain kinds of inquiry, and other. Much of what goes on in a – frequently only nominally – deliberative body such as a parliament is discursive in nature given the unlikelihood that parliamentary debate in itself will have a significant impact on legislation. All deliberative bodies are partly discursive institutions insofar as they are conducted in public or, at least, have their outcomes subject to public scrutiny.

All kinds of discursive institution are participatory in quality in one or other sense of the term. In the classical framework of representative democracy, only the mass mediated public sphere and the voting system could be said to be *directly* participatory in any sense. In some variants of the political realism, described in Part I, only the influence exerted by voting is regarded as a legitimate form of public participation. At present, there is a growth in interest in direct participatory institutions and a significant upward estimation of their value (Bacqué and Sintomer, 2011; O'Sullivan, 2011). Innovations in discursive institutions offer a new context for democratic justice. These innovations bridge the respective activities of cognitive elaboration and normative specification. They abstract from the immediate pressures of decision-making to address the very foundations of building possible kinds of agreements, though rarely consensus, at the level of cultural models. These innovations are an important new component to the range of arenas of public communication.

The assumed participation deficit has given rise, albeit uneasily and ambivalently, to a new wave of direct participatory institutions, spanning law, public administration, parliament, and civil society (Abels and Bora, 2004). These institutions arise in the space between calls for governance institutions to democratize areas of society, for example those areas that generate unacceptable risk, and the existing 'processing capacity' of democratically regulated communication arenas. Where the latter prove to be insufficient, new institutions fill the space and illustrate how new substantive problems generate additional procedural responses. These innovative discursive institutions are not always classed as institutions because of their weak practical import. Indeed, one of the principal research questions they generate is the trajectory of their possible institutionalization. They include institutions for citizen participation, such as public hearings and public forums, and for citizen deliberation, such as consensus conferences and citizen juries.

They also include, somewhat more loosely, more traditional legal mechanisms of involving citizens or providing citizens with avenues for redress such as jury trials and judicial review. More loosely still, they could include discursive components of other institutional arrangements such as rights of objection, public consultative meetings, or policy deliberation processes with citizen involvement. These institutions are specialized around questions of cognitive innovation within a general discourse of justification. They typically arise when the consequential, outcome-oriented role of other institutions encounters legitimacy problems (Abels and Bora, 2004). Their growth therefore signifies the increase in legitimacy problems of existing institutions confronted with disputes over the kind and nature of knowledge, arising from such characteristic contemporary issues as scientific-technical and environmental controversies and identity politics (Stehr, 2001).

Such institutions are located in an intermediate space between public discourse in the public sphere and formal legal-political institutions. The actual role they have in decision-making or general policy-making is mostly not very strong. They appear rather to generate politically relevant knowledge, perhaps even policy learning, through expressing the views of the observing public. Discursive institutions give the public a recognizable voice; they channel their views to political actors and other institutions. Such indirect effects may be transformed over time to more direct effects, if these institutions acquire more clearly defined decision-making or policy-making functions in circumstances where intractable disputes over rival knowledge claims continue to generate legitimacy problems. These functions might include a more defined role in the normative steering of trajectories of knowledge-generating institutions, a prospect envisaged by Fuller (Fuller, 2000), a development that would indicate the will to institutionalize some aspects of cognitive-communicative learning processes along the lines of the democratic inquiry Dewey envisaged as the role of philosophy and social science (Bohman, 1999; Dewey, 1927).

A cognitive-communicative learning approach means that public discourse, whether in specialized institutions or in the wider public sphere, should be analysed within the contexts provided by the cognitive order and socio-cultural models. Two reductive tendencies are unsuited to the communicative and epistemic complexity of modern societies. The first, already a target of policy learning approaches, is that of an Archimedean standpoint and associated procedures entailed in the assumption of a single truth revealed by positivist-styled inquiry. Policy co-ordination in a communication society requires extended networks of communication that generate awareness, monitoring, reflexivity, and even legitimacy (Apel, 1984; Trenz and Eder, 2004). Hence, politically relevant knowledge should be less conceived in terms of the aggregation of facts and more in relation to the communicative construction of collective schemata that determine the relevance of facts. The reductive tendency to be avoided here, therefore, is to conceive of policy knowledge without recognition of the discursive communication that brings collective learning into play.

If the first reductive tendency is to conceive of knowledge without discourse, the second is to conceive of political discourse as a specialized and restricted activity that exists outside of the general context of societal knowledge. This leads to an 'over political' conception of discourse that cannot do justice to knowledge schemata and practices that lie beyond the formal political sphere. This does not mean that discursive political 'steering' of other social spheres is not possible. This has already been anticipated in the account of cultural models that is provided in Chapter 13 above. Formally organized spheres should not be denied necessary autonomy by excessive subordination to discursively generated political steering. However, reflexive, discursive kinds of political steering have a better chance than hierarchical ones of respecting necessary 'tolerance limits' of formally organized spheres with regard to intrusions on their autonomy. Such steering must therefore, on the one hand, take account of the normative requirements contained in the democratic interest in justice and the relative autonomy of the functional symbolic media that also steer formally organized spheres. Appropriate mixes of discursive and media steering will diminish the likelihood that such spheres will burden their environments with excessive externalities, as has evidently been the case with the excessive autonomy enjoyed by the financially driven economic system in the last number of decades. This is a clear indication of deficiencies in needed discursive steering.

Discursive steering of this kind, at least ideally, is inclusive, reflexive, and revisable. The extension of such steering is consistent with the more radical impulses of deliberative theory. Current discursive innovations have not been able to operate in this way. Major shortcomings have included low general institutional status and strongly polarized positions, for example with respect to public hearings on the risk of new technologies. Nonetheless, the cumulative case for innovative discursive institutions, extending across all the various manifestations, is strong. Cumulative learning from such experiments may over time be realized in changes in cultural models, normative structures and, ultimately, the general relationship between democratic institutions and other social spheres. This would entail fundamental collective learning. A limitation of the scholarship, both theoretical and empirical, has been to concentrate mainly on possible direct effects of discursive institutions, in the sense of manifest effects on decision and policy-making, and less on indirect cultural effects within the wider spectrum of established and innovative communicative arenas, associated modes of governance, and deep-lying cultural resonance. The democratization of knowledge, in this latter sense, must be put more centre-stage, as it is a critical part of the extension of democratic justice.

Communication Structures and the Cognitive Order

In the previous chapter, and in the last section, the structures that shape public communication have been provisionally outlined. The previous chapter laid out general societal structures, followed above by an outline of

The Dynamics of Public Communication 417

the meso-level arena structures in which public discourse is institutionally structured in both a cognitive and normative sense. The communicative structure of the meso-level is at the heart of the discursive capacity of the public sphere. The task that opens up from this, in the light of the foregoing, is how these structures and associated processes can be set within the context of the cognitive order as outlined in detail in Part III. This task is addressed in the current section. And beyond this task, which amounts to interrelating social and cultural structures of public communication, arises that of relating these structural contexts to communication dynamics. This will be taken up in the following section.

Figure 6 revisits Figure 1, at the end of Part II, in which the respective emphases of political philosophies within normative culture were outlined. As explained there, Figure 1 integrates two eras of Habermas's work, his earlier work in which the public sphere occupied the space between state

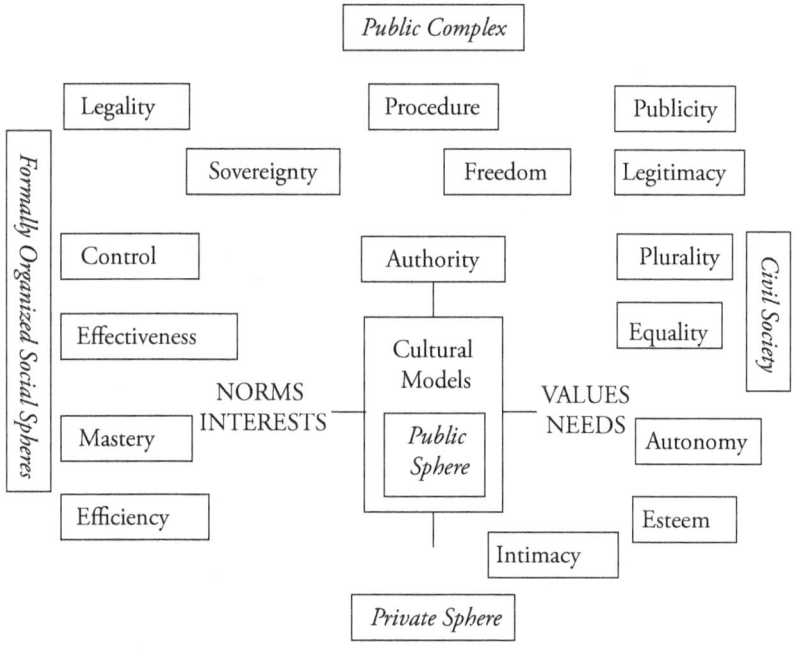

Figure 6: Societal Spheres and the Cognitive Order

and civil society, and a later era when the context formed by his account of system and lifeworld must also be incorporated. The public sphere in the figure is, therefore, positioned within a quadrilateral framework with the addition of the later system/lifeworld axis. It also adds a third era in Habermas's work by including the deliberative and discursive complex, placed at the centre of Figure 6. The parametric axes in Figure 1, which respectively run vertically from structure to agency and horizontally from system to lifeworld, reflect the first two paradigms. The discursive and deliberative complex at the centre reflects the third.

Figure 6, using the same basic framework as Figure 1, is placed within the cognitive order of modernity, which involves two specific dimensions being added, cognitive principles and cultural models. The cognitive principles that serve as presuppositions of modern action systems are ranged around the outer margin of the figure. In a list that is by no means exhaustive, they extend from functionally relevant principles on the left hand side (efficiency, effectiveness, mastery of nature); include the principes underpinning the functional component of governance around the top left-hand quadrant (control, legality, sovereignty); go on to include the constitutional and quasi-constitutional normative culture of the formal-political dimension of civil society ranging around the top right-hand quadrant (freedom, publicity, plurality, legitimacy); and include the less formal normative culture of civil society around the bottom right-hand quadrant (authenticity, sincerity, expressive identity, the good life in its many manifestations).

Cultural models are at the very core of Figure 6, located within, but also anchoring, the deliberative-discursive complex, and placed in the figure at the meeting point of the axes. Structurally conditioned immanent discourses, translating between communication arenas, through collective learning processes span immanent contexts of action and the cognitive order. The latter is composed of the cognitive rule principles around the outside of the diagram and the combined status of cognitive cultural models and socio-cultural models at the centre. Society-spanning discursive processes, circulating within and between communication arenas, therefore lead to selections from these cognitive principles being made over time that are symbolically packaged into cultural models. Cultural models then guide norm-building processes and the general processes of

The Dynamics of Public Communication

social integration described in Chapter 13. The cultural organization of society through plural cultural models both shapes public discourse and actors' cognitive models and, reciprocally, is discursively transformed by discourses emanating from micro- and meso-levels.

In Figure 7, complementing Figure 6, the three cognitive cultural systems and dimensions of social integration, outlined in Part III, are laid out. Whereas these dimensions, functional, moral and evaluative, are basic to all areas of social life, and cannot be reduced to a functional form of societal steering as with Luhmann, each of them nonetheless is respectively more

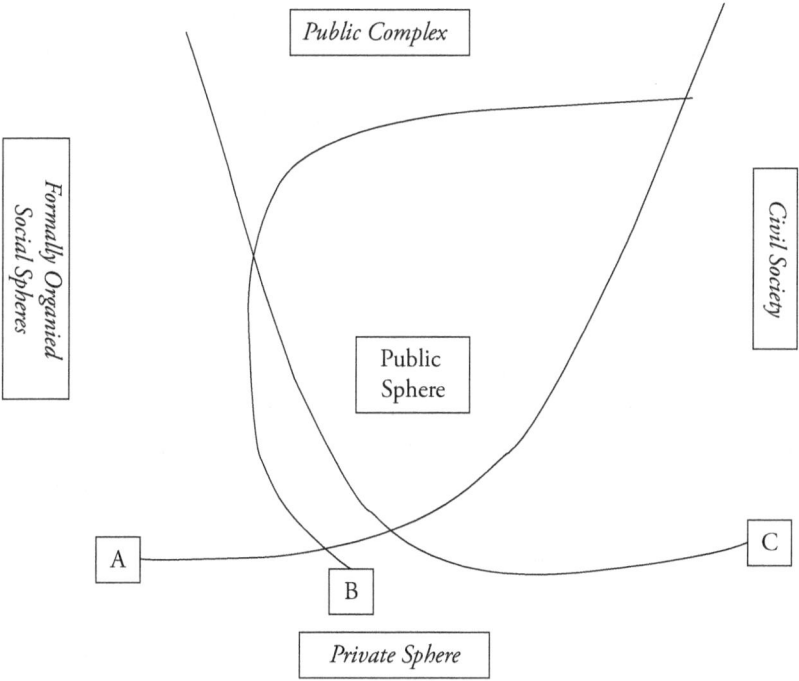

Figure 7: The Cognitive Framework of the Public Sphere

Legend:
A is the functional cultural structure;
B is the moral-legal cultural structure;
C is the ethical-evaluative structure.

prominent in certain social spheres. The functional power of symbolically generalized media of communication is prominent and, in certain respects, constitutive in formally organized spheres. A clear example is the use of money in the economic system. But these steering media are, nonetheless, embedded within normatively and ethically integrated forms of social organization. System integration and social integration are combined in various ways in different spheres of life, rather than being regarded as entirely belonging to qualitatively different domains. Structuring by moral norms and communicative power is, by contrast, prominent and constitutive in the public complex and the organized part of civil society. And, finally, structuring by ethical values and social power is more prominent in the more informal parts of civil society and in private life. As argued in Part II with regard to discourse ethics, it is more difficult to distinguish moral and ethical norms, and the respective orders of power, from one another than it is to distinguish them both from functional media and pragmatic norms.

From a cognitive perspective, the various principles that correspond with these three spheres, enter in through discourses that elaborate or fundamentally challenge existing orders, both so to speak 'internally', as new moral claims challenge existing moral norms institutionalized in law, as counter-cultural identities challenge institutionalized norms, and as functional codes are reconstructed for new purposes – but also 'externally' as the various symbolically generalized media and norms interpenetrate one another, generating innovative potentials. These three cultural structures also correspond closely with Figure 4 in Chapter 13, which emphasizes the respective social spaces occupied by three kinds of democratic communication, purposive-rational, deliberative, and general public communication.

The top two quadrants of Figure 6, complementing Figure 1 in Chapter 10, comprise the dominant sites of the macro-political order. Here, the quasi-transcendent order of cognitive principles is made immanent by means of orienting cultural models that interpenetrate moral, legal, and evaluative dimensions of normative culture. The deliberative-discursive complex that mediates between the top and bottom halves of the figure composes the meso-level of deliberation and public discourse. The communicative forms of social integration, consensus, rational dissensus,

The Dynamics of Public Communication 421

compromise, and repressive hegemony, also developed in Part III above, and represented in Figure 8, may also be aligned with this typological distinction of cultural spheres.

The four communicative modes of social integration in Figure 8 are (1) consensus, or its contrary, repressive hegemony, (2) rational dissensus, (3) compromise, and (4) general norm conformity or its contrary, counter-normative reason. Compromise (3) can be aligned with bargaining; (1) consensus, is predominantly deliberative but in a context shaped by general public discourse; consensus can also be procured through repressive ideological domination; (2) rational dissensus comprises an admixture of deliberation and discourse, but discourse more fundamentally; and (4) an alternative of affirmation as norm conforming meaning or critique in the form of critical discourse. These are consistent with the philosophies outlined in Part II, that is, with Rawls (consensus), political realism (compromise); republicanism (rational dissensus), radical democracy (counter-normative critique), and discursive-deliberative democracy as a spanning theory. These modes of co-ordination align with their more general functions as laid out in Figure 1, Chapter 10, respectively oriented towards reproducing and elaborating norms, values, and interests and articulating claims associated with unmet needs.

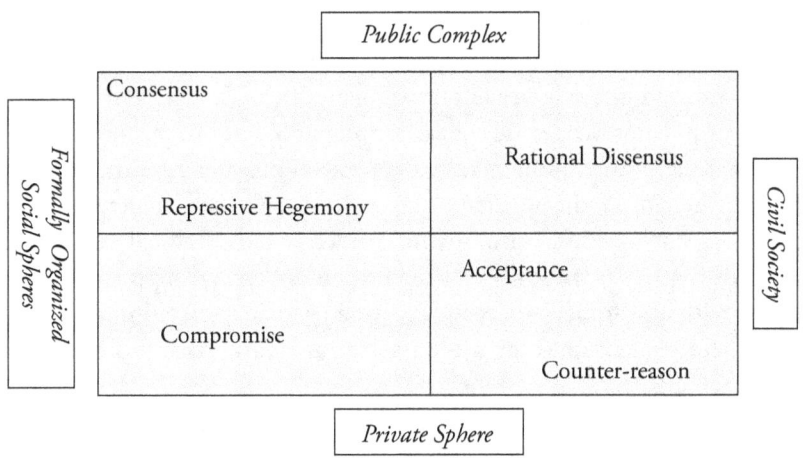

Figure 8: Communicative Modes of Social Integration

In Part II, Habermas's discursive-deliberative theory, together with his earlier social theory of communicative action, was given a general role spanning the various foci of the other political philosophies in norms, values, interests, and needs. In Figure 8 above, this deliberative-discursive core has been opened up and broken into components that reflect the distinctive modes of reasoning of the other philosophies, consensus, rational dissensus, compromise, and counter-normative reasoning. The overarching theory, associated with communicative action and discourse ethics, as adapted here takes on the role of discursive co-ordination within the broad cognitive framework outlined in Part III. In short, the communicative modalities outlined in Figure 8 are meta-discursive compositional modalities that give form to discursive elaboration of what is cognitively achievable. They prescribe how the spectrum of meaning represented in cultural models is communicatively organized.

Figure 8 moves downwards from macro to micro on the vertical axis. Correspondingly, the initiation of the kind of counter-normative claims already theorized in Chapter 10 above is located in the lower right-hand quadrant. This therefore involves the separable or combined logics of the articulation both, on the one hand, of social interests and social needs that are claimed to be unmet and, on the other, radical projects for the structuring of the organizational and cultural foundations of social relations. In terms of fundamental social change, the bottom right-hand quadrant is primary, reaching beyond interest-dominated distributive conflicts, which are crystallized in the lower-left hand quadrant, to the reconstruction of identities and moral order. Of course, various mobilizations that incorporate both material and symbolic claims and projections often fuse and support one another. Yet, radical distributive projects have little chance without becoming anchored in culturally interpreted needs. Radical projects of all kinds that are first ideally articulated acquire critical support by resonating with and sometimes reconstituting particular social milieus, and, from there, generating compatible associational forms that more securely carry their claims.

Radical micro-cognitive models therefore emerge in the informal sphere of civil society as it meets private life. But micro-cognitive models are not confined to this sphere. The socio-communicative order as a whole, described in the various figures, generates agents with distinctive micro-cognitive models. In other words, the micro- to macro-level vertical movement in the figures, especially from the lower right-hand quadrant of Figure 1 and Figure 8, to the two upper quadrants, only captures the oppositional discourses that may have radical import for political order. At a second stage, once the transformative implications of a new idea system gain social traction, micro-cognitive models that carry these ideas may diffuse throughout all social spheres. Networked social positions that derive from particular societal loci, formally organized spheres, the public complex, and civil society, characterize political issues. These social positions are both discursively and topically organized and either operate within the constraints of cultural models or begin to recombine cognitive principles and social practices into cultural models. Occasionally, where radical social change is at issue, they also begin to significantly change a number of cognitive principles, or elaborate one or more new principles.

*Communication Dynamics: Argumentation,
Deliberation, and the Cognitive Order*

This section moves on to address communication dynamics within its macro- and meso-structural contexts. Public discourse is composed of illocutionary acts that have perlocutionary force in the sense of shaping 'cognizing' entities that include human agents, institutions, and systems. The significance of discourse cannot be fully derived from its structural context. It is neither a by-product of the social positions of its producers nor of the social contexts of its reception. The discourses that circle in and between them shape the communicative structures and processes documented in this and the previous chapter. Neither social structural nor cultural structural assumptions, alone or together, can fully explain its dynamics, even if sometimes they can go a long way.

For discourse is not just an effect of structures, it is constitutive of them. Understood according to the cognitive paradigm developed here, discourse penetrates into and combines different cognitive principles as they are manifested in various social spheres, forging and revising connections between them, and making the process available to publics of all kinds whose argumentation is eventually resolved into cultural models. Discourse therefore contributes to structural ordering and yet frequently exceeds the learning built into such orders. Society cannot be fully comprehended from a structural perspective; it can only be comprehended from a relational perspective that combines structures and the discourses that both bind and constitute them. Structural patterns may endure for long periods conditioning discourses but discourses, in the end, transform them.

Discourse in the contemporary idiom of social theory is a kind of flow between and within the manifest structural nodes of society. Public discourse is the intrinsic currency of the democratic order because it is what enables politics to respond to the contingency of modern life, either stabilizing this contingency in enduring dimensions of normative culture or focalizing it to elaborate or transform that culture. Based on the foregoing analysis in this book, three key dimensions intrinsic to understanding how democratic public discourse operate are *public argumentation*, including thematization, collective argumentation and reception processes, *collective learning as cognitive-cultural structure formation*, and *deliberation* with strong or weak public involvement. These three dimensions are consistent with the account given in Chapter 13.[1]

Public argumentation includes the activities of initial thematization, general collective argumentation, and reception. Thematization refers to the process whereby, from the range of issues that could be made salient, certain issues actually become so. How this happens is far from predictable. It partly depends on the historical canon of what counts as relevant in a society. Amongst other factors, this includes the alignments and relative strength of various parties in respect of functional, social, and communicative power, the structure of public memory, the role of journalists and other cultural producers like academics, churches, and knowledge-producing associations of all kinds, the ideological orientation of the media, the balance of power between different forces, and the consolidation of effective

---

[1] It might be useful for the reader to look back at Chapter 13, in particular at the synthetic Figure 2, as it is relevant for much of the following text.

micro-cognitive models in milieus and amongst publics. A society in which there is a strong history of civil societal mobilization and autonomy will tend to generate a different kind of agenda to one in which civil society has been rendered weak by repressive hegemony and remains insufficiently differentiated from any or all of political authority, formally organized spheres, and private life.

It also matters what political cultural model – liberal, republican, radical, and many in-between variants – has been dominant or, more accurately, how strongly the different philosophies are represented in the general political cultural model. Increasingly, today, thematization relates to the difference between media forms. Do issues become selected through new or old media of communication? What role do information brokers such as journalists play in these media forms? Thematization occurs at the beginning of an issue cycle, but it can recur many times throughout it as a response to feedback through resonance. Thematization is not simply a shift in the collective argumentation process, though it is partly that; it is most fundamentally the effect of significant changes or innovations in micro-cognitive models.

Thematization can be distinguished into two kinds: conventional agenda setting, which is primarily top-down, or bottom-up agenda-building processes. In the former case, influential insiders such as politicians, journalists, public bureaucracies, and influential interest groups *set* the agenda; in the latter, a broader coalition of social movements, civil societal associations, campaigning individuals, oppositional political parties, amongst others, *build* the agenda. The respective strengths of the two positions, which of course don't exclude one another, have given rise to much debate in literature on the mass media as discussed in Chapter 15.

Agenda-building thematization is likely to become more prominent, to some extent already has, with the advent of the Internet and social media. In the latter case too, a vast expansion in modalities of political communication may be witnessed. Initial and recurring thematization is bound up with these different modalities, which include a variety of message forms in mass or new media associated with particular communicative conventions, ranging from narrative depictions, to opinion giving, to factual reporting and many more. The interaction of text generation, dissemination, and reception generates continuous reciprocal feedback between them. In the course of issue cultures, they become topically organized into a finite set of resonant positions, a factor that Hilgartner and Bosk attribute to limits of available bandwidth (Hilgartner and Bosk, 1988; O'Mahony and Schäfer, 2005). The manner in which issues evolve depends on the balance of power, institutional structures, and the cognitive and cultural order.

Thematization is pivotal to public communication. It connects the micro-generative mechanisms of society to the amplification produced by mass media and other arenas of communication. The thematization of radical agendas, in particular, involves the introduction into public discourse of beliefs, commitments, and evaluations that frequently were previously not even latently present. Radical thematization of this kind is often associated with diverse kinds of social movement. Radical issues, once thematized, may enter into mainstream fora of collective argumentation and, further, may in the right circumstances become cognitively and normatively institutionalized, leading over the long term to demobilization of movements' innovative cognitive models that were responsible for putting the issue on the agenda at the outset (Eder, 1996; O'Mahony and Delanty, 2001). But it remains of the first importance to understand the process whereby cultural innovation initially takes root. This does not primarily happen through a process of non-public communication in private contexts of life, but through a type of quasi-public incubation of new cognitive models in the associational spheres of the civil societal periphery, though this process may be profoundly influenced by 'private' experiences that are thus made public. Feminism is the paradigmatic example of this kind of private/public translation.

Collective public argumentation is in some respects difficult to separate from thematization and reception, because thematization and reception are intrinsic to it. The distinction is therefore more one of scale. Collective public argumentation is a society-wide process, concerned with an issue of high public salience. Another indication of the progression from initial thematization to collective argumentation is the wider range of communicative arenas that are implicated. Even deliberation, which has a distinctive role, is frequently absorbed into processes of collective argumentation, from which it eventually seeks a certain level of autonomy in order to proceed with intertwined moral, legal, and ethical norm building. Collective argumentation is characterized by a wide range of actors that operate across a full range of arenas. Collective argumentation entails multiple kinds of resonance with, and feedback loops from, its broader societal context. It represents public discourse at its most comprehensive and complex.

A new emphasis on the process of interpreting media messages began to emerge in the sociological and cultural studies literature on the mass media a number of decades ago, partly because the various macro-structural paradigms that had dominated the social sciences for some time had begun to wane. This new emphasis suggested that reception was not solely determined by the message, but that it emerged from a complex process of decoding in which existing cultural schemata of the viewer, reader, or listener afforded her a perspective with which to reconstruct the text, rather than simply to accept its manifest import (Hall, 1997). The general viewpoint on reception is not necessarily incompatible with adopting an agenda-setting perspective on the process of thematization; dominant cultures and institutions could still engage in agenda-setting, but message producers could not determine the culture of issues on their own, given the variability and autonomy of responses to these messages. An agenda-building perspective accentuates still more the importance of reception. From such a perspective, thematization and collective argumentation should be understood as being formed by a series of interrelated discourses and interpreting schemata held by multiple producers and multiple receivers.

The agenda-building perspective already begins to anticipate the question of dissemination that has become perceived as a much more important dimension of reception in recent times with the advent of the new media. Dissemination structures and processes are frequently not formally considered in the literature on media influence. Yet the manner in which media messages are disseminated is extremely important. Mass media forms of dissemination are first of all closely related to the milieus that the given media outlet characteristically services. It matters whether media organizations have wide reach across milieus and publics so that the spectrum of possible opinion is fully serviced. With the advent of the Internet, the question of dissemination takes on an entirely new importance. Distribution no longer consists in getting a cultural commodity in front of a reader, hearer, or listener, but of getting a message to any member of an unlimited audience who can, in many cases, also respond. The distinction between producer and receiver, though far from entirely dissipated, is reduced in importance. While this is a new freedom and power granted to civil society, as Sunstein and others point out, there are also dangers of the fragmentation of meaning given wide-ranging and rapid dissemination potential along with the heterogeneity of sources of text generation.

Some recent sociological scholarship has made the concept of resonance central to the idea of reception (Luhmann, 1989; Strydom, 2003; Trenz and Eder, 2004). Resonance describes the impact that a given 'message' will have on different kinds of 'audience', where the idea of an audience takes on structural connotations and, potentially, a temporally extended form. In Figure 9, five kinds of resonance are identified; systemic, governance, associational, public, and cultural. Not alone the concept of audience, but also that of 'message', has to be rethought to capture the complexity induced by the nature of resonance. The concept of message has been extensively used in much media research, but it needs to be semiotically developed to capture the density of meaning that arises from communication processes that go on at many levels and time frames. Messages are semiotically organized signs in a given communicative act that are oriented to contexts of reception such as systems, cultural orders, associations, publics, and governance institutions, and yet also influenced by the effect of resonance from them. All of this induces an interpretive process with no necessary agreement emerging on what the message unequivocally means. Messages pass through various kinds of cultural filters before they generate an interpretation that makes possible a responsive action, even if the responsive action is only to settle on an interpretation. This process is what is conveyed by the sociological concept of resonance.

The five kinds of resonance identified in Figure 9 are all complex multifaceted processes. The challenge of understanding their interrelation generates even more complexity. Expressed relatively simply, systemic resonance refers to resonance on symbolically generalized media of communication, such as power or money, that are constitutive of formally organized spheres; governance resonance refers to resonance on the institutional complex of pragmatic, moral, ethical, and legal schemata that underpin political normative structures; cultural resonance refers to resonance on cultural interpretation systems generally and, most decisively, on the cognitive cultural level; associational resonance refers to resonance on the micro-cognitive models of associations, whether these are understood in a reproductive or transformative manner; finally, public resonance refers to resonance on the cognitive models of publics. The cognitive-cultural dimensions of such resonance for each of the major structural orders of society are outlined also in Figure 9, in a manner consistent with the cognitive order outlined in Figure 6 above.

Discursively carried messages generate resonance in some way and to some degree by 'disturbing' the cognitive-cultural foundations of particular social spheres, as for example systems, the associational and public culture of civil society, the culture of everyday life, and the institutional self-understandings of the legal-political order. These cultural orders are depicted on the outside of Figure 9. In cases of far-reaching and sustained resonance, the cognitive cultural models and/or socio-cultural models that regulate how social spheres are independently and interdependently culturally organized are brought into question. At this point, the second dimension of communication dynamics, *collective learning as cognitive structure formation* comes into play.

Structure formation is distinguished from resonance in that such structures convert the collective learning that may emerge from various kinds of resonance into temporally enduring cultural models – cognitive cultural or socio-cultural – that in turn shape the normative production of co-ordinated action rules. But cultural models are a long way down the structure-forming road. Of more immediate significance is another kind of cultural structure that emerges from public communication. These are the discursive structures emphasized both by Miller and by Forst. Discourse structures emerge from sustained episodes of collective argumentation, including argumentation standpoints offered by various kinds of agents and the distinctive patterns of resonance drawn from the various kinds listed above. Discourse structures in this sense, as already suggested above in Part III, organize argumentation. Expressed in the language of framing, a distinct range of frames may organize argumentation on given issues: for example, on environmental issues, frames such as responsibility, sustainability, and natural harmony may be dominant.

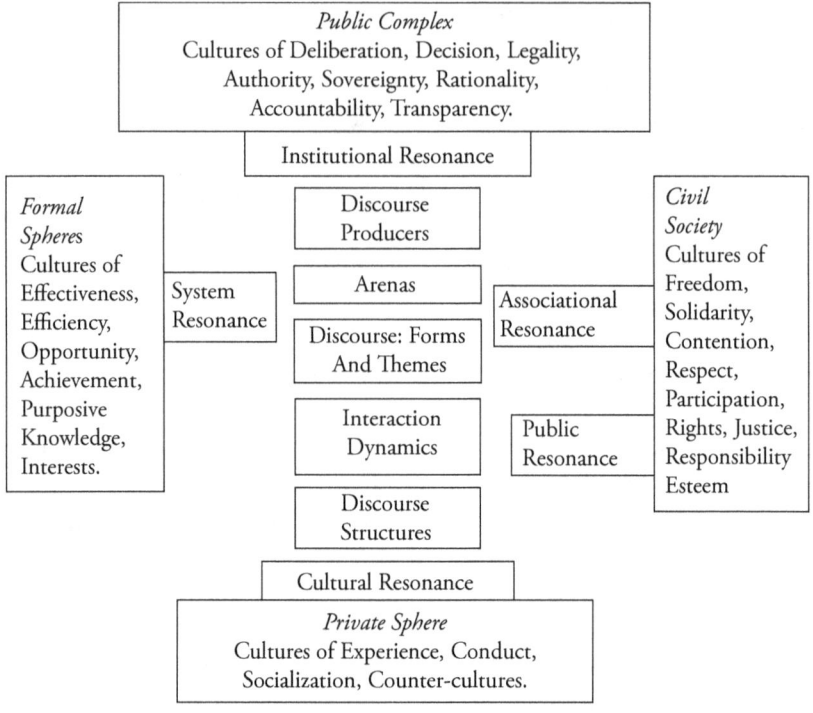

Figure 9: Societal Spheres: Discourse, Culture, and Resonance

Frame positions held by social agents are developed with respect to these frames, and framing strategies are used to represent such frame positions to their best advantages as they engage with one another. Patterns emerge in that some frames become more dominant, frame positions acquire consistency from frame to frame, and also frame positions lead to the consistent utilization of certain framing strategies. This process leads to the generation of discourse structures that are partly shaped by existing cultural models and partly reflect collective learning processes that reach beyond these existing models and may lead to their elaboration or transformation.

Transformative micro-cognitive models, which mostly first originate on the societal periphery, animate collective learning processes. On the macro-level, collective learning takes the form of emergent cultural models. It represents potentials that may or may not make their way into the dominant socio-cultural models that guide norm building, though emergent socio-cultural models can have some practical influence even if they fail to make that final step. The step before the achievement of collective learning in emergent cultural models is that of the consolidation of discourse structures. Discourse structures are mostly topically restricted within the broad semantic space offered by existing cultural models, and engage either with modest changes to these models or simply engage with changes to the normative order itself, without impacting on the orienting cultural models. The latter kind of change will be less radical, as fundamental change animated by collective learning requires the construction of emergent cultural models that ultimately lead to the transformation of existing cultural models.

The dynamics of cognitive structure formation reach all the way from micro-cognitive models, to meso-level discursive structures, to macro-level cognitive principles, and to both cognitive cultural models and socio-cultural models. Drawing from Figure 2 in Chapter 13, learning is possible at all levels, micro, meso, and macro. Micro-level learning involves the formation, on the basis of reflection on experience, of a new way of looking at the natural, technical, and social world. This primary impetus to learning then leads on to secondary learning in the public sphere that results in the creation of discursive structures arising from processes of wide-ranging collective argumentation. These discursive structures, if they involve significant changes to cultural models, carry collective learning processes that may prove to be significant on the societal level. They may also embody a kind of collective learning that could lead to the blocking of innovation and promote domination, collective pathology, or both. Finally, fundamental collective learning results in a sustained challenge to an existing dominant cultural model that, if ultimately successful, leads on the changes in normative action rules. It should be kept in mind, though too complex to outline fully here, that all these processes of learning and structure formation are filtered through complex resonance processes of different kinds and of short and long duration.[2]

---

2   Another book would be required to fully document all these processes with an appropriate level of discursive, cultural, and sequential sensitivity. This would also

The third dimension of the dynamics of public communication under consideration here is *deliberation*. Deliberation is understood as a procedure for translating discursively achieved collective learning on the cognitive-cultural plane into the setting of norms. Deliberation is understood not simply normatively in terms of how to achieve a high standard of inclusion of themes and social positions, but also descriptively as a means of political 'finalization'. Strong normative accounts of deliberation tend to also depend on strong counterfactual claims, since actual forms of such deliberation do not exist. Or at least they do not exist in Habermas's sense of *public deliberation* as distinct from Rawls's more restricted sense of public reason. The idea of deliberation utilized here is more normatively relaxed in terms of attempting to grasp how political deliberation in its actual forms can be grasped. Hence, it includes and distinguishes between cabinet, parliamentary, legal, public participatory, and committee forms of deliberation. As currently manifested, these forms of deliberation are far from the strong normative models that appear in much of the literature. Indeed in many of these cases, if strong standards of what constitutes deliberation are brought to bear, then they hardly qualify as deliberative at all. They are counted as deliberative here because, though imperfect, they cumulatively provide a means of realizing cognitively generated learning potentials on the normative plane. On this cumulative level, rather than individually, a reflective and argumentative process is conducted that may, in aggregate, be regarded as a process of deliberation.

In one part, deliberative processes contribute to collective learning, whether they are to be regarded from certain normative standards as progressive or pathological. This observation runs against the sharp break that Habermas utilizes in *Between Facts and Norms* between discursive political will formation and political deliberation. While in the end a distinction can be drawn, since the political process has the moral and legal responsibility to settle on normative arrangements, salient issues remain public political issues in the sense that processes of political deliberation always take

---

be best done, in the first instance at least, through the analysis of a concrete issue set within its broader contexts.

place in a cognitive-cultural context shaped by the public. These processes are continuously informed by triple contingent learning characterized by a virtually present observing public (Strydom, 1999). Beyond the formal legitimacy of politics as the right to follow certain courses of action once procedures are observed, there is also the issue of wider communicative legitimacy in which the adequacy and fairness of political outcomes are judged in terms of their fidelity with the expression of public will. This distinction mirrors that which arises between a cognitively contextualized normative approach and one where the normative paradigm is mistakenly assumed to dominate the cognitive dimension by means of strong counterfactual assumptions about procedurally generated rightness.

Immanence, Transcendence, and Communicative Democratization

Much of the emphasis placed on the nature of 'good' normative principles in the theory of justice over the last half-century rests on strong counterfactual arguments. A good deal of political philosophy derives hypothetical standards from beyond immanent social life, but as outlined in Part I greater intra-philosophical criticism has emerged of such strong 'transcendentalism'. From a sociological perspective, this philosophical self-critique presents both a danger and an opportunity; a danger in that much sociology has always hidden the counterfactual foundations of normative diagnosis or critique and could be encouraged by the new developments in political philosophy to continue in that vein; but it also presents an opportunity, in that sociology can join philosophy in exploring how transcendent and immanent horizons can be brought together in analyzing social actuality and in normative reflection that 'transcends' it, while yet offering a prognostics that could be feasibly realized within it.

Viewed sociologically, counterfactual standards normally operate by latently structuring social life. That is to say, they are operative in a wide variety of action situations where the force they possess is not explicitly recognized. Counterfactuals in this sense operate as phenomenological presuppositions or implicit rules of action that lie behind the explicit self-understanding of actors. They can only be reconstructed and made explicit by special devices of discursive explication that demonstrate that such implicit rules had first to be in place for the action in question to be executed. Generally, in sociological theory and research, the counterfactual dimension of democracy, understood in this sense of implicit reasoning competences that cognitively structure culture, institutions, and publics, is given little attention. What by and large has been missing is attending to the capacity of public discourse to make explicit, where the situation requires it, what normally remains implicit. In other words, what is missing is the perception of the capacity of publics to reconstruct cognitive meta-rules and to use them as standards against which small- and large-scale social practices should be justified. This implies that such meta-rules can in normal cases function latently in social practices sustained by established procedures, normative commitments, and various kinds of cognitive structure in circumstances that correspond with Habermas's idea of the public sphere when at rest as opposed to mobilized (Habermas, 1996).

In Kantian-inspired democratic theory with its phenomenological heritage, counterfactual arguments are used, both in Rawls's original position and in Apel and Habermas's idea of the counterfactual force of the better argument. These counterfactual approaches mix latency with explication. The counterfactual devices can never be fully socially realized, but they make possible claims for the social immanence of moral norms. The reason, applying in both cases, that the counterfactual device could not be socially realized is that the discursive and cultural structures that could fully carry them are not foreseeable. Insofar as these counterfactual devices are used to justify principles that should guide normative arrangements they, nonetheless, raise immanent claims to validity.

It is at this point, while being of orienting value, that over-extended use of counterfactuals becomes problematic. No real processes are demonstrated within the theories that would correspond to the immanent realization of counterfactual presuppositions for fear of weakening their deontological force. A supplementary counterfactual position would improve the normative force of the arguments. Counterfactuals operate in social life to an empirically varying extent, and the question raised is how counterfactuals can be shown to translate into immanent processes in real social situations. Habermas's position, in one sense, is stronger than Rawls's, as his discursive-deliberative theory of democracy can be used to diagnose the actual or possible social instantiation of counterfactual potentials. In another sense, though, Rawls, contra Habermas's extreme proceduralism, comes up with an actual substantive principle in the difference principle. In so doing, though, Rawls is problematically forced to move to a third party observer perspective, removed from anything political agents could *actually* construct. In his case, this move is founded on a strong transcendental device, the original position and its mundane equivalent of public reason, that leaves aside actual *publicly* anchored capacities for justification.

As argued in this text, the complexity of social life means that substantive projections of normative standards and institutional arrangements must constantly be generated. While these projections will sometimes result in enduring normative commitments and institutional path dependencies, and can thus be argued for normatively as does Rawls, they should be constructed through a democratized system of public communication. Democratization of the means of communication is essential if the multiplicity of standpoints that characterize modern societies are to come into play, generating their own arguments rather than having arguments attributed to them. Further democratization of the public sphere would allow potential publics to become actual publics. The improved rationality level of public discourse would then better contribute to building normative standards. And manifold problems of democracy show that the price of not doing so is very high.

Both the latent 'everyday' phenomenological understanding used in sociological accounts of implicit practices, and political philosophical positions that abstract from feasible public justification, nonetheless concur in the view that reconstructing counterfactuals has social implications. The first assumes that the reconstructed counterfactuals are already present in social life, the second that they have normative implications that should be recognized in designing political institutions. From the latter philosophical standpoint, it is a question of feasibly closing the gap to the counterfactual standard, whether that is understood more substantively in Rawls or more procedurally in Habermas. What is, so to speak in a naïve attitude, 'clear' is that empirical-theoretically reconstructing counterfactuals that are latently present in socio-political life is a reconstructive task of considerable magnitude. From a sociological standpoint, oriented to understanding the realization and possible realization of communicative democratization, how could this task be advanced?

If recourse is once again made to Figure 1 at the end of Part II, where various political philosophies were located on a societal theoretical grid, two kinds of consideration can be brought into play to help understanding of how counterfactual principles operate, or could operate, immanently in social life. The first consideration relates to the nature of 'political' counterfactuals and, the second to the nature of 'non-political' counterfactuals. An overarching question is how are these counterfactuals related?

With regard to these considerations, in Figure 1 all five philosophical positions utilize counterfactuals in diagnosing political issues and prescribing the normative conditions for realizing a better future. These counterfactuals are the Rawlsian position of moral constitutionalism based on the original position; the republican position of recovering historically achieved normative cultures and/or realizing contemporary models of non-domination; the radical position of the openness to occupation by multiple social projects of the 'empty space' of the political; the liberal realist position of settling for a functionally efficacious, minimal, formal democratic proceduralism; and the deliberative position of the unconstrained force of the better argument.

All five positions also advance non-political – in the strong sense – counterfactuals. Classical liberalism advances a claim to the desirability of regulative – non-normative and pragmatic – rules in social life; political liberalism involves assumptions about the 'fair' interrelation of liberty and equality in social arrangements; communitarian republicanism advances the idea of defending or reasserting a historically realized concrete democratic ethos; political radicalism and non-communitarian republicanism advocate non-domination realized by an appropriate democratic politics; and deliberation argues for the societal value of deliberatively achieved justice.

These counterfactuals bridge immanent and transcendent horizons. In different combinations and to different degrees, they are both immanent and transcendent. Cumulatively, they provide a conceptual repertoire of counterfactual standards that are actually used in political argumentation and norm building and that also are the subject of different kinds of scholarly reconstruction. The more profound and significant in terms of social evolution these public arguments are, the more they reach into the counterfactual imagination of democracy and raise the issue of the horizons of normative realization of various potentials. But freedom to engage the counterfactual imagination in this democratic sense meets the resistance of social life in several forms; it meets the resistance of non-democratic counterfactual standards that political ideologies variously take up; and it meets the resistance of limits to normative realization in the complex experimental laboratory of society itself.

Following the above remarks, the standard of communicative non-domination cannot simply revert to the latent and implicit counterfactual standard that sociology has for long predominantly utilized, as alternatively a sociology that operates, on the one hand, with a standpoint that does not incorporate either critique or justification, or a critical sociology that operates with negative critique alone. The alternative to the strong transcendentalism that, particularly in its Rawlsian version, has come under fire in political philosophy in recent times from a variety of positions that include revitalized classical liberalism, critical liberalism, and Roman republicanism, is not to adopt a merely negative standard masking a still strong transcendentalism. What is needed is engagement with the task of describing the manner in which the transcending imagination or, with Peirce, the potential for situation-transcending abduction, is both present, and yet is misrecognized, in available potentials within cognitive structures. A standard of communicative non-domination, built on this basis, would therefore look, firstly, to the communicatively relevant structures and dynamics that shape the collective learning potentials latent in the different micro-, meso-, and macro-levels of the cognitive order, and then to the relationship between these learning potentials and the deliberative foundations of normative procedures. If one substantive trend can be recognized amidst these complex relations, it is that the blockages to fundamental democratic learning, whether understood cognitively or normatively, are currently too strong.

CHAPTER 18

Cosmopolitanism and the Transnational Institutionalization of the Public Sphere

Since the beginning of the 1980s, the spatial reach of the territorial legal-political order has become partly displaced from the smaller scale of the nation-state to a broader scale, reaching from macro-regional 'weak' transnational territories to the global level. In this transition, the tendency to view 'society' as consistent with a legal-politically, culturally, and structurally integrated and largely self-organizing national social space has now been rendered deeply problematic. The idea of isolated national societies was in some ways always problematic. It implicitly diminished the sense of intra-societal cultural differences, hypostatized antagonistic national identities, implicitly justified an unjust international division of resources, emphasized evolutionary progress rather than the effects of war and violence, and ignored the international system of states in which these societies were embedded (Delanty and O'Mahony, 2002; von Trotha, 2006). Nevertheless, shorn of its stronger normative connotations of claiming to be an acceptable spatial 'container', using Giddens' word, the term did correspond to real entities that, in some normative respects, could be defended as giving rise to opportunity, solidarity, and a sense of belonging, at least for those fortunate enough to live in a 'successful' nation-state (Giddens, 1987).

The plausibility of using the term 'society' as synonymous with national society has eroded. In academic analysis, this erosion has mostly been seen as a consequence of functional action systems that outgrow their national contexts. These deterritorialized action systems actively shape structural interdependencies on a transnational level. Both the action systems and their consequences pose fundamental challenges to existing democracies, as they do to the potential extension and deepening of democracy through discursive democratization.

In the recent, broadly sociological, literature, this state of affairs has elicited various responses. Systems theory, with its strong evolutionary foundation, has articulated the necessity of a world systems society that would eliminate the need for not alone the legal-political form of the nation-state, but also those transnational legal-political and territorial forms that might attempt to replace it (Albert and Hilkermeier, 2004; Teubner and Korth, 2010). This approach offers a radical polycentric vision of a functionally organized world society that would sweep away the assumed historically effective, but now allegedly diminishing, hegemony of its legal-political institutions. Bourdieu, by contrast, reflects much of sociology in viewing the unlimited free rein of functional systems as a neo-liberal dystopia that in reality articulates the ethos of a transnational elite as opposed to a merely necessary functional response to complexity. International social fields are forming that potentially overwhelm the order of justice that was institutionalized in the nation-state, albeit in a contradictory and incomplete manner (Bourdieu, 1986; Trubek, Dezalay, Buchanan, and Davis, 1995).

If these theories, the systems theory and legal pluralism of Luhmann and Teubner and the constructivist structuralism of Bourdieu, respectively emphasize the first two pillars of the cultural order of modernity, functional codes and ethos, Habermas, in advocating morally justifiable procedures that span national and transnational orders, emphasizes the third (Habermas, 2006). Habermas goes some way to following Kant by accepting that the moral foundations of legitimate government must include the arguments of all those affected by norms, and that a cosmopolitan international law must be a law of individuals and not of states, though he does not follow him all the way towards a world government. For Habermas, the thoroughgoing constitutionalization of the nation-state means the normative core of the public use of reason only fully operates in that setting. Over time, however, democratic learning processes may allow the integration of transnational and national levels of government in a way that would still respect the democratic role of nation-states and preserve, on the transnational level, the normative core of the public use of reason.

As with his general theory of democracy, Habermas's position is, at least partly, synthetic in the transnational sphere too. He criticizes legal pluralism for robbing citizens of their status and abandoning them to the vagaries of an unmanageably complex society. And he also criticizes post-Marxist positions, which share a lot with Bourdieu, that assume that the international arena is only composed of 'vampiristic centres' and 'desiccated peripheries', positions that do not take into account the intrinsic normative dynamics of legal developments (ibid.). Habermas's position is directed by the necessity of overcoming the functional interdependencies and complexity that systems theory analyses, on the one hand, and, on the other, of maintaining and further developing a 'civic solidarity', whose disappearance is of such concern to Bourdieu, as opposed to merely moral-legal integration. Civic solidarity on the transnational level depends for Habermas, as Bohman critically observes, on the retention of the category of territorial political identity – in the form of postnational identity – and with it the notion of demos (Bohman, 2007).

The contemporary situation in the European Union serves as a reference point for illustrating these phenomena in more than a particular and local manner. The communicatively relevant structural forms of society and the account of communication dynamics that were outlined in Chapters 16 and 17 will be used to guide the argument.

Between National and Transnational Society: Propitiating Societal Conditions

For the second time in less than 200 years, European societies, for all the immense social change that happens in the interim, stand at a crossroads that has certain similarities. In the slow gestation of the European welfare state towards the end of the nineteenth century, which had commenced as a response to the liberal capitalist-industrial order that had transformed the world in less than a century, it was in the end established that techno-economic advance might run ahead of, but should ultimately serve, broader societal goals. To some degree, this state of affairs mirrors the present. The establishment of a liberal capitalist order in the beginning of the nineteenth century was part of a more encompassing movement involving the separation of political authority and civil society, and the constitutionalization of their relationship to one another, as well as of civil society in its own right. As such, the private freedom that arose with the establishment of the modern economy, initially a major carrier of civil society, over-reached itself and required restraint through the generalization of right (Lefort, 1988).

In the contemporary period, what is sometimes presented across different shades of the political spectrum as the necessary unshackling of the restrictive structure of the paternalistic welfare state has, on the contrary, generated a crisis-ridden imbalance that can be compared with the nineteenth-century liberal-capitalist era. This state of affairs has been the sustained focus of sociological criticism. An era of deregulation has accompanied the relentless criticism of the welfare-state model. Though the regime established across the western world, combining gradual deinstitutionalization of the welfare state with an increasingly deregulated economy and a more individualistic society, is currently in crisis, it is not clear whether it is coming to a close or is merely galvanizing for a further period of hegemony.

These quickly sketched macro-societal developments may be depicted in terms of Figure 1 in Chapter 10 above. In terms of this figure, transnational polity formation in the EU is currently proceeding on a classical liberal path, that is, building from the left-hand-side quadrants of the diagram emphasizing interest articulation, functionally oriented network formation, market liberalization, and general purposive rationalization by means of a controlling bureaucracy. Some limited transnational constitutionalization of human rights has also been put in place, and even if this has proved to be significant at the national level in some cases, it has not led to a formal constitution.[1] Beyond this minimal framework of rights, the right-hand-side of the diagram referencing the normative culture of civil society in the form of solidaristic moral commitments, values, and everyday needs, is not comparably addressed in the existing transnationalization process. This is, in large part, because these spheres are the preserve of nation-states that

1   The fact that *individuals* can take human rights cases at the transnational level nonetheless *does* indicate one important cosmopolitan criterion for the efficacy of a cosmopolitan law beyond the law of states.

have more fully developed constitutional and solidarity regimes than that existing on the transnational plane. This imbalance does not, nonetheless, amount to a potentially harmonious division of powers. It also accords with a transnational socio-economic cultural model that emphasizes liberalization and competition.

All of this amounts to the existence of a weak territorial form on the transnational level of the European Union. It has maintained legitimacy through its perceived contribution to realizing functional goals and, perhaps even more fundamentally, through serving as an institutional symbol of a historical learning process leading to the renunciation of recurrent violence between European nation-states, including internal genocide of some categories of people. However, the attempt to build an integrated governance regime to organize functional flows by developing an integrated private and public law, common standards, and above all by the ill-fated design of European Monetary Union, has resulted in not just crisis symptoms of functional disorganization, but a vast range of secondary problems. These are above all centred on morally sharpened questions of collective responsibility and solidarity that extend to the very survival of a democracy founded on the model of communicative organized public sovereignty, not just at the transnational level but also at national level, given the radical implications of these transnational developments.

Between National and Transnational Democracy: Structures and Dynamics of Communication and Culture

The European Union is well suited to serve as a case study that would explore Habermas's idea of the possibility of democratic learning that over time *might* balance out governance powers and solidarities at national and transnational political levels (Habermas, 2006). At present, general pessimism reigns about its future. A centre composed of the most prosperous and powerful countries and a periphery of poorer and weaker countries have emerged that appear to entrench distributive injustice, and even to undercut the fledging transnational democratic process. This suspicion is given more weight by the apparent irrelevance of the European Parliament as the most far-reaching crisis in the history of European transnationalism unfolds.

When Habermas refers to democratic learning he primarily refers to normative learning processes, for example arising from the interplay of deliberative forums operating on different vertical levels of democracy. Such learning could extend to encompass the more diffuse cognitive learning located in processes of democratic will formation. The problem with this understanding is not that it is wrong, but that the cognitive learning process is too smoothly assimilated to a strong counterfactually grounded account of normative learning, denying it a differentiated and self-standing autonomy. James Bohman offers an interesting critique of writers such as Habermas and Held with respect to their ideas on transnational governance that partly complements this analysis (Bohman, 2007). Bohman claims that, though Held has part of the answer in his ideas about differentiated institutions, levels of governance, and civil societal inclusion, both he and Habermas still seek out something equivalent to the self-legislating demos that would guide the normative process. Such a demos would, according to Bohman, anchor the traditional equation of political identity and political membership that produces rigid and pre-given normative commitments and leads to the exclusion of non-citizens from democratic processes.

Bohman advocates, instead, a more flexible and responsive kind of relevance setting and norm building that would not be anchored in the fixed cultural form of the demos but in more dynamic normative cultures generated across demoi by transnational democratic interaction. This kind of interaction would require fairly organized dialogical procedures that would be responsive to the networks and relations that exist within transnational society. Such flexibility would allow multiple democratic forms to be generated by publics and individuals properly equipped with the 'democratic minimum' of normative powers and status. Democracy would not be confined to such normative arrangements. It would also take on a cognitive form through the generation of better information by means of co-operative modes of inquiry and associated better problem-solving capacity.

Bohman works with a flexible account of structure formation that, translated into evolutionary terms, emphasizes the generation of variety within the framework of cognitive cultural models of democracy. This variety would open up innovative selective options rather than seeking premature institutionalization of norms and procedures on the basis of the established demotic model. Trenz and Eder offer what is in some respects close to an institutional-theoretical translation of this perspective (Trenz and Eder, 2004). For these authors, the democratic performance of the European Union arises from the interplay between governance institutions and the governed, with the interplay regulated by counterfactual expectations of democracy, held on all sides, which gradually become more immanent as explicit democratic practices. These counterfactual expectations lurk in the structure of communicative interplay between democratic institutions and social agents and, in the end, they point the way towards transnational communicative democratization.

For Trenz and Eder, the public sphere mediates between governing institutions and the governed and it links the unfolding transnational spaces of political communication to the democratization of the institutional system of the EU. Though the EU has so far not been successful in developing a constitution, democratic constitutionalization has nonetheless informally proceeded with political communication as its institutional software. The authors observe that two related mechanisms are conducive to the development of a European public sphere. The first is increased communication within EU institutional environments and its networked context, generating double contingent learning, and the second is the public audience's increased awareness and attention to communication regarding governance, generating the possibility of triple contingent learning. The general argument is that the 'democratic functional' requirements of political communication lead through various intermediate stages of learning towards a fully developed mass-media public sphere in which the kind of triple contingent collective learning is made possible that could adequately address transnational societal problems.

Both these approaches have considerable value. They emphasize in different ways that transnational democratization is a long-term project and that it is currently at an early stage, if indeed it continues. They concentrate on the meso-level: in Bohman's case emphasizing a post-demotic order that would use a wider range of modalities of deliberation, and perhaps even wider communicative governance through the democratization of the mode of inquiry itself; in Trenz and Eder's case, exploring how the counter-factual idea of democracy eventually comes to the fore as it structures EU level political communication. Even with these approaches, it is nonetheless still the case that the problem associated with Habermas's account of the cognitive level persists. With both Bohman and Trenz and Eder, the accounts are incomplete because they concentrate too much on the meso-level of political processes and move from there to the level of normative implications and structure formation. Absent from these accounts are the advantages that are conferred by a multi-level cognitive approach that is concerned with the communicative production of cognitive structures and their societal implications.

Cognitive Sociology and European Transnationalism

The contemporary EU situation reveals certain patterns from the vantage point of a cognitive-communicative analysis. The arena structure of communication, both internal to the arenas themselves and transversally across them, is under-developed by comparison with national-level public spheres. This is true at the formal democratic level, where the European Parliament is one of the most advanced of parliamentary regimes in its internal organization, but has little public resonance and, as the contemporary crisis indicates, little agenda-setting or norm-specifying public role. The lack of direct public and cultural resonance characterizes all the European institutions that have a communicative role. With respect to wider democratic communication, national public spheres remain dominant and European issues are translated into national level discourse and resonance, rather than having an independent European standing. On the popular level at least, but extending also into expert and political levels, the construction of the publics of other countries is mostly based on stereotypes amidst deficient information (Hedetoft, 1995). Consistent with the account of double and triple contingent learning offered above, the European public spheres may be regarded as primarily double contingently structured, currently allowing only interests and stereotypical cultural constructions to become prominent. The absence of a strong, transnationally generalized public perspective up to the present, consistent with Trenz and Eder, means triple contingent learning remains a distant prospect. The absence of this necessary kind of democratic learning applies not just to the vertical relationship between European institutions and publics, where publics are only seen as nationally specific publics, but also to the relationship between the various national publics whose communication does not adequately resonate with other public spheres.

From one vantage point, the contemporary transnational situation in Europe appears to be characterized by national interest bargaining not so far removed from the realist theory of international relations, leavened by a framework of co-ordinating transnational institutions. Viewed this way, European institutions, including the inter-national institutions like the powerful Council of Ministers, insofar as they arrogate to themselves in a quasi-democratic manner powers that were previously the democratic prerogative of nation-states might be regarded as more of a threat to democracy than a further necessary level. This is certainly the view of many political and academic currents from both left and right.[2] Viewed from another vantage point, that of Beck's methodological cosmopolitanism stressing the degree of actual structural and cultural commonality that has characterized various national societies for a long time and now

---

2 Such a view is captured by the term executive-federalism that Habermas uses to capture the current interventionist regime emerging under German leadership within the Euro area that has insisted on technocratic governments in Greece and Italy to address the financial crisis from 2008 onwards. More generally, the important academic stream of liberal inter-governmentalism questions whether the EU should be regarded as an emergent democracy. Any transnational democratic role in this view is strictly secondary to national-level democracy and the representatives of these democracies should be regarded as the principal carriers of democratic values and executors of democratic procedures on the transnational level (Moravcsik, 2005).

growing, the situation appears different (Beck, 2006; Delanty, 2006). Taken up in terms of a communicative cognitive sociology, the prospects for transnational democracy in Europe correspondingly appear more promising or, at least, the cognitive-cultural foundations are far from entirely antithetical to it.

On the micro-cognitive level, while potential transnational democratic subjects in Europe are presently still greatly influenced by their national habitus, a cosmopolitan current has emerged relatively strongly and is growing in significance. This is partly for reasons connected with long-run historical memory and collective learning about the destructive potential of partisan national identities, partly because of a common continental European culture of everyday life, partly because of the formation of transnational networks and contexts of experience, and partly because of what Trenz and Eder emphasize, a response to the extension of EU governance to various fields so as to profoundly affect people's lives (Trenz and Eder, 2004). While, for these reasons, micro-level cognitive models in European countries are no longer so securely embedded in the national habitus and therefore appear open to a more cosmopolitan orientation, profound uncertainty about the wider macro-cognitive, normatively relevant culture and about normative arrangements themselves continue to generate opacity about what is possible on the transnational level. In these circumstances, the micro-cognitive situation is profoundly mutable and unstable, generating movements of various kinds with populist and chauvinist tendencies that interact with and disturb the relatively long-run democratic political cultures that characterize individual societies.

The structural and cultural instability that assails individuals and groups trying to work out a relationship to the transnational order is compounded by a general crisis in the socio-economic cultural model that long preceded the crisis of the social model itself. The broad direction of the European project that has emphasized non-normative, functional, transnational integration has been complemented by a similar project on a global scale that has left the egalitarian justice model of the post-war period, furthest developed on the European continent, under threat (Streeck, 2009). At present, then, contemporary Europe exhibits symptoms to which reconstructivist constructivism appears to be the appropriate academic response to address circumstances of destructuration and contingency, leading to moral confusion about the grounding principles of an appropriate transnational normative order. In this case, the reconstructivist intention must as much respectfully follow the popular constructivist impulse as attempt to guide it. Potentialities for cosmopolitan solidarity are located in the presuppositions of cognitive principles, and organized and made visible in the associated horizons offered by cognitive cultural models, above all the emergence of a cosmopolitan cognitive cultural model (Strydom, 2012). As both Bohman and Habermas observe, European transnationalism is already far along the road towards a postnational order. But much recontextualizing collective learning is required to fully embed a solidaristic emphasis in the cognitive cultural model of transnationalism and, on this basis, to develop a transnational socio-cultural model that does not usurp the place of national socio-cultural models unless it is to allow democratic gains to be made.

The last remarks above bring the focus back to the micro- and meso-levels. At the macro-cultural level, the European normative order has been rendered extremely unstable, partly because of the long-run crisis in the normative orientation of western societies, together with the profound additional challenge generated by a transnational order, itself now in crisis, that was supposed to correct such problems but, apparently, has only succeeded in exacerbating them. In the contemporary situation, the cognitive cultural model of cosmopolitanism is reflected in a kind of cognitive dissonance at the micro-cognitive level. To some degree like environmentalism in the nineteenth century, no clear social evolutionary pathway to a cosmopolitan society is apparent; but, unlike environmentalism, no other pathway offering an alternative social model opens up either. In addition, the cognitive-cultural and institutional foundations of twenty-first-century cosmopolitanism are much stronger than nineteenth-century environmentalism. Uncertainty at the level of micro-cognitive models is reflected in a multiplicity of competing and sometimes overlapping thematizations of potential transnational options that selectively combine different cognitive principles. These multiple thematizations generate an extremely complex reaction on the cultural structural level, especially at the level of discursive structures on the meso-level that presently exhibit a deep-lying conflict structure. Both patterns of thematization and discursive structures are shaped by competing ideological orientations. In the contemporary EU, these competing orientations and ideologies are not organized within integrating cultural models, but they rather exhibit a conflict structure that harbour potentials for either pathological or progressive collective learning in Miller's sense.

The potentials for pathological – regressive, defensive, ideological, authoritarian – collective learning are clearly manifest in the contemporary situation. Above all, danger lurks in the attempt to operate strictly at the level of double contingent learning and, at most, minimally include the third term of the public where absolutely necessary while, on some issues, to actively exclude them. The cult of expertise, galvanized by some versions of the cognitive revolution and by the status accorded to certain kinds of economics, greatly encourages the idea of the sufficiency of double-contingent learning. Because of its peculiar architecture that left the reproduction of the lifeworld to national contexts and systems to the transnational order, the European Union has so far proved to be a principal source of a conservative political realism. This kind of functional world making makes for pathological collective learning as it forgets the historical lesson of the need to embed functional systems in the lifeworld with a morally shaped democratic order at its core. Democratic world making has therefore to take the lead from functional world making, if the cosmopolitan transnational project is to be saved. Otherwise, its critics are right and it had better be rapidly abandoned. Functional world making on non-egalitarian democratic and social premises will not generate a rationalist utopia but, instead, a dystopia of disappointed expectations, ressentiment, demoralization, humiliation, and other sources of aggression and violence.

In the light of such a terrible prospect, progressive collective learning that would be intrinsically triple contingent in form is as necessary as it may prove difficult to achieve. While remaining a long way off, and perhaps never finally arriving, such learning may at least be reconstrively anticipated. In the current situation, a first challenge, the first of many, would be the construction on the transnational plane of two interrelated socio-cultural models derived from micro- and meso-level dynamics. The first model would align economic goals with distributive justice goals on the transnational plane, and the second would address how a compatible procedural-democratic order could be envisaged.

These models are interrelated insofar as a cultural model articulating the ground rules of a key element of the system of co-operation has always historically coexisted with a democratic political model. The latter has the complementary role of reliably 'deliberating' on and specifying appropriate norms for that system of co-operation, even if the problem of differences in social power that qualify the inclusivity of its process of justification has persisted. Extensive difficulties obstruct the putting in place of these interrelated models, including the general complexity of transnational governance with its enlargement of scale and multiplicity of demoi, the problems besetting the ideologically dominant liberalization model on a global level and, even more fundamentally, the challenges arising from the shift to a more, if far from fully, polycentrically organized global society in which function systems and social spheres acquire relatively greater levels of autonomy.

There is a tendency in both intellectual and practical reflection on the EU situation to immediately address normative innovation. Yet the reconstructive, cognitive challenge appears more fundamental in the sense of the need to address the cultural horizons of just and feasible normative innovation in which transnational publics are vested with normative powers. The idea that just and feasible democratic innovation is what is required on the transnational level immediately makes apparent what is deficient in contemporary European debate – sustained attention to what Forst describes in a two-fold sense as a basic structure of justification and a justified basic structure (Forst, 2007b).

The first, a basic structure of justification, specifies the requirements of a fully inclusive justificatory process that would be anchored in social relations of justification and that would overcome recurrent tendencies towards 'bad' justification due to the effects of domination; the second refers to the basic structure of society that, if fully justified by subjects themselves, would generate non-domination.[3] Neither of these standards, respectively

---

3 Forst's position here is close to the cognitive position that is argued for in this book. Though Forst rightly adds a constructivist dimension to his political philosophy in

of fundamental and maximal justice, can be met by a functionally inspired socio-economic model that is dominant on the European stage and which is based on politically 'liberating' the steering media of money and power complemented by interest bargaining. The task, therefore, is to specify from the full set of available quasi-transcendent cognitive principles and discursively generated collective learning what just and feasible cognitive cultural and socio-cultural models could be on the transnational level, cultural models that would address, in Forst's terms, issues of fundamental justice in the form of democratic procedures and the maximal justice of a fully justified basic structure.

The above is a task that both embraces and extends beyond imaginatively constructing what might constitute the principles of formal constitutionalization. Formal constitutionalization underpins the basic structure of institutional responsibilities, private rights, and responsibilities, and the legal foundations of democratic procedures. But, alongside formal constitutionalization, informal constitutionalization must also develop, as the former only covers those matters on which consensus can be reached and hence leaves out much of the modern cognitive and normative order. For example, even in those modern constitutions where cultural, social, and ecological rights are represented, they do not enjoy the same practical status as private and political rights and, consequently, are mostly realized

---

the sense of a strong emphasis on reasoning by political agents themselves, an overly strong normative standpoint still persists in that he does not demonstrate how such a constructivistically understood rule of reason could emerge. Therefore, not unlike Habermas, what exactly such relations of justification would consist of, where they would be located, and what they would do, is not fully apparent. The default position then appears as something like perfect procedural justice that stands beyond society. As stressed throughout the book, this idea has important counterfactual value, but neglects the problem of how this counterfactual can make inroads into real democratic arrangements that currently exist or could be anticipated. A fully developed cognitive complement would draw attention to societal complexity and the multiple locations and kinds of reasoning, temporal disjunctions in reasoning given the status of the public as a third point of view, and diffuse and temporally extended collective learning processes – including pathological and power-saturated learning – leading to the social organization of 'real' counterfactuals in cultural models.

by social and political processes beyond constitutional law. To the extent that the present is a period that foregrounds rational dissensus as a mode of political organization, collective moral and ethical collective learning in civil society comes more firmly into the picture. Rational dissensus is the carrier of informal constitutionalization and this process belongs to the first phase of building trans-European cultural models that contain an outline sense of the principles underlying a justified basic transnational structure.

Both formal and informal constitutionalization will be long processes. Using a formulation drawn from Trenz and Eder, the legitimacy of double contingent functional learning processes has been exhausted on the European Union level. Now, deeper processes of triple contingent justification involving publics are required that constitutively address moral and ethical considerations within a framework of rational dissensus. There has been an inexorable rise in the Europeanization of public discourse since the economic crisis that commenced in 2008, which indicates precisely the kind of democratic, hence triple contingent, learning process between national and transnational levels that Habermas envisages (Habermas, 2001). But the process is diffuse, with discourse structures carrying potentially progressive collective learning processes within civil society elaborated in a manner that, while to some degree compatible across national public spheres – recurrent debates about austerity versus stimulus in economic policy, for example – is not organized so as to make the respective public discourses reciprocally observable and thereby to generate transnational collective learning and democratically justified structure formation.

If this diffuse and incomplete form of publicity is to be remedied, a more unified transnational public sphere needs to be brought into being. Without the substrate of a fully inclusive, thematically comprehensive, and multiply resonating public sphere, democratic collective learning and macro-cognitive structure formation is not possible. But such a public sphere will not be likely to emerge unless a normative complex on the institutional level is put in place, structured in terms of deliberation and rational dissensus, rather than the current model of national-level bargaining and compromise. To direct and anchor processes of thematization and discourse structuration, and to make cognitive structure formation possible, a deliberative complex needs to be established that serves as an analogue on the transnational stage for national parliaments. The European Parliament partly fulfils this role but, as currently constituted, simply does not do so adequately. There are various possible routes to reforming this body, but without its powers being radically strengthened with respect to the Council of Ministers and European Commission none of them will be very meaningful. One option, for example, is for the various groupings of the parliament that already represent most of the major ideological orientations in Europe to stand separately from national political parties in European elections as carriers of Europe-relevant issue cultures. This would prevent the absorption of European level politics into national politics, which ineluctably follows from its representatives emanating from national level parties, ensuring that when it really counts the European Parliament will stand down before the legitimacy and power of national governments.

Tom Burns has made interesting proposals on the future of parliamentary systems, including chairing a committee that produced a Green Paper on the subject for the European Parliament in 2000 (Burns, 1999; Burns, Jaeger, Liberatore, Meny, and Nanz, 2000). He advocates the idea of organic democracy over against formal parliamentary democracy. Organic democracy would recognize that there is something of a participation revolution currently taking place, with more members of the public engaging directly in political activity of all kinds, ranging from participation in NGOs to professional self-regulation. Moreover, the various kinds of problems that contemporary democracies face, extending from identity conflicts to issues of expertise and risk, are not easily resolved. A majority mandate to govern is simply not enough in the face of the kind of intractable conflict that characterizes many issues. Burns advocates, like Bohman, a multi-modal deliberative system and, like him too, sees this as an alternative to the integrating idea of the demos (Bohman, 2007). A citizenship capable of deliberation, rather than the demos, would be the principal democratic agent. Deliberation and discursive will formation in multiple public spheres could take many forms and acquire stronger cognitive as well as normative functions. Burns views a continued role for the parliamentary complex, but now more as the supervisor of a wide range of governance forms than a sovereign legislator in its own right. This would go with the drift of devising a democratic response to those structural interdependencies and governance innovations alike that increasingly reach across and beyond territorial borders – and to an even greater extent will do so in the future.

These ideas appear particularly well suited to the challenge of transnational governance though, as Burns intends, they also can be applied to national democracies. They allow for differentiated modalities of governance that could take account of the fuzzy boundaries that might characterize transnational authority. Their implementation would require radical rethinking of what a transnational parliamentary system would look like, even though in its internal operations the European Parliament already has some of the basic prerequisites. Such a parliamentary-deliberative complex would be highly consistent with the cognitive-communicative framework outlined above. It would make possible greater capacity to translate between cognitive and normative realms, so that discourse structures could be flexibly translated into both substantive and procedural cognitive cultural models and the innovations of both civil society and formal organizations correspondingly recognized. In this scenario, what Bohman objects to in the concept of demos, a citizenry that would largely passively endorse political authority, could be translated into a structuring culture of another kind, one that would be responsive to the pluralistic articulation of discourses, but nonetheless providing a minimally stable orienting normative culture for democratic and non-democratic affairs alike.

From the standpoint of the architecture of the public sphere, yet more arenas would be countenanced that would reach across all the quadrants outlined in Figure 1 and also reach across formally organized spheres, the public complex, and civil society. The multiple networks and relations flowing in and between these complexes would continue to be translated into various kinds of discursive and deliberative governance, but this would be done by means of a more joined-up architecture that would not be so subject to overwhelming normative power from the existing state complex. The parliamentary complex, potentially one of the heartbeats of democracy, does not have to be vitiated by the often remote and separate power of cabinet government. As a co-ordinating and supervisory agency, it can enable more direct forms of democracy to take hold that might involve societal self-organization in various spheres and at various levels, the combination of agencies with different kinds of involvement by the public, and much else. Without falling into the naïve utopianism that sometimes attends to assessment of new technology, the new more flexible media of communication, still in their infancy, have the potential to support innovative forms of communicative governance that overcome scale and distance. The beginning of the modern public sphere in small urban communities was accompanied by a huge increase in political communication prompted by the printing press (Zaret, 1992). Today, there is a similar rise in political communication that, even if the media potentials reach beyond the contemporary institutional forms, can be expected to creatively intertwine with new modes of communicative governance, not least on a transnational level of forging democratic, just, responsible, and viable cultural models.

The contemporary European situation crystallizes the tension between, on the one side, a demos that is closely entwined with ethnos on the nation-state level and on the other, the pull of a transnational cosmopolitanism that would at least vie with demos as a source of political orientation. At present in Europe, the profound stakes associated with this tension lie latent in the discourse, inflected not just with material interests and present claims to solidarity within national contexts, but also with historical memories of war and violence that has made, at least minimal, cosmopolitanism necessary. Cosmopolitanism on the European scale would still, contra Bohman and Burns, require some form of demos, but a demos shorn of a strong attachment to ethnicity and nation as an excluding rallying call. Such a demos, extending Habermas's idea of constitutional patriotism, should extend to the informal constitution that inheres in cultural models. Cosmopolitanism is one of the necessary cognitive cultural models and it is being constituted and reconstituted from discursive struggles that reflect a wide variety of social positions (Strydom, 2012).

Cosmopolitan solidarity requires cosmopolitan publicity and both require further profound changes in transnational democratic cultures and institutional forms, changes that presently are only being anticipated and are fragile and reversible. Brunkhorst's observation that there has been a shift from state-embedded publics to public-embedded states captures the challenge well (Brunkhorst, 2005, 2007). Public autonomy has been to a considerable extent displaced from its constitutional foundations in nation-states and is currently forced to substantially operate on a transnational footing without these foundations. Brunkhorst also observes how the nation-state – though never stable and beset with problems – helped to diminish and mostly eliminate the disruptive influence of wars of religion, extreme class conflicts, and constitutional fights over public autonomy. The decline of the powers of states and the rise of the supra-national level has weakened public autonomy. In the terms developed in this book, the three facets of the nation-state era identified by Brunkhorst were part of the cultural models of democratically organized nation-states. New transnational cultural models, which could solve the problems of the present and obviate the recurrence of problems of the past, are urgently needed.

A promising way of exploring this latter question is that proposed by Levy and Sznaider with respect to the genesis and consolidation of human rights regimes (Levy and Sznaider, 2006; Skillington, 2012; Skillington, 2013a, 2014). They argue that the memory of gross human rights violations animate the contemporary escalation of human rights norms. They intrinsically associate the framing of such violations following Finnemore and Sikking with successive stages in norm building (Finnemore and Sikking, 1998). They claim that rhetorical entrepreneurs find ways of making certain frames resonate with public sensibilities, leading to the gestation of international norms that to be sustained must be institutionalized in treaties, conventions, and organizations. A second stage is the 'cascading' of such norms through their adoption in multiple countries. A third is the decontestation of these norms, as they become internalized and acquire a taken for granted quality.

In cognitive sociological terms, the first stage involves the construction of first phase cultural models that are then amplified and consolidated in the course of the norm-building process. The formation of cultural models, related to but distinct from norm formation, involves symbolic consolidation; in this example, publics becomes transposed onto the transnational level and the mechanisms of framing and resonance are used by them in such a way as to lead over time to moral norm building. But the cognitive apparatus remains, as framing, resonance, and cognitive structure formation processes continue, now partly consolidating around normative complexes and norm-building procedures on the transnational level.

These two vantage points, the one outlining the challenge to public autonomy from the weakening of the nation-state and the other emphasizing how it can be rebuilt on the transnational level, crystallize a key dimension of the contemporary conjuncture. The practice of democracy, intrinsically sustained by public autonomy, has fallen on hard times, but the ideals of democracy live on. The besetting question is whether these ideals, suitably adapted to new circumstances and renewed horizons of fundamental and maximal justice, can operate as real counterfactuals that make their way into the emergent forms of cosmopolitan democracy.

Conclusion: The Public Sphere and Democracy

The manner in which the category of the public sphere was introduced into mainstream sociological thinking by Habermas, continuing the work of figures such as Dewey and Mills, fully fifty years ago has, as discussed in the introduction, created a challenge for the discipline that has not been adequately met ever since. This challenge is to develop a normative sociology that would not evade but incorporate normative claims of democratic theory, directing attention towards the status of publicity and publics, inclusion in and exclusion from the means of communication, the relationship between public autonomy and territory, and the relationship between freedom and discourse. The challenge has been if anything sharpened in the following years as Habermas has moved from the largely negative critique of the early Frankfurt School towards the more strongly counterfactual, disclosing critique of deliberative theory. Though it may have intellectually sharpened the challenge, it also provided a new focus of criticism in the claimed 'idealism' of this new normative standpoint

The nature of the critique of Habermas within sociology on the ground of an alleged idealism has been partly responsible for the fact that the normative implications of the public sphere have never been fully developed within the discipline, or on its frontiers with other disciplines. An aim of the book has been to begin the task of rectifying that situation. Here, the emphasis has been on the frontier with political philosophy with a view to advancing the theory of the *political* public sphere. But it could equally be said that other important frontiers – touched on here only tangentially, at least with respect to the actual literature – that include literary and cultural theory in one direction, and communication theory in another, lie equally underdeveloped.

Other factors have also contributed to the challenges posed by the concept of public sphere that are less directly traceable to the theoretical form in which it emerged. The first is that the public sphere is a concept of such wide structural import that it requires the theory of society to construct an adequate context for its normative implications. The early Habermas relied on a neo-Marxist critical theory of society. Crucial critical concepts in *Structural Transformation* such as 'refeudalization' or the implications of the commodity form of media ownership were drawn from that tradition. Neither Marxism, nor the rival theory of structural functionalism that Habermas creatively combined it with in the early 1980s, have been sustained as working models of the theory of society for decades now. Sociological analysis, at least explicitly, has all but relinquished those theory traditions, which had originally supported it, and no clear alternative has been put in its place. Recognizing the need, Habermas has at various times combined a theory of quasi-segmentary differentiation between core and periphery with functional differentiation of social systems to support the theory. These, jointly and separately, unquestionably have their place, but in the case of the theory of functional differentiation in particular, it is not well suited to serving as the dominant basis of description of social structures for a theory of communicative learning and communicative power (Habermas, 1996; 2006).

The absence of a workable theory of society has partly been responsible for another challenge that proved disorienting. The theory of the public sphere depends on a wide communicative theory of politics in which a theory of the mass media should play a prominent but not dominating role. Much of the scholarship on the public sphere, especially that with an empirical orientation, has focused predominantly on the media. But the theoretical implications of the concept of the public sphere cannot be properly satisfied without a wider theory of both communicative arenas and processes. While the theoretical and empirical study of the mass media remains a vital component of public sphere scholarship, it is not a substitute for a wider theory of communication in both these aspects. When even a few of the dimensions of this wider theory are listed, such as the nature of resonance, communication and structure formation, and deliberative democracy, it can easily be seen that the theory of the public sphere is much wider than media theory. The indirect and unsatisfactory nature of normative theorizing, together with the decline of the theory of society, have in their way contributed importantly to the substantial narrowing of public sphere theory towards a theory of media.

Conclusion: The Public Sphere and Democracy

If the above challenges could, either directly or indirectly, be traced back to the original formulation of the public sphere by Habermas, then another, relating to the substantial weakening of its nation-state context, has independently rapidly progressed in the last few decades (Habermas, 2001; Fraser, 2007). Fraser, for example, who *does* link this dimension back to Habermas's nation-centric *Structural Transformation*, argues that public opinion increasingly takes on a post-territorial form in that it is no longer centred along Westphalian lines on a dominant sovereign state. This is an argument shared by Bohman with his idea that the implications of plural demoi on the transnational level have replaced the integrating role of demos in the nation-state (Bohman, 2007). Both Fraser and Bohman argue that it is necessary to move to a post-demotic conception of publicity in which, not citizenship, but something like Dewey's old concept of the circle of affectedness, now transnationally articulated, should be the decisive factor for understanding how publics are constituted. Others, like David Miller, argue that, on the contrary, public autonomy and solidarity are best developed within existing nation-states and that excessive weakening of the nation-state will result in greater injustice (Miller, 1995).

Habermas himself has something of a middle position in that his idea of postnationalism envisages the continuation of nation-state democracy and public spheres complemented by an emerging transnational order of which the European Union offers a good example. What is in little doubt from empirical trends is that the high degree of democratic autonomy enjoyed by nation-states has been significantly diminished by the macro-regionalization and globalization of public opinion in the context of a major expansion in migratory, economic, geo-political, and cultural circles of affectedness (Brunkhorst, 2005). Correspondingly, the integrity and autonomy of national public spheres has also been diminished, a situation that generates a major theoretical and practical challenge.

This book has sought to make some modest progress with regard to the scale of the above challenges. To address the ultimately central challenge of advancing a normative sociology of critical publicity, it has sought to explore the degree to which normative claims rest on cognitive foundations that are revealed through the combined analysis of, respectively, the dynamics of public discourse, how such discourse triggers collective learning within the cognitive order of modernity, the formation of cultural models as an outcome of these learning processes, and institutional norm-building guided by these models. By means of this cognitive-communicative paradigm, the constructivist orientation of the social sciences meets halfway the reconstructivist orientation of the Kantian philosophical heritage, a heritage whose reconstructivist methodology can be extended to non-Kantian traditions. In this way too, advances towards a normative sociology of critical publicity, which can demonstrate by means of its constructivist methodology the reconstructive accomplishments of publics in their political discourses and practices, challenges political philosophy in return to incorporate these accomplishments and thereby to qualify its hitherto dominant third-party normative standpoint.

The cognitive-communicative approach, therefore, opens the way to understanding how normative arguments emerge within cognitively grounded complexes of meaning. The mostly implicit, or at least mostly not fully adumbrated, communicative constructs of political philosophy, joined with a communicative-oriented sociology, together provide the means to comprehend how society communicatively develops, justifies and applies its normative standards. Sociology has, in return, to join with political philosophy in exploring not just what is the case, but also what could and should – or should not – be the case. The latter task circumscribes the challenge that the fully developed concept of the public sphere poses as a requirement of a normative sociology of critical publicity.

The other challenges outlined in the paragraphs above are defined in relation to this central one. One word, 'society', incorporates all of them. Firstly, the concept of public sphere incorporates societal communication structures and processes of general political significance and not simply those of the mass or even new media, even if the latter pose all kinds of new challenges through altering the nature of mediated communication. Secondly, the theory of society seeks to understand how democratic communication across all social spheres is both formed by and impacts on existing societal structures, both cultural and social. Thirdly, the nature of society today, and with it the future of democratic communication and critical publicity, can no longer be comprehended in terms of the unitary nation-state, but in terms of conditions of co-dependency on many levels within a postnational constellation. These developments generate an analytic challenge that is also a normative one. How can the ideal of public sovereignty be upheld through its only available means, that is, through public discourse that has appropriate normative status?

The approach to the study of public discourse laid out in this book is intended to clarify the prerequisites of a kind of analysis that would conjoin the theory of society and normative reflection. These prerequisites involve the socio-historical, processual, and structural understanding of how publics do or could reason and how such understanding may be used to sustain and deepen democracy. The framework of the book seeks to show how the public remains a central category, one for too long excessively diminished in importance in empirical-theoretical social science. A reorientation in these disciplines towards incorporating the normative status of the category of public would require not just the perspective of negative critique, which explains why the public has not been able to function in an adequate and appropriate manner because of structural forces ranged against it. It would also require the perspective of a disclosing critique that would show, taking knowledge generated by explanatory negative critique into account, how the actions of publics can change normative arrangements. Central to both tasks is the manner in which the cognitive order opens a space for societal reflection in multiple dimensions that goes beyond present institutional arrangements, and makes possible what Honneth calls social freedom (Honneth, 2011).

It is generally the case that academics can only go with the flow of reality. Their contribution to shaping it depends on epistemic alliances with those variations on publics, for example, social movements and a multiplicity of other social forces that actually generate social change. Publics themselves, with or without academics, engage in reconstructive learning and normative world making. It would be unwise to be normatively naïve and assume that publics will make the world that some academics desire, especially given that academics themselves desire very different worlds. In fact, while the category of public, as distinct from those of mass or crowd, does have democratic presuppositions, the variety of publics can nonetheless be expected to be capable of producing very different worlds.

Accepting difference and pluralism as integral to the cognitive order, which itself consists of competing as well as complementary perspectives, means that the capacity of academics – social scientists or philosophers – to advance normative standards on behalf of society diminishes, but does not entirely disappear. The challenge of producing a tolerable and fair world may be principally a matter for publics, but the recognition of what is intolerable and unfair and how it could be corrected still requires an academic contribution. Such an academic contribution in some part depends on the capacity of academics to argue out their own differences so that the various societal standpoints from which they argue do not always have to be antagonistically represented, even if they frequently must be. In this pluralist age, any prospectively valuable outcome of these arguments will have to be one that engages reciprocally with the many different standpoints, an insight, here applied reflexively to academics, that is so central to the many shades of difference democracy and to the later work of Habermas and Rawls.

Neither in societal or academic argumentation processes, even when characterized by good faith and inclusion, is it foreseeable that democratic procedures can provide for all the voices to be equally heard and for the one good argument to emerge, though this remains a good counterfactual standard. The cognitive perspective allows the *societal* discursive work to which the public fundamentally contributes, and from which learning processes and structures emerge, to become fully apparent. It is only through the building of democratic cognitive cultural models of how democracy *should* regulate other social spheres, without dominating them, that multiple publics can comprehend and normatively organize pluralism, differentiation, and complexity. Today, differentiation and complexity pose fundamental challenges to normatively organizing pluralism. But the kinds of epistemic and practical pessimism animated by the sense of a world out of control should be leavened by the sense of a normative project of modernity that needs to be completed and the deep injustices that arose with that project as it was concretely realized removed, or at least tolerably alleviated (Brunkhorst, 2007). It is undoubtedly too optimistic to suggest that the current spectrum of conflict, disorganization, growing injustice, and epistemic confusion offers just the kind of opportunity to remedy these accumulated injustices as well as the malign consequences

Conclusion: The Public Sphere and Democracy   465

of selective rationalization and contradictory institutionalization on local, national, and global planes. But it would be too pessimistic to assume that problems currently unsolved, or at various stages of being addressed, do not provide opportunity to build on some of the achievements of modernity.

The ideal theoretical metaphor of bringing people together in one place to sort out issues of such great complexity and sensitivity has counterfactual value, but the implications of this counterfactual must be shown to be effective in social life. And beyond this counterfactual ideal of consensus, lies the social reality of continuing conflict and dissensus. Rather than only, as typically argued, counterposing this reality to the ideal of consensus and finding it wanting, the counterfactual ideals for creatively addressing such conflicts should also be advanced. From the standpoint of the social sciences, this above all means empirical-theoretically investigating the 'fair value' of counterfactuals as they really operate, so to speak 'real counterfactuals'. One of the primary insights of cognitive approaches of the kind advanced here is that such real counterfactuals do not lie beyond social life, but actively structure it. Empirical studies are needed that demonstrate these structures in action.

Continuing this theme, further empirical studies are also needed to properly demonstrate the theoretical and normative value of what has been abstractly outlined in this book. These studies would not merely be downstream applications of what is theoretically developed here, but would also serve as theory reconstructing. Here, too, the wider and complex world of methodologies for the analysis of public discourse, scarcely addressed in this volume, would come to centre stage. But what should animate these studies is not simply the goal of explanatory critique of a bad reality, but also the goal of complementary normative articulation of the prospect of a better reality. For this, as Karl-Otto Apel makes clear, social scientists must not be afraid to disclose what it is they are arguing for and not simply against. The constructivist turn in the social sciences, necessary, on one side, to qualify the predominantly third-party normative arguments of political philosophy, should not, on the other side, be used to hide the normative arguments of social scientists but, instead, to make them apparent as responsible acts. This is what a truly reflexive relation to the public sphere necessarily entails.

Bibliography

Abels, G., and Bora, A. (2004). *Demokratische Technikbewertung*. Bielefeld: Transcript.
Albert, M., and Hilkermeier, L. (2004). *Observing International Relations:Niklas Luhmann and World Politics*. London: Routledge.
Alexander, J., Giesen, B., Munch, R., and Smelser, N. J. (eds). (1984). *Discourse, Participation, and Sociological Theory*. Berkeley: University of California Press.
Alexy, R. (1993). Justification and Application of Norms. *Ratio Juris*, 6(2), 157–170.
Alford, C. F. (1985). Is Jurgen Habermas's Reconstructive Science Really Science? *Theory and Society*, 14(3), 321–340.
Anderson, B. (1983). *Imagined Communities: Reflections on the Origin and Spread of Nationalism*. London: Verso.
Apel, K. O. (1975). *Diskurs und Verantwortung: das Problem des Übergangs zur postkonventionellen Moral*. Frankfurt: Suhrkamp.
Apel, K. O. (1978). The Conflicts of our Times and the Problem of Political Ethics. In F. R. Dallmayr (ed.), *From Contract to Community: Political Theory at the Crossroads*. New York: Marcel Dekker.
Apel, K. O. (1980). *Towards a Transformation of Philosophy*. London: Routledge and Kegan Paul.
Apel, K. O. (1984). *Understanding and Explanation: A Transcendental-Pragmatic Perspective*. Cambridge, MA: MIT Press.
Apel, K. O. (1987). The Problem of a Macroethic of Responsibility to the Future in the Crisis of Technological Civilization: An attempt to come to terms with Hans Jonas's 'Principle of Responsibility'. *Man and World*, 20(1), 3–40.
Apel, K. O. (1993). Discourse Ethics as a Response to the Novel Challenges of Today's Reality to Coresponsibility. *The Journal of Religion*, 73(4), 496–513.
Apel, K. O. (2001). Regarding the Relationship of Morality, Law, and Democracy: On Habermas's Philosophy of Law (1992) from a Transcendental-pragmatic Point of View. In M. Aboulafia, M. Bookman and C. Kemp (eds), *Habermas and Pragmatism*. London: Routledge.
Apel, K. O., and Papastephanou, M. (1998). *From a Transcendental-semiotic Point of View*. Manchester: Manchester University Press.
Archer, M. (1984). *Culture and Agency: The Place of Culture in Social Theory*. Cambridge: Cambridge University Press.
Arendt, H. (1958). *The Human Condition*. Chicago: University of Chicago Press.

Arjomand, S. (2003). Law, Political Reconstruction, and Constitutional Politics. *International Sociology*, *18*(1), 19–34.

Audard, C. (2009). *Qu'est-ce que le Libéralisme? Éthique, Politique, Société*. Paris: Gallimard.

Bachtiger, A., Niemeyer, S., Neblo, M., Steenbergen, M. R., and Steiner, J. (2010). Disentangling Diversity in Deliberative Democracy: Competing Theories, their Blind Spots and Complementarities. *Journal of Political Philosophy*, *18*(1), 32–63.

Bacqué, M. H., and Sintomer, Y. (eds). (2011). *La Démocratie Participative: Histoire et Généalogie*. Paris: La Decouverte.

Ballantyne, G. (2007). *Creativity and Critique: Subjectivity and Agency in Touraine and Ricoeur*. Leiden: Brill.

Barber, B. (1984). *Strong Democracy*. Berkeley: University of California Press.

Barry, B. (1995). John Rawls and the Search for Stability. *Ethics*, *105(4)*(4), 874–915.

Barthe, Y., Callon, M., and Lascoumes, P. (2001). *Agir dans un Monde Incertain. Essai sur la Démocratie Technique*. Paris: Seuil.

Baynes, K. (1992). Constructivism and Practical Reason in Rawls. *Analyse & Kritik*, *14*, 18–32.

Beck, U. (2006) *The Cosmopolitan Vision*. Cambridge: Polity Press.

Benhabib, S. (1987). The Generalized and the Concrete Other: The Kohlberg-Gilligan Controversy and Feminist Theory. In S. Benhabib and D. Cornell (eds), *Feminism as Critique*. Minneapolis: University of Minnesota Press.

Benhabib, S. (1996). Toward a Deliberative Model of Democratic Legitimacy. In S. Benhabib (ed.), *Democracy and Difference: Contesting the Boundaries of the Political* (pp. 67–94). Princeton, NJ: Princeton University Press.

Berg, M., and Geyer, M. H. (2002). *Two Cultures of Rights: The Quest for Inclusion and Participation in Modern America and Germany*. Cambridge: Cambridge University Press.

Billig, M. (1995). *Banal Nationalism*. London: Sage.

Bobbio, N. (1984). *The Future of Democracy: A Defence of the Rules of the Game*. Cambridge: Polity Press.

Böhler, D. (2003). Dialogreflexive Sinnkritik als Kernstück der Transzendentalpragmatik: Karl-Otto Apels Athene im Rücken. In D. Böhler, M. Kettner and G. Skirbekk (ed.), *Reflexion und Verantwortung: Auseinandersetzungen mit Karl-Otto Apel*. Frankfurt: Suhrkamp.

Bohman, J. (1994). Complexity, Pluralism and the Constitutional State: On Habermas's Faktizitat und Geltung. *Law and Society Review*, *28*(4), 897–930.

Bohman, J. (1998). Survey Article: The Coming of Age of Deliberative Democracy. *Journal of Political Philosophy*, *6*(4), 400–425.

Bohman, J. (1999). Democracy as Inquiry, Inquiry as Democratic: Pragmatism, Social Science, and the Cognitive Division of Labor. *American Journal of Political Science*, *43*(2), 590–607.

Bohman, J. (2000). *Public deliberation: Pluralism, Complexity, and Democracy.* Cambridge, MA: MIT Press.

Bohman, J. (2004a). Republican Cosmopolitanism. *Journal of Political Philosophy*, *12*(3), 336–352.

Bohman, J. (2004b). Expanding Dialogue: The Public Sphere, the Internet, and Transnational Democracy. N. Crossley, and J. M. Roberts (eds), *After Habermas: New Perspectives on the Public Sphere.* Oxford: Wiley.

Bohman, J. (2007). *Democracy across Borders: from Dêmos to Dêmoi.* Cambridge, MA: MIT Press.

Bohman, J. (2010). Participation through Publics: Did Dewey Answer Lippmann? *Contemporary Pragmatism*, *7*(1), 49–68.

Bohman, J. (2013). Jus Post Bellum as a Deliberative Process: Transnationalizing Peacebuilding. *Irish Journal of Sociology*, *20*(2), 10–27.

Bohman, J., and Regh, W. (2002). *Deliberative Democracy: Essays on Reason and Politics.* Cambridge, MA: MIT Press.

Boltanski, L., and Chiapello, E. (2005). *The New Spirit of Capitalism.* London: Verso.

Boltanski, L., and Thévenot, L. (2000). The Reality of Moral Expectations: A Sociology of Situated Judgement. *Philosophical Explorations*, *3*(3), 208–231.

Boltanski, L., and Thévenot, L. (2006). *On Justification: Economies of Worth.* Princeton, NJ: Princeton University Press.

Bonnell, V. E., Hunt, L., and White, H. (eds). (1999). *Beyond the Cultural Turn: New Directions in the Study of Society and Culture.* Berkeley: University of California Press.

Bora, A. (1999). Discourse Formations and Constellatoins of Conflict. In P. O'Mahony (ed.), *Nature, Risk and Responsibility: Discourses of Biotechnology.* London: Macmillan.

Bora, A., and Hausendorf, H. (2006). Communicating Citizenship and Social Positioning. In A. Bora and H. Hausendorf (eds), *Analyzing Citizenship Talk: Social Positioning in Political and Legal Decision-Making Processes.* Amsterdam: John Benjamins.

Boudon, R. (1986). *Theories of Social Change.* Cambridge: Polity Press.

Boudon, R. (2007). *Essais sur la Théorie Générale de la Rationalité.* Paris: Presses Universitaires de France.

Bourdieu, P. (1977). *Outline of a Theory of Practice.* Cambridge: Cambridge University Press.

Bourdieu, P. (1984). *Distinction: A Social Critique of the Judgement of Taste*. Cambridge, MA: Harvard University Press.
Bourdieu, P. (1985). The Genesis of the Concepts of Habitus and Field. *Sociocriticism*, 2(2), 11–24.
Bourdieu, P. (1998). *Practical Reason*. Cambridge: Polity Press.
Bourdieu, P. (1986). The Force of Law: Toward a Sociology of the Juridical Field. *Hastings Law Journal*, 38(5), 814–853.
Bourdieu, P., and Wacquant, L. J. D. (1992). *An Invitation to Reflexive Sociology*. Chicago: University of Chicago Press.
Bouvier, A. (2007). An Argumentativist Point of View in Cognitive Sociology. *European Journal of Social Theory*, 10(3), 465–480.
Brandom, R. (1998). *Making it Explicit: Reasoning, Representing, and Discursive Commitment*. Cambridge, MA: Harvard University Press.
Brinkley, A. (1995). *The End of Reform: New Deal Liberalism in Recession and War*. New York: Vintage.
Brunkhorst, H. (2005). *Solidarity: From Civic Friendship to a Global Legal Community*. Cambridge, MA: MIT Press.
Brunkhorst, H. (2007). Globalizing Solidarity: The Destiny of Democratic Solidarity in the Times of Global Capitalism, Global Religion, and the Global Public. *Journal of Social Philosophy*, 38(1), 91–109.
Bufacchi, V. (2011). *Social Injustice: Essays in Political Philosophy*. London: Palgrave.
Burns, T. R. (1999). The Evolution of Parliaments and Societies in Europe. *European Journal of Social Theory*, 2(2), 167–194.
Burns, T. R., Jaeger, C., Liberatore, A., Meny, Y., and Nanz, P. (2000). *Green Paper: The Future of Parliamentary Democracy: Transition and Challenge in European Governance*. Brussels: Commission of the European Communities.
Calhoun, C. (ed.) (1992). *Habermas and the Public Sphere*. Cambridge, MA: MIT Press.
Canovan, M. (1999). Trust the People! Populism and the Two Faces of Democracy. *Political studies*, 47(1), 2–16.
Carpini, M. X. D., Cook, F. L., and Jacobs, L. R. (2004). Public Deliberation, Discursive Participation, and Citizen Engagement: A Review of the Empirical Literature. *Annual Review of Political Science*, 7, 315–344.
Castoriadis, C. (1998). *The Imaginary Institution of Society*. Cambridge, MA: MIT Press.
Celikates, R. (2006). From Critical Social Theory to a Social Theory of Critique: On the Critique of Ideology after the Pragmatic Turn. *Constelllations*, 13(1), 21–40.
Charney, E. (1998). Political Liberalism, Deliberative Democracy, and the Public Sphere. *American Political Science Review*, 92(1), 97–110.

Christiano, T. (2008). *The Constitution of Equality: Democratic Authority and its Limits.* Oxford: Oxford University Press.
Cicourel, A. V. (1974). *Cognitive Sociology. Language and Meaning in Social Interaction.* New York: Free Press.
Cicourel, A. V. (1981). Notes on the Integration of Micro-and Macro-Levels of Analysis. In K. Knorr-Cetina and A. V. Cicourel (eds), *Advances in Social Theory and Methodology: Toward an Integration of Micro- and Macro-Sociologies.* Boston, MA: Routledge and Kegan Paul.
Cobb, R., and Elder, C. (1983). *Participation in American Politics: The Dynamics of Agenda-Building.* Baltimore, MD: Johns Hopkins University Press.
Cohen, J. (1989). Deliberation and Democratic Legitimacy. In A. Hamlin and P. Pettit (eds), *The Good Polity.* London: Wiley.
Cohen, J., and Fung, A. (2004). Radical democracy. *Swiss Journal of Political Science*, 10(4), 23–34.
Cohen, J., and Sabel, C. (1997). Directly-Deliberative Polyarchy. *European Law Journal*, 3(4), 313–342.
Cohen, J. L., and Arato, A. (1994). *Civil Society and Political Theory.* Cambridge, MA: MIT Press.
Connolly, W. E. (2002). *Identity\Difference: Democratic Negotiations of Political Paradox.* Minneapolis: University of Minnesota Press.
Cooke, M. (2006). *Represesenting the Good Society.* Cambridge, MA: MIT Press.
Delanty, G. (2006). The Cosmopolitan Imagination and Social Theory. *British Journal of Sociology*, 57(1), 25–47.
Delanty, G., and O'Mahony, P. (2002). *Nationalism and Social Theory: Modernity and the Recalcitrance of the Nation.* London: Sage.
Deranty, J. P. (2009). *Beyond Communication. A Critical Study of Axel Honneth's Social Philosophy.* Leiden: Brill.
Dewey, J. (1927). *The Public and its Problems.* New York: Holt.
Dewey, J. (1985). *The Later Works, 1925–1953.* Carbondale: Southern Illinois University Press.
DiMaggio, P., Hargittai, E., Neumann, W. R., and Robinson, J. P. (2001). Social Implications of the Internet. *Annual Review of Sociology*, 27(1), 307–336.
Dryzek, J. S. (1987). Discursive Designs: Critical Theory and Political Institutions. *American journal of Political Science*, 31(3), 656–679.
Dryzek, J. S. (1994). *Discursive Democracy: Politics, Policy, and Political Science.* Cambridge: Cambridge University Press.
Dryzek, J. S. (2000). *Deliberative Democracy and Beyond: Liberals, Critics, Contestations.* New York: Oxford University Press.
Edelman, M. (1988). *Constructing the Political Spectacle.* Chicago: University of Chicago Press.

Eder, K. (1985). *Geschichte als Lernprozeß? Zur Pathogenese politischer Modernität in Deutschland.* Frankfurt: Suhrkamp.

Eder, K. (1996). *The Social Construction of Nature: A Sociology of Ecological Enlightenment.* London: Sage.

Eder, K. (1999). Societies Learn and Yet the World is Hard to Change. *European Journal of Social Theory, 2*(2), 195–215.

Eder, K. (2006). The Public Sphere. *Theory, Culture & Society, 23*(2–3), 607–611.

Eder, K. (2007). Cognitive Sociology and the Theory of Communicative Action: The Role of Communication and Language in the Making of the Social Bond. *European Journal of Social Theory, 10*(3), 389–408.

Edwards, D., and Potter, J. (1992). *Discursive Psychology.* London: Sage.

Elias, N. (1992). *Studien über die Deutschen: Machtkämpfe und Habitusentwicklung im 19. und 20. Jahrhundert.* Frankfurt: Suhrkamp.

Elkin, S. L. (2006). *Reconstructing the Commercial Republic: Constitutional Design after Madison.* Chicago: University of Chicago Press.

Elster, J. (1989). *The Cement of Society: A Study of Social Order.* Cambridge: Cambridge University Press.

Emirbayer, M. (1997). Manifesto for a Relational Sociology. *American Journal of Sociology, 103*(2), 281–317.

Emirbayer, M., and Mische, A. (1998). What Is Agency? *American Journal of Sociology, 103*(4), 962–1023.

Emirbayer, M., and Sheller, M. (1998). Publics in History. *Theory and Society, 27*(6), 727–779.

Esping-Andersen, G. (1990). *The Three Worlds of Welfare Capitalism.* Princeton, NJ: Princeton University Press

Estlund, D. (1997). Beyond Fairness and Deliberation: The Epistemic Dimension of Democratic Authority.: In W. Rehg and J. Bohman (eds), *Deliberative Democracy: Essays on Reason and Politics.* Cambridge, Mass: MIT Press.

Ezrahi, Y. (1990). *The Descent of Icarus: Science and the Transformation of Contemporary Democracy.* Cambridge, MA: Harvard University Press.

Ferree, M. M., Gamson, W. A., Gerhards, J., and Rucht, D. (2002a). *Shaping Abortion Discourse: Democracy and the Public Sphere in Germany and the United States.* Cambridge: Cambridge University Press.

Ferree, M. M., Gamson, W. A., Gerhards, J., and Rucht, D. (2002b). Four Models of the Public Sphere in Modern Democracies. *Theory and Society, 31*(3), 289–324.

Fesmire, S. (2003). *John Dewey and Moral Imagination: Pragmatism in Ethics.* Bloomington: Indiana University Press.

Finnemore, M., and Sikking, K. (1998). International Norm Dynamics and Political Change. *International Organization, 52*(4), 887–917.

Forst, R. (2002). *Contexts of Justice: Political Philosophy beyond Liberalism and Communitarianism.* Los Angeles: University of California Press.

Forst, R. (2007a). First Things First: Redistribution, Recognition, and Justification. *European Journal of Political Theory, 6*(3), 291–304.

Forst, R. (2007b). *The Right to Justification: Elements of a Constructivist Theory of Justice.* New York: Columbia University Press.

Fraser, N. (1992). Rethinking the Public Sphere: A Contribution to the Critique of Actually Existing Democracy. In C. Calhoun (ed.), *Habermas and the Public Sphere.* Cambridge, MA: MIT Press.

Fraser, N. (2007). Special Section: Transnational Public Sphere: Transnationalizing the Public Sphere: On the Legitimacy and Efficacy of Public Opinion in a Post-Westphalian World. *Theory, Culture & Society, 24*(4), 7–30.

Fraser, N. (2008). Abnormal Justice. *Critical Inquiry, 34*(3), 393–422.

Fraser, N., and Honneth, A. (2003). *Redistribution or Recognition?: A Political-philosophical Exchange.* London: Verso.

Freeden, M. (1996). *Ideologies and Political Theory: A Conceptual Approach.* Oxford: Oxford University Press.

Fricker, M. (2007). *Epistemic Injustice: Power and the Ethics of Knowing.* Oxford: Oxford University Press.

Fung, A. (2002). Creating deliberative publics: Governance after Devolution and Democratic Centralism. *The Good Society, 11*(1), 66–71.

Galston, W. (2010). Realism in Political Theory. *European Journal of Political Theory, 9*(4), 385–411.

Gamson, W. (1992). *Talking Politics* Cambridge: Cambridge University Press.

Gamson, W., and Lasch, K. (1983). The Political Culture of Social Welfare Policy. In S. Spiro and E. Gudmahyaar (eds), *Evaluating the Welfare State: Social and Ethical Perspectives* (New York: Academic Press).

Gaus, G. F. (2003). *Contemporary Theories of Liberalism: Public Reason as a Post-Enlightenment Project.* London: Sage.

Gerhards, J. (1997). Diskursive versus Liberale Öffentlichkeit. Eine Empirische Auseinandersetzung mit Jürgen Habermas. *Kolner Zeitschrift fur Soziologie und Sozialpsychologie, 49*, 1–34.

Giddens, A. (1984). *The Constitution of Society: Outline of the Theory of Structuration.* Berkeley: University of California Press.

Giddens, A. (1987). *The Nation-State and Violence: Volume 2 of A Contemporary Critique of Historical Materialism.* Berkeley: University of California Press.

Giddens, A. (1991). *The Consequences of Modernity.* Palo Alto, CA: Stanford University Press.

Gilligan, C. (1982). *In A Different Voice: Psychological Theory and Women's Development.* Cambridge, MA: Harvard University Press.
Goffman, E. (1983). The Interaction Order. *The American Sociology Review, 48*(1), 1–17.
Goffman, E. (1986). *Frame Analysis: An Essay on the Organization of Experience.* Boston, MA: Northeastern University Press.
Goodin, R. E. (2003). *Reflective Democracy.* Oxford: Oxford University Press.
Gottweis, H. (1998). *Governing Molecules: The Discursive Politics of Genetic Engineering in Europe and the United States.* Cambridge, MA: MIT Press.
Gould, M. (2005). Looming Catastrophe: How and Why 'Law and Economics' Undermines Fiduciary Duties in Corporate Law. In R. C. Fox, V. M. Lidz and H. J. Bershady (eds), *After Parsons – A Theory of Social Action for the Twenty-First Century.*
Greenfeld, L. (1993). *Nationalism: Five Roads to Modernity.* Cambridge, MA: Harvard University Press.
Gunnell, J. G. (2004). *Imagining the American Polity: Political Science and the Discourse of Democracy.* Philadelphia: Pennsylvania State University Press.
Günther, K. (1993). *The Sense of Appropriateness: Application Discourses in Morality and Law.* New York: Suny Press.
Gutmann, A., and Thompson, D. (1996). *Democracy and Deliberation.* Cambridge, MA: Harvard University Press.
Habermas, J. (1973). A Postscript to *Knowledge and Human Interests. Philosophy of the Social Sciences, 3,* 158–161.
Habermas, J. (1984). *The Theory of Communicative Action, vol. 1: Reason and the Rationalization of Society.* London: Heinemann.
Habermas, J. (1987). *The Theory of Communicative Action, Volume 2: Lifeworld and System: A Critique of Functionaist Reason.* Boston, MA: Beacon.
Habermas, J. (1989). *The Structural Transformation of the Public Sphere: An Inquiry into a Category of Bourgeois Society.* Cambridge, MA: MIT Press.
Habermas, J. (1990). *Moral Consciousness and Communicative Action.* Cambridge: Polity Press.
Habermas, J. (1992). Further Reflections on the Public Sphere. In C. Calhoun (ed.), *Habermas and the Public Sphere.*
Habermas, J. (1993). *Justification and Application: Remarks on Discourse Ethics.* Cambridge: Polity Press.
Habermas, J. (1994). Three Normative Models of Democracy. *Constellations, 1*(1), 1–10.
Habermas, J. (1995). Reconciliation Through the Public Use of Reason: Remarks on John. Rawls's Political Liberalism. *Journal of Philosophy, 92*(3), 109–131.
Habermas, J. (1996). *Between Facts and Norms: Contributions to a Discourse Theory of Law and Democracy.* Cambridge, MA: MIT Press.

Habermas, J. (2000). From Kant to Hegel: On Robert Brandom's Pragmatic Philosophy of Language. *European Journal of Philosophy*, *8*(3), 323–355.
Habermas, J. (2001a). From Kant's 'Ideas' of Pure Reason to the 'Idealizing' Presuppositions of Communicative Action: Reflections on the Detranscendentalized 'Use of Reason'. In W. Rehg and J. Bohman (eds), *Pluralism and the Pragmatic Turn: The Transformation of Critical Theory: Essays in Honour of Thomas McCarthy*. Cambridge, MA: MIT Press.
Habermas, J. (2001b). *The Postnational Constellation: Political Essays*. Cambridge: Polity Press.
Habermas, J. (2003). *Truth and Justification*. Cambridge, MA: MIT Press.
Habermas, J. (2006). Political Communication in Media Society: Does Democracy Still Enjoy an Epistemic Dimension? The Impact of Normative Theory on Empirical Research. *Communication Theory*, *16*(4), 411–426.
Habermas, J. (2008). *Between Naturalism and Religion*. Cambridge: Polity Press.
Hall, S. (1997). *Representation: Cultural Representations and Signifying Practices*. London: Sage.
Hansen, M. (1993). Unstable Mixtures, Dilated Spheres: Negt and Kluge's The Public Sphere and Experience, Twenty Years Later. *Public Culture*, *5*(2), 179–213.
Haraway, D. J. (1991). *Simians, Cyborgs, and Women: The Reinvention of Nature*. New York: Routledge.
Harrington, J. (1992). *The Commonwealth of Oceana; And A system of Politics*. Cambridge: Cambridge University Press.
Hauser, G. (1998). Civil Society and the Principle of the Public Sphere. *Philosophy and Rhetoric*, *31*(1), 19–40.
Hauser, G. (1999). *Vernacular Voices: The Rhetoric of Publics and Public Spheres*. Columbia: University of South Carolina Press.
Hedetoft, U. (1995). *Signs of Nations: Studies in the Political Semiotics of Self and Other in Contemporary European Nationalism*. Dartmouth: University of Michigan Press.
Hilgartner, S., and Bosk, C. L. (1988). The Rise and Fall of Social Problems: A Public Arenas Model. *The American Journal of Sociology*, *94*(1), 53–78.
Hirst, P. (1993). *Associative Democracy*. Cambridge: Polity Press.
Honig, B. (1993). *Political Theory and the Displacement of Politics*. Ithaca, NY: Cornell University Press.
Honneth, A. (1996). *The Struggle for Recognition: The Moral Grammar of Social Conflicts*. Cambridge, MA: MIT Press.
Honneth, A. (1997). Recognition and Moral Obligation. *Social Research*, *64*(1), 16–35.
Honneth, A. (1998). Democracy as Reflexive Cooperation: John Dewey and the Theory of Democracy Today. *Political Theory*, *26*(6), 763–783.

Honneth A. (2004a). Recognition and Justice: Outline of a Plural Theory of Justice. *Acta Sociologica*, *47*(4), 351–354.
Honneth, A. (2004b). From Struggles for Recognition to a Plural Concept of Justice: An Interview with Axel Honneth. *Acta Sociologica*, *47*(4), 383–391.
Honneth, A. (2007). *Disrespect: The Normative Foundations of Critical Theory*. Cambridge: Polity Press.
Honneth, A. (2011). *Das Recht der Freiheit: Grundriß einer Demokratischen Sittlichkeit*. Frankfurt: Suhrkamp.
Honneth, A., Butler, J., Geuss, R., and Lear, J. (2008). *Reification: A New Look at an Old Idea*. Oxford: Oxford University Press.
Horkheimer, M. (1982). *Critical theory: Selected Essays* (1). London: Continuum.
Isaac, J. C., Filner, M. F., and Bivins, J. C. (1999). American Democracy and the New Christian Right: A Critique of Apolitical Liberalism. In I. Shapiro and C. Hacker-Cordon (eds), *Democracy's Edges*. Cambridge: Cambridge University Press.
Jacobs, L. R., Cook, F. L., and delli Carpini, M. X. D. (2009). *Talking Together: Public Deliberation and Political Participation in America*. Chicago: University of Chicago Press.
Joas, H. (1996). *The Creativity of Action*. Cambridge: Polity Press.
Johnson, P. (2006). *Jurgen Habermas: Rescuing the Public Sphere*. New York: Routledge.
Jonas, H. (1979). *Das Prinzip Verantwortung*. Frankfurt: Suhrkamp.
Kant, I. (1917). *Perpetual Peace: A Philosophical Essay*. London: Allen & Unwin.
Kelly, E. (2011). *Public Reason as a Collective Capability*. Proceedings from Symposium on Sen's 'The Idea of Justice', New York.
Kelly, T. (2001). Sociological not Political: Rawls and the Reconstructive Social Sciences. *Philosophy of the Social Sciences*, *31*(3), 3–19.
Kitschelt, H. (1986). Political Opportunity Structures and Political Protest: Anti-Nuclear Movements in Four Democracies. *British Journal of Political Science*, *15*(1), 58–85.
Kitschelt, H., and McGann, A. J. (1997). *The Radical Right in Western Europe: A Comparative Analysis*. Ann Arbor: University of Michigan Press.
Kjaer, P. (2006). Systems in context: on the outcomes of the Habermas/Luhmann Debate. *Ancilla Juris*, *1*, 66–77.
Knorr-Cetina, K. (1981). The Micro-Sociological Challenge of Macro-Sociology: Towards a Reconstruction of Social Theory and Methodology. In K. Knorr-Cetina and A. V. Cicourel (eds), *Advances in Social Theory and Methodology: Toward an Integration of Micro- and Macro-Sociologies*. Boston, MA: Routledge and Kegan Paul.
Koopman, C. (2009). *Pragmatism as Transition: Historicity and Hope in James, Dewey, and Rorty*. New York: Columbia University Press.

Koselleck, R. (1998). *Critique and Crisis: Enlightenment and the Pathogenesis of Modern Society*. Cambridge, MA: MIT Press.
Laclau, E. (1996). *Emancipation(s)*. London: Verso.
Lamont, M., and Thévenot, L. (2000). *Rethinking Comparative Cultural Sociology*. Cambridge: Cambridge University Press.
Landes, J. B. (1988). *Women and the Public Sphere in the Age of the French Revolution*. Ithaca, NY: Cornell University Press.
Landes, J. B. (1995). The Public and the Private Sphere: A Feminist Reconsideration. In J. B. Landes (ed.), *Feminist, the Public and the Private*. Oxford: Oxford University Press.
Lange, S., and Schimank, U. (2004). A Political Sociology for Complex Societies. In E. Amenta, K. Nash, and Scott, A. (eds), *The Blackwell Companion to Political Sociology*. Oxford: Blackwell.
Lefort, C. (1988). *Democracy and Political Theory*. Cambridge: Polity Press.
Levy, D., and Sznaider, N. (2006). Sovereignty Transformed: A Sociology of Human Rights. *British Journal of Sociology*, 57(4), 657–676.
Luhmann, N. (1980). *Gesellschaftsstruktur und Semantik: Studien zur Wissenssoziologie der modernen Gesellschaft*. Frankfurt: Suhrkamp.
Luhmann, N. (1982). *The Differentiation of Society*. New York: Columbia University Press.
Luhmann, N. (1989). *Ecological Communication*. Cambridge: Polity Press.
Luhmann, N. (1990). *Political Theory in the Welfare State*. Berlin: de Gruyter.
Luhmann, N. (1993). *Legitimation durce Verfahren*. Frankfurt: Suhrkamp.
Luhmann, N. (1996). *The Reality of the Mass Media*. Stanford, CA: Stanford University Press.
Luhmann, N. (1997). *Die Gesellschaft der Gesellschaft*. Two volumes. Frankfurt: Suhrkamp.
Luhmann, N. (1998). *Observations on Modernity*. Palo Alto, CA: Stanford University Press.
Luhmann, N. (2000). *Die Politik der Gesellschaft*. Frankfurt: Suhrkamp.
Luhmann, N. (2004). *Law as a Social System*. Oxford: Oxford University Press.
Lukes, S. (1974). *Power: A Radical View*. London: Palgrave.
Lynch, M. (1997). *Scientific Practice and Ordinary Action: Ethnomethodology and Social Studies of Science*. Cambridge: Cambridge University Press.
McCarthy, T. (1995). Legitimacy and Diversity: Dialectical Reflections on Analytical Distinctions. *Cardozo Law Review*, 17, 1083–1126.
McCarthy, T. (2001). Die politische Philosophie und das Problem der Rasse. In L. Wingert and K. Gunther (eds), *Die Öffentlichkeit der Vernunft und die Vernunft der Öffentlichkeit: Festschrift für Jürgen Habermas*. Frankfurt am Main: Suhrkamp.

McCombs, M. (2004). *Setting the Agenda: The Mass Media, and American Politics.* Oxford: Wiley.
McIntyre, A. (1981). *After Virtue: A Study in Moral Theory.* London: Allen Lane.
Mannheim, K. (1935). *Ideology and Utopia: an Introduction to the Sociology of Knowledge.* London: Routledge & Kegan Paul.
Mansbridge, J., Bohman, J., Chambers, S., Estlund, D., Follesdal, A., Fung, A. (2010). The Place of Self Interest and the Role of Power in Deliberative Democracy. *Journal of Political Philosophy*, *18*(1), 64–100.
Mayhew, L. (1997). *The New Public: Professional Communication and the Means of Social Influence.* Cambridge: Cambridge University Press.
Mead, G. H. (1934). *Mind, Self, and Society from the Standpoint of a Social Behaviourist.* Chicago: University of Chicago Press.
Merton, R. K. (1936). Puritanism, Pietism, and Science. *The Sociological Review*, *28*(1), 1–30.
Merton, R. K. (1938). Science, Technology and Society in Seventeenth Century England. *Osiris*, *4*, 360–632.
Merton, R. K. (1973). The Normative Structure of Science. In *The Sociology of Science.* Chicago: University of Chicago Press.
Meyer, T. (2002). *Media democracy: How the Media Colonize Politics.* Cambridge: Polity Press.
Michelman, F. (1997). How can the People ever Make the Laws? A Critique of Deliberative Democracy. In J. Bohman and W. Rehg (eds), Cambridge, MA: MIT Press.
Miller, D. (1995). *On Nationality.* Oxford: Clarendon Press.
Miller, M. (1986). *Kollektive Lernprozesse: Studien zur Grundlegung einer soziologischen Lerntheorie.* Frankfurt: Suhrkamp.
Miller, M. (1992). Rationaler Dissens. Zur gesellschaftlichen Funktion sozialer Konflikte. In H.-J. Giegel (ed.), *Kommunikation und Konsens in modernen Gesellschaften.* Frankfurt: Suhrkamp.
Miller, M. (2002). Some Theoretical Aspects of Systemic Learning. *Sozialersinn*, *3*, 379–421.
Mills, C. W. (1968). *The Power Elite.* Oxford: Oxford University Press.
Moller, H. G. (2009). *The Moral Fool: A Case for Amorality.* New York: Columbia University Press.
Moody, M., and Thévenot, L. (2000). Forms of Valuing Nature: Arguments and Modes of Justification in French and American Environmental Disputes. In M. Lamont and L. Thévenot (eds), *Rethinking Comparative Cultural Sociology: Repertoires of Evaluation in France and the United States.* Cambridge: Cambridge University Press.

Moravcsik, A. (2005). The European Constitutional Compromise and the Neofunctionalist Legacy. *Journal of European Public Policy* 12(2), 349–386.
Mouffe, C. (1990). Radical Democracy or Liberal Democracy? *Socialist Review*, 2, 57–66.
Mouffe, C. (1996). Radical Democracy or Liberal Democracy? In D. Trend (ed.), *Radical democracy: Identity, citizenship and the State*. New York: Routledge.
Mouffe, C. (2000). *The Democratic Paradox*. London: Verso.
Nash, K. (2007). *Contemporary Political Sociology: Globalization, Politics, and Power.* Oxford: Blackwell.
Negt, O., and Kluge, A. (1993). *Public Sphere and Experience*. Minneapolis: University of Minnesota Press.
Nelkin, D. (ed.) (1992). *Controversy: Politics of Technical Decisions*. Dartmouth: University of Michigan Press.
Nine, C. (2008). A Lockean Theory of Territory. *Political Studies*, 56(1), 148–165.
Nine, C. (2012). *Territory and Global Justice*. Oxford: Oxford University Press.
Nine, C. (2013). Compromise, Democracy, and Territory. *Irish Journal of Sociology*, 20(2), 91–210.
Nino, C. S. (1998). *The Constitution of Deliberative Democracy*. New Haven, CT: Yale University Press.
Niquet, M. (2003). Reziprozität und Befolgungsgültigkeit. Grundzüge einer realistischen Moraltheorie'. In D. Böhler, M. Kettner and G. Skirbeck (ed.), *Reflexion und Verantwortung: Auseinandersetzungen mit Karl-Otto Apel*. Frankfurt: Suhrkamp.
Nussbaum, M. (2000). *Women and Human Development: The Capabilities Approach*. Cambridge: Cambridge University Press.
Nussbaum, M. (2011). Perfectionist Liberalism and Political Liberalism. *Philosophy and Public Affairs*, 39(1), 3–45.
Offe, C. (1987). The Utopia of the Zero Option: Modernity and Modernization as Normative Political Criteria in *Praxis International*, 7(1), 1–24.
Offe, C. (1992). Bindings, Shackles, Brakes: On Self-limitation Strategies. In A. Honneth, T. McCarthy, C. Offe, and A. Wellmer (eds), *Cultural-Political Interventions in the Unfinished Project of Enlightenment*. Cambridge, MA: MIT Press.
O'Mahony, P. (2002). Citizenship, Digitization and Citizen Services in Ireland. In S. W. R. Authority (ed.), *Changing Aspects: ICT supported development in rural areas*. Cork: South Western Regional Authority.
O'Mahony, P. (2009). Sociological Theory, Discourse, and the Cognitive Construction of Participation. *Comparative Sociology*, 8(4), 490–516.
O'Mahony, P. (2010). Habermas and Communicative Power. *Journal of Power*, 3(1), 53–73.

O'Mahony, P. (2011a). Irish Environmental Discourse: Towards an Ecological Ethic? In P. O'Mahony and K. Keohane (eds), *Irish Environmental Politics after the Communicative Turn*. Manchester: Manchester University Press.

O'Mahony, P. (2011b). Social Theory and the Critique of Capitalism in a Communication Society. *Irish Journal of Sociology*, *19*(1), 150–175.

O'Mahony, P., and Delanty, G. (2001). *Rethinking Irish History: Nationalism, Identity, and Ideology*. London: Macmillan.

O'Mahony, P., and O'Sullivan, S. (2006). Procedure and Participation: The Genetically Modified Plants Controversy in the UK and Ireland. In A. Bora and H. Hausendorf (eds), *Analyzing Citizenship Talk: Social Positioning in Political and Legal Decision-Making Processes*. Amsterdam: John Benjamins.

O'Mahony, P., and Schäfer, M. S. (2005). The 'Book of Life' in the Press: Comparing German and Irish Media Discourse on Human Genome Research. *Social Studies of Science*, *35*(1), 99–130.

O'Mahony, P. (ed.) (1999). *Nature, Risk and Responsibility: Discourses of Biotechnology*. London: Macmillan.

O'Sullivan, S. (2011). Towards Democratic Justice. *Irish Journal of Public Policy* 3(2).

Park, R. E. (1972). *The Crowd and the Public, and Other Essays*. Chicago: University of Chicago Press.

Parkinson, J., and Mansbridge, J. (eds). (2012). *Deliberative Systems: Deliberative Democracy at the Large Scale*. Cambridge: Cambrridge University Press.

Parsons, T. (1963). On the Concept of Political Power. *Proceedings of the American Philosophical Association*, *107*, 232–262.

Parsons, T. (1967). *Sociological Theory and Modern Society*. New York: The Free Press.

Pateman, C. (1976). *Participation and Democratic Theory*. Cambridge: Cambridge University Press.

Peters, B. (1993). *Die Integration moderner Gesellschaften*. Frankfurt: Suhrkamp.

Peters, B. (2001). Deliberative Öffentlichkeit. In K. L. G. Wingert (ed.), *Die Öffentlichkeit der Vernunft und die Vernunft der Öffentlichkeit: Festschrift für Jürgen Habermas*. Frankfurt am Main: Suhrkamp.

Peters, B. (2008). *Public Deliberation and Public Culture; The Writings of Bernhard Peters 1993–2005*. London: Palgrave Macmillan.

Piaget, J. (1932). *The Moral Judgement of the Child*. London: Routledge.

Pettit, P. (1998). Reworking Sandel's republicanism. *The Journal of Philosophy*, *95(2)* (2), 73–96.

Pettit, P. (1999). *Republicanism: A Theory of Freedom and Government*. Oxford: Oxford University Press.

Pharo, P. (2004). *Morale et Sociologie: Le Sens et les Valeurs entre Nature et Culture*. Paris: Gallimard.

Philp, M. (2007). *Political Conduct*. Cambridge, MA: Harvard University Press.

Philp, M. (2010). What is to be Done? Political Theory and Political Realism. *European Journal of Political Theory*, *9*(4), 466–484.
Powell, W. W., and DiMaggio, P. J. (1991) *The New Institutionalism in Organizational Analysis*. Chicago: University of Chicago Press.
Putnam, H. (2002). *The Collapse of the Fact/Value Dichotomy and Other Essays*. Cambridge, MA: Harvard University Press.
Rawls, J. (1971). *A Theory of Justice*. Cambridge, MA: Harvard University Press.
Rawls, J. (1985). Justice as Fairness: Political not Metaphysical. *Philosophy and Public Affairs*, *14*(3), 223–251.
Rawls, J. (1993). *Political Liberalism*. New York: Columbia University Press.
Rawls, J. (1997). The Idea of Public Reason Revisited. *The University of Chicago Law Review*, *64*(3), 765–807.
Rawls, J. (1999). *The Law of Peoples*. Cambridge, MA: Harvard University Press.
Rawls, J. (2001). *Justice as Fairness: A Restatement*. Cambridge, MA: Harvard University Press.
Rehg, W. (1994). *Insight and Solidarity: A Study in the Discourse Ethics of Jürgen Habermas*. Berkeley: University of California Press.
Rehg, W., and Bohman, J. (eds). (2001). *Pluralism and the Pragmatic Turn: The Transformation of Critical Theory*. Cambridge, MA: MIT Press.
Rorty, R. (1982). *Consequences of Pragmatism: Essays, 1972–1980*. Minneapolis: University of Minnesota Press.
Rorty, R. (1991). The Priority of Democracy to Philosophy. *Objectivity, Relativism and Truth*, 178–196.
Rose, N. (1999). *Powers of Freedom: Reframing Political Thought*. Cambridge: Cambridge University Press.
Rosenfeld, M. (1998). Can Rights, Democracy, and Justice be Reconciled through Discourse Theory. In M. Rosenfeld, A. Arato (eds), *Habermas on Law and Democracy: Critical Exchanges*. Berkeley: University of California Press.
Sabatier, P. A., and Jenkins-Smith, H. C. (1993). *Policy Change and Learning: An Advocacy Coalition Approach*. Boulder, CO: Westview Press.
Sandel, M. J. (1984). The Procedural Republic and the Unencumbered Self. *Political Theory*, *12*(1), 81–96.
Sandel, M. J. (1996). *Democracy's Discontent*. Cambridge, MA: Belknap Press of Harvard University Press.
Sandel, M. J. (1998). *Liberalism and the Limits of Justice*. Cambridge: Cambridge University Press.
Sartori, G. (1987). *The Theory of Democracy Revisited*. Chatham, NJ: Chatham House.

Saward, M. (2002). Rawls and Deliberative Democracy. In M. Passerin-D'Entreves (ed.), *Democracy as Public Deliberation: New perspectives*. Manchester: Manchester University Press.

Schapiro, I. (1986). *The Evolution of Rights in Liberal Theory*. New York: Cambridge University Press.

Schapiro, I. (2005). *The State of Democratic Theory*. Princeton, NJ: Princeton University Press.

Schimank, U. (1996). *Theorien Gesellschaftlicher Differenzierung*. Opladen: Leske and Budrich.

Schnadelbach, H. (1987). What is Neo-Aristotelianism? *Praxis International*, *7*(3–4), 225–238.

Schon, D. A., and Rein, M. (1994). *Frame Reflection: Towards the Resolution of Intractable Policy Controversies*. New York: Basic Books.

Schumpeter, J. A. (1942). *Capitalism, Socialism, and Democracy*. New York: Harper Bros.

Scott, R. W. (2001). *Institutions and Organisations*. London: Sage.

Seidman, S. (1983). *Liberalism and the Origins of European Social Theory*. Berkeley: University of California Press.

Seligman, A. B. (1995) *The Idea of Civil Society*. Princeton, NJ: Princeton University Press.

Sen, A. (2009). *The Idea of Justice*. London: Allen Lane.

Shklar, J. N. (1991). *American citizenship: The Quest for Inclusion*. Cambridge, MA: Harvard University Press.

Shklar, J. N. (1992). *The Faces of Injustice*. New Haven, CT: Yale University Press.

Sintomer, Y. (2011). Democratie Participative et Imperatif Deliberatif: Enjeux d'une Confrontation. In M. H. Bacqué and Y. Sintomer (eds), *La Démocratie Participative: Histoire et Généalogie*. Paris: La Découverte.

Skillington, T. (1997). Politics and the Struggle to Define: A Discourse Analysis of the Framing Strategies of Competing Actors in a 'New' Participatory Forum. *British Journal of Sociology*, *48*(3), 493–513.

Skillington, T. (2012). Climate Change and the Human Rights Challenge: Reframing Justice beyond the Borders of the Nation State. *International Journal of Human Rights*, *16*(8), 1196–1212.

Skillington, T. (2013a). Climate Change and Cosmopolitan Justice: Expanding the Scope of Peace or Violence in a Resource Challenged World? *Irish Journal of Sociology*, *20*(2), 132–152.

Skillington, T. (2013b). The Borders of Contemporary Europe: Territory, Justice, Rights. In L. Bora and A. Czajka (eds), *Europe after Derrida*. Edinburgh: Edinburgh University Press.

Skillington, T. (2014). *Climate Justice and Human Rights*. London: Palgrave.
Somers, M. R. (1993). Citizenship and the Place of the Public Sphere: Law, Community, and Political Culture in the Transition to Democracy. *American Sociological Review*, 587–620.
Somers, M. R. (1995a). What's Political or Cultural about Political Culture and the Public Sphere? Toward an Historical Sociology of Concept Formation. *Sociological Theory*, *13*(2), 113–144.
Somers, M. R. (1995b). Narrating and Naturalizing Civil Society and Citizenship Theory: The Place of Political Culture and the Public Sphere. *Sociological Theory*, *13*(3), 229–274.
Somers, M. R. (2008). *Genealogies of Citizenship: Markets, Statelessness, and the Right to have Rights*. Cambridge: Cambridge University Press.
Splichal, S. (1999). *Public Opinion: Developments and Controversies in the Twentieth Century*. Lanham, MD: Rowman and Littlefield.
Splichal, S. (2006). In Search of a Strong European Public Sphere: Some Critical Observations on Conceptualizations of Publicness and the (European) Public Sphere. *Media, Culture and Society*, *28*(5), 695–714.
Splichal, S. (2010). Eclipse of 'the public': From the Public to (Transnational) Public Sphere. Conceptual Shifts in the Twentieth Century. In J. Gripsrud, and H. Moe (eds), *The Digital Public Sphere: Challenges for Media Policy*. Göteborg: Nordicom, Göteborgs Universitet.
Stehr, N. (2001). *Knowledge Politics: Governing the Consequences of Science and Technology*. Boulder, CO: Paradigm.
Streeck, W. (2009). *Re-Forming Capitalism: Institutional Change in the German Political Economy*. Oxford: Oxford University Press.
Strydom, P. (1987). Collective Learning: Habermas's Concessions and their Theoretical Implications. *Philosophy and Social Criticism*, *13*(3), 265–281.
Strydom, P. (1999). Triple contingency: The Theoretical Problem of the Public in Communication Society. *Philosophy & Social Criticism*, *25*(2), 1–25.
Strydom, P. (2000). *Discourse and Knowledge: The Making of Enlightenment Sociology*. Liverpool: Liverpool University Press.
Strydom, P. (2003). Resonance: Triggering a Dormant Dimension of the Public Sphere. In V. Kultygin and V. Shukov (eds), *European Social Theory*. Moscow: European Sociological Association.
Strydom, P. (2006). Contemporary European cognitive Social Theory. In G. Delanty (ed.), *Handbook of Contemporary European Social Theory*. London: Routledge.
Strydom, P. (2007). Introduction: A cartography of Contemporary Cognitive Social Theory: Special Issue on 'Social Theory after the Cognitive Revolution: Types

of Contemporary Cognitive Sociology'. *European Journal of Social Theory*, *10*(3), 339–356.
Strydom, P. (2011). *Contemporary Critical Theory and Methodology*. London: Routledge.
Strydom, P. (2012). Cosmopolitanism, the Cognitive Order of Modernity, and Conflicting Models of World Openness: On the Prospects of Collective Learning. In A. Giri (ed.), *Cosmopolitanism and Beyond: Towards A Multiverse of Transformations*. India: Duwamish Books.
Strydom, P. (2013). On the Age of Responsibility: The Responsibility Discourse, and the Prospects of a Responsible Society: Approches Multidisciplinaires. In A. Marchildon and A. Duhamel (eds), *Quels Lendemains pour la Responsibilite*. Quebec.
Sunstein, C. R. (1988). Beyond the Republican Revival. *Yale Law Journal*, *97*, 1493–1537.
Sunstein, C. R. (2002). *Republic.com*. Princeton, NJ: Princeton University Press.
Tarrow, S. (1998). *Power in Movement: Collective Action, Social Movements and Politics*. Cambridge: Cambridge University Press.
Taylor, C. (1989). *Sources of the Self: The Making of the Modern Identity*. Cambridge, MA: Harvard University Press.
Taylor, C. (2004). *Modern Social Imaginaries*. Durham, NC: Duke University Press.
Teubner, G., and Korth, P. (2010). Two Kinds of Legal Pluralism: Collision of Transnational Regimes in the Double Fragmentation of World Society. In M. Young (ed.), *Regime Interaction in International Law: Facing Fragmentation*. Oxford: Oxford University Press.
Thévenot, L., Moody, M., and Lafaye, C. (2000). Comparing Models of Strategy, Interests and the Public Good in French and American Environmental Disputes. In M. Lamont and L. Thévenot (eds), *Rethinking Comparative Cultural Sociology: Repertoires of Evaluation in France and the United States*. Cambridge: Cambridge University Press.
Tönnies, F. (1992). *Kritik der öffentlichen Meinung*. Berlin: Springer.
Touraine, A. (1971). *The Post-industrial Society: Tomorrow's Social History: Classes, Conflicts and Culture in the Programmed Society*. New York: Random House.
Touraine, A. (1977). *The Self-Production of Society*. Chicago: University of Chicago Press.
Touraine, A. (1981). *The Voice and the Eye: An Analysis of Social Movements*. Cambridge: Cambridge University Press.
Touraine, A. (1995). *Critique of Modernity*. Oxford: Blackwell:.
Touraine, A. (1997). *What is Democracy*. Boulder, CO: Westview.
Trenz, H.-J., and Eder, K. (2004). The Democratizing Dynamics of a European Public Sphere: Towards a Theory of Democratic Functionalism. *European Journal of Social Theory*, *7*(1), 5–25.

Trubek, D. M., Dezalay, Y., Buchanan, R., and Davis, J. R. (1995). Global Resructuring and the Law: Studies of the Internatinalization of Legal Fields and the Creation of Transnational Arenas. *Case Western Reserve Law Review, 44*, 407–498.
Tschentscher, A. (1997). The Function of Procedural Justice in Theories of Justice. In K. F. Rohl and S. Machura (eds), *Procedural Justice*. Aldershot: Ashgate.
Turner, S. P. (2010). *Explaining the Normative*. Cambridge: Polity Press.
Vester, M., v. Oertzen, P., Geiling, P., Hermann, T., and Müller, D. (1993). *Soziale Milieus im gesellschaltlichen Structurwandel*. Köln: Bund-Verlag.
Von Trotha, T. (2006). Perspektiven der politischen Soziologie. *Soziologie, 35*(3), 283–302.
Walzer, M. (1990). The Communitarian Critique of Liberalism. *Political Theory, 18*(1), 6–23.
Warren, M. E. (2001). *Democracy and Association*. Princeton, NJ: Princeton University Press.
Warren, M. E. (2007). Institutionalizing Deliberative Democracy. In S. W. Rosenberg (ed.), *Deliberation, Participation, and Democracy: Can the People Govern*. London: Palgrave Macmillan.
Weber, M., and Kalberg, S. (2001). *The Protestant Ethic and the Spirit of Capitalism*. London: Routledge.
Wellmer, A. (2000). *Endgames: The Irreconcilable Nature of Modernity: Essays and Lectures*. Cambridge, MA: MIT Press.
Wenzel, H. (2005). Social Order as Communication: Parson's Theory on the Move from Moral Consensus to Trust. In R. C. Fox, V. M. Lidz, and H. J. Bershady (eds), *After Parsons: A Theory of Social Action for the 21st Century*. New York: Russell Sage Foundation.
Williams, B. A. O. (2005). *In the Beginning was the Deed: Realism and Moralism in Political Argument*. Princeton, NJ: Princeton University Press.
Willke, H. (1992). *Ironie des Staates: Grundlinien einer Staatstheorie polyzentrischer Gesellschaft*. Frankfurt: Suhrkamp.
Young, I. M. (2000). *Inclusion and Democracy*. Oxford: Oxford University Press.
Young, I. M. (2010). Representation and Social Perspective. In M. L. Krook, and S. Childs (eds), *Women, Gender, and Politics: A Reader*. Oxford: Oxford University Press.
Zaret, D. (1992). Religion, Science, and Printing in the Public Spheres in Seventeenth-century England. In C. Calhoun (ed.), *Habermas and the Public Sphere*. Cambridge, MA: MIT Press.
Zerubavel, E. (1997). *Social Mindscapes: An Invitation to Cognitive Sociology*. Cambridge, MA: Harvard University Press.
Zolo, D. (1992). *Democracy and Complexity: A Realist Approach*. Philadelphia: Pennsylvania State University Press.

Index

Abduction 263, 273, 344, 346
Abortion 30, 42, 306
Academics, standpoint of 3, 39, 62, 74,
    193, 243, 321, 334, 337, 366, 391,
    404, 405, 411, 413–414, 424, 439,
    448, 451, 463–464
Administration 24, 25, 124, 181, 183, 186,
    188, 191, 207, 232, 293, 227, 228,
    fn 11, 230, 287, 296, 324, 326, 377,
    391, 393, 394–395, 400, 402–403,
    405, 412, 413
Adorno, Theodor 13, 93
Agency 2, 4, 5, 8, 10, 16, 17, 33, 43, 45, 71,
    72, 79, 80, fn 5, 95, 96–97, 102,
    106, 132, 136, 138, 139, 141, 150,
    166, 169, 175, 176, 178, fn 8, 198,
    200–201, 202, 205, 209, 215, 216–
    222, 228, 230–231, 236, 243, 246,
    257, 258, 259, 261–276, 277, 279,
    315, 316, 317, 318, 320, 323, 324, 325,
    339, 340, 341, 342, 343, 344–346,
    358, 390, 396, 402, 418, 424, 429,
    430, 435, 445, 452fn, 454, 455
Agonistic 5, 91, 92, 95, 96
Anthropology 213, 215, 316
Apel, Karl-Otto 32–33, 64, 113, 164–170,
    179–180, 205, 218, 242, 298, 302,
    307, 308–309, 415, 434
Archer, Margaret 261, 270
Arendt, Hannah 71, 81, 207
Argumentation 11, 26, 28, 30, 33, 80,
    130, 136, 141, 142, 143, 150, 155,
    167–168, 172, 174, 178, 179,
    182, 195, 217, 218, 233, 253, 274,
    277–278, 289, 292, 295, 299, 307,
    310, 327–328, 332, 336, 338, 346,
    348, 355, 356, 359, 360, 366, 369,
    391, 393, 395, 398, 423, 423–433,
    436, 464
Association 8, 55, 60, 66, 67–68, 102,
    106, 115, 122, 148, 185, 186, 190,
    196, 201, 217, 220, 225, 227, 275,
    294, 297, 302, 321, 331, 336, 337,
    338, 365, 378, 379, 391, 395–399,
    402, 403–406, 412, 422, 424,
    425, 426, 428, 429, 430
Authoritarianism 31, 92, 94, 98, 101,
    211–212, 303, 309, 312, 324, 325,
    339, 341, 450
Authority, Political, *see* governance
Autonomy 8, 18, 24, 95, 96, 104, 105, 123,
    151, 152, 158, 166, 171–172, 175,
    180, 182, 184, 187–188, 189–190,
    200, 204, 224, 228, 243, 247, 254,
    263, 266, 267, 268, 272, 280, 306,
    316, 323, 323, 324, 327, 331, 332,
    362, 380, 381, 361, 392, 393, 402,
    415–416, 417, 425, 426, 427, 444,
    451, 461
    private 12, 41, 51, 53, 91, 114, 115,
        136, 137, 177, 224–225, 256,
        309, 383
    public 12, 46, 53, 56, 64–67, 69,
        71–89, 91, 93, 134, 136, 142, 173,
        177, 181, 191–192, 211, 225–226,
        229, 256, 295, 369, 410–411,
        456–457, 458, 459, 461
    see also public sovereignty

Bacon, Frances 405
Barber, Benjamin 103
Benhabib, Seyla 57–58, 62, 102
Bentham, Jeremy 357–359
Bohman, James 21, 22, 45, 77, 85–88, 89, 91, 137, 277, 359, 376, 386, 441, 445–446, 446, 449, 454–455, 456, 361
Boltanski, Luc 6, 30, 42–43, 84, 265, 273–275
Boudon, Raymond 260
Bourdieu, Pierre 12, 84, 152, 261–264, 267–268, 270, 271, 273, 305, 313, 315–317, 319, 341, 368, 402, 410, 440, 441
Bouvier, Alban 260
Bourgeois 9–23, 373, 400
    bourgeois-masculinist public sphere 18, 21
Brunkhorst, Hauke 456
Bufacchi, Vittorio 40, fn 2
Burns, Tom 139, 454–456

Capabilities 60, 267
Capitalism 13–15, 40, fn 1, 50, fn 1, 61, fn 13, 92, 106, 191, 204, 216, fn 8, 297, 301, 329, 441, 450
Castoriadis, Cornelius 94–97, 101
Charney, Evan 67–68
Cicourel, Aaron 263, 264–265, 268, 276, 278, 317
Citizenship 7, 8, 10, 19, 41, 43–44, 50–51, 53–56, 58–59, 62, 65–67, 75, 79, 82, 86, 87, 93, 100, 104, 105, 112, 115, 120–121, 130, 132–135, 138, 139, 149, fn 12, 151, fn 1, 157, 183, 188, 320, 332, 357–358, 361–363, 380–381, 383, 385, 394, 397, 400, 414, 440, 444, 454–455, 461
Civil society 7, 8, 17, 21, 24, 55, fn 8, 56, 58, 65, 67–69, 81, 91, 94, 96, 102, 105–107, 114–115, 122, 127, 145, 148, 150, 182, 183, 184, 185, 186, 208, 210, 211, 225, 227, 229, 230, 232, 234, 324, 326, 326, 336–337, 349, 351, 380–381, 389, 390–391, 395–401, 403–406, 412–413, 418, 419, 422–430, 442, 444, 453, 455
Class 1, 2, 75, 185, 191, 297, 302, 306, 313, 329, 369, 402, 457
Cognitive 103, 140, 254–259, 264, 356–357, 377–378, 380, 387, 412, 415, 444
    cognitive-normative relation 152, 159, 197, 206, 222, 236, 253, 280, 281–282, 283–284, 288, 293–314, 356, 361, 380, 387, 393, 396, 403, 407, 409, 413–414, 461, 462
    cultural models 80, 170, 289, 292, 386, 413
    order 35, 36, 39, 47, 92, fn 1, 97, fn 5, 221, 288, 290–291, 292, 355, 361–371, 409–410, 411, 416–418
    rule systems 201, 282, 288, 291, 292, 382
    sociology 31, 34–35, 47, 101, 150, 159, 164, 165, 223, 253, 254, 259–280, 281, 283, 286, 315–351, 389, 445, 446–458, 463–465
    structures 16, 36, 80, 156, 157, 159, 196, 221, 254, 289, 290–291, 385, 393
    see also counterfactual, democratic, immanent, learning, normative, public, transcendent
Common good 18, 20, 27, 40, 54, 66, 71, 75, 88, fn 11, 99, 118, 120, 294, 343, 396–398, 404, 406
Communication community 23, 33, 84, 167–169, 174, 195, 249, 293, 298–304, 318
Communitarian 65, 71–74, 77, 80, 81, 83–84, 87, 88, 111, 146, 172, 191,

Index

213, 233, 254, fn 1, 232, fn 13, 313,
 fn 4, 328, 331, 375, 390, 436
Community 10, 19, 23, 41, 42, 65, 71–74,
 77, 80, 82–84, 85, 86, 88, 94, 99,
 115, 116, 122, 123, 141, 150, 173, 188,
 190, 225, 240, 245, 247, 249, 275,
 294, 375, 385, 398, 456
Competition, political 32, 46, 96,
 109–127, 157, 203, 253, 297, 260
Compromise 28, 43, 112, 114,142, 155,
 160, 219, 246, 251, 293, 297,
 307–313, 325, 329, 330, 333–336,
 338, 350, fn 7, 421, 422, 453
Conflict 12, 20, 21, 28, 43, 91, 94, 95,
 96, 102, 114, 118, 146, 153, 168,
 172, 175 188, 196, 201, 204, 214,
 241, 253, 262, 274, 282, 287,
 289, 299, 305–309, 311–313, 321,
 326–27, 329, 333, 343, 348, 366,
 394, 422, 449, 450, 454, 457,
 464, 465
Connolly, William 96, 97
Consequential 5, 77–81, 82, 414
Conservatism 61, fn 13, 329
Constitutional 8, 9, 13–15, 17, 19, 23–25,
 28, 29, 47, 49, 50, 50, 50 fn 1, 52,
 54–57, 59, 62, 67–69, 78, 96, 109,
 113, 125, 126, 142, 146, 173, 182,
 184, 195, 209, 218, 220, 221, 225,
 232, 235, 237, 241, 303, 307, 308,
 310, 315, 316, 316, fn 1, 317, 329,
 344, 369, 370, 380, 395, 396, 396,
 fn 1, 418, 436, 440, 442, 443,
 445, 452, 453, 456, 457
 informal constitutionalization 113,
 195, 209, 232, 235, 452
Constructivism 2, fn 2, 19, 47–48, 49,
 62, fn 15, 132, 141, 151, 156, 157,
 160, 164, 171, 172, 193, 197, 199,
 202, 204, 221, 222, 243, 246, 262,
 263, 265, 268, 283–285, 288, 315,

366, 368, 369, 389, 409, 440, 448,
 449, 451, fn 3, 462, 465
Consumption 378, 379, 385, 399
Contestability 77, 80, 81, 100, fn 7,
 357
Controversy 268, 393–394, 411
Co-operation, system of 82, 88, 88, fn 12,
 147, 174, 175, 277, 291–292, 305,
 309, 327, 341, 343, 451
Cosmopolitanism 19, 22–23, 36, 89, 233,
 325, 328, 439–458
Counter-cultural 399, 420, 430
Counterfactual 6, 11, 11, fn 5, 12, 16, 23,
 29, 57, 61–64, 69, 84, 121, 130, 130,
 fn 2, 134, 135, 137, 138, 141, 143,
 149, 150, 159, 160, 167, 169, 177,
 181, 182, 193, 196, 197, 198, 204,
 205, 206, 209, 216, 221, 231, 239,
 240, 242, 289, 290, 296, 298–301,
 303, 309, 316, 318, 327, 336, 338,
 343, 358, 361, 363, 367, 401, 432,
 433–437, 444, 445, 451, fn 3, 458,
 459, 465
Critique 2, 3, 15, 16, 22, 25, 31, 32, 34, 47,
 53, fn 2, 62, fn, 14, 114, 151, 157,
 163, 164, 170, 188, 193, 198, 207,
 209, 213, 214, 215, 217, 240, 259,
 268, 273, 275, 284, 287, 290, 300,
 321, 325, 331, 344, 363, 365, 370,
 399, 401, 409, 421, 433, 437, 459,
 461, 463, 465
Culture, political 17, 30, 39, 42, 54–57,
 60, 63, 64, 153, 154, 154, fn 3, 191,
 331, 337, 362, 363, 383, 398, 425,
 448

Deduction 260, 346
Democracy 10–12, 41–42, 324, 329,
 347
 communication theory of 39–47,
 212–213, 246–249, 254, 275,

276–278, 280, 285, 289–290,
356–355, 364–365, 374, 380,
402–403, 462–463
see also public communication
deliberative democracy 2, 27, 32,
40–42, 44–46, 56–60, 71, 76–77,
81, 84, 87–88, 129–150, 151–160,
197, 219, 277, 282, 287, 361, 407
democracy-society relation 5, 16,
19–20, 163–192, 179–192, 195, 211,
fn 5, 217, 291–292, 366–377, 369,
410, 416, 464
democratic elitism 114, 117, 118–121,
127
democratic functionalism 445
democratic innovation 86, 100–101,
207, 211–212, 291, 342, 411, 451,
454–455
see also democratization, public
participation
democratic inquiry 415, 446
democratic legitimacy 26–28, 81, 114,
322, 345
democratic minimum 153, 444
democratic procedures, *see* justice,
democratic
democratic publicity 2, 2, fn 2, 6,
7–9, 14, 16, 26–29, 31, 36, 42,
88, 99, 106, 134–136, 142, 168,
172, 177, 256, 286, 320, 323–324,
357–361, 373, 375, 382, 393–394,
397, 399–400, 404, 411–423, 453,
456, 467, 459, 462
democratic theory 3, 6, 16, 21, 32–34,
37–160, 158–160, 165, 197–198,
223–249, 302, 343, 364, 403,
fn 3, 421
democratization 17, 22, 34, 85–86,
94, 105, 110, 196, 273, 331–332,
334–335, 336, 342, 343–344,
355, 384, 387, 397, 413–414, 416,
433–437, 439, 445

discursive democracy 6, 189, 226,
263, 439
see also public discourse
economic theory of 110, 119–120
formal democracy 6, 47, 85, 101, 109,
211, 310, 334, 337, fn 5, 383, 406,
446
see also public participation
majoritarian 27, 77, 118, 127, 133, 136,
137, 137, fn 7, 138, 211, 290, 301,
308, 309, 358, 454
radical 3, 32, 39–47, 91–107, 109, 111,
fn 1, 113, 117, 129, 132, 134, 135, 136,
139, fn 7, 140, 142–143, 145, 146,
152, 156, 163, 166, 176, 192, 193,
198, 199, 210, fn 4, 217, 225, 226,
229, 235, 248, 359, 380, 385, 397,
403, fn 3, 412 416, 421–422,
436, 464
social 40, fn 1, 50–51, fn 1, 61, fn 13,
94, 365
transnational 21–23, 36, 439–458
see also autonomy, cognitive, justice,
liberalism, normative, public,
political realism, republicanism
Deontological 5, 73, 77–81, 92, 97, fn
4, 99–101, 112, 113, fn 3, 139, fn 7,
147, 164, 172–173, 193–222, 226,
390, 434
Derrida, Jacques 17
Dewey, John 8, 11, 40, fn 2, 46, 65, 88,
fn 12, 129, 153, 196, 275, 358, 415,
459, 461
Diachronic 147, 220, 370, 371, 404
Discourse ethics 5, 24, 28, 33, 34, 130,
fn 2, 157, 158, 160, 163–192, 193–
197, 200, 204, 209, 214, 217–218,
223, 228, 231, 234, 238, 240, 241,
246, 253, 284, 292, 295, 295, 298,
302, 316, 326, 355, 367, 420, 422
Dissensus, rational 20, 28, 153, 159, 160,
219, 233, 277, 289, 291, 205, 297,

Index 491

307–311, 313, 327, 330, 333, 334, 348, 366, 367, 421–422, 453
Domination 6, 8, 14, 15, 17, 21, 98, 105, 112, 116, 118, 120, 151, 157, 209, 210, 233, 244, 267, 305–307, 313, 332, 333, 380, 382, 437
   non-domination 74–86, 100, fn 7, 145, 152, 159, 168, 171, 174, 177, 311, 367, 436
   see also critique, freedom
Down, Anthony 110
Dryzek, John 102, 129, 131–132, 135–136, 142
Durkheim, Emile 85, 93, 242, 262, 264, 271, 282, 291, 302, 341

Eastern Europe 67–68, 397, 403
Ecology, *see* environment
Economy 13, 40, fn 1, 50, fn 1, 51, 53, 54, 59, 61, fn 12, 83, 104, 105, 110, 114, 115, 122, 137, 148, 184, 185, 186, 188, 208, 209, 227, 230, 237, fn 16 241, 255, 256, 273, 300, 304, 306, 307, 323, 324, 329, 330, 337, 343, 345, 346, 350, 368, 370, 371, 379, 381, 392, 395, 400, 403, 405, 406, 416, 420, 441, 442, 443, 448, 450, 452, 453, 461
Elias, Norbert 271
Elitism 4, 42, 57, 99, 109, 114, 115, 117, 118–121, 126, 127, 157, 183, 231, 246, 310, 360, 365, 440
Elkin, Stephen 112
Elster, Jan 302
Emancipation 14–17, 405
Emirbayer, Mustafa 261, 368
Emotion 146, 177, 213, 214, 235, 257, 308, 384
Enlightenment 2, 13, 23, 73, 171, 179, 382, 405
Environment 5, 137, 139, 158, 178, 187, 206, 220, 232, 258, 266, 294, 301, 306, 308, 314, 325, 329, 340, 343, 346, 348, 414, 429, 449
Epistemology 1, 2, 32, 46, 115, 130–132, 156, 197, 240, 279, 283, 315, 350, 369
   communicative 85, 157, 164, 165–179
   see also constructivism
Equality, inequality 4, 5, 7, 8, 13, 15, 18, 19, 42, 50, 50, fn 2, 51, 52, 53, 54, 66, 69, 87, fn 11, 93, 96. 99. 101, 102, 114, 137, 148, 158, 175, 177, 182, 184, 194, 201, 204, 213, 249, 284, 295, 297, 307, 310, 324, 340, 345, 358, 417, 436
Esping-Andersen 40, fn 1
Ethical 2, 5, 25, 28, 32, 34, 35, 41, 46, 47, 65, 66, 80, 82, 83, 84, 86, 89, 96, 111, 112, 131, 135, 146, 155, 156, 166–170, 173, 175, 177–183, 188, 190, 196, 204–206, 213, 219, 232–236, 245–247, 254, 261, 262, 264, 265, 266, 268, 272–279, 293, 294–297, 299, 300, 302–304, 306, 307, 309, 322–330, 335, 350, 366, 368, 370, 377, 395, 403, 412, 419, 420, 427, 428, 453
   see also communitarianism, community, discourse ethics
European Union 439–458
Expertise 121, 153, 154, 190, 350, 363, 382–383, 400, 405, 446, 450, 454

Feminism 17, 18, 94, 102, 106, 186, 220, 225, 227, 329, 347, 401, 426
Ferree, Myra Max 30, 39, 42, 44, 157, 255
Finnemore, Martha 457
Forst, Rainer 6, 10, 50, 99–101, 130, 209–210, 216, 233, 244, 245, 249, 297, 337, 343, 410, 429, 451, 451, fn 3, 452
Foucault, Michel 93, 377, 405

Fraser, Nancy 6, 16, 18–23, 27, 92, 97, 97, fn 4, 97, fn 5, 99–102, 105, 185, 209, 287, 461
Freedom 4, 5, 8, 44, 50, 51, 67, 77, 78, 79, 81, 85, 98, 114, 116, 118, 135, 157, 166, 180, 201, 224, 225, 254, 304, 309, 323, 332, 333, 341, 357, 369, 381, 395, 400, 417–418, 428, 430, 437, 442, 459, 463
  communicative 85, 86, 89, 225, 357, 381
  as non-domination, *see* domination
Functional, *see* functional power, Luhmann, pragmatic, Willke

Galston, William 111, 112, 127, fn 9
Gamson, William 337
Gaus, Gerard 56
Gender 21, 209, 218, 300, 306, 329, 337, 369, 401, 402
Genetically modified crops 306
Global 29, 84, fn 7, 86, 169, 186, 284, 342–343, 375, 381, 384, 386, 402, 439, 451, 461, 465, 470
Goffman, William 245, 278, 279, 337
Gottweis, Hubert 98, 403, fn 3
Governance 15, 25, 60–68, 89, 71, 75, 80, 82, 96, 104, 109, 110, 112, 115, 118, 119, 124, 125, 126, 136, 137, 137, fn 6, 140, 149, 153, 172, 186, 194, 212, 224, 229, 265, 287, 289, 335, 343, 355, 358, 359, 360, 363, 377, 393, 394, 397, 399, 400, 404, 405, 413, 416, 418, 424, 428, 440, 442–448, 459, 451, 454–456
  see also democracy, power, public
Gutmann, Amy 58–59, 62, 77

Habermas, Jürgen 2–3, 6, 7, 8, 9–34, 41–43, 44, 57, 77
Habitus 156, 193, 261, 262, 267, 271, 313–314, 402, 448

Haraway, Donna 91
Hauser, Gerard 27–28
Hegel, Georg W. 12, 66, 84, 189, 198, 334, 379
Hermeneutic 64, 228, 405
Historicity 94, 156, 221, 476
Hobbes, Thomas 43, 59, 62, 64, 112, 115, 116, 119, 122, 123, 190, 394
Honneth, Axel 12, 29, 30, 32, 33, 43, 46, 101–102, 148, 156, 168, 198, 209, 210, 212–217, 228, 245, 302, 312, 334, 335, 339, 369, 463
Honig, Bonnie 91–92, 95, 97, 111, 113

Identity 17, 19, 22, 26, 61, 62, 86, 91, 92, 97, 105, 107, 114, 156, 181, 234, 235, 241, 244, 245, 246, 270, 275, 276, 287, 306, 325, 326, 329, 340, 341, 368, 369, 378, 386, 401, 403, 414, 418, 441, 444, 454
  see also ethical
Ideology 10, 13, 15, 29, 39, 41, 72, 79, 122, 127, 143, 154, 156, 157, 166, 203, 206, 233, 236, 237, 253, 267, 289, 290, 297, 306, 312, 324, 325, 329, 331, 336, 337, 339, 340, 344, 346, 361–366, 381, 383, 398, 402, 421, 424, 437, 450, 451, 454
Imaginary 94, 96, 97, 101, 346, 386
Immanence, social 11, 16, 35, 62–64, 94, 98, 101, 138, 142, 143, 155, 160, 165, 169, 173, 188, 193, 195, 196, 201, 204–206, 213, 214, 221, 224, 226, 240, 257, 258, 260, 261, 268, 285, 292, 298, 310, 316, 319–321, 323, 326, 328–330, 344, 370, 418, 420, 433–434, 436, 445
Induction 260, 346
Inequality, *see* equality
Injustice, *see* justice
Institutions, *see* normative
International relations 180, 447

Index

Internet 14, 375, 376, 378, 385, 386, 387, 425, 427
Intersubjective 32, 64, 66, 79, 94, 116, 131, 151, 152, 157, 158, 159, 166, 167, 168, 171, 174, 175, 176, 178, 179, 181, 192, 225, 228, 238, 243, 260, 262, 274, 277, 283, 286, 288, 295, 303, 338, 339, 344, 358

Joas, Hans 105, 273, 342
Jonas, Hans 203, fn 3
Journalism 378, 379, 424, 425
Justice 40, 42–43, 49–69, 73, 74, 79, 80, 82, 83, 86, 97, 152, 158, 159, 168, 169, 172, 173, 182, 186, 205–210, 212–216, 218, 225, 241, 242–245, 257, 280, 430, 433, 436, 440, 448, 452, 458
  democratic 55, 100, 103, 106, 139, fn 7, 141, 160, 172, 177, 194, 196, 198–207, 207–210, 210, fn 4, 216, 241, 243–244, 302, 324, 329, 343, 363–363, 366, 385, 410, 411, 452
  distributive 60–62, 205, 306, 307, 422, 444, 450
  injustice 32, 60, 80, fn 5, 92, 95, 119, 132, 177, 197–198, 210, 216, 218, 221, 241, 369, 370, 443, 461, 464
  Rawls, principles of 51–54, 59, 61–64, 84, 88–89, 111, 113–114, 155, 157, 178–179, 200–201, 202, fn 2, 206–207, 232
  sense of 55–6
  substantive foundations of 92, 244, 309, 303, 306, 308, 320, 347

Kant, Immanuel 2, 5, 33, 49, 59, 62, 110, 115, 121–122, 152, 167–168, 171, 173, 175, 203, 206, 274, 284, 322, 343, 357, 358, 434, 440, 462
Kelly, Erin 59–60

Knorr-Cetina, Karen 263–265, 268–271, 273, 276, 317
Knowledge 28, 31, 52, 56, 66, 91, 133, 139, 176, 223, 224, 243, 261–263, 269, 271, 274, 285, 299, 318, 322, 334, 338, 368, 377, 387, 396, 404, 409–411, 414–416, 424, 430, 463
Kuhn, Thomas 258

Laclau, Ernesto 91, 92, 95, 97
Lamont, Michele 84
Lange, Stefan 123–125
Latour, Bruno 263
Law 2, 4,18, 20, 23–25, 29, 40, 47, 54, 55, 57, 62, 67, 72, 74, 77, 81–83, 85–86, 91, 93, 101, 102, 104, 109, 111, 112, 116, 122, 124, 126, 132, 135, 146, 149, 150, 155, 156, 158, 167, 169, 170, 172, 173, 175, 177, 181, 182–186, 191, 195, 200, 201, 204–207, 209–218, 223–225, 228–232, 237, 239, 240, 241, 243, 244, 247, 248, 253, 255, 256, 261, 265, 279, 291, 293–297, 209, 302–304, 306, 308, 309, 310, 311, 313, 314, 320, 322–329, 331, 334–336, 339, 342, 345, 348, 349, 351, 358, 366, 369, 370, 391–395, 399, 400, 403, 411–414, 417–420, 427–430, 432, 439–443, 452, 453
  natural law 54, 114–115, 122
  see also constitutional, democracy, normative
Learning, collective 5, 16, 21, 26, 30, 68, 69, 78, 88, 101, 126, 137, 142, 153, fn 2, 159, 164, 167, 177, 179, 187, 188, 194, 197, 205, 206, 207, 211, 212, 215, 219, 220–223, 226, 231, 234, 240, 243, 253, 254, 256, 257, 258, 259, 261, 262, 263265, 266, 267, 268, 269, 270, 271, 272, 275, 276, 277, 279, 280, 281–314, 315,

316, 318–321, 324–328, 330–332, 338–347, 350, 351, 355, 356, 360, 361, 365–371, 389, 394, 406, 409, 414–416, 418 424, 429–433, 437, 440, 443–445, 447–450, 452, 453, 460, 462–464
Lefort, Claude 95–101
Levy, Daniel 445–465
Liberalism 40–42, 45, 46, 47, 49–69, 71–72, 73, 75, 76, 77, 78, 81, 82, 85, 86, 87, fn 11, 92, 93, 95, 96, 97, 98, 99, 102, 105, 107, 110, 111, 112, 113–117, 118, 119, 120, 121, 125, 129, 131, 135, 145, 146, 154, 156, 163, 168, 172, 173, 182, 186, 191, 192, 197, 216, 223, 224, 225, 226, 229, 236, 237, 256, 264, 274, 297, 308, 309, 329, 331, 332, 350, 361, 362, 370, 381, 390, 395, 401, 425, 436, 437, 441, 442, 443, 447, fn2, 451
Libertarianism 50, 107, 115, 118, 119, 331
Linguistic 7, 167, 174, 239, 260, 268, 279, 284, 340
Lippmann, Walter 110, 360
Locke, John 43, 44, 59, 110, 112, 115, 115, fn 5, 123, 152, 166
Luhmann, Niklas 17, 94, 104, 122–127, 184, 187, 189, 199, 200, 201, 202, 203, 205, 211, 214, 230, 235, 236, 237, 242, 243, 263, 254, 254, 266, 267, 268, 279, 294, 315, 316, 316, fn 1, 317, 320, 326, 327, 328, 331, 360, 384, 389, 392, 419, 428, 440
Lukes, Steven 103
Lynch, Michael 127, fn 9, 263, 270

McIntyre, Alasdair 71, 73
Mansbridge, Jennifer 130, fn 2, 142, 146, 148, 359
Marx, Karl 10, 92, 93, 122, 246, 302, 335, 367

Marxism 13, 23, 105, 109, 122, 123, 181, 199, 362, 441, 460
Mead, George Herbert 167, 262, 270, 271, 282, 283, 340, 402
Media 9, 13, 14, 31, 36, 152, 185, 186, 199, 208, 229, 256, 277, 326, 337,339, 356, 360, 371, 373–387, 390 393, 396, 397, 403, 413, 416, 420, 424–428, 452, 456, 460, 462
Mediation 24, 35, 40, fn1, 51, 95, 97,98, 114, 116–118, 126, 127, 131, 139, 148, 150, 151, 157, 175, 176, 179, 181, 185, 191, 200, 215, 221, 224, 227, 241, 242, 262, 266, 267, 272, 274, 277, 279, 283, 288, 293, 296, 297, 305, 315- 317, 322, 323, 327, 329, 331, 332, 334, 338, 356, 360, 369, 375, 376, 379, 380, 382, 384, 400, 406, 412, 413, 420, 445, 462
Memory 259, 269, 271, 317, 338, 377–379, 385, 424, 448, 457
Merton, Robert 127, fn 9, 409
Michelman, Frank 76, 80
Michels, Robert 110, 360
Middle East 68
Miller, David 461
Miller, Max 20, 28, 34, 159, 163, 204, 211, 212, 219, 233, 265, 266, 271, 277, 282, 283, 285, 289, 291, 293, 297, 302, 306, 397, 311, 312, 318, 337, 339, 341, 345, 346, 360, 366, 429, 450
Mills, Charles, W. 8
Mische, Anne 261, 264, 268
Mobilization 35, 106, 184, 191, 210, 246, 292, 422, 425
Modernity 3, 4, 6, 22, 33, 35, 44, 73, 82, 93, 101, 114, 137, 156, 171, 179, 194, 213, 221, 257, 266, 284, 316, fn1,319, 320, 323, 325, 328, 329, 330, 339, 340, 342, 349, 379, 380, 405, 418, 440, 462, 464, 465

Index

Moral 2, 5, 9, 10–12, 19, 20, 21, 25, 27–29, 34, 35, 40–44, 47, 51, 53–55, 59, 62, 65, 66, 72, 73, 78, 79, 82, 86, 88, 89, 97, 99, 102, 111–114, 116, 117, 122, 123, 137, 142, 146, 147, 155–158, 163, 166–168, 170–176, 178–180, 182–184, 188–191, 193, 195, 196, 198, 200–202, 204–207, 209–211, 213–219, 221, 222, 229, 231–237, 240–247, 254, 255, 261, 262, 265, 266, 268, 271–276, 278, 279, 283-285, 291- 297, 299–304, 306–311, 313, 314, 316–318, 321, 322, 324–331, 335, 340, 341, 343, 345, 346, 348–351, 357, 358, 364, 366, 367, 369, 370, 377, 395, 403, 412, 419, 420, 422, 427, 428, 432, 434, 436, 440–442, 449, 450, 453, 457
Mouffe, Chantal 16, 91, 92, 95- 99, 100, 102, 111, 111, fn 1, 113

Narrative 175, 345, 365, 369, 426
Nation 22, 26, 42, 56, 63–66, 74, 82, 84, 86, 86, fn 9, 87, 87, fn 10, 88, 116, 156, 245, 294, 296, 306, 328, 329, 337, 375, 378, 386, 401, 439, 440, 442, 443–446, 447, 448, 450, 453, 456, 457, 458, 461, 463, 465
Needs 135, 179, 188, 213, 226, 229, 230, 235, 237, 245, 280, 324, 417, 421, 442
Negt and Kluge 7, 12–19, 23, 103, 104
Networks 8, 95, 187, 199, 280, 330, 338, 377, 379, 380, 386, 399, 405, 406, 415, 423, 442, 444, 445, 448, 455
Nine, Cara 84, fn 7, 115, fn 5
Niquet, Marcel 195–196, 203, 206, 209, 218, 234
Non-domination, *see* domination
Normative 1–6, 9–13, 15–19, 21–27, 29–36, 39–47, 49, 54–56, 62–64, 66, 71-, 72, 74, 78, 80–83, 85–89, 92, 97, 98, 100–102, 104–106, 110, 113, 114, 117, 119, 121, 122, 125–127, 129, 132–141, 143–147, 149, 150–156, 158–160, 163–165, 167, 169, 170–174, 178, 179 181–192, 193–203, 206, 207, 209, 210, 212–216, 218–222, 223–227, 229, 231–233, 235–240, 242–244, 246–248, 253–256, 258, 259, 261, 263, 268, 269, 271–274, 276–288, 290–294, 296–305, 309–311, 314, 317–322, 325, 326, 328, 331–339, 341, 343, 345, 348, 350, 351, 355–371, 377, 378, 380–382, 384, 387, 389, 392, 394–396, 398, 400, 403, 404–407, 409, 410, 412, 413, 415–418, 420, 421, 422, 424, 426, 429, 431–437, 439, 440, 441, 446, 448, 449, 451–455, 457, 459–465
counter-normative 33, 106, 256, 348, 350, 404, 422
culture 3, 6, 16, 31, 32, 35, 63, 71, 81, 86, 89, 100, 155, 159, 184, 188, 196, 197, 209, 220, 253, 281, 319, 322, 350, 362, 363, 396, 404, 417, 418, 420, 424, 442, 455
see also public culture
models 37–162, 163, 165, 194–202, 224–226, 229, 321, 322, 325, 326, 333, 335–338, 343, 432, 436
standards 10, 174, 178, 178, fn 8, 179–183, 206–207, 213–214, 221–222, 254, 334, 432–437
see also cognitive, communication community, co-operation, counterfactual, critique, democracy, inequality, justice, public

Offe, Claus 102, 187

Paine, Thomas 115
Park, Robert E. 8
Parkinson, John 359
Pathology, *see* critical, learning
Peirce, Charles Sanders 33, 84, 167, 174, 272, 282, 292, 298, 346, 437
Peters, Bernhard 26–29
Pettit, Philip 39, 73, 74- 81, 82, 85, 98, 100, fn 7, 129, 152, 357
Phenomenology 182, 199, 227, 228, 263, 271, 279, 317, 328, 389, 390, 433–435
Philp, Mark 111, 127, fn 9
Pluralism 2, 4, 45, 50, 53, 74, 76, 88, 93, 95–98, 98–100, 111, 114, 120–122, 127, 133, 149, fn 12, 158, 160, 168, 175, 201, 203, 219, 231, 233, 236, 245, 294, 300, 360, 440, 455, 464
Politics, *see* cognitive, democracy, governance, normative, power, public
Political culture, *see* public culture
Positivism 409, 415
Post-conventional 35, 166, 228, 275
Post-structuralism 3, 17, 179
Post-metaphysical 26, 294
Postnational 86
Power 3, 17, 18, 21, 22, 26, 50, fn 1, 76, 81, 85, 93, 96, 98, 99, 100, 103, 105, 106, 106, fn 10, 110. 111, 112–113, 113, fn 3, 117, 118, 119, 145–146, 150, 153, 154, 156, 157, 167, 206, 236, 258, 295, 307, 313–314, 322, 331, 336, 340, 341, 350, 385, 385, fn 2, 387, 443, 443–444, 456, 457, 460
    communicative 15, 16, 133, 181, 184, 186, 187, 190, 191, 194, 200, 207–212, 220, 226, 228, fn 11, 230, 231, 239, 245, 305, 324–326, 366, 383–384, 412, 420, 424–425, 443, 444
    functional 24, 25–26, 123–126, 153, 180–181, 186, 198–199, 207–212, 227, 228, fn11, 230, 236–237, 265–267, 304–305, 324–326, 335, 336, 392–393, 403–404, 419–420, 424–425, 428–429
    social 14, 75, 135, 156, 177–178, 185–186, 190, 198, 208–213, 242–243, 244, 248–249, 267, 299, 303, 305, 307, 309, 314, 324–326, 333, 366, 419–418, 424–425, 428, 459, 452
    see also conflict, domination
Pragmatic rationality 26, 47, 111, 131, 204–205, 233–234, 247, 255–256, 257, 273, 293, 296, 299, 303, 304, 307, 309, 312, 314, 313, 336, 399, 412, 420, 428
Pragmatics 10, 33, 85, 160, 167, 168, 177, 183, 193, 198, 214, 220, 221, fn 10, 229, 248, 267, 274, 276, 277, 278, 283–288, 292, 293, 317, 318, 320, 327, 338, 368, 369, 402
Pragmatism 33, 40, fn 2, 45, 85, 262, 264, 268, 271, 275, 279, 321, 348
Psychology 264, 270, 271
Public
    communication 1, 6, 8, 9, 13, 14, 16, 23–24, 31–32, 33, 35, 42, 47, 56, 109, 110, 117, 121, 125, 126, 127, 130, 143, 151, 152, 154, 156–157, 181, 185–189, 192, 196, 210, 223, 238, 276–277, 280, 305, 310, 322, 326, 335, 344, 349, 351, 355, 356–357, 359, 360, 362, 367, 371, 373–437, 445, 446–447, 455–456
    see also democracy, communication theory of, public discourse, public justification

Index

competence 121–122, 126, 141, 186, 208, 230, 231, 257, 325, 335, 339–341, 383, 385, 434
contestation 2, 5, 5, fn 3, 19, 46, 47, 71, 91–107, 112–113, 117, 229, 234, 235, 237, 248, 256, 268, 330, 456–457
see also conflict, contestability
culture 8–9, 22, 28–29, 30–31, 33–34, 39, 40, 41–42, 43, 56, 67–68, 71, 72, 86, 93–94, 101, 229, 232, 234–235, 256, 268, 315, 321, 330, 339, 341, 350–351, 362, 380, 385, fn 2, 399, 428–429, 456
see also normative culture, political culture
deliberation 42, 46–47, 77, 121, 130, fn 1, 131, 132, 139–140, 144, 145, fn 12, 147,148–150, 152, 155, 157, 158, 243, 277, 289, 348, 369, 361, 393, 432
see also deliberative democracy
discourse 2, fn 2, 3, 4, 11, 20, 24, 25, 27–29, 31–32, 39, 41, 43, 47, 55, 55, fn 7, 56, 62, 67, 68, 85, 97, 150, 155, 157, 159, 160, 183, 184, 186, 190, 194, 196, 198, 203, 208, 214, 217, 218, 219, 232, 239, 242, 243, 244, 255–256, 266, 268, 276, 277, 281, 284, 285, 286, 287, fn 2, 290, 299, 306, 310, 315, 318, 319, 336, 338, 344, 346, 375, 389, 390, 391, 400, 401, 406, 407, 410, 412, 414, 415, 419, 420, 423, 424, 426, 434, 435, 453, 462, 463, 465
see also democracy, communicative theory of, public communication
justification 3, 4–5, 6, 25, 26, 30, 43, 53, 57, 62, fn 14, 64, 69, 72, 88, 94, 100, 100, fn 7, 101, 115, 115, fn 5, 142, 147, 149, 165–170, 171, 172–173, 178, 180, 183, 191–192, 193, 196, 197, 198, 207, 209–212, 216–219, 232, 243, 244, 249, 256, 276, 272, 273, 275, 277, 280, 288, 290, 293–294, 294–296, 305, 307–308, 314, 322, 325, 327, 338, 343–345, 349, 357, 363, 364, 366, 394, 395, 414, 435, 437, 451–453
memory 259, 269, 271, 317, 338, 377, 379, 385, 424, 448, 457
participation 9, 18, 32, 41, 46, 47, 62, 65, 77, 81, 83, 93, 103, 104, 124, 134, 135, 170–171, 184, 196, 212, 232, 289, 289, fn 3, 292, 320, 321, 335, 373, 374, 384, 410, 413–414, 432
see also democratic innovation, democratization
reason 4–5, 9, 30, 31, 32, 46, 49–69, 102, 116, fn 6, 150, 155, 182–183, 201–202, 203, 204, 229, 231–232, 237, 341, 342, 349, 382, 432, 435
sovereignty 8–9, 18, 46, 50, 109–110, 112, 115, fn 5, 117, 119, 125, 132, 135, 140–144, 151, 152, 181, 197, 218, 221, 223, 290, 291, 320, 356, 357, 359, 360, 361, 364, 383, 4171–418, 463
strong and weak publics 21, 26
will formation 27, 41, 71, 77, 381, 444
Puritan 405

Race 106, fn 10, 209, 304, 329, 369, 402
Rational choice 110, 118, 236
Rawls, John 4–5, 29, 32, 44, 46, 47, 49–69, 78–80, 84, 89, 94, 95, 96, 99, 101, 102, 106, fn 10, 110, 111, 112, 113, 114, 116, 121, 125, 129, 131, 139, 140, 141, 146, 148, 152, 155, 156, 171, 173, 176, 178, 182, 183, 191, 200–206, 214, 225, 229, 231, 232,

233, 234, 235, 243, 247, 264, 284, 308, 319, 320, 335, 343, 350, 357, 421, 423, 434, 435, 436, 437, 464
original position 51, 52, 56, 58, 61–65
see also public reason
Realism, political 32, 45, 46, 109–127, 145, 156, 157, 176, 179, 182, 191, 197, 218, 236, 263, 290, 413, 450
Recognition, see Honneth, Axel
Reconstructivism 31, 39, 42, 43, 47, 65, 84, 106, 145, 157,159, 160, 163, 164, 166, 176, 187, 192, 193, 197, 204, 209, 221, 223, 228, 245, 247, 276, 283, 284, 285, 286, 288, 292, 321, 344, 345, 348, 366, 367, 402, 403, 409, 410, 420, 422,, 427, 433, 434, 435, 437, 449, 45, 462, 463, 465
Rehg, William 172, 174, 178, 277
Religion 156, 265, 329, 402, 457
Republicanism 32, 40–42, 44, 45, 46, 55, 71–89, 91, 93, 97, 99, 105, 117–120, 127, 129, 131, 135, 145, 146, 152, 155, 158, 163, 172, 176, 177, 191, 192, 217, 223, 224, 225, 226, 229, 232, 233, 248, 256, 264, fn 1, 331, 395, fn 1, 421, 425, 436, 437
Resonance 106, 123, 146, 235, 287, fn 2, 288, 289, 330, 349, 351, 392, 402, 406, 416, 425, 427–431, 446, 457, 460
Responsibility 5, 53, 78, 86, 158, 166, 168–169, 177, 182, 183, 186–190, 200, 203, fn 1, 205, 206, 207, 217, 218, 220, 255, 258, 259, 303, 308–309, 323, 328, 344, 346, 348, 370, 382, 394, 395, 400, 412, 429, 432, 443
Rhetoric 28, 65, fn 16, 103, 399, 401, 457
Rorty, Richard 46, 55, fn 5
Rousseau, Jean-Jacques 59

Saint-Simon, Henri 109
Sandel, Michael 61, fn 13, 71–75, 76, 81 83, 87, 89, 156
Saward, Michael 58
Schapiro, Ian 61, fn 13, 118, 119, 120, 121, 127
Schimank, Uwe 123–125, 279
Schumpeter, Joseph 110, 112, 119, 120–121, 123–124, 360
Schutz, Alfred 271
Sen, Amartya 40, fn 2, 59–61, 80, 80, fn 5, 113, 267, 369
Shklar, Judith 67
Sikking, Kathryn 457
Skillington, Tracey 87, 103, 457
Social change 34, 49, 83, 92, 132, 163, 181, 188, 220, 242, 259, 275, 276, 300, 302, 318, 336, 341–343, 368, 374, 394, 402, 422, 423, 441, 463
Social systems, see Luhmann, mediation, power, functional
Solidarity 24, 28, 51, 73, 84, 89, 156, 199, 241, 294, 310, 358, 386, 391, 395, 430, 439, 441, 442, 443, 449, 456, 461
Somers, Margaret 43–44, 65, 332, 362, 363, 381
Sovereignty 117, 123, 417, 430, 455, 461
Spatiality 5, 74, 84, 86, 248, 277, 288, 300, 301, 329, 357, 363, 368, 370, 374, 375, 376, 386, 387, 390, 407, 439
Splichal, Slavko 2, fn 2, 19, 21, 357, 367
Steiner, Jorg 367
Strydom, Piet 34, 62, fn 14, 125, fn 8, 203, 207, 214, 219, 259, 260, 276, 276, 283–293, 302, 318, 366
Subject formation 93, 94, 95, 156, 158, 217, 219, 220, 234, fn 4, 235, 340
Subjugation 91–107, 156
Sunstein, Cass 44, fn 3, 71, 87, fn 11, 129, 131, 376, 378, 382, 384, 428

Index 499

Synchronic 147, 220, 357, 370–371, 379, 387
Sznaider, Natan 457

Taylor, Charles 44, 73
Teleological 26, 40, fn 2, 78, 100, 121, 122, 139, fn 7, 174, 220, 238, 239, 265, 321
Temporality 5, 16, 167, 207, 216, 221, 248, 259, 271, 288, 293, 299, 330, 357, 368, 370, 379, 387, 389, 428, 429, 451, fn 3
Territory 21–22, 60, 83, 84, 89, 375, 386
Thévenot, Laurent 6, 30, 42, 84, 265, 273–275
Thomson, Dennis 58, 59, 62
Tönnies, Ferdinand 8
Touraine, Alain 93–95, 156, 217, 235, 255, 271, 332, 333, 334, 339, 340, 351
Transcendence 11, 16, 34, 35, 36, 40, fn 2, 41, 55, fn 5, 59, 61, 63, 64, 73, 84, 94, 113, 115, 165, 166, 168, 171–173, 176, 178, 192, 195, 196, 198, 199, 205, 206, 213, 214, 224, 226, 232, 248, 257, 258, 260, 264–267, 272, 273, 279, 283, 284, 287, 291, 292, 316, 319, 320, 321, 323, 324, 327–330, 336, 347, 367, 369, 381, 399, 400, 420, 433, 436, 437, 452
Trenz, Hans, Georg 276, 428, 445–448, 453
Triple contingency 203, 232, 283, 286, 287, 288, 325, 338, 361, 362, 400, 433, 445, 447, 450, 453

Violence 241, 284, 305, 316, fn 1, 439, 443, 450, 456

Waugh, Evelyn 384
Weber, Max 66, 93, 110, 112, 200, 234, 323
Wellmer, Albrecht 66
Westphalian 22, 461
Williams, Bernard 111
Willke, Helmut 104, 189–190

Young, Iris Marion 103, 398

New Visions of the Cosmopolitan

Series Editors: Patrick O'Mahony and Tracey Skillington

New Visions of the Cosmopolitan explores how the forces of contemporary social change release a cosmopolitan energy that dilutes the relevance of the nation-state. The 'transnational turn' creates tendencies toward greater world openness. A more pluralist, multi-perspectivist late modernity requires a cosmopolitan research framework capable of illustrating how world histories and futures are intricately connected under these new conditions. This series offers a body of work exploring how cosmopolitan ideas, emerging from encounters between local and global currents, generate impulses towards social, cultural, legal, political and economic transformation.

The series invites contributions that focalize this contemporary situation using theories, perspectives and methodologies drawn from multiple disciplines. Of particular, although not exclusive, interest are proposals exploring: transnational visions of justice and solidarity; cosmopolitan publics; researching cosmopolitan worlds; cosmopolitan memory; the cosmopolitics of contemporary global capitalism; borders of the cosmopolitan; cosmopolitanism in the non-western world; security, war and peace in a cosmopolitan age; multiple modernities; divergence and convergence; political culture and multi-level governance.

This peer-reviewed series publishes monographs and edited collections.

Vol. 1   Patrick O'Mahony
        The Contemporary Theory of the Public Sphere
        2013. ISBN 978-3-0343-0146-6 hb.
        2019. ISBN 978-1-78997-248-1 pb.

Vol. 2   Rebecka Lettevall and Kristian Petrov (eds)
        Critique of Cosmopolitan Reason: Timing and Spacing the Concept of World Citizenship
        2014. ISBN 978-3-0343-0898-4

Vol. 3   Aybige Yilmaz, Ruxandra Trandafoiu and Aris Mousoutzanis (eds)
        Media and Cosmopolitanism
        2015. ISBN 978-3-0343-0969-1

Vol. 4   Anastasia Marinopoulou (ed.)
         Cosmopolitan Modernity
         2015. ISBN 978-3-0343-0873-1

Vol. 5   Ulrike M. Vieten and Gill Valentine (eds)
         Cartographies of Differences: Interdisciplinary Perspectives
         2016. ISBN 978-3-0343-1859-4

Vol. 6   Georg Cavallar
         Theories of Dynamic Cosmopolitanism in Modern European History
         2017. ISBN 978-1-78707-487-3

www.ingramcontent.com/pod-product-compliance
Lightning Source LLC
Chambersburg PA
CBHW052009290426
44112CB00014B/2171